Citizens Adrift

Paul Howe

Citizens Adrift
The Democratic Disengagement
of Young Canadians

UBCPress · Vancouver · Toronto

20 19 18 17 16 15 14 13 12 11 10   5 4 3 2 1

Printed in Canada on FSC-certified ancient-forest-free paper
(100 percent post-consumer recycled) that is processed chlorine- and acid-free.

Library and Archives Canada Cataloguing in Publication

Howe, Paul, 1966-
  Citizens adrift : the democratic disengagement of young Canadians / Paul Howe.

Includes bibliographical references and index.
ISBN 978-0-7748-1875-9 (bound); 978-0-7748-1876-6 (pbk)

  1. Young adults – Political activity – Canada. 2. Political participation – Canada.
I. Title.

HQ799.9.P6H68 2010   323'.04208420971   C2010-905263-3

e-book ISBNs: 978-0-7748-1877-3 (pdf); 978-0-7748-1878-0 (epub)

Canadä

UBC Press gratefully acknowledges the financial support for our publishing program of the Government of Canada (through the Canada Book Fund), the Canada Council for the Arts, and the British Columbia Arts Council.

This book has been published with the help of a grant from the Canadian Federation for the Humanities and Social Sciences, through the Aid to Scholarly Publications Programme, using funds provided by the Social Sciences and Humanities Research Council of Canada.

Printed and bound in Canada by Friesens
Set in Stone by Artegraphica Design Co. Ltd.
Copy editor: Peter Colenbrander
Proofreader: Francis Chow
Indexer: Lillian Ashworth

UBC Press
The University of British Columbia
2029 West Mall
Vancouver, BC V6T 1Z2
www.ubcpress.ca

Contents

Appendices

Tables and Figures

Acknowledgments

When I began thinking about this project on democratic disengagement among young Canadians, I might have been considered part of that demographic group on a generous definition of the term. By any reckoning, that is no longer the case, which is a roundabout way of saying that the project has been a fair time in the making, from initial conception through to publication of this volume. Along the way, I have received generous support and encouragement from a number of individuals and organizations.

My engagement with debates about Canadian democracy began when I was serving as research director of the Governance Program at the Institute for Research on Public Policy (IRPP) from 1998 to 2001. Colleagues at the IRPP, including its then president, Hugh Segal, as well as academic collaborators Richard Johnston, André Blais, and many others, were enthusiastic supporters of, and contributors to, the Strengthening Canadian Democracy project initiated during my tenure. The interest kindled at the IRPP carried over to the University of New Brunswick, where the current project gradually took shape. Several seminar classes, at both the undergraduate and graduate level, on the theme of democratic disengagement have provided a valuable opportunity to discuss key ideas with members of the age cohort that constitutes the focal point of the study. Helping to move the project along at different stages were several bright and industrious research assistants: Vincent French, who, among other assignments, had the task of gathering datasets and conducting preliminary analysis for the comparative research presented in Chapter 3; Julie Kusiek, who carried out background research on various themes related to adolescence underpinning the analysis of Chapter 9; and Shane DeMerchant, who came to the project in its latter stages and provided assistance in tying up loose ends throughout.

The study makes extensive use of survey data to investigate relevant patterns of democratic engagement. The head of the Government Documents, Data and Maps department at the University of New Brunswick library, Elizabeth Hamilton, provided initial advice in locating relevant datasets, as well as ongoing assistance in securing materials in a timely manner. I also extend my thanks to the many researchers who have made their data available for secondary analysis. These researchers include all those involved in the Canadian election studies carried out on the occasion of each federal election. Their ongoing efforts have resulted in a valuable shared resource for the political science community in this country. The same recognition should be extended to the private polling firm Environics and its Quebec partner firm CROP, for the datasets they have provided to the Canadian Opinion Research Archive at Queen's University; and to other researchers, too numerous to list here, whose original data have been drawn upon extensively in different parts of the study (a full listing can be found in the references). While most of the data consulted were of the electronic variety, some were only to be found in the traditional format of dusty old reports. Roma Kail, reference librarian at Ryerson University, was most helpful in sorting through archived material of this type (a series of reports by the Bureau of Broadcast Measurement housed at Ryerson).

I also extend my gratitude to the participants in a nationwide telephone survey conducted for the project in late 2007 and early 2008. Nearly 2,000 Canadians volunteered twenty to twenty-five minutes of their time in this endeavour. I must acknowledge as well the professionalism and hard work of Jolicoeur et associés, the firm that conducted the survey, and more specifically Jean François Dion and Pierre-Alexandre Lacoste of Jolicoeur. Also providing assistance to the survey process was David Northrup of the Institute for Social Research at York University, who offered helpful thoughts in the planning stage on how to tackle the challenge of declining response rates faced by survey researchers nowadays.

Bill Cross and Richard Niemi reviewed the work closely and offered a range of insightful comments that helped strengthen the book in many ways. Their efforts are greatly appreciated, as are those of Randy Schmidt, Emily Andrew, and Laraine Coates of UBC Press in shepherding the manuscript through the publication process.

Generous support was given to the project by the Social Sciences and Humanities Research Council of Canada, which provided a research grant that was indispensable in supporting all facets of the work over a three-year period. Another grant from the Harrison McCain Foundation at the University of New Brunswick provided for a lighter teaching schedule during one year of the project and allowed the research to proceed more expeditiously.

Lastly, on a personal note, I would thank my family, Anna, Sophie, and Noah – engaged and inspired individuals all – for their love and encouragement over the course of completing the project and for their contagious enthusiasm for life's other diversions that helped lighten the load throughout the research and writing process.

Introduction

The suggestion that young Canadians are politically disengaged tends to provoke strong reactions. One is swift agreement accompanied by firm conviction that the problem can and should be fixed. A second is scepticism, reflecting the view that engagement comes in many different forms and young people should not be uniformly branded. There is a measure of truth in both responses. Political disengagement among young Canadians is real enough and can be ameliorated through concerted effort, but it is also multifaceted in both its manifestations and underlying causes, and does not admit of either simple summation or solution.

This study explores the phenomenon from various angles, searching for that which is most fundamental in the behavioural and attitudinal patterns sometimes cited as evidence of young people's disengagement. The position taken is that political disengagement involves more than just politics. Young people have not turned away simply because politics is uninteresting, the parties are all the same, elections are sometimes uncompetitive, or politicians are untrustworthy. If these are exacerbating factors, they do not constitute the primary reason for waning political engagement among younger Canadians or an adequate analytical foundation for developing proposals to address the issue. Instead, political disengagement reflects broader changes in political culture, that constellation of ingrained attitudes and dispositions that individuals bring to their understanding of democracy and their own role and responsibilities within the democratic system. Political culture includes not just political content, but all attitudes and dispositions of relevance to politics, including those more social and cultural in nature. The origins of political disengagement lie in this more encompassing realm.

The steep challenges involved in engaging Canadians politically have been evident in other democratic developments of late. Recent initiatives to change the electoral system in several provinces have broken new ground in Canadian democratic practice. They are the first to seriously contemplate the adoption of proportional representation (PR). Those provinces pushing xiv *Introduction*

furthest in the process – BC, PEI, and Ontario – have held referendums to give citizens the final say on whether to move ahead. In two of those cases, BC and Ontario, the referendum was preceded by a more innovative procedure still: a citizens' assembly assigned the task of deliberating at length on the merits of different electoral systems and presenting a recommended alternative to be put to a general vote. Many with an interest in democratic reform anticipated that Canadians, often frustrated at a lack of say in government, would jump at this opportunity to refashion (or defend) an important pillar of our electoral democracy. And sure enough, some did: those selected to participate in the assemblies displayed enthusiasm for and dedication to their work and others watching from the sidelines followed their deliberations with keen interest. Ultimately, however, the engagement of the general public with the issue was disappointing.

The first BC referendum, held at the same time as the provincial election of May 2005, was probably the high point. Fifty-seven percent of eligible voters participated in the referendum, with 58 percent supporting the proposed single-transferable vote (STV) system – a moral victory for advocates of change, but not enough to carry the day under the supra-majority threshold established by the government. The result was more sobering when British Columbians were given a second opportunity to express their views on STV in the May 2009 provincial election: the referendum turnout was down substantially to 49 percent of eligible voters, with only 39 percent now voting in favour of the proposal. In Prince Edward Island, the province normally recording the highest voter turnout in federal and provincial elections, the referendum of November 2005 was a stand-alone event. A scant 33 percent of registered voters turned out to cast a ballot and the referendum failed by a margin of nearly 2 to 1. Turnout was somewhat better in Ontario in October 2007, where the referendum again occurred in conjunction with a provincial election. However, this was an election that produced a record low turnout, so that only 51 percent of registered voters ended up casting a referendum ballot. Moreover, surveys revealed that at the end of the referendum campaign many remained vague on the details of the proposed PR model, and that those who knew little were more likely to oppose the change (Cutler and Fournier 2007). For advocates of reform, this was perhaps the most stubborn obstacle of all: ill-informed supporters of the status quo. The end result was the same as in PEI and the second BC referendum, a resounding victory for the No side. Even if other factors also contributed to these deflating outcomes – among them poor public education campaigns and a lack of strong advocates among party leaders (Seidle 2005; McKenna 2006) – the failure of citizens to rise to the democratic occasion cannot be denied.

Instead of helping to correct the problem, the democratic reform experience of the past few years has only underscored the challenges involved in engaging the citizenry at large. Even when a procedure is put in place that conforms to what many consider an ideal model of public deliberation, many Canadians remain indifferent to the proceedings. Advocates of reform will continue to press for change and it is to be hoped that their efforts will eventually bring about much needed modifications to our political structures and practices (Howe et al. 2005). However, it must also be recognized, in light of recent setbacks, that the revitalization of Canadian democracy rests at least as much on addressing the problem of citizen disengagement. Without this, progress on institutional reform – not to mention other issues where the quality and breadth of public engagement is critical to a successful outcome – will be halting. The possibility of a richer democracy will remain unrealized.

The fact that young Canadians are especially prominent among the ranks of the disengaged invites many questions. A preliminary one involves a simple point of clarification: what is meant by the phrase "young Canadians"? The answer is necessarily vague. Beyond underlining that it does not refer exclusively to "youth," a group I take to mean those no older than twenty-one, the age limits are flexible. Some researchers focus on those fifteen to twenty-four, others on those eighteen to twenty-nine, yet others on those twenty-one to thirty-five. The precise demarcation is not crucial, as the basic pattern on a number of key measures is one of gradually diminishing political engagement at younger ages. Moreover, the pitch of the age gradient is typically found to be steeper today than in the past, suggesting disengagement among today's young adults is not simply the replication of an age-old pattern. Instead it signals, at least partly, a generational change. It is this feature of democratic disengagement that is the most disconcerting, as it potentially carries significant consequences for the long-term vitality of Canadian democracy.

The past ten years have seen considerable discussion and analysis of this emergent issue in both academic circles and the public arena. Since the federal election of 2000, when overall voter turnout dropped sharply to just over 60 percent and the spotlight fell on the high abstention rates among young electors, a variety of studies have investigated the political disengagement of young Canadians. A handful of traditional academic papers have appeared, but the larger part of this work has been sponsored by think-tanks and government agencies, including papers produced under the auspices of the Institute for Research on Public Policy, the Centre for Research and Information on Canada, the Canadian Policy Research Networks, the Canada West Foundation, Elections Canada, Statistics Canada, and the New Brunswick Commission on Legislative Democracy.[1] This work has served an essential purpose, bringing the issue to public attention, setting out basic parameters of the debate, and identifying key findings that have anchored policy discussion. However, this prior work (my own included) has largely consisted of shorter pieces with a practical orientation that can take us only so far in our understanding of the issue.

Studies of greater depth and focus are needed at this stage. Works from elsewhere provide some general guidance as to the form these might take. These include a number that identify gradual evolution in the mores, habits, and values of citizens as the principal force giving rise to generationally driven changes in democratic engagement. One is Robert Putnam's influential tome *Bowling Alone*, which documents the sharp decline of "social capital" in the US over the past several decades and outlines its deleterious consequences for American democracy (2000). Another is Russell Dalton's rejoinder to Putnam, *The Good Citizen* (2008), which offers a more optimistic assessment of generational patterns of democratic engagement in the US and is grounded in his larger body of work in the same vein (Dalton 2004, 2006). Other relevant studies are comparative, including Martin Wattenberg's *Is Voting for Young People?*, a study of habits of news media use, political knowledge, and political participation among young people in the developed democracies (2008). There is a common recognition in these works that voter turnout is but one element in a larger syndrome of attitudes and behaviour and that political disengagement can only be understood in the context of broader social and cultural change. There are also important differences across these and other works in their general characterization of the changes taking place – some are relatively optimistic, others gloomier – and the identification of the root causes putatively responsible for reshaping patterns of political involvement among younger generations.

Such studies, and the theoretical perspectives they advance, have informed research on the political disengagement of young Canadians but have not yet been emulated in Canadian studies of comparable scope or depth. This, then, is the contribution this book seeks to make: to push beyond established findings in recent research on the disengagement of young Canadians to engage more fully with themes developed in the broader comparative literature. It aims for depth over breadth: rather than canvassing all facets of disengagement among young Canadians, the study concentrates on the two areas deemed most essential. These are the evolution of *political attentiveness,* which encompasses trends in political interest, political knowledge, and habits of news media use; and trends in *social integration*, the connections to community and the social norms that influence how people conduct their lives on a general plane and the extent and manner of their engagement with the political world.

The political attentiveness of the citizenry has been an abiding concern of political scientists ever since early public opinion research revealed some decades ago that the average citizen is not nearly as interested in, or knowledgeable about, politics as classical theories of democracy had commonly supposed. These shortfalls have taken on new significance in recent years as evidence has accumulated in a number of the developed democracies of a significant gap between younger and older citizens on various measures of political attentiveness. If the traditional concern was that citizens fell short of the lofty ideals of abstract democratic theory, the current apprehension is that younger generations are failing to meet the rather minimalist expectations typical of contemporary theorizing about the conditions necessary for democracy to work fairly and efficiently. Determining whether and why this is so, and how it might be remedied, constitutes one key piece of the disengagement puzzle.

Meanwhile, there is also widespread recognition that there are broader changes afoot contributing to the democratic disengagement of younger generations. The postwar period has seen significant changes in lifestyles and social norms that have, according to various theorists, gradually weakened the bonds of social integration in the developed democracies. Philosophical works taking up this theme sometimes adopt a longer time frame, underlining the historical ascendance of liberal individualism and the stress this has placed on values of community and solidarity in the modern period (Taylor 1991; Barber 2003). The treatment of these matters here is more empirical than philosophical, more contemporary than historical, but these broader perspectives hover in the background of the analysis. The general supposition borrowed from the philosophers is that community in some form or other is prior to democracy, that a healthy measure of social solidarity and shared public purpose is necessary for democracy to flourish. If there has indeed been some unravelling of the ties that bind among younger generations, this too represents an important seam to be exposed and explored in order to understand fully the origins and implications of rising disengagement among the young.

In identifying shortfalls in the current state of citizen engagement in Canadian democracy, the question naturally arises what a stronger democracy might look like. To my mind, the answer is necessarily vague because democracy is an open-ended proposition, the goalposts subject to repositioning as the expectations, ambitions, and capacities of "the people" evolve. Certainly a more vibrant democracy would be one in which there is a stronger sense of common purpose and solidarity among citizens, who manifest their solidarity in part by closely attending to, and regularly participating in, the political life of community and country. The end goal may be imprecisely defined, but the direction of change required at the present time is not.

Clearly, these themes and goals are not uniquely Canadian, and so in the chapters that follow significant effort is made to place the Canadian experience in a comparative perspective. In some instances, this means assembling information and data on Canada and other countries and drawing the relevant comparisons. In other places, the work is comparative in the sense that it is informed by theoretical perspectives generated elsewhere – including those of Putnam, Dalton, Wattenberg, and others – and is sensitive to the implications of findings emerging from the Canadian case. Sometimes, this is simply a matter of situating Canada within an extant theoretical framework, but in other cases it involves suggested amendment of existing theory to better accommodate findings from the Canadian case. Consequently, the book is not just an empirical study of democratic disengagement among young Canadians informed by broader theory, but also a case study that seeks to offer new theoretical insight that could be applied elsewhere. The hope is that the conceptual and empirical contributions resonate with audiences both inside and outside Canada and make some useful contribution to broader debates.

Exploring key thematic elements at length reflects the academic orientation of the study, but there is a practical purpose as well. The latter part of the book outlines ideas for policy initiatives large and small that could make a substantial difference to the political engagement of young Canadians. Some initiatives would require considerable effort and dedication, so their success will depend on the priority the issue receives. At this stage, the necessary sense of urgency does not seem to exist. The political disengagement of young Canadians has occasioned considerable handwringing and expressions of concern, but to date has produced no concerted effort to address the problem. A cynic might observe that parties in power probably do not stand to gain from making this a priority. Younger voters, at the federal level at least, show relatively greater support for small parties than the major players, the Liberals and Conservatives. One poll just prior to the 2008 federal election, for example, found that 48 percent of those under thirty-five were planning to vote for the NDP, Greens, or Bloc Québécois, compared to only 31 percent of those fifty and over (Strategic Counsel 2008). If voter turnout were suddenly to jump 30 points among those under thirty-five, the impact on election outcomes could be quite substantial. An optimist, on the other hand, would be impressed by the fact that leaders at both provincial and federal levels have undertaken certain reform initiatives, such as opening the door to electoral reform and introducing fixed election dates, that run counter to their own self-interest. With a firm push from various quarters – academics and others engaged in policy research, the media, election agencies, smaller political parties, factions within the larger parties, concerned citizens at large – reversing the disengagement of young Canadians could be made a higher public priority.

Methodology

This study is concerned with evolving trends in citizen attitudes and behaviours broadly relevant to democratic engagement. Consequently, the main method of investigation is quantitative, more precisely the analysis of large-scale surveys of the general population in Canada and other countries.

One key objective throughout is to distinguish those patterns and tendencies that are common to young people of different periods and those that have grown more pronounced among generations coming of age in recent times (more technically, the relative significance of life-cycle and cohort effects). The most effective way to do this is to track citizen attitudes and behavioural patterns over time, which necessitates turning to existing datasets from earlier and more recent periods. Bringing together a wide array of secondary data sources capturing different facets of citizen engagement provides insight into the longitudinal trends in political participation and disposition that have brought us to our current pass.

The book also draws extensively on a more current survey conducted specifically for the study and designed to fill a number of important gaps in our understanding of democratic engagement. The Canadian Citizen Engagement Survey 2007-08 (CCES 2007-08), a survey of nearly 2,000 Canadians, provides up-to-date measures on certain indicators, as well as allowing for exploration of areas not closely examined in prior survey research.[2]

This predominantly quantitative approach is complemented by other methods, including historical reflection, aimed at providing a richer understanding of past experience than can be captured by numbers alone, and philosophical inquiry, designed to anchor the empirical (and, in places, prescriptive) analysis in normative principles distinguishing desirable and undesirable democratic outcomes. As with other studies on the topic of democratic disengagement, the book is principally aimed at a scholarly audience but also endeavours to engage with readers outside academia with an interest in this important policy issue. Quantitative results, along with findings and theories from the scholarly literature, are presented in a manner designed to render them intelligible to readers who may not be deeply steeped in these matters.

The Book in Brief
The study is divided into four parts. Part 1 consists of two chapters: Chapter 1 sets the stage by examining patterns of political participation across age groups at different points in time and is followed by a preliminary assessment of the factors sometimes held responsible for declining involvement among the young (Chapter 2). This first cut at explaining disengagement raises as many questions as it answers, however, so much of Chapter 2 is devoted to identifying the issues that need to be addressed in order to arrive at a fuller understanding of the matter. In doing so, the chapter goes beyond the brief outline offered here to provide a more detailed foregrounding of subsequent chapters and the overall structure and logic of the inquiry.

Part 2 of the book, Chapters 3 to 5, examines contours of political attentiveness in the past and present – knowledge of politics, interest in politics, and patterns of news media use – in both Canada and other countries and considers the implications for political engagement. Part 3, Chapters 6 to 8, takes up the theme of social integration, considering how the ties that bind individuals to their communities have weakened over time, and the consequences for democratic involvement.

Part 4 synthesizes and summarizes in two distinct ways: by presenting a theory of social change that helps account for changing patterns of political attentiveness and social integration over the long haul (Chapter 9); and by distilling key findings to produce policy recommendations aimed at encouraging broader and deeper engagement among younger citizens (Chapter 10). The latter suggestions are tailored to Canada, but to the extent the general analytical framework of the book applies elsewhere, the policy recommendations probably do as well. Many of these will already be familiar to those immersed in the subject of democratic disengagement, while a few are more novel. The principal contribution is to suggest where emphasis should be placed in order to tackle the problem of young people's current disengagement from politics at its foundations.

Citizens Adrift

Part 1
Setting the Stage

1

Democratic Participation in Canada

Mention democratic disengagement and the issue that first springs to mind for most people is declining voter turnout. This is not necessarily because people put excessive stock in elections as a vehicle for citizen engagement. Indeed, many would insist there is more to democracy than simply casting a ballot every so often. However, from a practical standpoint, voter turnout is an indispensable measure because it is based on a census of all eligible citizens. On those occasions when *everyone* has the right and opportunity to participate in a democratic activity that requires only modest personal effort, how many actually do so?

The short answer is, fewer nowadays than in the past. The long answer, which offers greater insight into the meaning and significance of declining voter turnout, is more involved. It entails looking more closely at patterns of electoral participation among younger and older Canadians over time, as well as paying some attention to the methods by which voter turnout is measured. Much of this first chapter is devoted to a close examination along these lines of trends in electoral participation in Canada. The conclusion is that declining turnout and low levels of participation among young Canadians are portentous developments, signalling something seriously amiss with contemporary Canadian democracy.

Recognizing, however, that voting is but one form of democratic engagement, other forms of participation are considered as well, including involvement in other political activities, volunteering, and membership in groups within the community. Casting the net wider is necessary in order to address the important counter-argument, voiced both in Canada and elsewhere, that young people do not participate less, they simply participate in alternative ways more to their liking and of their own choosing. The empirical evidence brought to bear on the issue in the latter part of this first chapter suggests this argument is not without merit and necessitates some amendment of earlier observations. It does not, however, alter the essential conclusion: there is a sizable block of young Canadians, too large by any reasonable yardstick, whose disinclination to be involved in public affairs extends across a broad range of civic and political activities.

Attention turns in Chapter 2 to a preliminary investigation of factors that help explain this broad-based disengagement among a substantial vein of the young adult population. Three prime suspects are considered – disaffection with politics and government, inattentiveness to politics, and the weakening of social integration – but only two are retained for further consideration. If political discontent is alive and well from sea to shining sea, it does not seem to be a significant force undermining participation in politics, either in general or among young Canadians in particular. Political inattentiveness, on the other hand, more specifically low levels of political interest and knowledge and spotty attention to public affairs via news media, is having a deleterious effect on the political involvement of young Canadians. So too are the twin elements of diminished social integration outlined below, relatively weak attachments to community among younger Canadians, and heightened individualism.

This examination of different forms of political and civic participation and the reasons for the diminishing involvement of a significant swath of young Canadians sets the stage for the remainder of the book. More probing analysis of patterns of political attentiveness and social integration is undertaken in the six chapters comprising Parts 2 and 3, which form the book's core. The final two chapters in Part 4 address the origins of these important changes in the attitudinal and behavioural proclivities of younger generations and offer a series of ideas for encouraging young Canadians to re-engage with their democracy.

General Trends in Voter Turnout and Methodological Matters

The decline in voter turnout in Canada in recent times has been much discussed and analyzed. Since 1988, voter participation at the federal level has dropped from 75 percent, roughly the postwar norm, to below 65 percent in each of the elections of 2000, 2004, and 2006, and just under 60 percent in 2008 (Figure 1.1). Turnout in provincial elections has also been falling sharply over the same period. In Quebec, the 2008 election saw turnout drop dramatically, to below 60 percent, following a steady decline since 1994. In Nova Scotia, voter participation has slowly ebbed and also edged below 60 percent in 2009, while turnout in Ontario, normally in the 60 percent to 65 percent range in the 1970s and 1980s, tumbled to just over 50 percent in the provincial election of 2007. If space on the graph permitted, Figure 1.1 could be expanded to reveal that most other provinces, with the exception of Prince Edward Island, have witnessed a similar decline in electoral participation in recent times, including Alberta, where turnout in the 2008 provincial election fell to an historic low of 40.6 percent.[1]

Figure 1.1

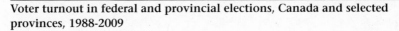

Voter turnout in federal and provincial elections, Canada and selected provinces, 1988-2009

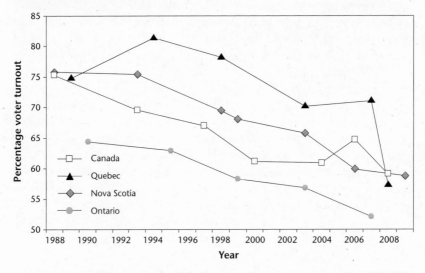

Sources: Directeur Général des Élections du Québec 2008; Élections Canada 2009; Elections Nova Scotia 2009; Elections Ontario 2007.

As researchers attentive to these trends have started to pay more attention to who votes and who does not, the most striking finding has been the low level of participation among young Canadians. Provincial turnout patterns are not generally scrutinized as closely, but a large gap in turnout between younger and older citizens has been reported for New Brunswick (Howe 2007b), British Columbia (Elections BC 2005, 33), Manitoba (Prairie Research Associates 2004, 4-5), and Alberta (Leger Marketing 2008, 36).

At the federal level, there has been closer study of age-based differences in turnout. One report appearing in 2003, based on a large national survey, produced the startling estimate that a mere 25 percent of those aged eighteen to twenty-four had voted in the 2000 federal election (Pammett and Leduc 2003a, 20). This figure caught the attention of many and gave added impetus to the public debate already underway on the political disengagement of young Canadians. As a survey-based estimate, however, it faced a common problem with this method of assessing political participation: significant inflation. The actual voter turnout reported by survey respondents was 82.3 percent overall and 50.1 percent among those under twenty-five.[2] The first of these figures was obviously inaccurate, since actual turnout in the 2000 election was only 61.2 percent.[3] The researchers made a statistical adjustment to the survey data to bring the overall turnout level down to that figure, this same adjustment yielding the 25 percent turnout estimate for those under twenty-five.

Other evidence would suggest that the study probably overshot the mark in pegging turnout among young voters that low. After the subsequent federal election in 2004, Elections Canada used a new method to estimate turnout by age group, based on a large sampling of voters list records after the election (Elections Canada 2005). This approach avoids the problem of inflated reporting, since it is based on administrative records of participation, which include the age of each elector. Using this method, the turnout level estimated for those aged eighteen to twenty-four in the 2004 election was 37 percent. While one interpretation of this result might be that turnout among young people moved sharply upwards between 2000 and 2004 – Elections Canada had, after all, launched numerous initiatives in that period to boost turnout among young voters – this does not square with other results. The same voters list study found that the true turnout levels in 2004 for older age groups were in the 65 to 75 percent range, on average about 9 percentage points *below* the adjusted survey-based estimates from the 2000 election (Pammett and Leduc 2003a, 20). Unless turnout in 2004 simultaneously jumped among young people and slumped among older voters, it would seem that the study of the 2000 election was off the mark in its statistical adjustment procedures.

The point is not to criticize the earlier study nor to suggest that the democratic impulse is alive and well among young Canadians, as 37 percent is hardly a stellar participation rate. It is simply to establish that there is no evidence that turnout among the young has spiked sharply upwards in more recent federal elections. With this new methodology providing more reliable estimates of turnout by age group, the gap between younger and older adults can be gauged more precisely. Since Elections Canada is continuing with this study at each federal election, it is also possible to use the 2004 study as a baseline to track changes in turnout across different age categories over time. Table 1.1 compares results of the studies conducted after the 2004, 2006, and 2008 elections. The table reveals an improvement in turnout among young Canadians in the 2006 election and a slight closing of the age gap. Turnout that year increased by 6 to 7 percentage points among younger age groups (those under forty-five) but by no more than 2 to 4 points among older groups. In 2008, participation among younger groups declined, in some cases back to 2004 levels, but at the same time fell by a greater margin among all older age categories (save the eldest). As a result, the turnout gap between young and old was again slightly reduced.[4]

These trends bear monitoring and as time goes by it may become possible to detect the arc of participation in particular demographic categories more

Table 1.1

Voter turnout in Canadian federal elections by age group (%)

Age	2004	2006	2008
18 to 24	37.0	43.8	37.4
25 to 34	44.0	49.8	48.0
35 to 44	54.5	61.6	53.9
45 to 54	66.0	70.0	59.7
55 to 64	72.9	75.4	65.6
65 to 74	75.5	77.5	68.4
75+	63.9	61.6	67.3

Sources: 2004 and 2006: Elections Canada 2008, 9; 2008: Elections Canada 2010, 8.

clearly. At this stage, the more consistent pattern that might be emphasized is that turnout among the most participatory age group, those sixty-five to seventy-four, has been more or less double that of young adults under twenty-five in each of the last three federal elections. The reasons for this stubborn gap and how it might be reduced more substantially are subjects that merit close investigation.

Efforts to probe the reasons behind electoral disengagement have, however, been hindered by mounting challenges in persuading people to talk about these matters. Survey response rates have been on the decline, slowly over the long haul and more precipitously in the last few years. Unbeknown to most casual consumers of polling research, the average response rate across the industry now sits at around 10 percent (PMRS Response Rate Committee 2003). The drop has been especially sharp among young adults, for reasons that are not entirely clear. Technological developments are certainly a factor (increased use of cellphones and call-screening, for example) but do not seem to explain the phenomenon fully. In any event, no polling organization has been immune from the problem, even those concentrating on academic survey research, which generally go to considerable lengths to capture hard-to-reach and reluctant respondents (and which still manage to secure overall response rates around 50 percent). The result has been a significant decline in the representation of young adults in the survey samples commonly used to track and analyze patterns of political engagement. In the 2004 Canadian election study, for example, the eighteen to twenty-nine age group comprised only 15.4 percent of the sample,[5] well below their estimated share of the population, 19.9 percent (Elections Canada 2005, Appendix, 2). Just four years earlier, in the 2000 Canadian election study, there was no such discrepancy between the representation of this age group in the survey sample and the population. The main concern with this abrupt decline in survey participation among young adults is not smaller sample sizes, but the representativeness of those samples. It is widely recognized that those with some interest in politics are more inclined to participate in surveys on political matters (one reason voter turnout rates on surveys are inflated). If response rates are lower or dropping more rapidly among young adults, over-representation of the politically engaged in that group may be especially acute. Consequently, the gap between young and old may appear less profound and downward trends among the young less pronounced than they would if the politically disengaged were fully present and accounted for in our survey samples.[6]

These are, however, new challenges to an unobstructed view of the landscape, and our understanding of the present rests at least as much on a clear assessment of the past. For this purpose, there is a rich body of prior survey research, dating back to a time when methodological barriers were less formidable, that can provide insight into earlier trends in citizen engagement that have brought us to our current pass. This study makes considerable use of such earlier data sources. It also draws extensively on one more current survey conducted specifically for the study, which was designed to fill a number of important gaps in our understanding of democratic engagement. These varied sources underwrite analysis and reflection on the decline in voter turnout along with other manifestations of waning civic involvement, as well as the broader social and cultural tides of change relevant to these developments.

Two Key Variables: Age and Electoral Participation

Before pursuing other lines of inquiry, however, there is considerably more to be said about the canary in the political disengagement coal mine, declining voter turnout. The observation that turnout is disconcertingly low among today's young adults can be taken further to provide new insight into the phenomenon, along with important grounding for a broader analysis of political disengagement. This elaboration involves recognizing that both age and electoral participation are more complex variables than is immediately apparent.

Life-Cycle and Cohort Effects

Age, for its part, marks two quite different characteristics: how old someone is and their year of birth. Both are potentially relevant to political engagement. How old someone is tells us something about their current stage of life, their likely level of maturity, their "stake" in society, and other factors that might reasonably be expected to influence political involvement. To link low voter turnout among young adults to these types of factors is to assume it is a function of the fact that they are in the early stages of adulthood. Two assumptions normally accompany this line of thinking: today's young adults will change their ways as they age, eventually attaining turnout levels as high as older adults; and a reduced propensity to vote is something that would have been evident among young adults of the past as well. It is, then, a relatively optimistic interpretation, suggesting that low voter turnout among today's young adults is simply a normal phase that each generation passes through on its way to reaching peak levels of political engagement later in life.

In addition to reflecting how old someone is, however, age also reflects one's year of birth, or more descriptively, the period in which one was born and came of age. Many believe that people's basic values and dispositions, including those relevant to political engagement, are shaped by the social and political environment prevailing during the early years of childhood and adolescence. These formative influences exert a strong and steady pull throughout a person's life, leading to abiding differences in certain attitudes and behaviours among those born at different points. To link low voter turnout among today's young Canadians to these types of factors is to suggest it reflects something distinctive about those who came of age in more recent times. The attendant expectations in this case are more pessimistic: lower turnout would not necessarily have been evident among young people of the past and today's young adults will remain relatively disengaged from electoral politics even as they age.

The technical terms for these two accounts of age-related differences are life-cycle and cohort effects. The first sees people's behaviours and attitudes as a function of changes people experience as they age and move through different stages of life. The second interprets them as reflections of the distinctive and abiding qualities of the birth cohort to which people belong. Researchers looking at voter participation have drawn on this conceptual distinction to provide some important grounding for our understanding of current patterns of turnout among young Canadians. Using the surveys conducted during each federal election from 1968 through 2000 (save 1972), the research team overseeing the Canadian election study has conducted analysis comparing young people of the present and past and tracking how voting tendencies have evolved as cohorts have aged – the necessary method to detect life-cycle and cohort effects. A pure life-cycle account would anticipate similar levels of turnout between young adults of the past and present, along with a pattern of increasing participation among young adults as they age over time. An unqualified cohort account would anticipate lower levels of turnout among younger cohorts joining the electorate and no increase in participation within these cohorts as they grow older.

There is also the possibility that *both* effects contribute to low voter turnout among today's young adults, and this, in fact, is what the empirical results reveal. Voter participation is affected by life-cycle dynamics, as turnout increases by roughly 15 percentage points between the ages of twenty and fifty (Blais et al. 2004, 224). Thus part of the current turnout gap between younger and older Canadians reflects an abiding tendency of young adulthood. In addition, however, there are substantial cohort effects that have produced lower participation rates in new birth cohorts joining the electorate over time. Even though people are more apt to vote as they grow older, turnout levels remain consistently lower than for earlier cohorts at the same age. These cohort effects date surprisingly far back: compared to those born before 1945, turnout levels are about 2 to 3 points lower in the 1945 to 1959 birth cohort, another 10 points lower in the 1960s cohort, and a further 10 points lower in the 1970s cohort (Blais et al. 2004, 225). Although this research has not been extended to those born in the 1980s, an approximate estimation is simple enough. The Elections Canada study of participation by age group in the 2004 election found that turnout was 7 percentage points lower among those aged eighteen to twenty-four (born in the 1980s) than among those aged twenty-five to thirty-four (born in the 1970s) (Elections Canada 2008, 9), and the difference between the two age groups was about the same in the 2006 study. The calculations by the election study team suggest that the life-cycle difference between the average ages for these groups – twenty and thirty, respectively – is 8 to 11 percentage points and therefore can account for this entire gap (Blais et al. 2004, 224). This suggests that the turnout decline among rising cohorts has levelled off: when life-cycle effects are taken into account, participation among the 1980s cohort is roughly the same as the 1970s cohort, which is to say, about 20 points below the turnout level of those born in the 1940s and earlier.

While both life-cycle and cohort effects contribute to a turnout gap between young and old, there are important differences between the two. One is that life-cycle effects are typically seen as the more readily explicable phenomenon. That people are less apt to vote when they are younger can be tied to any number of self-evident features of early adulthood: residential mobility (Highton 2000), a focus on personal goals that take priority over politics (higher education, establishing a career, finding a life partner – see Strate et al. 1989), or perhaps simply a general lack of life experience (Highton and Wolfinger 2001). That the young people of today are less likely to vote than young people of the past, by contrast, poses a greater mystery: what is it about younger cohorts, or their social and political environment, that has made them less apt to participate in electoral politics?

A second key difference lies in the impact of life-cycle and cohort effects on overall participation levels. A steady churn of younger non-voters gradually maturing into voters, the life-cycle dynamic, does not pull down aggregate turnout. Cohort effects, on other hand, do have this impact, as younger people less committed to voting take the place of more participatory older cohorts. This happens only slowly, of course, since generational turnover is a gradual process. This is why the downward pressure on turnout that started in the early 1970s among those born in the late 1940s and 1950s has only come to our attention in the past ten years or so. The impact at the outset was negligible: the decline in voting among the 1945 to 1959 cohort was small and this group represented only a fraction of the electorate at that time. Any downward effect was easily masked by the fluctuation produced by other factors that influence turnout in any given election. The aggregate impact only became noticeable as the turnout gap grew larger with successive cohorts (those born in the 1960s, 1970s, and 1980s) and as these cohorts came to account for more of the total electorate. The continuation of these processes would lead us to anticipate that turnout will remain on a downward trend (marked by less predictable short-term fluctuations) until cohorts less committed to voting eventually come to comprise the entire adult population. The one consolation is the apparent levelling-off of turnout decline among those born in the 1980s. If this continues to hold for this cohort and others to follow (a risky assumption, mind), there is a turnout floor in sight of about 55 percent, 20 points lower than the historic norm of around 75 percent. This would represent a new baseline for voter turnout in Canadian federal elections, with fluctuations around that figure dependent on a bevy of election-specific factors that make precise predictions impossible. In the absence of successful initiatives to reverse the downward trend, voter participation would presumably dip below 50 percent from time to time.

In light of the foregoing, there is a natural tendency to give greater heed to cohort differences in turnout than to the life-cycle dynamic. The latter, reasonably characterized as a "normal" and self-correcting tendency among the young, can appear relevant only as a confounding factor that must be taken into account to reveal the true magnitude of cohort effects, after which it can be safely set aside. The analysis that follows in subsequent chapters is not quite so dismissive. In employing the conceptual distinction to investigate various dimensions of democratic disengagement among young Canadians, the initial approach is to follow the standard logic, treating life cycle and cohort as separate demographic effects to be carefully separated, like white and yolk, through appropriate conceptual reasoning and analytical techniques. However, rather than discarding the one not required in the standard recipe, it is set aside for later purposes. As life-cycle patterns continue to materialize, they are gradually folded back into the mix by blending the two demographic effects in a theory designed to explain why younger generations have become increasingly disengaged over time. The distinction between life cycle and cohort thus serves a twofold purpose, helping to map the contours of young people's participation in order to distinguish the perennial from the new, but also setting the stage for a blending of the perennial and the new that offers a different understanding of the root causes of democratic disengagement.

Habitual and Intermittent Non-voting

If our understanding of age differences in voter turnout is enhanced by acknowledging the important distinction between life-cycle and cohort effects, it can also be advanced through further refinement of the concept of electoral participation. Whether an individual votes in any given election is simple enough and requires no great elaboration. But focusing on someone's actions (or inaction) in a single election can be misleading. People who normally vote may miss one election because they were otherwise occupied and unable to get to the polling station, or they may have deliberately abstained, but only for reasons specific to that electoral contest. Consequently, participation across multiple elections is a more meaningful measure: Does someone vote always, sometimes, or never? What about young people: Are they habitual voters, intermittent voters, or habitual abstainers? And how do they stack up in this respect against young people of the past? These are slightly more complex questions that can reveal more about the nature of declining voter turnout and the participatory tendencies of today's young adults.[7]

The expectation from some recent commentary would be that a good number of the non-voters among today's young adults are people who never vote. The same researchers responsible for the widely cited cohort analysis of Canadian voting patterns over time have elsewhere suggested that young Canadians have "tuned out" of electoral politics and are "turning their backs on electoral politics in unprecedented numbers" (Gidengil et al. 2003, 9). Another scholar who has written widely on the issue of political disengagement has warned that many of today's young Canadians can be characterized as "political dropouts" (Milner 2005). These pithy descriptions have not, however, been based on analysis of the participation of individuals over multiple elections. The presence of cohort effects among younger generations can certainly give the impression of electoral desertion, as it is easy to assume that consistently lower turnout means that some individuals within a given cohort must be failing to vote at each opportunity. However, this is not necessarily the case, as cohort effects only indicate stable behaviour at the group level, which can be consistent with a wide range of participatory tendencies at the individual level. To take a hypothetical example: if voter turnout in a particular cohort is a steady 50 percent over time, it may be that half the individual members of that cohort always vote and half never do; or it could be that *every* member of the cohort votes *half* the time, thereby generating 50 percent turnout at each election. Of course, between these two extremes is an infinite range of possibilities, since people can have a propensity to vote anywhere between 0 percent and 100 percent. As long as propensities remain stable – and this does not even have to be individual propensities, just aggregate propensities within the group – the behaviour of the cohort will be constant. So, stable turnout within a cohort does not provide sufficient evidence to draw conclusions about the participatory proclivities of individual voters.

The only way to find out what stability at the cohort level means is to analyze participation by individuals across multiple elections. While panel surveys in which respondents are interviewed at multiple points in time are one way to capture such information, these come with their own particular methodological challenges and are not frequently conducted. Cross-sectional surveys that ask respondents at a given point about their past participation in multiple elections are a more readily available source.

Table 1.2 uses two such studies separated by thirty years to assess voting propensities at two different points, along with change in those propensities over time. Respondents from the 1974 and 2004 Canadian election studies are categorized based on their reported participation in three elections: the federal elections of 1974 and 2004, the previous federal elections (in 1972 and 2000), and the most recent provincial election. For both periods, the youngest age group is limited to those aged twenty-five to twenty-nine, to ensure that all respondents would have been eligible to vote in all three elections in question.[8]

Table 1.2 reveals changing patterns of non-voting over time, changes that are most significant among younger adults. Consider first the earlier data. In 1974, there were exceedingly few habitual non-voters in the population as a whole. Only 1.3 percent reported voting in none of the three elections in question (total column). Furthermore, there were no more habitual non-voters among the youngest group than in older age categories – in fact, in what is partly a statistical quirk, there were none.[9] Thus non-voting among those under thirty was solely a reflection of an elevated proportion of inter-mittent voters; and within this category, occasional non-voters, who participated in two of three elections, were far more numerous (27.0 percent) than more frequent non-voters, who voted in only one (6.9 percent). The conclusion for the earlier period is unambiguous: lower turnout among young adults was solely due to their elevated propensity to vote intermittently rather than the presence of any significant block of habitual non-voters.

Nowadays, patterns of non-voting have changed significantly, especially among younger cohorts. The most important change is the emergence of a sizable contingent of habitual non-voters. In the 2004 data, the incidence of habitual non-voting among those aged twenty-five to twenty-nine, non-existent in 1974, sat at 11.1 percent. The incidence among those aged thirty to thirty-nine was also much higher in 2004 than in 1974 (9.9 percent versus 1.7 percent), and was modestly elevated in the forty to forty-nine age category (4.4 percent versus 0.7 percent). It is only among those fifty and older that habitual non-voting remained at the minimal levels seen in 1974.

Table 1.2

Multi-election voter participation, 1974 and 2004 (%)

Elections voted in	Age						Total
	25-29	30-39	40-49	50-59	60-69	70+	
1974							
None	0.0	1.7	0.7	1.2	2.3	2.3	1.3
One	6.9	6.7	2.5	2.6	2.7	2.3	4.0
Two	27.0	19.3	13.9	13.7	11.5	12.2	16.4
Three	66.0	72.3	82.9	82.5	83.5	83.1	78.3
(N)	(259)	(404)	(439)	(343)	(260)	(172)	(1,877)
2004							
None	11.1	9.9	4.4	2.4	2.6	1.8	4.9
One	15.7	10.9	4.8	1.4	1.4	3.0	5.3
Two	19.9	13.8	11.0	10.5	7.8	6.9	11.2
Three	53.2	65.4	79.7	85.7	88.2	88.2	78.6
(N)	(216)	(477)	(745)	(630)	(348)	(331)	(2,747)

General note: Columns in this and other tables may not add up to precisely 100 percent due to rounding. For tables based on survey data, weights supplied by the original investigators to produce representative national samples have been applied where available.

Note: The calculations are based on reported participation in the last two federal elections and most recent provincial election.

Sources: 1974 and 2004 Canadian Election Studies.

Meanwhile, there continued to be, as in 1974, elevated levels of intermittent voting among younger adults. Adding one- and two-time voters together, nearly 36 percent of those under thirty can be classified as intermittent voters in the 2004 data; among those fifty and over, this combined total drops to roughly 10 percent. Yet there is also an important change within the category of intermittent voters, as one-time voters have become more common, again among younger age groups in particular. Whereas the ratio of two- to one-time voters among the under thirty group in 1974 was about four-to-one (27 percent versus 6.9 percent), it is now almost one-to-one (19.9 percent versus 15.7 percent). A similar shift in this ratio, though less pronounced, appears in the thirty to thirty-nine and forty to forty-nine age groups. It is only among those fifty and over that the proportion of two- to one-time voters is more or less unchanged from 1974. In these changing patterns lies further evidence of a weakening disposition to vote among younger cohorts.

Clearly, considerable changes have occurred in the composition of the non-voting population, especially in younger cohorts. The simplest way to summarize the changes is to say there has been an increase in the lower two categories (habitual non-voters and one-time voters) at the expense of the upper two. A slightly more complex way to summarize the difference is to think about what the results suggest about general propensities to vote. The 1974 results come very close to what would be expected if *all* young voters at that time were generally disposed to vote at each opportunity. To be precise, statistical theory suggests that if *every* young voter had an 87 percent likelihood of voting in each of the three elections in question, we would expect to see 0 percent missing all three, 4.4 percent voting in one, 29.5 percent voting in two, and 65.9 percent voting in all three.[10] The fact that this very nearly matches the actual pattern in the 1974 data suggests that non-voting at that time was a largely random occurrence: most young people were generally inclined to vote at each opportunity, but due to random circumstance, a sizable number had missed one recent election and a handful had missed two. The 2004 results for young adults, on the other hand, cannot possibly be explained by assumptions of a uniform propensity to vote, not even assumptions of a *lower* uniform propensity to vote. The pattern that appears in Table 1.2 could only be produced if some of today's young adults are highly inclined to vote at any given opportunity and others are highly disinclined. So, another way to summarize the changes is to say that a new group – inveterate abstainers – has emerged on the electoral scene, as a result of which there is now, compared to thirty-some years ago, much greater variation in the propensity to vote among young adults.[11]

Further insight into the mechanisms behind habitual and intermittent non-voting can be gleaned from the reasons survey respondents offer for failing to vote at particular opportunities. For example, when non-voters were asked in the 2004 election study why they did not participate in that particular contest, 65 percent of habitual non-voters cited relatively substantial impediments – they did not know for whom to vote or what the issues were, had no interest in the election, felt their vote would make no difference, or (perhaps most tellingly) were not really sure why. Such reasons were cited by only 30 percent of intermittent voters who had missed the 2004 election. Meanwhile, 59 percent of the latter cited circumstantial reasons for not voting – they simply forgot, were too busy or too ill to vote, were absent on election day, were not registered, or were uncertain about where to vote – compared to only 19 percent of habitual non-voters (author's calculations based on 2004 Canadian election study).[12] The latter are reasons more clearly linked to happenstance and for that reason more likely to be random in their effects, preventing Person A from voting in one election, Person B in the next – in other words, producing intermittent abstention. More profound impediments to electoral participation, on the other hand, are more likely to be carried forward by the same individual from one election to the next and hence to be associated with habitual non-voting.

Pulling these findings together can help make sense of the general evolution of voting among young Canadians over time. In the past, turnout was somewhat lower among young adults mainly because of their greater tendency to vote intermittently. This is consistent with the notion that lower participation among the young at this time principally represented a life-cycle dynamic – a reflection, in other words, of the early stage of adulthood, when people are preoccupied with other matters and do not always find the time to vote, even if so inclined. This is a type of effect likely to impinge upon many if not most young adults, leading to an overall pattern, evident in the 1974 data, consistent with random abstention. As these young voters have aged, however, they have, in aggregate, changed their ways, just as life-cycle theory would predict. We can trace these changes by consulting Table 1.2 and noting that those who were in their twenties in 1974 are the same people (or at least a sample of the same people) who would have been in their fifties in 2004. Now that they are considerably older, their intermittent voting has tailed off (combined one- and two-time voting has declined from 33.9 percent to 11.9 percent) and habitual voting has increased by about the same amount (from 66.0 percent to 85.7 percent). Young intermittent voters of 1974, for the most part, had matured into middle-aged habitual voters by 2004.

There is no reason to think this life-cycle dynamic would have disappeared over time and the evidence in Table 1.2 suggests it has not. We continue to see higher levels of intermittent voting among the young than the old and would anticipate that many of today's sporadic twenty-something voters will eventually move on to become consistent electoral participants. What is new is the marked growth in the category of habitual non-voters. These individuals, their non-voting rooted in more profound motivational impediments, are more set in their ways. It is this group that distinguishes the young people of today from those of thirty years ago and that is responsible for the cohort effects that have seen turnout declining steadily among rising generations over the past number of years.

After much ado, then, the conclusion is that the characterizations in recent commentary do seem apt: some young people are electoral "dropouts," who are "turning their backs" on electoral politics. This established, a criticism arises concerning existing efforts to boost voter turnout. Most of these initiatives (some contained in a federal bill, C-16, that failed to pass prior to the dissolution of parliament in the fall of 2008) are unlikely to win over electoral dropouts and are instead designed to improve turnout among intermittent participants. These include such measures as providing more opportunity for advance voting, allowing for voting at regular polling stations on two consecutive days, including a day of rest (i.e., Sunday and Monday), and making it easier for unregistered voters to sign up to vote on the spot. Such measures address circumstantial reasons people with an inclination to vote sometimes fail to do so. That they are likely to influence intermittent non-voters only probably explains why their overall effects tend to be limited (Blais et al. 2007). To achieve more substantial effects, habitual non-voters must be targeted through a different set of initiatives.[13]

From a normative standpoint, moreover, intermittent voters are probably of lesser concern than those who never vote. Through their past behaviour, they have demonstrated the willingness and wherewithal to participate at least on occasion. If future occasion warrants – when issues they consider important are on the public agenda, arguably the most critical time for people to make their voices heard – the likelihood of their voting is high. By contrast, it is not nearly as clear that habitual non-voters will find their way to the polling station when issues that matter to them are at stake (or perhaps more precisely issues that *should* matter to them, since lack of political awareness, explored at some length in later chapters, is a distinguishing trait of habitual non-voters). The fact that elections agencies have focused on administrative measures aimed at the easy targets among the non-voting population is understandable, given the limited resources and policy tools at their disposal. However, if efforts to boost participation succeed only in increasing the frequency of voting by intermittent voters, they can be considered but a limited success. As we explore the factors giving rise to habitual non-voting and the deeper disengagement from public life underlying this pattern of behaviour, it will become clear that more far-reaching initiatives involving a broader range of players will be needed to turn the tide.

Habitual Non-voters: A Closer Look

If an emphasis on habitual non-voters provides a more defined conceptual and normative focus for the analysis of electoral disengagement, it can also have the appearance of diminishing the scope of the problem to the point of insignificance. After all, according to the estimate in Table 1.2, only about 11 percent of those aged twenty-five to twenty-nine could be deemed habitual non-voters in 2004. Compared to the more dramatic numbers for abstention rates among young voters in individual elections (50 percent or more), this seems a rather modest and manageable figure.

This would be a hasty conclusion, however, as the 11 percent figure vastly understates the true level of habitual non-voting. This is because the Canadian election studies, despite the best efforts of those involved, have not escaped the intractable problem of inflated estimates of voter turnout. For example, the turnout level reported by respondents in the 2004 study for the federal election just past was 86.4 percent, whereas the actual turnout on 28 June 2004 was 60.9 percent. If this discrepancy seems large, the flipside of these numbers, the incidence of non-voting, makes the distortion seem even greater: 13.6 percent non-voting reported on the survey versus 39.1 percent in the real world, almost a threefold difference.

There are two main reasons for this. One is that politically engaged individuals are more likely to agree to be surveyed. The other is that people will sometimes indicate they voted when in fact they did not, whether due to faulty recall, an inclination to give the socially acceptable response, or some combination of these. The first problem can be tackled by achieving a higher response rate on surveys in order to reach those less taken with politics. The only studies that are able to push significantly beyond the response rates achieved by the Canadian election studies (high-quality surveys that make maximization of response rates a priority) are those that are government-sponsored. For this reason, a Statistics Canada survey on social engagement conducted in 2003, the seventeenth in the General Social Survey (GSS) series, is an important source for more definitive assessments of voter participation patterns. Canadians may like to complain about their government, but should have no cause to criticize the data collection efforts of our national statistical agency. A high response rate of 78 percent, well above the 50-55 percent range achieved in recent election studies, means that the survey's estimates of voter turnout are more in line with reality. A large sample size of nearly 25,000 Canadians is another significant benefit, allowing for fine-grained analysis within narrowly defined subgroups, which allows for consideration and refinement of various propositions relating to the electoral participation of young Canadians.

With respect to voter turnout, the Statistics Canada survey asked respondents whether they had voted in the most recent federal, provincial, and municipal elections.[14] Table 1.3 displays voting patterns across the three elections for the same age groups as before. The finding that immediately leaps out is the sharply higher rate of habitual non-voting among young adults. Compared to the 11.1 percent estimate for those aged twenty-five to twenty-nine based on the 2004 Canadian election study data, the figure here is 33.8 percent, equal now to the percentage of habitual voters. The incidence of habitual non-voting is similarly elevated for other age categories compared to the earlier estimates: 25.7 percent among those aged thirty to thirty-nine, 16.3 percent among those forty to forty-nine, and roughly 10 percent among those fifty and over.

One small problem with these estimates is that the Statistics Canada study, unlike the election studies, was not restricted to those residents of Canada eligible to vote in elections, namely, Canadian citizens. Nor did it ask respondents about their citizenship status or inquire whether they had not voted because they did not hold Canadian citizenship. The survey did, however, ask all respondents whether they were born in Canada and, if not, when they had immigrated. Using this information, recent immigrants (1995-2003) less likely to have attained citizenship were excluded from the calculations in Table 1.3 (and in subsequent turnout calculations based on this study below). With pre-1995 immigrants still in the sample, a reasonable

educated (19 percent versus 7 percent) and a fourfold difference for the other groups: those with other postsecondary education (33 percent versus 8 percent), those with a high school diploma (43 percent versus 11 percent) and those with none of the above (50 percent versus 13 percent). Relevant too is the fact that those with some sort of postsecondary education represent the larger part of the young adult sample in the survey – university graduates 20 percent, those with other postsecondary education (some university, community college, or trade/technical training) another 58 percent. While these figures are slightly inflated compared to actual population figures, it remains the case that those with some postsecondary education are in the majority among Canadians under age thirty.[20] Given their substantial weight in the population, the large rise in habitual non-voting among younger cohorts that has taken place over the last number of years simply could not have occurred without a significant "contribution" from those at higher levels of educational attainment.

The same conclusions about patterns of habitual non-voting apply when we look at another important socioeconomic variable, income level (Figure 1.3). Among younger adults, the increase in habitual non-voting with decreasing household income is steep, the resulting gap between the most and least affluent considerable (18 percentage points), while among older Canadians habitual non-voting among those in the bottom income category is only slightly greater than in the high-income group (a difference of 6 percentage points).[21] Yet the fact that income shows a stronger connection to voter participation among the young does not mean that well-heeled young Canadians have remained above the fray. The pervasiveness of the turnout gap between young and old is revealed by a consistent fourfold difference in the level of habitual non-voting between younger and older respondents at each income level. The problem of habitual non-voting among young adults is clearly evident across the entire socioeconomic spectrum.

These results point to a twofold conclusion. If voting patterns associated with education and income remain stable as younger cohorts age, then the contours of habitual non-voting apparent in Figures 1.2 and 1.3 will gradually reshape the socioeconomic profile of the active electorate as a whole. Those disadvantaged in various ways will, relatively speaking, be substantially less involved in electoral politics than society's middle and upper crusts. As others have argued, differing rates of participation across social classes can have significant consequences, allowing for public policy changes – cuts to social programs, tax cuts for the well-to-do – that hurt the interests of lower classes (Lijphart 1997; Milner 2001). Habitual non-voters, though more likely to suffer the adverse consequences of such actions, are unlikely to vote en masse to stop them. The experience of the 1990s, when significant cuts were made to various social and welfare programs across most provinces with no obvious electoral response from disadvantaged strata of Canadian society,

Figure 1.3

Voting propensity by age and household income

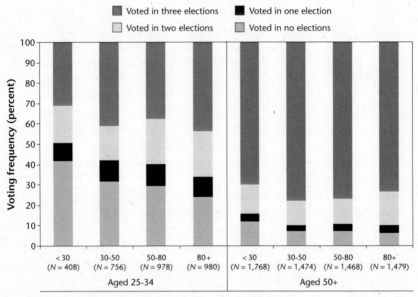

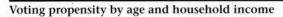

Source: Statistics Canada, GSS 17 (2003).

exemplifies these political dynamics in action. Greater inequalities in participation in future years are likely to continue the trend. At the same time, an exclusive focus on the impoverished and poorly educated is not an adequate response to what is clearly a broad-based disengagement from electoral politics among younger Canadians. To enhance engagement *and* ensure equal representation for all, a two-track strategy is needed: to boost involvement among younger cohorts in general, while paying particular attention to those disadvantaged in various ways, whose interests are unlikely to be adequately represented without their own active participation in politics.

Beyond Voting

Before proceeding to examine factors that might have given rise to the relatively acute form of electoral disengagement that is habitual non-voting, it is important to take account of other forms of involvement in Canadian politics and civic affairs. While voting is an important facet of democratic engagement, it is also unique among participatory acts in that it is the only one with a participation target – the notional target, at least – of 100 percent.

For other forms of political and civic activity, there is generally no expectation that all will participate. We expect and accept that only a section of the population, perhaps a relatively small minority, depending on how intensive and time-consuming the activity in question is, will engage. At the same time, however, in assessing patterns of involvement across multiple realms of civic and political involvement, the reasonable hope would be that aggregate rates of involvement would be significantly higher. If it is unrealistic to expect that everyone will do everything in the civic and political arena, a more realistic ambition for a vibrant democracy is that most citizens will do something beyond voting.

One form of more intensive democratic engagement is involvement in a political party. Despite the voluble criticism sometimes directed their way, parties remain vital cogs in the democratic system, serving as important vehicles for the articulation of interests and ideologies, as instigators and contributors to public debate, and as the principal agents in the implementation of public policy. Any decline in citizen involvement in political parties must be of concern, for parties without partisans are unlikely to fulfill these functions as effectively as parties with a more robust and active membership (Dalton and Wattenberg 2000).

With respect to young Canadians, there is clear evidence that voter participation patterns are mirrored in trends in party involvement. As in other countries, Canada's political parties suffer from a dearth of young members. A survey of nearly 4,000 Canadian party members carried out in 2000 found that only 6 percent were under age thirty, whereas 42 percent were sixty-five or older (Cross and Young 2004, 432). Furthermore, the available evidence suggests that this is a generational rather than a life-cycle phenomenon (as would seem to be true in other countries too; see Whiteley 2007). In earlier decades, concerns were sometimes voiced about the excessive prominence and influence of the youth wings of Canadian parties, an issue rarely mentioned nowadays (Young and Cross 2007, 1). Surveys confirm a significant drop in the proportion of adults under thirty who have ever been a member of a party, from just under 10 percent in 1990 to 5 percent in 2000, a sharp decline over a relatively short time (Gidengil et al. 2004, 129-30).

While there may be shortcomings of the parties partly to blame for these trends, there are broader issues to be considered relating to young people themselves and their propensity to participate in the political realm. Those who have closely studied the role of young people in Canada's political parties see their conspicuous absence as a reflection of "structurally grounded generational change" (Young and Cross 2007, 26). As with voting, there may be easy solutions that sound rather tempting (e.g., the parties should pay greater attention to issues of concern to young people), but these will not make a significant dent if the core of the problem lies elsewhere.

Yet there is more to democratic life than just voting and parties, and a broader perspective is required to take full stock of the problem. One important response to the debate on democratic disengagement, voiced in both Canada and other countries, is that young people *do* participate in the public life of the country, but that they simply go about it in different ways from older generations. This proposition goes hand in hand with the idea that the mores and methods of conventional politics – elections, political parties, parliament, and the rest – are out of sync with the sensibilities of today's younger generation, hence their disinclination to vote or join parties and their preference for other forms of public involvement.[22] Whether for this reason or others, it is undeniably the case that the participation gap between young and old is considerably smaller for a number of measures of political and civic engagement beyond voting and party membership. However, a closer look at these patterns of involvement, based on the Statistics Canada's General Social Survey of 2003, suggests that there remains significant cause for concern about the degree of public engagement among a sizable section of today's younger generation.

Of particular relevance to the optimistic interpretation of engagement among today's younger citizens are newer forms of participation motivated by a wide array of political and social concerns. On the Statistics Canada study, respondents were asked if they had engaged in the following activities in the past year: signing a petition, attending a protest or march, and boycotting or choosing a product for ethical reasons. These less conventional types of political activity have become popular methods of seeking to exert political influence in the past few decades. The survey also asked respondents about their engagement in three other, more traditional political activities beyond voting during the past year: expressing their views by contacting a newspaper or politician, attending a public meeting, and volunteering for a political party (a slightly broader question about party involvement than membership per se).

Figure 1.4 shows the percentage of respondents in different age groups who reported participating in at least one of these six activities in the past year, along with a breakdown into the incidence of involvement in traditional and non-traditional activities. The patterns contrast markedly with the sharp age trend for the core democratic activities of voting and party membership. For the six activities as a whole, levels of participation are more or less uniform, hovering around the 50 percent mark from ages fifteen to sixty-nine. The only sharp deviation is among those seventy and over, as the incidence of participation drops to 31 percent. Looking separately at traditional and non-traditional activities, the anticipated pattern emerges: the tendency for young people to be less engaged is more evident in the realm of traditional political activity. Among those in their twenties, the incidence of party volunteering, contacting a newspaper or politician, or attending a public

Figure 1.4

Beyond voting: Other political activities by age

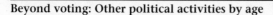

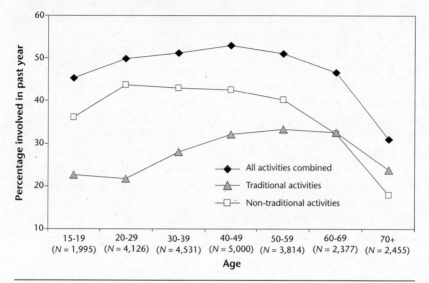

Source: Statistics Canada, GSS 17 (2003).

meeting is 22 percent, a figure that climbs to 33 percent among those in their fifties (a 50 percent increase). For the non-traditional activities – signing petitions, boycotting or choosing a product for ethical reasons, and participating in a demonstration – the pattern looks similar to that for all activities combined: fairly even participation across age groups, with the exception of a significant dip among those sixty and over.

We might be flinty in our assessment and note that, on the whole, young people, contrary to the impression that might be formed from media coverage of youth-led protests over globalization, the environment, and other contentious issues of recent times, are not exceptionally engaged in non-traditional forms of political activity. In the same vein, it could be added that middle-aged Canadians manage to be *equally* involved in non-traditional ways and *more* involved in traditional forms of politics, suggesting a more catholic approach to political activity that may be more productive in achieving change. Consistent with this observation, among those aged fifty to fifty-nine who reported involvement in at least one non-traditional activity, 55 percent also reported participating in a traditional one, compared to only a third (35 percent) of those in their twenties.

The bottom line, however, is that the general level of political activity "beyond voting" among young Canadians is comparable to that of older Canadians, suggesting the younger generation is holding its own outside the limited arena of voting and party politics. The same holds true of two other forms of public engagement more civic than political: volunteering and involvement in non-political groups. The first is based on a question asking respondents whether they had volunteered in the past year.[23] The second is based on questions asking about participation or membership in six different categories of groups: school group or neighbourhood associations, service club or fraternal organizations, religious-affiliated groups, cultural or educational or hobby organizations, sports or recreation organizations, and other groups. Figure 1.5 provides no indication of any shortfall among young Canadians in these other areas of public involvement. In fact, the most active are those aged fifteen to nineteen, whose levels of volunteering and group involvement are significantly higher than any others. While this could be taken as a harbinger of a dramatic rise in volunteering and group participation among this particular cohort, a more likely explanation is that this pattern represents a temporary life-cycle effect, indicating something distinctive about the adolescent stage of life that facilitates these kinds of involvement. Aside from this and a downward dip once again among the oldest respondents, the age trend is relatively flat. There is no sign here of any marked age divide akin to that for electoral participation.

Thus far, the case for optimism seems solid: looking beyond voting at a wide range of other civic and political activities, there are few apparent signs of broader civic disengagement among young Canadians. The assessment

Figure 1.5

Beyond voting: Volunteering and group memberships by age

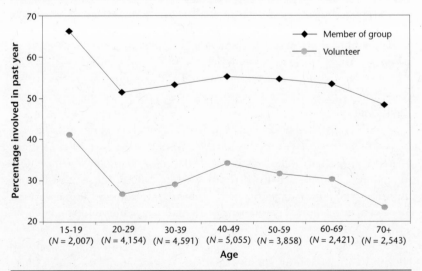

Source: Statistics Canada, GSS 17 (2003).

is less positive, however, when other socio-demographic factors that influence political and civic engagement are taken into account. Education, in particular, has a strong effect on all these extra-electoral activities and should be given due consideration in evaluating differences between age groups, given that younger cohorts on the whole have considerably higher levels of education. As would be anticipated, when each of the measures of engagement is examined within education levels, larger differences open up between the young and the not-so-young, especially among those with at least some postsecondary education. In the case of political activities (all six combined), the difference between those in their twenties and those in their fifties in Figure 1.4 (without controlling for education, that is) was just a single percentage point. When the same data are examined within educational categories, the younger group trails the older group by 9 percentage points among those with a university degree and by 4 percentage points among those with some postsecondary education but no degree. For volunteering, the uncontrolled difference in Figure 1.5 between twenty- and fifty-somethings is 5 points; the gap increases to 8 points among those with a degree, and 10 points among those with other postsecondary education. Finally, in the case of group activity, the uncontrolled difference of 3 points in Figure 1.5 becomes 6 points for those with a degree, and 12 points for those with other postsecondary education. While these age differences are not of the same order as those for electoral participation, neither can they be dismissed as negligible. And these higher educational categories, it should be recalled, represent the larger part of the under-thirty population, and indeed the more privileged segment that might be expected to be actively involved in civic and political affairs, given the well-documented benefits of higher education. Of course, without any analysis of civic involvement among young people of the past – analysis that would be difficult to undertake given the lack of suitable data sources – the possibility cannot be ruled out that the participatory proclivities of those in their twenties reflect a life-cycle pattern that will naturally correct itself with age, rather than a cohort effect portending generational decline. Still, the fact should be acknowledged that there are, once education is controlled, non-negligible differences between young and old in other areas of political and civic involvement.

The wisdom of applying such controls has been questioned by at least one observer (Arniel 2006, 100-4). It is mainly a matter of being careful about the implications that are drawn. To use education controls to argue that young adults are, contrary to appearances, less involved than older Canadians would be dubious reasoning. The level of participation in any given age group is what it is – inserting a control variable that ostensibly reveals the "true" level of engagement among younger citizens smacks of statistical sleight of hand. That said, it is surely worth pointing out that young people are less engaged than might be expected, given their education levels, and asking why the democratic dividend that would reasonably be anticipated from a sure and steady increase in levels of education down the years has failed to materialize. It is also worth contemplating what other factors might be at play serving to undermine the positive influence of education on various forms of public engagement. This is pertinent to a consideration of whether declining voter turnout among the young is an isolated phenomenon or part of a broader pattern of disengagement, for, as becomes clear in the subsequent chapter, some of the *same factors* that have a negative influence on electoral participation also tend to depress other forms of political and civic involvement. There is, then, value in drawing a circle around a broad range of political and civic activities and investigating some of their joint underlying determinants. In the one case, such analysis reveals why young adults vote significantly less than older Canadians and what might be done to close the gap. In the other, it indicates why young people are only holding their own in other realms of public involvement and what might be done to realize the full potential of their considerable educational reserves. The common objective is the enhancement of democracy through more wide-ranging participation by all citizens in different dimensions of the governing process (Barber 2003).

If the foregoing represents one reason to resist treating young people's involvement in other forms of political and civic activity as adequate compensation for shortfalls in the electoral arena, another emerges from closer consideration of who within the younger generation participates in these other ways and who does not. Pertinent here are the patterns of engagement across different categories of electoral participation. Figure 1.6 displays the percentage within each of the relevant categories – habitual non-voters, intermittent voters, and habitual voters – who reported engaging in various extra-electoral activities, for younger and older age categories. One would expect engagement of other varieties to decrease with a diminished propensity to vote, and Figure 1.6 reveals that indeed it does. Moreover, the pattern holds for both the younger and older age groups. There is no indication in these results that younger citizens who fail to vote are instead pouring their civic energies into other forms of public involvement.

There is, however, a more subtle difference between age categories worthy of note. Among older Canadians, the drop-off in electoral engagement is relatively consistent at each of two steps: from habitual voters to intermittent voters and from intermittent voters to habitual non-voters. For the younger group, aged twenty-five to thirty-four, the principal gap in extra-electoral engagement lies between those who vote occasionally and those who never vote; there is relatively little difference between intermittent and habitual voters (indeed in the case of non-traditional political activities and group memberships there is none).

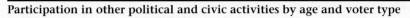

Figure 1.6

Participation in other political and civic activities by age and voter type

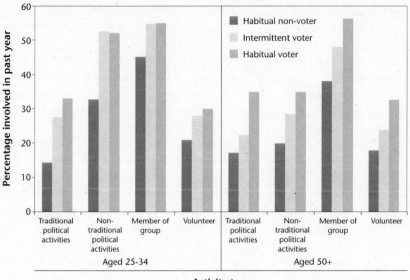

Source: Statistics Canada, GSS 17 (2003).

This pattern has a couple of implications. First, it suggests something about the character of intermittent voting in different age groups. For young Canadians, sporadic participation in elections seems to be consistent with being a relatively involved citizen, whereas for older Canadians it sends a stronger signal of more broad-based disengagement. One possible explanation for this is that conceptions of the "good citizen" (Dalton 2008) have undergone a generational redefinition, in that voting in elections is seen by younger cohorts as an optional element of citizenship, one of a larger array of potential modes of involvement to be taken up as one sees fit, whereas older generations treat consistent electoral participation as more essential. According to Stolle and Hooghe, there has been "a transition [among younger generations] from routine participation to a more reflexive and monitoring form of political involvement" (2005, 164). Yet there may also be a life-cycle dynamic underlying these patterns. It will be recalled from above that the high level of intermittent voting evident among young Canadians of both the past and present was interpreted as a reflection of ephemeral circumstances of young adulthood that impinge on voting, while the lower level among older adults was taken as evidence that intermittent young voters typically become habitual voters as they age and mature. The implication:

to be an intermittent voter at twenty-five is one thing, to still be one at fifty-five, quite another. As intermittent voting diminishes with age, it does become a clearer symptom of a deeper disengagement that goes beyond mere circumstantial non-participation. Early on, however, it does not carry the same significance. Thus the contrast between younger and older Canadians – the fact that young people who vote intermittently are otherwise just as participatory as habitual voters the same age – is not necessarily evidence of a new generational sensibility more inclined to monitorial and sporadic modes.of participation.

The other key point that emerges from Figure 1.6 is that habitual non-voting sends a more consistent and unambiguous signal: failure to vote election after election *is* a reliable indicator of a broader disengagement that manifests itself across other forms of political and civic involvement. Some young people nowadays may be participating in alternative ways and keeping levels of participation within their cohorts afloat, but they are *not*, for the most part, the electoral dropouts. It is this segment of the young adult population, a sizable minority, that is more clearly a generational force, their absence from the public arena serving to gradually sap overall levels of democratic participation. These habitual non-voters not only eschew the polling booth, they are also less present across other sectors of political and civic life.

This important general conclusion should not be overstated, however. Habitual non-voters, whether young or old, are not completely absent from other arenas of political and community involvement. While they are relatively thin on the ground compared to more electorally active Canadians, some do volunteer, join community groups, attend public meetings, sign petitions, and so on. To provide a sense of the number who are uninvolved across all sectors, as well as a more encompassing portrait of engagement patterns, a global summary of the participatory dispositions of different age groups is offered in Table 1.5. To create the table, a score of 1 was assigned for engaging in any of the six political activities, for volunteering in the past year, and for participation in any of the six categories of group involvement (thus a scale from 0 to 3). Added to this was another score between 0 and 3 representing the number of most recent elections in which respondents had voted. Thus scores at the extremes of the overall scale (0 or 6) are unambiguous in their meaning, while intermediate categories represent various possible combinations of electoral participation and other forms of political and civic involvement.

Others have taken a more nuanced approach to summary measures of engagement. Zukin et al., for example, use a similar array of survey measures to identify "political specialists" and "civic specialists," along with those who are both – "dual activists" – and those who are neither (2006, 63-65). However, it is important to underline that there are fairly significant correlations across different categories of participation: in the General Social Survey data, these range from 0.21 to 0.46 for volunteering, group memberships, and the two types of political activities, traditional and non-traditional. The same concentration of activism has been found in European countries, where party members are more likely to volunteer and be involved in social movements (Whiteley 2007, 19), and those who engage in high levels of political consumerism are more apt to vote, to work in political parties, and to contact politicians (Stolle and Cruz 2005, 96-97). Certainly, we could take the 2003 General Social Survey data and isolate some respondents who are civically but not politically active, and others who are involved politically but not civically. However, the more compelling pattern is that it is the same people, to a significant degree, who participate in a range of different activities in the broadly defined public sphere. A simple summary index reflects this idea that civic and political participation are of a piece.

At the top end of the aggregate engagement scale in Table 1.5 are those Canadians whose engagement runs both wide and deep – habitual voters who were also broadly active in the past year in the political and civic realms. According to the 2003 General Social Survey estimates, about 15 percent of Canadians fifty and over fit this description, compared to 7 percent of those twenty-five to thirty-four. Just behind these civic stalwarts are those Canadians participating in all but one of the relevant activities – that is to say, failing to vote in just one of three elections or not being active in one of the three general categories of extra-electoral involvement in the past year. A further 20 percent of those fifty and over, and another 14 percent of younger adults, fall into this stratum. Adding the two together, just over one-third of older Canadians and just over one-fifth of younger Canadians can be considered relatively deeply engaged by this accounting.

Table 1.5

Aggregate political and civic activities by age (%)		
Aggregate engagement score	Age	
	25-34	50+
0	11.4	4.9
1	12.7	4.2
2	14.6	7.1
3	20.3	25.8
4	19.5	23.0
5	14.2	20.2
6	7.3	14.8
(*N*)	(3,642)	(8,236)

Note: See text for method of calculating scores.
Source: Statistics Canada, GSS 17 (2003).

At the other end of the aggregate engagement scale are those who are both habitual non-voters and who report no involvement in other activities in the past year, whether political or civic. Just over 10 percent of those aged twenty-five to thirty-four and about 5 percent of those fifty and over qualify as inveterately disengaged by this measure. Next are the minimally engaged with a score of 1, who report voting in just one of three elections *or* indicate involvement in only one of three extra-electoral activities – a further 13 percent of the younger group, but only another 4 percent of the older group. Adding the two bottom categories together, about one-quarter of young Canadian adults can be considered minimally engaged, compared to just under 10 percent of older Canadians, a sharp contrast. When comparisons are drawn within educational categories, starker differences emerge, as before: among those who have not graduated high school, about half (49 percent) of the younger group score 0 or 1, compared to only 13 percent of those fifty and over. Among high school graduates, the minimally engaged comprise 39 percent of the younger group but only 11 percent of the older one. In the higher educational categories, those with some postsecondary education and those with a university degree, the differences between age groups are less dramatic but sizable still: 25 percent versus 7 percent and 12 percent versus 5 percent, respectively. Given the aforementioned concerns about biases in survey-based approaches to measuring public engagement, all these should probably be considered lower-end estimates.

These final categorizations and observations are consistent with the general approach informing much of the analysis in this first chapter. The average incidence of a given behaviour in a particular age category is not always particularly informative and more is revealed by concentrating on subgroups that exhibit more general syndromes of behaviours and characteristics. There are some young people today who vote intermittently, as young people have tended to do in the past as well, and who are engaged at reasonable levels in other ways. This segment of the population is clearly not of principal concern. But there are other young adults who are more profoundly disengaged from public life, and their numbers appear to have increased markedly among rising generations. Rather than despairing of the state of civic and political engagement among young people in general, the focus should fall on the core of the problem: those within younger cohorts who participate substantially less than their peers and their elders across a broad array of potential avenues of political and civic engagement, and whose absence from the public arena, given their concentration in lower socioeconomic categories, is not inconsequential.

Understanding this significant strand of chronic disengagement among younger generations of Canadians is the principal objective of this study. The starting point in the following chapter is a preliminary overview of possible explanatory factors and an outline of questions raised by these initial observations. This sets the stage for more intensive analysis in later sections of the book that further probe the more critical sources of disengagement.

2
The Wellsprings of Disengagement

The image of a democracy peopled by citizens in a steady state of civic and political animation is an attractive, but probably unattainable, ideal. A more realistic goal is to ensure that all citizens participate from time to time through voting and other activities of their choice, and that all are in a position to recognize when further political involvement on their part is warranted. By this yardstick, the significant rise in the number of younger Canadians displaying symptoms of chronic disengagement, such as habitual non-voting, is deeply problematic. Understanding the origins of the phenomenon requires investigation of substantial and enduring impediments to participation that could potentially explain such patterns of consistent non-involvement.

As a preliminary test, those factors worthy of further investigation must, on the one hand, clearly distinguish younger and older Canadians, and, on the other, show significant relationships to different forms of political and civic participation. Three general factors are considered in this chapter: disaffection with politics and government, inattentiveness to politics, and diminished levels of social integration. Of the three, only the latter two seem to offer significant explanatory purchase. Political disaffection is certainly a live issue in Canadian politics, but it is far from clear that it has significantly eroded the willingness of citizens, young or old, to be involved in political or civic affairs. A lack of attention to politics among younger Canadians, on the other hand, does seem to have negatively affected their participation in public life. The same is true of the twin elements of diminished social integration described below, relatively weak attachments to community among younger Canadians and their heightened individualism. It is, then, the latter two factors that become the main focus in seeking to develop a compelling account of the principal underlying forces giving rise to political disengagement among young Canadians.

In addition to presenting some initial findings that anchor the subsequent investigation, Chapter 2 also articulates a variety of empirical and normative questions that might reasonably be raised in response to these preliminary results and conclusions. The latter part of this chapter explains how these questions are addressed in later chapters and where they fit within the larger analytical framework of the study, thus providing a detailed roadmap to the book as a whole.

Methods and Approaches to Researching Participation

Of the different forms of public participation, voter turnout has been looked at most extensively in previous research. Most of that work involves analysis of participation in a single election, in contrast to the present focus on habitual non-voting. Nonetheless, there is considerable overlap with the current analysis for two reasons. First, inveterate non-voters account for the lion's share of the abstention among young Canadians, so naturally many of the factors that explain abstention as a single discrete act also explain the broader disposition that is habitual non-voting. Second, previous research, rather than investigating the minor and incidental factors that might affect the participation of those disposed to vote – modelling how much time people have available in their day to get to the polling station, for example – has instead tended to concentrate on the more compelling issue of fundamental motivations and dispositions that influence democratic involvement. For these reasons, the study of non-voting in Canada to date has, for the most part, implicitly been the study of habitual non-voting. Still, it is worth making this focus more explicit, both in our conceptual reasoning and empirical analysis.

Some hints of the larger impediments to political and civic participation can be found in what non-participants themselves have to say about the matter. One method, in the context of a structured survey or a more open-ended interview, is to put the question directly to non-voters: why did you not vote? However, responses to such questions can be misleading, as many will focus only on the immediate reasons for their abstention. This may be an adequate explanation for some, but not for others. If an intermittent voter says she did not have time to vote, this may be all there is to the matter, but the same explanation offered by a habitual non-voter does not really ring true. When it is known that someone habitually abstains, a follow-up question seems reasonable: Why did you not *make* the time to vote? Or more pointedly: Why is it you *never* seem to make the time to vote?

Such follow-up queries are typically not posed in the survey context, not just to avoid premature termination of the interview, but also because they call for a degree of reflection and self-awareness that may be unrealistic to expect of people who have probably not given the matter much thought. Asking people why they did not do something can be a fruitful tack if they made a conscious decision not to do so, but is less useful if they simply failed to do so (Zukin et al. 2006, 92). If someone were to ask me why I never scuba dive, I would be hard pressed to explain. Pushed harder, I might come up with a reason, might even mention issues or concerns that could make me appear anti-scuba diving. This would amount to squeezing water from a stone, however, and would not uncover the true reasons for my failing to take up the sport. A more fruitful method of investigation would be gathering information from various people on a range of demographic traits, attitudinal qualities, and behavioural tendencies thought to be relevant to participation in underwater sporting activities, and from there undertake a systematic comparison of scuba divers and non-scuba divers to see which factors are most relevant. The same approach is a more effective way of plumbing the true reasons for failure to engage in voting and other forms of political and civic participation.

By this reasoning, the value of the survey method (the primary source of information in what follows) lies not only in the standard defence that it involves large sample sizes that provide greater confidence in the generalizability of findings, but also in the structure of the information-gathering process. This involves querying people about a wide range of matters that they can, one by one, speak to clearly and confidently. These are then brought together by the researcher at the analysis stage to see how they correlate with one another and with different forms of political participation, drawing connections of which respondents themselves may not be fully aware. While there are insights to be gained from different styles of research, large-scale surveys covering a broad range of relatively disparate topics can help in identifying less evident connections that may be of considerable importance to understanding the root causes of political disengagement.

Dissatisfaction with Politics and Government
If the decisive rejection of proposed new voting systems in the referendums held in Prince Edward Island (2005), Ontario (2007), and British Columbia (2009) signalled that many citizens are not chomping at the bit for electoral reform, this should not be taken as evidence that all is well with the institutions of Canadian democracy. While these particular proportional representation proposals left some confused and others cold, there is, nonetheless, ample evidence that Canadians are far from fully content with their current political system. Asked about the way in which their political institutions function, their trust in political leaders and parties, or their general satisfaction with government, many Canadians offer negative assessments (Zussman 1997). Moreover, this political discontent has increased over time, suggesting it could well have been fuelled by rising dissatisfaction among younger generations, and might represent an important precipitant of political disengagement.

Despite the plausibility of the idea, previous studies have been largely consistent in concluding that the evidence in support of such a diagnosis is

Figure 2.1

Confidence in institutions by age

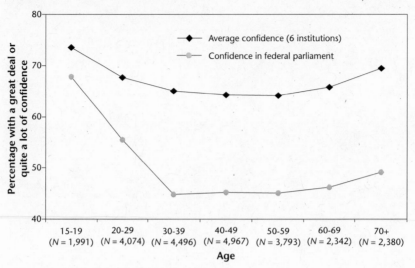

Source: Statistics Canada, GSS 17 (2003).

weak. Neither of the relationships needed to support the case – higher levels of dissatisfaction among the young, and a significant link between dissatisfaction and political disengagement – is to be found. Compared to older Canadians, young adults are no less satisfied with democracy, no less confident in public institutions, no less trusting of political parties and politicians (O'Neill 2001). Nor is there evidence that they hold distinct issue preferences that they feel are being given short shrift in the political process (Gidengil et al. 2005). Even if young Canadians were especially malcontent, this would make relatively little difference to their political participation, since negative evaluations of this type are not strongly associated with lower levels of political involvement (Howe 2007b, 260).

The 2003 Statistics Canada study on social engagement reinforces these previous conclusions. Figure 2.1 displays levels of confidence in various public institutions across age groups. One line shows the average percentage of respondents who indicate confidence in six different public institutions: the police, justice system or courts, health care system, school system, welfare system, and the federal parliament. The second line singles out confidence levels in the institution most likely to generate disaffection bearing on electoral participation, the federal parliament. The figure reveals that young people are slightly more, not less, confident in institutions than older Canadians. Their faith in public institutions is particularly elevated in the case of the Canadian parliament. The only institution of the six that young people

Figure 2.2

Levels of confidence in institutions and voting

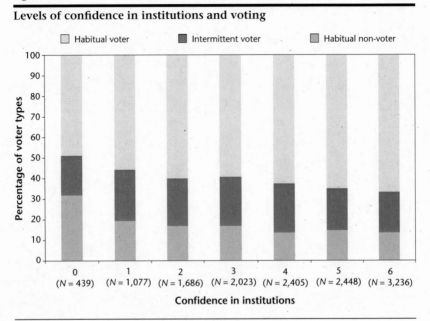

Source: Statistics Canada, GSS 17 (2003).

hold in lower esteem is the police (though levels of confidence in this instance are high across the board – over 80 percent in all age groups).

Figure 2.2 shows the relationship between confidence in public institutions and electoral participation, the bars in the graph displaying the distribution of voter types – habitual voters, intermittent voters, and habitual non-voters – within groups of respondents with varying levels of institutional confidence (voter type is based on respondents' reported participation in the most recent federal, provincial, and municipal elections).[1] One result stands out in seeming contradiction of the idea that distrust in government has little bearing on electoral involvement: the high level of habitual non-voting (31 percent) among those who indicate confidence in *none* of the six public institutions. Critical to note, however, is the limited range of this effect, as a mere 3.3 percent of survey respondents fall into the bottom category of institutional trust ($N = 439$). And while there is also an elevated level of habitual non-voting in the adjacent category (those with confidence in only one of six institutions), accounting for another 8 percent of the respondents, it is only slightly above the norm at 19 percent. Outside these two groups, the effects of institutional confidence on voter participation are minimal. Moving rightwards across the graph, there is no obvious trend in the level of habitual non-voting with increasing trust in institutions:

it ranges from 14 to 17 percent with no significant upward or downward movement. Levels of intermittent voting are slightly higher among the moderately confident (two to four institutions), and levels of habitual voting a notch higher among the most confident (five to six), but these differences are relatively slight and immaterial to the most critical manifestation of electoral disengagement, habitual abstention. In short, lack of confidence in government, if sufficiently profound, does seem to turn people off voting, but its impact is quite limited in the current Canadian context. In any event, this would not explain why young people are voting less, since they tend to be equally or more confident in public institutions relative to older citizens.

The case is weaker still when attention turns to other forms of public engagement and the relationship to institutional confidence, an area not much explored in previous Canadian research. Across a broad range of categories of political and civic engagement – traditional political activities, non-traditional activities, volunteering, and involvement in groups – the most engaged Canadians are found in the middling categories of institutional confidence, while at the extremes – confidence in no institutions and confidence in all six – engagement is invariably lower (Figure 2.3). For example, the rate of past-year participation in traditional political activities peaks among those confident in just one institution out of six (36 percent), is significantly lower among those confident in none (29 percent) and falls to its lowest level among those with confidence in all six (25 percent). The pattern is similar for non-traditional political acts, where the incidence of participation is highest among those who are confident in two of six institutions (50 percent) and drops rather sharply among those with the greatest confidence (35 percent). For volunteering and group involvements, participation is at its nadir among those confident in no institutions, but is also lower among the most confident by 5 or 6 percentage points compared to the peak intermediate confidence categories.

These results are consistent with what most studies have concluded: dissatisfaction with government is not of critical importance to the political disengagement of young Canadians. Young Canadians are, if anything, more confident in government, while a lack of confidence and trust puts only a small dent in voter turnout and, in modest doses, has a positive effect on other forms of political and civic engagement. Yet, on reflection, none of this should really come as a great surprise. After all, dissatisfaction has historically been a catalyst for political activism and demands for change, rather than withdrawal from the political arena (Howe 2007b). Kept within tolerable limits, harnessed in the service of constructive reform, a certain measure of distrust can be a healthy feature of a robust democracy (Schudson 1998, 302). This is particularly evident when a wider range of civic and political activities beyond voting is considered.

Figure 2.3

Levels of confidence in institutions and other types of engagement

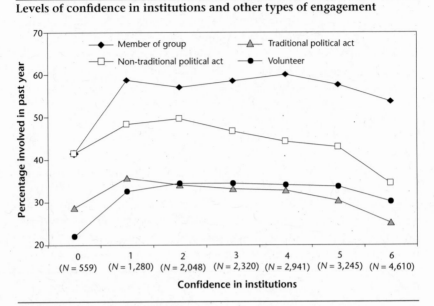

Source: Statistics Canada, GSS 17 (2003).

There are dissenting opinions on the matter, however. One researcher, using other surveys with somewhat different questions, has argued that young Canadians do in fact exhibit distinctive attitudes towards democracy and have particular issue preferences that are not being adequately addressed by Canada's political parties, both of these considerations explaining why they are "less interested" in voting (Turcotte 2005; Turcotte 2007, 6). A review of this research reveals, however, that the differences uncovered between age groups tend to be relatively small (certainly nothing that matches the differences described below for other factors relevant to political disengagement) and are counterbalanced by any number of attitudes where there is no gap between the young and not-so-young. The research also fails to provide any analysis of the second crucial link in the argument, the alleged connection between political discontent and waning electoral participation (or indeed any other form of political or civic engagement). It is not enough simply to assume that discontent breeds disengagement; it must be shown that those with critical attitudes or unfulfilled issue preferences are significantly less likely to participate than others. Qualitative studies from Canada and elsewhere making the case that the political system is responsible for young people's disengagement from politics (White et al. 2000; O'Toole et al. 2003a, 2003b; Canadian Policy Research Networks 2007) are not necessarily any more persuasive. It is hardly surprising that young people brought together in a workshop or focus group for a discussion of politics voice certain concerns about the political system. That some of these concerns have a distinctive youth colouring is not unexpected either (though rarely demonstrated convincingly, since most qualitative studies fail to solicit the views of any older citizens for comparative purposes). Yet none of this establishes that the views extracted through these methods represent precipitants of political disengagement. Without some corroboration from quantitative studies showing that young people hold distinctive attitudes and opinions towards relevant facets of the democratic system and that these attitudes, in turn, are linked to lower levels of political engagement, the findings from these qualitative investigations remain unconvincing.

None of this is to suggest that concerns about the political system voiced by young Canadians are without substance or merit. Even if diminished participation is not one of the principal consequences, scepticism and distrust of the political system only serve a constructive purpose if acknowledged and addressed. The recent wave of debate on democratic reform and some of the innovative approaches being used to explore the options before us – most notably, the citizen assemblies on electoral reform held in BC and Ontario – are crucial parts of the necessary response to widespread scepticism about current political structures and practices. To the extent younger generations have distinct democratic sensibilities, these should inform ongoing discussions on institutional reform. This is, however, a largely separate political project and distinct research agenda from the democratic disengagement debate.

Rather than concentrating on the political system and its shortcomings, there is a need to look squarely at citizens themselves, focusing on the ways young adults do differ markedly from the not-so-young in the behavioural dispositions and personal and social values relevant to political engagement. It is important not to mistake this redirection of attention for an attempt to pin disengagement on nothing more complicated than the civic lassitude of young Canadians (the seeming concern of some keen to link it to the political system).[2] People's behaviour is always guided, their values influenced, by larger structural factors that condition how they think and act. The point to emphasize is that the behavioural and attitudinal tendencies underlying young people's political disengagement are conditioned by structural influences that lie beyond the political realm, this the subject of further elaboration in chapters to come.

Political Inattentiveness

If not political disaffection, then what? One characteristic of younger Canadians of apparent relevance to their disengagement from politics is what might be termed their political inattentiveness. This inattentiveness encompasses both attitudinal and behavioural dimensions: low levels of interest

Figure 2.4

Following the news by age

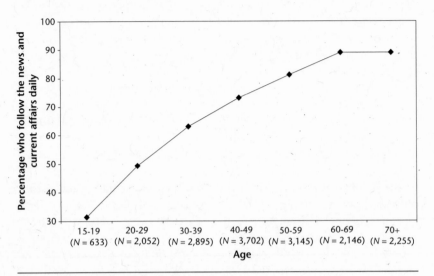

Source: Statistics Canada, GSS 17 (2003).

in politics, a tendency not to keep up with politics by reading and listening to political news, an inadequate base of knowledge about public affairs. The connection to political participation is not hard to surmise. Voting, for example, entails making a choice between competing candidates, parties, campaign platforms, and ideologies. Those who do not pay attention to politics are less likely to be in a position to make such a choice with any degree of certainty or commitment. Similarly, demonstrations and public meetings are less likely to be attended, petitions less likely to be signed, by those lacking familiarity with the pressing issues of the day. In the absence of political attentiveness, the formulation of political preferences is stunted, and it becomes easier to let the opinions of others more knowledgeable about public affairs carry the day. The evidence produced to date, for both Canada and other countries, suggests this is an important part of the story behind young people's disengagement from politics.[3]

One question from the 2003 Statistics Canada study exemplifies the typically strong linkages between measures of political attentiveness and manifestations of disengagement among young Canadians. It asks respondents how often they follow the news and current affairs – daily, several times a week, several times a month, or rarely or never. As Figure 2.4 reveals, young respondents are much less likely to be regular news consumers. Whereas nearly 90 percent of those over age sixty report taking in the news on a daily basis, this figure diminishes steadily with decreasing age, falling to 63 percent

Figure 2.5

Following the news and voting

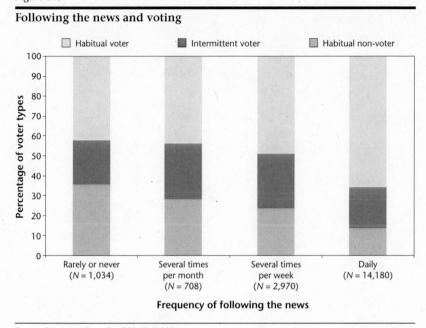

Legend:
☐ Habitual voter   ■ Intermittent voter   ☐ Habitual non-voter

Y-axis: Percentage of voter types (0 to 100)

X-axis (Frequency of following the news):
- Rarely or never (N = 1,034)
- Several times per month (N = 708)
- Several times per week (N = 2,970)
- Daily (N = 14,180)

Source: Statistics Canada, GSS 17 (2003).

among those in their thirties, 49 percent among those in their twenties, and 31 percent among those between ages fifteen and nineteen.

Meanwhile, Figure 2.5 displays how failing to keep up with the news is connected to voter abstention. While 36 percent of those who rarely or never follow the news are habitual non-voters, the incidence falls to 24 percent among those who partake several times a week and 14 percent among daily news consumers. The figure for those at the upper end of the news consumption scale undoubtedly masks further nuance, as this group accounts for a large majority of the Canadian population (68 percent). There is almost certainly further variation in both the amount of news consumption and the incidence of habitual non-voting among this large segment of the Canadian population who claim to be faithful adherents to the news of the day.

If following the news has a strong effect on voting, it also heavily influences other forms of involvement in public affairs (Figure 2.6). The linkage to political activities beyond voting is particularly strong: the percentage reporting at least one traditional activity in the past year climbs from just over 10 percent to a shade over 30 percent in moving from one end of the news attentiveness scale to the other, while non-traditional activity doubles from 20 percent to 40 percent. Volunteering and membership in groups also increase by about 10 percentage points in moving across the graph. Again, for all of these measures, there is likely further variation at the upper end

Figure 2.6

Following the news and other types of engagement

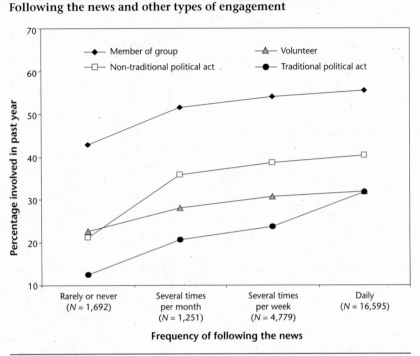

Source: Statistics Canada, GSS 17 (2003).

of the attentiveness axis, as the rates of participation for those who are particularly keen followers of news and current affairs would almost certainly be higher.

If the strength of these empirical relationships is plain to see, the larger implications are less self-evident. To observe that people who are not attentive to politics are less likely to participate in civic and political affairs might not seem like an obvious path to enlightenment about the nature and sources of disengagement among the young. This insight is so self-evident as to perhaps appear trivial. Indeed, some have suggested that rather than treating political inattentiveness as a precipitant of political disengagement, it is more sensibly seen as part and parcel of disengagement, the causes of which remain to be uncovered (Johnston and Matthews 2004, 10; Rubenson et al. 2004, 417). The fact that reasons reflecting political inattentiveness are regularly cited by respondents in response to open-ended queries about why they do not vote – "not interested," "don't know enough," and the like – suggests that at most this should be considered a proximate cause of disengagement, something sufficiently close to the surface as to be readily apparent to the disengaged themselves.

These points are well taken. The response is to emphasize that the relationship between political inattentiveness and disengagement among the young is but a starting point, serving as an important signpost towards a certain path of inquiry that must be pursued further to yield a deeper understanding. This involves addressing a series of follow-up questions that naturally arise in response to the basic correlation between age and political attentiveness, the most obvious of which is *why* young people pay relatively little attention to politics (Rubenson et al. 2004, 418).

An adequate response involves several distinct components. One is to probe causal linkages, asking whether any of the constituent elements of political inattentiveness can be considered more fundamental than the others, can be seen as the leading force behind broader changes in the political attentiveness of younger Canadians. The answer might seem obvious: interest in politics is the motivational starting point that would prompt someone to follow what is happening in politics, thereby leading to greater knowledge of political issues and debates and a basis for preference formation and meaningful participation. But while this is certainly a plausible chain of causality, there are other possibilities to consider, less self-evident but on reflection no less reasonable. Even if no definitive answer to this first question is possible, acknowledging the issue enhances our understanding of the full range of possible causal scenarios underlying processes of political (in)attentiveness.

A second necessary part of the analysis is to ask whether current differences between young and old reflect life-cycle or cohort effects. That is to say, is inattention to politics a condition common to young people of different periods, which tends to ameliorate with age, or are today's young adults, the cohorts who have come of age in recent years, distinctively inattentive to politics and likely to remain that way as they grow older? The answer to the question is relevant in several ways. It first promises to reveal whether inattentiveness among today's young adults is relevant to the cohort or life-cycle components of political disengagement in areas such as electoral participation. It also foreshadows how their political attentiveness will evolve as they age, and whether generational turnover will gradually lead to diminished levels of political attentiveness in the population as a whole. And finally, it offers guidance as to which underlying causes of political inattentiveness – those linked to life-cycle dynamics or to distinctive cohort experiences – should be considered most likely.

A third analytical dimension that arises in working through these initial questions concerns the adequacy of existing methods of gauging political attentiveness and each of its three constituent elements. Do the survey questions typically asked to assess political interest, political knowledge, and following politics in the media accurately capture the degree to which, and the ways in which, people pay attention to politics in the real world? Or are

Canadians attentive in ways, or to aspects of politics, that have escaped detection through existing methods of inquiry? An accurate picture of the current contours of political attentiveness among different age groups in Canada is important in assessing how young Canadians are faring in this regard, as well as pinpointing areas where the political attention deficit is most glaring.

These various avenues of inquiry are pursued in Chapters 3, 4, and 5. Chapter 3 starts by taking up the question of causal connections between interest, knowledge, and following politics in the media, establishing why it is important to keep this conceptual issue in mind in seeking to make sense of empirical patterns. The principal focus of the chapter is an analysis of life-cycle and cohort effects with respect to political attentiveness. The analysis is longitudinal, investigating levels of knowledge, interest, and attention to politics in the media over time and across age groups, the necessary method of teasing out the two effects. The focus is not restricted to Canada, drawing instead on a wide range of surveys conducted in six different countries – Canada, the US, and four European states – with an eye to assessing what is common to their experiences. The answer is a good deal more than might be anticipated, suggesting that whatever explanation is developed for political inattentiveness among young Canadians should be applicable to young adults in other places as well. The commonalities include significant cohort effects, strengthening the case that political attentiveness can be linked to this important component of declining electoral participation among the young. Yet life-cycle effects of considerable magnitude and consistency also appear. In reflecting on the broader implications of these results, the theory considered most closely is the prominent one that changes in the media environment that have greatly expanded the range of choice available to citizens have led to a decline in the captive audience for news and current affairs, a process that has undermined attention to politics among younger generations in particular (Wattenberg 2008). The results, which allow us to consider patterns of political attentiveness at times and in places where the media environment has varied in relevant ways, suggest this is not an adequate explanation. A changing media environment has probably exacerbated pre-existing tendencies, but does not constitute an adequate explanation in itself. The most important of these pre-existing tendencies is the marked life-cycle pattern of lower levels of political attentiveness in the early stages of adult life revealed by the analysis. The pattern and the idea are flagged in Chapter 3, the fuller implications for a broader account of the origins of disengagement left aside until a later chapter.

Chapter 4 focuses on the matter of measuring political attentiveness fully and accurately. It rests principally upon a survey conducted specifically for this study, a national sampling of nearly 2,000 Canadians conducted from December 2007 through April 2008, the Canadian Citizen Engagement

Survey (CCES). In light of some of the measurement shortcomings in existing data sources, one of the purposes of the survey was to probe aspects of political attentiveness that had not been fully considered in prior Canadian research. The main focus is on political knowledge and following public affairs in the media. One objective was to address the concern that previous efforts to assess political knowledge have tended to focus excessively on trivial pieces of information relating to conventional electoral politics – whether people can recall the names of the leaders of the main political parties, for example. The CCES endeavoured to assess Canadians' knowledge across a wider ambit of more substantive political matters, including basic mechanics of government, public policy issues of enduring importance, and issues outside the political mainstream sometimes thought to be of greater interest and relevance to young people. For news media use, the focus is not so much uncharted territory as it is meticulous coverage of known territory. The survey assessed how much time and attention people really devote to "following the news" by asking a series of relatively detailed questions about different types of news media use. This allows for the development of a relatively fine-tuned measure of news consumption and the pinpointing of specific areas where young people lag behind older Canadians. Latter sections of Chapter 4 draw on these relatively comprehensive and robust measures to re-examine important issues, such as the strength of the relationship between news media consumption and political knowledge.

Chapter 5 considers the consequences of political inattentiveness – knowledge in particular – for democratic engagement. Offering further evidence of the powerful linkages between political attentiveness and participation, the analysis adds nuance by examining variations in those effects across different forms of participation. It also moves beyond simply tallying the numbers participating in politics to consider the quality of citizens' contributions to public affairs – their capacity for critical judgment, their ability to formulate cogent policy preferences. Not surprisingly, political inattentiveness is found to be broadly detrimental to democratic engagement, undermining both the quantity and quality of citizen involvement in politics.

Social Integration

If attentiveness to politics is an individual attribute that disposes someone to participate in public affairs, and deficiencies in this area help explain lower levels of engagement among young Canadians, another critical factor has more to do with how individuals are connected to one another. Social integration, more precisely the weakening of social integration among young Canadians, is a second critical area to consider. This broad syndrome reveals itself in various ways, only some of obvious relevance to political involvement. For example, one manifestation, widely cited in studies of voter turnout, is that young adults in Canada (and other countries) are less likely to accept the norm that voting is a civic duty (Blais et al. 2002, 58; Clarke et al. 2003; Pammett and Leduc 2003a, 38-9; Zukin et al. 2006, 97-103; Howe 2007b, 247-48; Wattenberg 2008, 127-38). Since adherence to the norm is strongly linked to electoral participation, this helps explain lower voter turnout among the young. Despite wide circulation of the finding, however, few actually suggest that the route to electoral re-engagement is to impress upon younger citizens their obligation to vote. Some are probably uncomfortable with a finger-wagging approach, but there also seems to be general acknowledgment that it would simply not be effective. The reason is precisely that the larger extent of the condition is widely understood, if not always expressly articulated: scepticism towards voting as a civic duty is not a stand-alone attitude that can be treated in isolation, but is instead embedded within a larger constellation of sentiments and dispositions – scepticism towards community norms in general, resistance to societal claims upon the individual – that is not easily altered. Addressing this element of political disengagement requires fuller probing of different dimensions of social integration in order to pinpoint more clearly the nature and trajectory of the most relevant changes.

In attempting to encapsulate this important source of disengagement, two broad components of diminished social integration are identified in this study. One is the relatively tepid feelings of community attachment among young Canadians. The Statistics Canada study of 2003 again offers a preview of the types of variables and the strength of the relationships that suggest this is a phenomenon meriting further investigation. Three questions on the survey ask respondents how strong their sense of belonging is to their local community, their province, and to Canada: very strong, somewhat strong, somewhat weak, or very weak. While there is a general tendency for respondents to report quite strong attachments across the board – in all three cases, a large majority say their sense of belonging is at least somewhat strong – there is, nonetheless, evidence of an age gap that is far from negligible. When all three measures are brought together in a combined scale, almost 70 percent among the oldest age group lie in the upper portion of that scale. This percentage drops steadily with decreasing age, falling below 40 percent among those under age thirty (Figure 2.7). More detailed analysis later breaks down this summary index and attends more closely to the significance and meaning of these substantial age differences.

Meanwhile, both voting and other forms of political and civic engagement are strongly related to this general index of community attachment. Habitual non-voting decreases steadily, from 36 percent to 12 percent, in moving from the weak to strong pole of community attachment (Figure 2.8). The same progression from weak to strong attachments is associated with marked increases in other types of political activity, volunteering, and involvement in groups (Figure 2.9). The connection to civic participation is somewhat

Figure 2.7

Community attachments by age

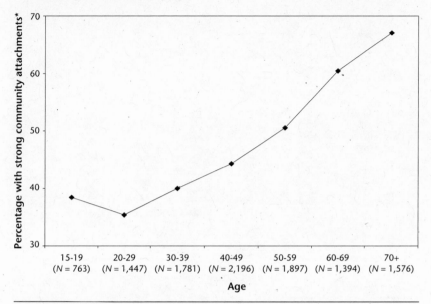

* Local, provincial, and national combined.
Source: Statistics Canada, GSS 17 (2003).

stronger: about a twenty-point difference in group membership and volunteering between one end of the community attachment scale and the other.
For political activities, the effect (about 10 percentage points) is limited to
traditional activities. For the non-traditional activities (demonstrations,
petitions, and the like) the trend is essentially flat across different levels of
community attachment – not entirely surprising, since these are more contentious forms of political activism that sometimes see groups vehemently
criticizing the policies or viewpoints of others within Canadian society,
activity from which those strongly wedded to community might shy. This
result aside, the significant influence of community attachments on different
forms of civic and political engagement is clear.

The second critical component of diminished social integration, closely
related to less robust feelings of community attachment, is the relatively
pronounced individualism that exists among younger Canadians. In this
case, there are no questions from the Statistics Canada study sufficiently on
target to capture this quality and provide an initial impression of the relationships that support the claim, so evidence of the individualistic tendencies
of younger Canadians and the connection to involvement in public affairs
is left until later chapters. As a preliminary statement, individualism can be

Figure 2.8

Community attachments and voting

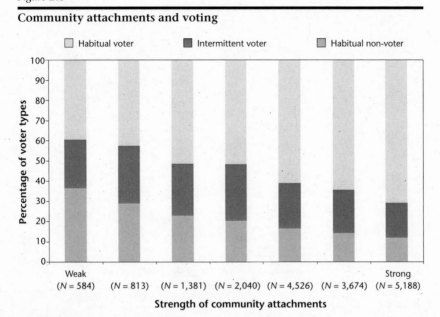

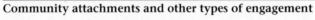

Source: Statistics Canada, GSS 17 (2003).

Figure 2.9

Community attachments and other types of engagement

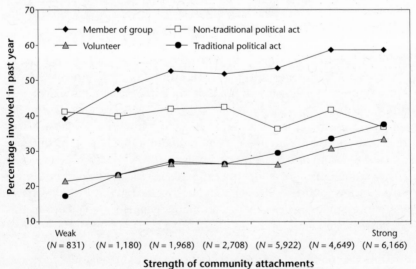

Source: Statistics Canada, GSS 17 (2003).

defined as a focus on the self – one's own interests, concerns, priorities, and ideas – that weakens social integration by altering the motivations that lead people to become involved in a wide range of common endeavours.

These two components of diminished social integration, less robust attachments to community and heightened individualism, are examples of explanatory factors that are not of obvious relevance to political engagement and, for this reason, unlikely to be cited by non-participants themselves when asked about reasons for their lack of participation. Yet the connections that appear in Figures 2.7 through 2.9, the gaps between young and old and the link to different forms of public involvement, suggest that waning social connectedness is an important factor that needs to be part of any comprehensive account of political disengagement. Once again, the primary thrust in pressing further is to tease out the fuller meaning of the concepts and identify more precisely what it means to say that social integration among young Canadians is lacking. Given the less evident connection to political disengagement, the greater remove between cause and effect, considerable emphasis must also be placed on tracing the connections that link strength of community attachment and individualistic proclivities to involvement in public affairs.

There are a number of separate matters to consider. The first is exploration and explication of the basic concepts. Even more so than political attentiveness, attachment to community and individualism are broad, indeed contentious, categories. They encompass a wide range of behavioural and attitudinal propensities, but also, when deployed in different contexts, carry significant normative overtones. Thus, an important first step is conceptual clarification and normative transparency. Already in making a preliminary case, there has been some blurring of relevant distinction in aggregating sentiments of belonging that are not obviously fungible: attachments to local community, province, and Canada. In later chapters, these are considered separately, alongside other measures that capture different ways of conceptualizing "attachment to community." Normative concerns are also considered, through acknowledgment that "community" can serve as a binding and restrictive notion in some respects, but can also be seen as embodying important values of solidarity and public commitment. Individualism is likewise a complex and multifaceted phenomenon, encompassing diverse values such as freedom, autonomy, self-regard, and self-reliance. To say that young Canadians are more individualistic than older Canadians is not sufficiently precise to provide much real analytical insight or normative guidance. Teasing apart the concept in order to draw meaningful distinctions allows for more useful empirical and prescriptive assessment. An essential first step, then, is to specify what it means to say young Canadians are less taken with community, more inclined to individualism, and to be clear about the potential good and bad in this.

A second element of conceptual clarification is consideration of the link between community and individualism. The simple interpretation would be that each is but the logical complement of the other: a strong attachment to community necessarily implies less emphasis on the self, while robust individualism naturally equates to weaker community bonds. There is some truth to this simple formulation, which then raises a question akin to that articulated for the different dimensions of political attentiveness: is one of these elements of social integration more fundamental than the other? If change has occurred over time, if younger generations have become less socially integrated, is the process more aptly characterized as an erosion of community creating a social vacuum in which individualism has taken root, or an ascendance of individualism that has pushed aside traditional attachments to community? As with political attentiveness, there is no definitive answer to this complex question of cause and effect, but there is value, nonetheless, in thinking through different possibilities. Yet at the same time as acknowledging the intimate connection between community and individualism, issue is also implicitly taken below with the conceptualization of the two as the simple complement of one another. In the course of adding nuance and distinction to these concepts, the position will emerge that they are not opposite ends of a single spectrum of variation, but rather two distinct concepts with spheres of shared influence. Differently stated, some forms of reasonably robust individualism are consistent with some forms of reasonably cohesive community. The task of strengthening social integration as part of the larger project of reviving public engagement in Canada is not, then, simply a matter of "more" community and "less" individualism, but rather a matter of identifying and working towards an attainable and attractive blend of a certain type of individualism and a certain understanding of community.

Alongside these conceptual issues, a second key question is the relative significance of life-cycle and cohort dynamics in explaining patterns of community attachment and individualism among younger Canadians. Where an age gap exists on any given measure of these concepts, is it a reflection of an abiding tendency of young adults of the past and present, a distinctive quality of younger birth cohorts, or a combination of the two? While suitable longitudinal data with relevant measures do not generally exist to answer such questions definitively, they remain ever present throughout the analysis and are addressed with various forms of evidence. Close scrutiny of current age patterns and reflection on theoretical expectations can provide fair insight into which of the two accounts is more plausible. As with other dimensions of disengagement, the evidence points towards mixed effects: differences between birth cohorts on key measures of social integration are considerable and have likely contributed to escalating disengagement over time, yet there are also clear life-cycle patterns that must be given due consideration.

In addressing these conceptual and empirical questions in subsequent chapters, community attachments and individualism are treated one at a time, though given their close connection they cannot be entirely pulled apart. The state of community among young Canadians is the main focus of Chapter 6, patterns of individualism the subject matter of Chapter 7. In the course of this analysis, another interpretation of waning social integration is introduced: Robert Putnam's account of declining social capital in the US (2000). Putnam's work has become a touchstone for those seeking to understand the role of social integration in the erosion of public engagement over time. His basic argument is that social capital – the intricate and diverse connections between individuals resulting from personal relationships and involvement in informal and formal groups in neighbourhoods and larger communities – is the essential marrow of community; and as these connections have atrophied over time in the US, so too have the larger commitments to public life built upon this social capital infrastructure. The approach in this study, while in the same broad vein as Putnam's influential account, diverges in important ways. The principal difference lies in Putnam's emphasis on social integration "on the ground," the tangible connections to others that knit people into the fabric of community, and the contrary emphasis here on social integration "of the mind" – the sentiments and ideas that strengthen bonds of community. The latter, specifically *feelings* of attachment to community and individualistic *norms*, powerfully govern how people conduct their lives on the ground and are, so the argument runs, more fundamental. Differences also emerge between Putnam's near-exclusive emphasis on cohort differences in levels of social capital in the US and the blend of life-cycle and cohort patterns for measures of attachment to community and individualism found in the Canadian case. Both the conceptual and empirical differences have significant implications for mapping out a relevant agenda for strengthening social integration in Canada.

Chapter 8 looks at implications of waning social integration for Canadian democracy, articulating how attachments to community and individualistic norms influence political participation. Changes in the relative influence of different motivations for personal engagement in politics are one consequence considered. Another is the impact on processes of interpersonal mobilization – the way people consciously and unconsciously seek to persuade others to be involved in politics and civic affairs. Also explored are some *positive* consequences that can plausibly be linked to the weakening of community sentiment and heightened individualism. This involves looking beyond political engagement at other qualities valued in a democratic society – in particular social and political tolerance. The fact that there are other values at stake has implications for how we might go about seeking to strengthen social integration in order to enhance Canadian democracy.

Looking Back, Looking Forward

The preliminary analysis and discussion of Chapters 1 and 2 lays the groundwork for much of what follows. The starting point was to consider the low levels of voter turnout among young Canadians in recent Canadian elections. The significance of this pattern, and others associated with it, hinges on important conceptual distinctions. The first, between life-cycle and cohort accounts of age differences, has informed earlier research on voter turnout in Canada. The second, between intermittent and consistent failure to participate – from one election to the next and across different realms of political and civic activity – has not been as closely considered. Overlaying the two conceptual distinctions sheds new light on the nature of life-cycle and cohort influences on participation and reinforces concern about engagement trends among young Canadians. Cohort decline is substantial, portending continued change as younger generations take the place of older ones more committed to various forms of public participation. These cohort effects, moreover, reflect a pattern of consistent non-involvement on the part of some, underlining the inveterate quality of the behaviour and raising important normative concerns particular to political dropouts. That these tendencies are disproportionately concentrated among young adults of modest means and sub-par educational attainment only heightens the normative urgency of the matter.

Having conceptualized the problem in this manner, the task became to identify substantial barriers to participation that might be responsible for patterns of chronic disengagement. Three have been considered in Chapter 2, but only two have been retained for further consideration. Dissatisfaction with government, a plausible precipitant of political disengagement in light of growing public disenchantment with politics and politicians over the past number of years, does not stand up under empirical scrutiny. Two other general factors offer more explanatory clout: inattentiveness to public affairs and diminished social integration, the latter comprising two closely related phenomena, less robust attachments to community and more marked individualism. Parts 2 and 3 of the book probe these areas more thoroughly in order to elucidate more fully the implications for democratic engagement.

At the end of these chapters, however, two burning questions remain: what is the origin of these sea changes in Canadian society that have given rise to democratic disengagement, and what is to be done? Part 4 of the book tackles these ultimate questions most fully and directly. Chapter 9 speaks to root causes, presenting a theory that pinpoints a specific social process that has played a significant role in precipitating waning attentiveness to politics and diminished social integration over time. Starting with the mechanism of causation associated with cohort effects – the deep impact of early experiences on who we become and who we remain as we age – the theory identifies a significant change in those experiences that would have occurred in the first half of the twentieth century with the emergence of adolescence as a distinct life stage, separated more neatly than before from both childhood and adulthood. This change in the social structure meant that certain tendencies of adolescence relevant to attentiveness to public affairs and social integration – abiding tendencies of adolescence, which is to say life-cycle tendencies – came to express themselves more fully. Critical to the argument is the proposition that the effect was seen not just in adolescents, but also in the adults that adolescents eventually became, though the latter effect unfolded only gradually in successive waves over time. By this account, changes among rising generations relevant to disengagement (the cohort account) reflect tendencies that have always been present among young people (the life-cycle account), but which have slowly been allowed freer expression in the "age of adolescence." It is here that the promised blending of life-cycle and cohort accounts occurs, as findings about abiding qualities of young people are integrated into an explanation of long-term generational change. Considered in conjunction with other broad social changes of the twentieth century that have been identified as important determinants of the evolution of modern democracy, it is suggested that the "age of adolescence" thesis can enhance our understanding of key social dynamics relevant to important changes in public engagement over time.

If Chapter 9 looks back, far back, to explain how we arrived at our current pass, Chapter 10 looks forward, drawing on the accumulated analysis to develop specific proposals for addressing political disengagement among young Canadians. The different facets of the study, some dealing with more technical and immediate matters, others addressing more fundamental issues, lend themselves to a multilayered set of proposals. The first tier focuses on immediate manifestations of disengagement, such as declining voter participation, speaking to the importance of developing strategies that address habitual non-voting and the more general disposition to inaction that is associated with this behaviour. A second layer involves addressing underlying dimensions of disengagement. Enhancing political attentiveness requires encouraging interest and knowledge of politics, changes most likely to be achieved through renewed emphasis on civics education in our schools. Stemming the erosion of social integration requires a shift in emphasis in the ideas and norms that govern our lives, change that can be partly achieved through transformation of political and civic discourse, which in turn probably means some alterations to the institutional structures and political practices that shape such discourse. A third layer focuses on the social structure that has been a critical wellspring of long-term social and political change: the relative segregation of adolescence from adult society in modern times. The ideas offered on this point involve creating linkages that better bridge the transition from youth to adulthood, allowing for earlier and more seamless entry by young people into the "adult" world of political and civic engagement.

As these introductory chapters make clear, this study encompasses a wide range of matters, eventually broaching relatively fundamental questions about the changing nature of Canadian society, indeed the changing nature of Canadians. It points to gradual social and political transformations that are slowly altering the quality of our democracy to largely negative effect. The subtlety of the processes makes them more difficult to apprehend: at this point, we continue to drift in a direction that may not be entirely to our liking without being entirely cognizant why it is happening or fully aroused to the deleterious consequences. The possibility of a vicious circle arises: as disengagement from public life proceeds apace, we become less exercised about it, less likely to act in concert to change it. Turning matters around will require a conscious effort brought about by wider recognition that something is awry with the current state of citizen engagement in Canada. The ideas and analysis presented here are one contribution to what will, it is hoped, develop into a fuller public deliberation on the future of the democracy we all share.

Part 2
Political Attentiveness

3

The Evolution of Political Attentiveness: A Six-Country Comparison

An essential underpinning of political involvement is awareness and understanding of politics. Expertise is not required, but a basic grasp of the workings of the political world and comprehension of political issues is necessary. The fact that many young Canadians fall below this modest threshold has become increasingly apparent in recent times. A disproportionate number express little interest in politics, are unfamiliar with basic facts about the political world, and spend little time trying to keep up with political issues and developments through the various media sources available to them.

Further probing of the cluster of characteristics and proclivities that constitute political attentiveness is needed to better understand this apparent deficit. Shortfalls among younger citizens across different dimensions of political attentiveness have been the focus of prior research in both Canada and other countries (Bennett 1998; McAllister 1998; Zukin et al. 2006; Pew Research Center for People and the Press 2007; Wattenberg 2008). A broad comparative perspective can provide a better grasp of the significance of Canadian trends and deepen our understanding of the reasons for low levels of political attentiveness among younger citizens.

The first question that arises is whether there have always been sizable differences in political attentiveness between young and old, or whether current differences represent a new development – in other words, the relative significance of life-cycle and birth-cohort accounts of age differences. To answer this question, longitudinal analysis based on comparable measures over time is essential. Where cohort effects appear, it must then be asked what might have precipitated diminished levels of attentiveness among younger generations? This question, in turn, can be tackled from two angles. The first is to probe causal linkages within the tight knot of correlated tendencies that comprise political attentiveness and ask whether any – political interest, knowledge, or news media attentiveness – should be seen as causally prior to the others and, therefore, the likely catalyst of broader change.

The second is to ask what structural or environmental factors might have acted upon this catalyst to produce the changes in political attentiveness seen among younger generations. These are the essential questions taken up in this chapter.

Where We Currently Stand: Canada in Comparative Perspective

Prior to assessing trends over time, it is helpful to take stock of where we stand at present. Since there is no absolute yardstick for judging whether current levels of political attentiveness in Canada are high, middling, or low, this entails looking at how Canadians rank against citizens of other democracies. Comparative assessment offers a sense of the upper and lower bounds of citizen attentiveness in comparable jurisdictions, as well as the implications of any erosion that might be occurring in this country. If we are currently at a high point, relatively speaking, we can perhaps weather some decline, but if we are at the low end of the scale and dropping further still, then any erosion occurring among younger generations takes on greater significance.

Previous comparisons have produced mixed results. Henry Milner has argued most pointedly that Canada suffers from significant shortcomings in levels of political attentiveness among citizens. In his book *Civic Literacy* and in shorter papers (2001, 2002, 2005), he draws a variety of telling cross-national comparisons, including rates of newspaper reading and levels of political knowledge in different countries, two factors he considers critical to the vitality of a democratic citizenry. On these important benchmarks, Canada sits in the lower ranks of the developed democracies, alongside countries such as the US and Britain and significantly below many European countries, particularly those of Northern Europe. His conclusions concerning political knowledge are supported by a study sponsored by the National Geographic Study in 2002, which tested geopolitical knowledge among samples of eighteen- to twenty-four-year-olds in nine countries. Young Canadians fared poorly on this test relative to their European counterparts, ranking third from the bottom, ahead of only the US and Mexico (RoperASW 2002, 17). The research team behind the Canadian election studies, on the other hand, point to more encouraging results in their broad overview of citizen engagement in Canada. Looking at a different barometer of attentiveness, political interest, they note that Canada ranked fourth among seventeen established Western democracies in the 1990 World Values Survey – though the survey was carried out shortly prior to the demise of the Meech Lake Accord, a time of intense political discussion in the country (Gidengil et al. 2004, 20). Martin Wattenberg, using a more recent wave of the same study (1999-2001), presents comparative data showing the percentage in different countries that follow politics in the news every day. The results for this measure look similar to Milner's, as Canadians in most age groups (sixty-five and over being the exception) sit in the bottom four of fourteen countries, joined there by the US, Japan, and Great Britain (2008, 83).

The inconsistency in these conclusions may simply reflect the fact that they focus on different dimensions of political attentiveness – knowledge and attention to news media on the one hand, political interest on the other. They could also reflect the different times at which the data were collected. To establish up-to-date comparisons, two questions about media use that appear consistently on Eurobarometer polls (surveys conducted on a regular basis in all member states of the European Union) were replicated on the 2007-08 Canadian Citizen Engagement Survey (CCES). Another question on the CCES concerning political interest was similar to a question posed on the European Social Survey,[1] another multi-country study conducted intermittently in recent years. Table 3.1 shows comparative results on these measures for selected countries. The results for media use – daily newspaper reading and daily TV news viewing – are consistent with Milner's conclusion that Canadians lag behind comparable countries in these areas. The reported incidence of daily newspaper reading is half that of certain Northern European countries and only moderately higher than various Southern European countries, where low education levels (and relatively high rates of illiteracy) among older respondents (fifty-five and over) pull down the overall average significantly. Nor do Canadians make up any ground through attention to

Table 3.1

Comparative measures of political attentiveness (%)

	Daily newspaper reading	Daily TV news viewing	Political interest (very or somewhat interested)
Spain	23	58	26
Portugal	25	75	28
Italy	26	65	32
France	29	65	45
Canada	*31*	*50*	*59*
Britain	39	71	52
Germany	50	69	54
Denmark	52	75	68
Netherlands	60	76	61
Sweden	70	72	62

Notes and sources:
Canada: Canadian Citizen Engagement Survey 2007-08. For media questions, $N = 1,103$, for political interest, $N = 1,922$.
EU countries, media questions: Eurobarometer 65.2, March-May 2006. Approximate N for each country is 1,000.
EU countries, political interest: European Social Survey, Round 3, 2006; Round 2, 2004 for Netherlands; and Round 1, 2002 for Italy. N varies from 1,198 (Italy) to 2,393 (UK).

television news, ranking at the very bottom of these ten countries in the percentage who report viewing the news daily. The results for political interest, on the other hand, are considerably better: Canada sits in the upper range, with average interest levels much higher than in the Southern European countries and not much below civic-literacy stalwarts such as Sweden and Denmark. Political interest, however, is a subjective measure and probably less meaningful if not accompanied by behavioural manifestations of attentiveness to politics. Overall, then, these mixed findings do not offer any reason for complacency. If an analysis of trends in political attentiveness over time reveals substantial decline among younger generations in Canada, there is not an abundant societal reservoir available to mitigate the negative effects.

Theoretical Conceptions and the Value of Longitudinal, Comparative Study

The second order of business before delving into the data is to pause and reflect on theoretical understandings that may prove useful in making sense of the empirical patterns that emerge. For while the finding that young people are relatively inattentive to politics has cropped up regularly in recent studies in Canada and other countries, less progress has been made in advancing beyond these empirical observations to a compelling theoretical account of the emergence and evolution of political inattentiveness among the young. The challenge lies in the fact that the three elements of political inattentiveness are deeply intertwined. This makes it difficult to say whether inattentiveness is primarily a product of lack of interest in politics, disinclination to follow politics in the media, paucity of political knowledge, or some combination thereof. This, in turn, makes it difficult to pinpoint structural factors that might have precipitated relevant attitudinal or behavioural changes in political attentiveness.

That said, many would be inclined to presume that interest in politics is the catalyst behind broader changes in political attentiveness. Interest provides the necessary motivation for someone to follow what is happening in politics and current affairs, which in turn generates greater knowledge of political issues. So, if attentiveness has waned among the young, a decline in political interest is the most likely reason. This assumption, if correct, would point to a certain category of potential explanations, those focusing on factors and forces that might have impinged on the political interest of younger generations.

This reasoning is plausible, but so too are other causal scenarios. It is reasonable to posit, for example, that knowledge of a subject can stimulate interest, since that which is intelligible is generally more interesting. Anyone who has ever watched an unfamiliar game or sport, be it baseball, cricket, or Australian rules tiddlywinks, will attest that without some understanding of the rules and strategies guiding the game, its appeal can be rather limited. Likewise, politics in its various forms, be it the horse-race of an election campaign or the rhetoric and nuance of ideological debate, is more interesting when someone has the necessary knowledge to make sense of what is being done or said by the protagonists. So it is reasonable to imagine knowledge leading to interest, as much as the reverse. And it is reasonable to further suppose that knowledge of politics might be an important reason people choose to pay attention to news media, as greater comprehension of what one is reading or hearing would render the activity more fulfilling. By this reasoning, a decline in knowledge could have been the precipitant of a broader erosion in political attentiveness among younger Canadians. Thus, the search for reasons and solutions to the problem might fruitfully concentrate on factors that could have generated a burgeoning knowledge deficit among the young.

Yet, to consider another possibility, it is also the case that simple exposure to a subject can catalyze interest therein and knowledge thereof. Someone, for example, who finds herself snowbound with a group of avid followers of Australian rules tiddlywinks keen to watch every minute of the world championships on satellite TV may discover that this fortuitous exposure ends up sparking a new interest. Interests are not set in stone. Among young people in particular it is reasonable to posit a certain malleability of interests and fluidity of attention that is likely to permit mere exposure – by peers and parents, through the media – to play a significant role in the development of interests. It is conceivable, then, that a decline in exposure to politics could have impinged on both political interest and political knowledge and that simply increasing such exposure among young people might rectify the problem.

Recognizing the foregoing, one influential study has concluded that *all* the causal linkages outlined in these hypothetical examples probably hold. Pippa Norris (2000) suggests that knowledge, interest, and attention to politics in the media form an interlocking circle of causation: a "virtuous circle," as Norris phrases it, among the politically attentive, a vicious circle (presumably) among the politically inattentive.[2] It is, Norris freely admits, a conclusion resting more on intrinsic plausibility than conclusive evidence, since it is difficult to prove that any of the correlations between knowledge, interest, and attentiveness to news media represent true causal effects. It is, nonetheless, a useful perspective to bear in mind and suggests two conclusions when applied to the phenomenon of declining political attentiveness among the young. The first is that change for the worse could have been precipitated by deterioriation in any, and perhaps all, of the different dimensions of political attentiveness, so it is important to entertain a variety of causal scenarios. The second is that efforts to address the matter can perhaps target various points on the virtuous circle of political attentiveness – can seek to pique political interest, enhance political knowledge, or encourage greater attentiveness to news media on the part of younger citizens – to positive effect. Whatever it is that has precipitated a decline in political attentiveness, there may be multiple ways to effect a solution.

The virtuous/vicious circle formulation is also useful when encountering the conclusions of other researchers less circumspect than Norris, who single out a particular strand of inattentiveness among the young as the key precipitant of broader change, without evident justification. It has been suggested, for example, that the principal reason for the political disengagement of younger citizens is that they have simply lost interest in politics. This idea is often voiced in the UK, where disengagement among the young and the attendant public debate over the past decade have closely paralleled Canadian developments (Jowell and Park 1998, 8; White et al. 2000; Park 2005, 29-32). The same theme is echoed in the US by researchers whose main focus is declining attention to politics in the media and the state of political knowledge among citizens, yet who are drawn to the conclusion that, in the final analysis, indifference to politics is the probable root cause of the disquieting trends they uncover (Bennett 1998, 539; Delli Carpini and Keeter 1991, 607). Canadian studies have drawn similar conclusions, though often stipulating that it is traditional electoral politics that young people have primarily disavowed, as they remain enthusiastic about alternative forms of civic and political involvement felt to be more meaningful and effective (Barnard et al. 2003; MacKinnon et al. 2007; Turcotte 2007). The common view emerging from such studies is that the solution to disengagement lies in politics itself. Political practices and institutional structures need to be reformed to conform more closely to the preferences and sensibilities of younger citizens and thereby rekindle their political interest.

Others shift the explanatory emphasis to other dimensions of political inattentiveness. Martin Wattenberg, for example, finding low levels of knowledge, political interest, and attention to news media among American adults under thirty, concludes that "a rapidly changing media environment" is to blame, and more particularly that "the shift from broadcasting to narrowcasting has dramatically altered how much exposure a young adult has received to politics while growing up" (2002, 90). The same conclusion is advanced in his comparative analysis of the long-established democracies (2003, 164-65; 2008). Still others, however, in advocating enhanced civics education as the remedy of choice (Galston 2001, 2007), imply that knowledge is the gateway to political engagement and can overcome obstacles presented by a lack of political interest among young people or their disinclination to follow politics in the media. Equip young people with a basic grasp of politics, it is implied, and other facets of political attentiveness will naturally follow. Each account is plausible, but none offers a compelling reason to privilege one particular strand of political inattentiveness in either our diagnoses of the problem or prescriptions for resolving it.

This chapter seeks to make headway on these matters by assembling a broad array of relevant evidence. Without claiming to unravel fully the knotty causal linkages between knowledge, interest, and habits of news media use, the analysis is structured to provide some useful conclusions about the plausibility of different causal scenarios by analyzing evolving patterns of political attentiveness over time and place. Survey data are consulted from the past and present for six countries: Canada, the US, Britain, Sweden, the Netherlands, and Norway. The choice of cases is principally driven by the availability of relevant data. The countries included have accessible survey data, both current and historical, with reasonably consistent measures of political knowledge, political interest, and habits of news media use. Yet fortuitously, the six cases can be seen as forming two distinct groupings of analytical relevance. Milner, in his comparative work on civic literacy (2001, 2002), groups Canada with the US and Britain, suggesting these Anglo-American countries are marked by low levels of political knowledge and spotty consumption of politically informative news media. By contrast, he places the Northern European states, particularly the Scandinavian countries, at the high end of his civic literacy spectrum. Evidence generally supporting this classification can be found in the comparative statistics provided in Table 3.1 above. While Milner does not focus extensively on generational differences in political attentiveness in *Civic Literacy*, he does suggest that countries like Sweden seem particularly determined to ensure that levels of civic literacy are maintained through various policy measures (179-80). In elsewhere analyzing political disengagement among young Canadians, he has more pointedly proposed that the decline in civic literacy is particularly acute in North America (2005, 7). It seems, moreover, a reasonable extension of the general argument that a society rich in information resources and possessing a politically attentive citizenry would be more successful in imparting the requisite civic skills and dispositions to younger cohorts than one lacking in these areas. The Anglo-American and Northern European countries thus present contrasting expectations with respect to trends in political inattentiveness among the young, and hence a useful set of cases for comparative analysis.

Political Knowledge

We begin with the element of political attentiveness that is perhaps most crucial to effective citizenship: political knowledge. Previous research has undertaken some investigation of trends in knowledge over time in various places. In the American case, earlier research has found a growing knowledge gap between young and old over the past several decades (Times Mirror

Center 1990; Delli Carpini and Keeter 1996, 172). A previous study by the current author identified a similar pattern in both Canada and one of the Northern European cases, the Netherlands (Howe 2006). Another work published at the time of writing this book undertakes a much broader comparative analysis, comparing age differences in political knowledge across a wide array of countries. It finds evidence that the gaps between younger and older citizens have grown larger in recent times (Wattenberg 2008). However, the clusters of countries examined at different points are not consistent and there is a rather long interval between early and later measurements (1970 to the late 1990s and early 2000s). This section extends this recent comparative work by taking a more meticulous look at six countries, drawing on a fuller set of surveys and questions to trace the trajectory of political knowledge differences between young and old over several decades.

In doing so, certain measurement issues must be considered. First, even in places where political knowledge has been regularly measured, there is little replication of specific questions. Even where the same question has been asked on multiple occasions, it is generally not sensible to treat this as a consistent barometer of knowledge, given fluctuations in the salience of different offices, office-holders, and political issues over time. For example, it is not surprising that respondents were increasingly successful in identifying William Rehnquist as the Chief Justice of the US Supreme Court when the question was posed on successive iterations of the American National Election Study from 1988 to 2004. Nor is it remarkable, given differences in the tenure and public profile of the incumbents, that 63 percent of Canadian respondents could identify Paul Martin as the federal finance minister in 2000 but only 7 percent could name Ralph Goodale as his successor four years later. Given this basic obstacle, there is generally no reliable way to assess how knowledge levels among younger and older groups have been evolving in *absolute* terms. Instead, we must utilize an alternative strategy, focusing on *relative* levels of political knowledge – differences in knowledge between young and old – to see whether this gap has been growing over time.

It is also necessary, in assembling comparative data, to take account of distinct types of political knowledge captured by survey measures. Previous studies (Delli Carpini and Keeter 1991; Jennings 1996) identify three general types: surveillance knowledge, civics knowledge, and historical knowledge. The most common questions appearing on national election studies and other surveys are surveillance items, in particular, the names of political office-holders and knowledge of current political issues. Civics questions designed to assess knowledge of institutions and political processes appear more occasionally, while historical items – knowledge of past events and political players – are relatively uncommon. Since previous research has found that age differences vary across categories of knowledge (Delli Carpini and Keeter

1996, 145; Jennings 1996), aggregating different types of knowledge items is ill-advised. The strategy adopted here is to examine only the most common category of knowledge items, surveillance knowledge. A longitudinal analysis of the other two categories is simply not feasible for the range of countries under consideration.

Table 3.2 reports results based on forty-five surveys conducted between 1956 and 2006 in the six countries.[3] The number of knowledge items used for any given survey ranges from three to thirty. Most inquire about mainstream electoral politics: identifying political leaders (party leaders and cabinet ministers), current government policies, and policy positions or campaign promises associated with specific political parties.[4] While the bulk of the questions focus on domestic political matters, a handful ask about international political figures and developments. Greater detail on the specific questions used in Table 3.2 can be found in Appendix B.

For each survey, a single statistic is reported: the mean percentage of correct items for those aged twenty-one to twenty-nine, less the mean percentage for those fifty to sixty-five (a minus sign thus indicating lower knowledge in the younger group).[5] Two notable findings emerge from Table 3.2. First, it is apparent that the gap in surveillance knowledge between young and old has grown considerably over time. Prior to 1979, the percentage point difference was in the single digits at every point but one. Since that year it has nearly always been in the double digits. Secondly, this pattern is consistent across the six countries, and the two general categories of countries, the Anglo-American and the Northern European. All have witnessed a growing gap between young and old in levels of surveillance knowledge over the past several decades.

Summary statistics make this clear. Prior to 1979, the mean knowledge gap between younger and older respondents across all countries and surveys was –4.3. For the Anglo-American countries in this period, it was –4.4, for the Northern European countries, –4.3. Since 1979, the mean gap for all countries has been –17.1: for the Anglo-American countries, –15.6, for the Northern European, –18.7. Whatever the differences in political attentiveness between the two categories of countries, they display a common pattern of a growing knowledge gap between younger and older adults over the past several decades.

Further calculations underscore the magnitude of the current knowledge deficit among the young in these six countries. The distribution of respondents on knowledge scales is typically bell-shaped, with the larger part of the sample clustered in the middle and relatively few at the extremes. Thus an average knowledge gap of 17.1 percentage points between younger and older adults represents a considerable spread. Another method of comparison that makes this more apparent is to locate the median respondent in the twenty-one to twenty-nine age group on the knowledge distribution for the fifty to

Table 3.2

Political knowledge age gap for six countries, 1956-2005

Year	Britain	Canada	US	Netherlands	Norway	Sweden
1956		-6				-1
1959	-4					
1960a			-3			
1960b			-10			-6
1964			-4			-6
1965					1	
1968			2			
1969	-6				-9	
1971				-2		
1973					-3	
1977				-8		
1979	-17					
1981				-10		
1984		-10	-10			
1985						-19
1986				-16		
1988			-20			-21
1989				-17		
1991						-26
1992			-17			
1993		-11				
1994a	-14			-13		
1994b				-15		-24
1996			-9			
1997		-15			-18	
1998				-19		-22
2000		-24	-13			
2001	-11				-19	
2002						-23
2004		-21	-14			
2005	-23					
2006		-21				

Notes: Entries are the mean percentage of correct responses for those aged 21 to 29, less the mean percentage for those aged 50 to 65. In some cases, age is a categorized variable in the dataset and the categories do not perfectly align with the 21 to 29 and 50 to 65 age bands. These are:

- Canada 1956: age groups are 21-29 and 50+
- Britain 1959 and United States 1960a: age groups are 18-30 and 51-60
- Netherlands 1989: age groups are 21-30 and 51-65.

Sources: Other than the following, all data are from the national election studies of each country. Canada, 1956: combined results for CIPO 250 and 252 (Gallup polls); Britain, 1959: Civic Culture Study; United States, 1960a: Civic Culture Study; Britain, 1969: combined results for Gallup polls 972d and 973a; Britain and Netherlands, 1994a: European Election Study 1994.

sixty-five group. In the 2004 Canadian data, for example, the median young respondent lies at the 20th percentile of the knowledge distribution for the fifty to sixty-five age group.[6] In other words, 80 percent of older Canadians know more about politics than the typical young adult. The same calculation for the other countries (for the most recent survey years) situates the median young respondent as follows: Britain, at the 22nd percentile; the US, the 33rd percentile; Sweden, the 13th percentile; Netherlands, the 24th percentile; and Norway, the 23rd percentile.[7] These are considerable gaps and again are largely consistent across the two categories of countries. This first finding is one of surprising consistency across the six countries and the two general categories of cases.

The sizable increase in the knowledge gap between young and old suggests that the current knowledge deficit among young Canadians principally reflects a cohort, not life-cycle, effect. It is *not* the case that young Canadians (or young people elsewhere) have always been markedly less knowledgeable about politics than older adults. Instead, this is a pattern that has slowly emerged among younger cohorts over several decades. Recalling the earlier discussion of electoral participation and the joint influence of life-cycle and cohort effects on low turnout among the young, the finding suggests that political knowledge can be linked to the more troublesome of the two effects, the cohort gap, and thereby to the habitual non-voting associated with this dimension of turnout patterns. A paucity of political knowledge is not a factor hindering participation in early adulthood that improves reliably with age, but instead a distinctive characteristic of today's younger generations weighing down their electoral participation in a more enduring manner.

These conclusions are, of course, based on measures of political knowledge that vary over time: different questions asked at different points that gauge relative, not absolute, levels of knowledge among the young. Some might be suspicious of this method, arguing that citizens on the whole have grown more politically aware and attuned over time – some certainly subscribe to this view (Norris 2000; Dalton 2006) – so that if the gap between young and old has increased, this does not necessarily mean that today's young adults are less knowledgeable than their counterparts of thirty or forty years ago. To shore up our conclusions, one further piece of evidence can be cited that draws on a particular survey question posed at multiple points that can be considered a reasonably consistent gauge of political knowledge. The question asks respondents to name the premier of their province, a fairly elementary piece of political information. In the 1984 Canadian election study, 88 percent of those aged twenty-one to twenty-nine were able to come up with the correct name. In the three election studies of 2000, 2004, and 2006, the average percentage of correct responses to the same question in this age group was only 60 percent. If we eliminate the 2004 study on the grounds that many provincial elections had taken place the previous year, leading to a number of newcomers in office and making the question a little more challenging, the figure for 2000 and 2006 climbs to 64 percent. If we eliminate Quebec from the 1984 calculations on the grounds that then Premier Réné Lévesque was a tremendously renowned public figure, the percentage of correct responses for that year drops to 84 percent. Even with these adjustments, the conclusion remains: young adults today are much less likely to know at least one simple political fact than their counterparts of the early 1980s.

Why might such a decline in surveillance knowledge have occurred? One possible answer, explored in subsequent sections, is that political interest and/or attention to politics in the media have ebbed over time, dragging political knowledge down with them. Before examining that possibility, it is worth considering whether there might be any changing conditions or circumstances that could have impinged on political knowledge directly. One possibility is the emphasis given to civics education. If there has been reduced time and effort given to the teaching of civics over the years, it could help to explain why knowledge of political affairs has declined considerably among younger generations. At first blush, this might seem an implausible account. Civics education tends to focus on institutional processes and generic knowledge of politics rather than the type of current events information picked up by survey questions measuring surveillance knowledge, and any facts about current political events that students might acquire in their high school civics classes would soon be out of date. It is important to recognize, however, that an understanding of principle facilitates retention of detail. Someone is, for example, more likely to remember that it is the Conservative Party pledging to reduce income taxes if he understands that cutting taxes is a policy initiative consistent with a conservative political philosophy. One study that speaks to this point found that the best predictor of people's ability to recall factual information about recent current events was not the amount of news they had recently read or watched, but their background level of political knowledge about more enduring elements of the political landscape (Price and Zaller 1993). So, it is certainly worth considering the possibility that a decline in civics instruction might have contributed to an erosion in knowledge of current politics among young Canadians.

Despite the plausibility of the hypothesis, however, there is reason to believe that inadequate attention to civics instruction is not a principal reason behind the growing political knowledge deficit. The reason is simple: there is no evidence to suggest that all six countries where the knowledge gap has grown substantially over the years witnessed a sharp reduction in the emphasis accorded civics education over the same period. While the potential for civics education to bolster civic engagement is often affirmed,[8] and a number of countries have been seeking to enhance this part of the school curriculum in recent years, there is nothing to indicate that civics instruction came to be widely de-emphasized in all these places some thirty to forty years ago.[9]

This is not to say that the teaching of politics in our classrooms has no role to play in addressing the knowledge deficit and the broader problem of political inattentiveness among young Canadians. If Norris is right about the virtuous circle connecting knowledge, interest, and news media consumption, then enhanced civics education almost certainly has a part to play in imparting fresh momentum to these mutually reinforcing dynamics. Thus, civics education is a subject that merits revisiting, but it is set aside for the moment as other dimensions of evolving political attentiveness over time that may offer different insights are probed.

Political Interest

If political interest provides the motivation to keep up with current events, it is plausible to think that this may be the root source of the inattentiveness to politics manifested in declining levels of political knowledge. There has previously been relatively limited investigation of the evolution of political interest across age groups in various countries, and the results have been mixed. Wattenberg analyzes a consistent question from the American National Election Studies and concludes that there has been a sharp decline in political interest among younger cohorts (2002, 88-90). He does not, however, examine evolving levels of political interest in his more recent comparative study of patterns of political attentiveness in the established democracies (2008). Dalton, on the other hand, looking at aggregate levels of political interest in the US, UK, France, and Germany from the mid-1950s to mid-1990s, finds a secular increase that would not be expected if interest in younger cohorts was falling off sharply (2006, 25). A similar analysis for the Netherlands likewise finds increasing political interest in the aggregate over the 1974-90 period (van den Broek 1994, 184-85) but a more recent study finds lower levels of interest among younger cohorts, particularly those born since 1970 (van Deth 2000, 257-58). A UK study finds evidence of both life-cycle and cohort effects, again suggesting that the latter effects are concentrated among the youngest cohorts (Park 2005, 30-32). Gidengil et al., on the other hand, looking at the Canadian case, suggest that political interest follows a life-cycle arc of increasing interest with age (2004, 22). No previous studies appear to have undertaken a more comprehensive comparative evaluation of the evolution of political interest across age groups over time.

It is possible for each of the six cases, using election study data supplemented by other sources, to assemble comparative data that can be used for this purpose. Indeed, for some countries the task is greatly facilitated by the consistent inclusion in national election studies of a single question aimed at measuring general political interest. This is the case for Sweden and the

Netherlands, and for the US from 1968 to the present; response categories for the 1964 US election study can be collapsed to render it comparable as well. In Norway and the UK, the wording of the political interest question has been highly consistent, but response categories have been altered over time. Again, collapsing of categories yields essentially comparable groupings. Given the relative stability in question wording for these cases, trends in absolute levels of political interest among the young are considered in this section, along with the gap between young and old.

In Canada, questions aimed at gauging general political interest have been less consistent. In some election studies, they are lacking altogether, and it is necessary to fall back on items querying interest in the upcoming election rather than politics in general. Given that the time series is imperfect in this way, early measures of election interest from 1949 and 1957 are added for the Canadian case to provide the longest time perspective possible. In light of the inconsistencies in question wording, the focus for Canada is on relative levels of interest between young and old, with no attempt made to assess absolute levels of interest for either group.

As with political knowledge, where a focus on the percentage of items answered correctly produces a scale ranging from 0 to 100, responses to the political interest items are rescaled to a 0 to 100 range.[10] The results are presented in Table 3.3. For the five countries where political interest measures are sufficiently consistent over time, the gap in mean interest between younger and older respondents is presented, followed by the mean for each group in parentheses. For Canada, only the difference between the younger and older age groups is reported.

The results are not quite as tidy as those for political knowledge above, but the essential pattern is clear enough: there is no evidence of a sharp decline in political interest among young adults across the six cases. In the Northern European countries, the moderate difference in mean levels of interest between young and old has remained essentially constant down to the present day. Prior to 1979, the mean gap across all three countries was –4.5. Since 1979, it has been –5.2. For the two countries that offer an unbroken string of question replication, the Netherlands and Sweden, the mean level of reported interest among those aged twenty-one to twenty-nine has declined not one whit over this long period. These results suggest an age gap that represents a life-cycle pattern only, not differences between birth cohorts.

For the Anglo-American countries, there was a fair-sized gap in political interest in earlier periods: –9.0 on average up to 1979. This has since become slightly more pronounced, growing to –12.8 in subsequent years. The increase, however, is driven by the North American countries. The political interest gap between young and old has remained essentially stable in the UK, as have absolute levels of interest among the young.

Yet even in the Canadian and American cases, growth in the interest gap

Table 3.3

Political interest age gap for six countries, 1949-2005

Year	Britain	Canada	US	Netherlands	Norway	Sweden
1956		−6				−1
1949		−12 (e)				
1957		−9 (e)				
1960						−8 (42, 50)
1964			−10 (56, 66)			−3 (44, 47)
1965		−9			−6 (29, 35)	
1968		−8 (e)	−6 (57, 63)			−1 (50, 51)
1969					−10 (28, 38)	
1970						0 (49, 49)
1971				−5 (30, 35)		
1972			0 (68, 68)			
1973					−12 (33, 45)	0 (52, 52)
1974	−9 (56, 65)	−16				
1976			−11 (60, 71)			−2 (52, 54)
1977				−4 (35, 39)	−6 (33, 39)	
1979	−5 (53, 58)	−15				−1 (52, 53)
1980			−13 (51, 64)			
1981				2 (42, 40)	0 (39, 39)	
1982						−3 (49, 52)
1983	−10 (45, 55)					
1984		−23	−13 (52, 65)			
1985					−6 (19, 25)	−3 (49, 52)
1986				−8 (38, 46)		
1988a	−14 (42, 56)					
1988b		−16	−11 (48, 59)			−7 (46, 53)
1989	−2 (50, 52)					
1989				−10 (41, 51)	−4 (33, 37)	
1990	−8 (47, 55)					
1991						−2 (50, 52)
1992			−12 (54, 66)			
1993		−15 (e)			−7 (29, 36)	
1994a	−4 (48, 52)					
1994b				−4 (42, 46)		−9 (49, 58)
1996			−18 (47, 65)			
1997	−7 (53, 60)	−18			−9 (30, 39)	
1998				−6 (39, 45)		−10 (48, 58)
2000		−20	−20 (41, 61)			
2001	−9 (49, 58)				−7 (32, 39)	
2002						−5 (50, 55)
2004		−17	−17 (51, 68)			
2005	−7 (53, 60)					
2006		−18				

Notes: Entries are the mean interest score for those aged 21 to 29, less the mean score for those aged 50 to 65, followed in parentheses by the mean score for each group, respectively. Canadian results based on election interest are indicated with (e).

Sources: Other than the following, all data are from the national election studies of each country. Canada, 1949: combined data for CIPO 186 and 189 (Gallup polls); Canada, 1957: combined data for CIPO 257 and 258 (Gallup polls); Britain and the Netherlands, 1983, 1988a, 1989, 1990, and 1994a: Eurobarometer polls from the Mannheim Eurobarometer Trend File 1970-2002.

between young and old is less pronounced than the changes in relative political knowledge seen above. The Canadian case is best suited to drawing comparisons. Recent election studies use an eleven-point scale for measuring political interest that allows for reasonably precise calculation of percentile scores. Using the same procedure as above, based on the 2004 Canadian election study, we find that the median respondent in the under-thirty age category lies at the 31st percentile of the interest distribution for the older age group, compared to the previously noted 20th percentile for political knowledge. From Table 3.3, it is also quite clear, in contrast to the knowledge results above, that a good part of this interest gap represents a longstanding difference between young and old rather than a newly emergent pattern – in other words, a life-cycle rather than cohort effect. While inconsistencies in measurement methods preclude putting too fine a point on these assessments, the general result seems clear. Despite a consistent decline in levels of knowledge, there is little evidence of a commensurate decline in political interest over the past forty years among young people in the six countries under consideration. Accounts of disengagement that emphasize low levels of political interest must recognize that young people, in these six countries at least, have always been somewhat less interested in politics than older adults and that current age differences are not exceptional.

News Media Use
The prior two findings – that there exists a significant gap in political knowledge between young and old in six different countries dating back to at least the late 1970s, and that there has been no apparent decline in political interest among the young that can readily explain this – would seem to bolster the plausibility of another prominent account of the origins of political inattentiveness among the young: that it is an inadvertent outcome of changing patterns of media consumption produced by major changes in the media environment. Two distinct processes are typically highlighted. The first emphasizes the drop in newspaper reading that followed the widespread penetration of television into people's homes and lives (Wattenberg 2008, 15; Milner 2002, 92). The second underlines the proliferation of TV viewing options that came with the widespread adoption of cable and related technologies and the consequent reduction in exposure to TV news and other public affairs programming (Baum and Kernell 1999; Pew Research Center 2004; Prior 2007; Wattenberg 2008). In both cases, the argument is that younger cohorts, their reading and viewing habits less fully formed than those of their elders, were most heavily influenced by these changes.

The timing of these transformations in the media environment varies to some degree from country to country. TV first swept across the US, where by 1960 there was a set in virtually every household. As Table 3.4 indicates, the same was true of Canada by about 1965 and Britain by the early 1970s.

Table 3.4

Television penetration in six countries, 1953-80

Year	Britain	Canada	US	Netherlands	Norway	Sweden
TV sets per 1,000 inhabitants						
1953	58	40	169	1	0	0.1
1955	105	121	227	7	0	1
1960	211	219	310	· 69	13	156
1965	248	270	362	171	132	270
1970	294	333	413	237	220	312
1975	361	413	560	267	260	355
1980	404	443	684	296	292	381
Approximate household penetration (%)						
1953	19	16	57	0	0	0
1955	34	47	75	3	0	0
1960	65	85	100	25	4	44
1965	74	100	100	60	40	73
1970	85	100	100	81	64	81
1975	100	100	100	85	73	85
1980	100	100	100	89	79	88

Notes: Average household size data have been used to calculate number of TV sets per 1,000 inhabitants required for 100 percent household penetration in different years (e.g., if average household is 3.0 persons, this number is 333, assuming no more than one set per household). Precise household size data are used for years where available. For other years, estimates are based on interpolated values.

TV data for the Netherlands, Norway, Sweden, and the UK (1953-70) are based on number of licences, not receivers, which may slightly underestimate penetration. However, the assumption that there are no multi-TV households may slightly overestimate penetration (e.g., other sources indicate a household penetration rate of just below 90 percent for the US in 1960, not 100 percent – see Prior 2007, 59).

Sources: TV data, 1953-60: UNESCO *Statistical Yearbook 1965*; TV data, 1965-80: UNESCO *Statistical Yearbook 1986*; average household size data: *United Nations Demographic Yearbook 1955, 1962, 1963, 1971, 1976*, and *1987*.

By contrast, take-up was considerably slower in the three Northern European countries. In the mid-1960s, estimated penetration rates ranged from 40 percent (Norway) to 73 percent (Sweden), and even by the end of the 1970s, the technology was only prevalent, not ubiquitous, in all three places.

The expansion of choice in channels and programming also proceeded unevenly. In some places, a measure of choice was present from the beginning. Americans could choose from among several private broadcasters. Many Canadians, by virtue of living close to the American border, could also watch these channels, in addition to their own public broadcaster, CBC, and a private network (CTV) that started airing in 1962. In Britain, viewers could choose between the BBC and the private broadcaster, ITV (launched in 1955), while a second public channel, BBC2, began broadcasting in 1964. Meanwhile, in continental Europe, a sole public broadcaster was the norm in the early days of television. The Netherlands added a second public channel in 1964, as did Sweden in 1968. Norway did not do so until 1996, though in 1992 a private channel was established.

Of course, even in countries with multiple channels, viewing choice in the early years of television was often limited, particularly with respect to news broadcasts, as these were often shown simultaneously on different channels. The widespread adoption of cable (followed later by satellite television and now TV over the Internet), which greatly expanded the menu of viewing options, is typically seen as the critical development that reduced exposure to news and current affairs programming (Wattenberg 2008, 5). This happened earliest in Canada, where cable was already present in 45 percent of homes by 1975 (McFayden et al. 1980, 16) and in more than 60 percent by 1985 (Sciadis 2002, 8). The US was not far behind: slow growth through to 1980, at which point about 20 percent of homes had cable, was followed by a period of rapid expansion, leading to 43 percent household penetration by 1985, and 67 percent by 1997 (Statistical Abstract of the United States 1999). In most of Europe, cable and satellite technology, along with private broadcasters, first appeared in the 1980s but only came to be widely adopted in the 1990s (Holtz-Bacha and Norris 2001). However, there remained significant variations in penetration rates across countries. As of 1997, cable or satellite penetration stood at 31 percent in the UK, 57 percent in Norway, 64 percent in Sweden, and 99 percent in the Netherlands (Norris 2000, 96). The uneven timing of the relevant developments across these countries is to be kept in mind in seeking to assess the impact of changes in the media environment on evolving patterns of news media consumption.

Newspaper reading

To consider the arguments in turn, we turn first to patterns of newspaper reading over time. One limitation that arises is the lack of consistent measurements of this activity prior to the introduction of television, a challenge that others have also confronted. Robert Putnam, for example, in his analysis of newspaper reading in *Bowling Alone* (2000, 219), uses data from the General Social Survey starting in 1972. Seeing evidence of cohort effects since that time, he infers that differences between older cohorts are indicative of a decline in newspaper reading that emerged around the time that television first arrived on the scene. Other studies of newspaper reading habits likewise rely on data first collected well after television was firmly established (Peiser 2000; Lauf 2001; Wattenberg 2008).

So it is with the principal data source used here, the Multinational Time Use Study, which compiles surveys from numerous countries from 1965 to the present, all based on detailed diaries of respondents' activities for a single day (or in the Dutch case, multiple days).[11] There are three reasons for choosing this source. The first is coverage: the time-use surveys, using a reasonably consistent survey methodology, encompass numerous countries of interest over a significant stretch of time.[12] The second is measurement precision: time-use surveys gauge not simply whether or how often respondents read the paper, but the amount of time spent reading on a given day. The third relates to measurement bias, though here there are concerns with both traditional survey approaches and time-use diaries. The potential problems are underlined by a striking finding on the 2005 Canadian time-use survey. In addition to asking respondents to complete a time diary by detailing their activities for the previous day, the survey included a series of additional questions. One asked respondents how often they read the paper "as a leisure activity." Of those who reported reading the newspaper for leisure "daily," only *one-quarter* actually reported any time spent reading newspapers on the time-diary portion of the interview (25.3 percent). Moreover, this discrepancy was especially pronounced for young respondents. A mere 5.2 percent of "daily" newspaper readers aged twenty to twenty-nine reported reading a newspaper on the time diary, compared to 31.1 percent of those fifty to sixty-four and 45.7 percent of those in their seventies.[13]

The reason for the discrepancy between the two methods of reporting is likely twofold. On the one hand, there is undoubtedly over-reporting of newspaper reading on questions that simply ask about the general frequency of reading, which others have discovered can be quite dramatic (Zaller 2002, 311). However, there is also probable under-reporting through the diary method, due to a failure to record activities of short duration, an acknowledged problem with time-use diaries (on the 2005 Canadian time-use study, few report reading times of less than fifteen minutes).[14] If young people are especially apt to read for brief periods – and there is evidence for this in both European countries and Canada[15] – this would help to explain the exceptionally high percentage of young "daily" newspaper readers who fail to record any time reading the paper on their time diaries. Neither method is ideal then. However, time-diary surveys, used occasionally in previous studies of trends in newspaper reading (Robinson 1980; Raeymaeckers 2002), do offer a number of advantages.

One unfortunate feature of the aggregated Multinational Time Use Study database is that newspaper reading is not a separate category of activity, but is instead grouped together with magazine reading. This means that the data represent maximum estimates of newspaper reading time. To gain a more precise sense of the effects of using this measure, the 2005 Canadian time-use study, which offers a finer breakdown of activities, is again consulted. In that study, the mean time spent on magazine reading accounts for a relatively modest 19 percent of the total time spent on newspapers and magazines combined.[16]

Table 3.5

Newspaper and magazine reading, age difference for six countries, 1965-2000

Year	Britain	Canada	US	Netherlands	Norway	Sweden
1965			.44 (16, 36)			
1971		.52 (14, 27)			.72 (21, 29)	
1975	.49 (11, 23)		.45 (13, 29)	.64 (34, 53)		
1980				.64 (29, 45)		
1981		.36 (9, 25)			.63 (26, 41)	
1983	.33 (7, 21)					
1985			.33 (8, 24)	.53 (25, 47)		
1986		.33 (5, 15)				
1987	.35 (7, 20)					
1990				.43 (19, 44)	.47 (18, 38)	
1992		.33 (7, 21)	.32 (8, 25)			
1995	.27 (7, 26)			.33 (14, 42)		
1998		.24 (4, 17)	.24 (4, 17)			
2000	.28 (5, 18)			.30 (11, 37)	.37 (13, 35)	.27 (7, 26)
2005		.15 (2, 13)				

Notes: Entries are the ratio of mean reading time (newspapers and magazines) for those aged 21 to 29 compared to those aged 50 to 65, followed in parentheses by the mean time in minutes for each group, respectively. Swedish data are based on published results using age groups 20 to 24 and 45 to 64.

Sources: Multinational Time Use Study, Version 5.5.2.

Table 3.5 reports results. Individual cells display the ratio of the mean reading time (younger/older) recorded by respondents on the time diary. Shown in parentheses are the mean number of minutes for each group (twenty-one to twenty-nine, fifty to sixty-five) respectively, from which the ratio is calculated (it should be borne in mind that many respondents report no reading time whatsoever, thus explaining some of the very low mean values). Data are missing for Sweden due to the exclusion of this country's time-use datasets from the combined data file; published results for 2000 are the only figures available.

The table first reveals that a gap between young and old in time dedicated to the reading of newspapers (and magazines) is hardly new. In all cases, there is a considerable difference in average reading time between the two age groups at the earliest measurement point. The table also provides clear evidence of a sharp decline in newspaper reading among young people: in Canada, for example, the average time among those under thirty drops from fourteen minutes in 1971 to two minutes in 2005. However, reading time has declined substantially among the older comparison group as well (in all cases but Norway). That said, the drop among the young has been more precipitous. Thus the ratio of reading time for younger and older respondents has fallen substantially over the past thirty to forty years, from a range of one-half to three-quarters in the 1965 to 1975 period, to a range of one-quarter to about one-third in recent years – and in the most recent Canadian study in 2005, to just one-sixth.

This is a useful first cut at the data, but given the degree of change occurring among both younger and older adults, is not really adequate to the task of sorting out life-cycle and cohort effects. Comparing age groups at different points in time was sufficient in the earlier analysis of political knowledge and interest, as inconsistencies in question wording over time and/or relatively clear-cut results rendered more elaborate and precise methods inadvisable and unnecessary. But here the measurement method – average time reading per day as captured by time diaries – is consistent and the results harder to interpret. What, for example, is to be made of the age gap that is evident at the beginning of the time series in each country? Does it represent a life-cycle effect, meaning that considerable increases in newspaper reading should be anticipated for today's youngest cohorts as they grow older? Or could it represent a difference between the birth cohorts represented by the twenty-one to twenty-nine and fifty to sixty-five age groups at the start of the time series? Or is it a reflection of both? Instead of simply comparing younger and older groups at different points in time, to answer such questions a more structured cohort analysis is required in order to determine more conclusively the relative importance of birth year and age to newspaper reading propensities.

In doing so, one additional potential effect must also be considered: period effects affecting people of all ages and birth cohorts at a given point. Sometimes period effects represent a permanent shift in attitudes or behaviour manifested by young and old alike; in other cases, they represent more ephemeral changes. Time spent reading newspapers, for example, can be temporarily influenced by whether there is a particularly gripping news story unfolding at the time of data collection, or by the time of year data are gathered if there is seasonal variation in reading patterns (e.g., less time reading the paper in the summer months). Whatever their precise nature, potential period effects must be taken into account in order to sort out accurately the effects of aging and birth cohort.

Table 3.6, based on the same data as Table 3.5, provides results of a cohort analysis of mean reading time (newspapers and magazines) for each of the countries save Sweden. Rather than the cohort tables that are sometimes used to carry out such analysis, which can be cumbersome to evaluate, the results are based on OLS regression models designed to capture relevant life-cycle, cohort, and period effects in a more succinct fashion. Period effects were identified from an inspection of cross-tabulations for mean reading time by birth cohort at different points. Reasons for these are generally not obvious, but they appear to reflect ephemeral influences, as they affect single years only. The life-cycle effect is captured with a single variable, the respondent's age.[17] Cohort effects are modelled with dummy variables for five-year birth cohorts. Those born in 1920 or earlier form the comparison cohort against which subsequent cohorts are measured.

The constant in the model, the estimated value of the dependent variable when all independent variables take the value 0, represents in this case the estimated mean reading time for those born in 1920 or earlier at age twenty-one – in Canada, 27.1 minutes. The cohort effects indicate the estimated reduction (or increase) in reading time around this value for successive cohorts at the same age. In Canada, the coefficient of –25.6 for the 1981-84 cohort means that estimated reading time among this group at age twenty-one is 1.5 minutes, a rather stark contrast to say the least. The life-cycle effect estimates the impact of aging, assumed to be constant for all birth cohorts. In the Canadian model, this takes the value of 2.4, indicating a relatively minimal increase in reading time between the ages of twenty one and sixty-five. Finally, the period effects pick up shifts in mean reading time affecting all cohorts at particular points (the one salient effect in the Canadian case being a reduction of 5.5 minutes in 1986).

It is easy to see in considering the Canadian results along with those for the other countries why life-cycle effects might get shunted aside when juxtaposed with cohort effects. Not only do they speak to the dimension of diminished newspaper reading among the young that improves with age, they would also appear to be relatively minor. It is nonetheless worth noting that the results in Table 3.6 reveal consistent life-cycle effects, statistically significant in every case, varying from small to moderate across the five countries. The coefficients suggest an increase in reading time of two to sixteen minutes per day in moving from age twenty-one to age sixty-five. Thus part of the age gap in reading time appears to represent an abiding difference between people of different ages.

But clearly this result is less salient than the powerful cohort differences in reading activity apparent in all five countries. The decline among the youngest cohorts, those born in the 1960s and 1970s (and for Canada, the 1980s), is the most striking. These cohorts are estimated to spend a small fraction of the time on newspaper reading that was spent by the oldest cohorts at the same age. A considerable gap is also apparent for those birth cohorts that would have formed the twenty-one to twenty-nine age group when the first time-diary surveys were done back in the 1960s or 1970s – people born in the 1940s or 1950s, depending on the particular country. But the differences do not end there: the decline in reading time, measured against the benchmark of the pre-1920 cohort, stretches back to those born as early as between 1921 and 1925 (Britain, Canada, and the US) and 1926 and 1930 (the Netherlands and Norway). While differences for the latter groups might appear rather slight, perhaps even trivial, seen within the

Table 3.6

Cohort analysis of reading time per day (magazines and newspapers) in five countries, 1965-2005 (OLS regression)

		Britain		Canada		US		Netherlands		Norway	
		B	(SE)	B	(SE)	B	(SE)	B	(SE)	B	(SE)
Constant		16.4	(1.0)	27.1	(0.8)	31.5	(1.2)	48.1	(1.6)	29.6	(1.8)
Birth cohorts	1921-25	-1.4	(0.7)	-1.5	(0.7)	-7.8	(1.0)	-1.8*	(1.1)	0.1*	(1.0)
	1926-30	-7.5	(0.6)	-5.4	(0.7)	-11.1	(1.0)	-2.5	(1.1)	-2.7	(1.1)
	1931-35	-6.4	(0.7)	-7.6	(0.7)	-13.2	(1.1)	-9.2	(1.2)	-3.4	(1.2)
	1936-40	-7.0	(0.7)	-10.3	(0.7)	-13.8	(1.1)	-14.5	(1.2)	-5.9	(1.3)
	1941-45	-9.8	(0.8)	-12.6	(0.7)	-16.3	(1.1)	-13.1	(1.3)	-6.4	(1.3)
	1946-50	-9.0	(0.8)	-15.0	(0.7)	-17.5	(1.2)	-14.6	(1.3)	-5.7	(1.4)
	1951-55	-10.6	(0.9)	-17.5	(0.7)	-20.0	(1.2)	-20.4	(1.4)	-9.2	(1.6)
	1956-60	-12.0	(0.9)	-19.5	(0.7)	-24.1	(1.3)	-24.9	(1.5)	-9.2	(1.7)
	1961-65	-12.0	(1.0)	-19.7	(0.8)	-25.6	(1.4)	-28.8	(1.6)	-13.2	(1.8)
	1966-70	-15.3	(1.1)	-22.4	(0.9)	-25.8	(1.6)	-32.4	(1.7)	-17.4	(1.9)
	1971-75	-14.4	(1.2)	-23.6	(1.0)	-27.3	(2.0)	-36.2	(2.0)	-17.3	(2.2)
	1976-80	-12.3	(1.6)	-25.2	(1.2)	-31.5	(3.2)	-37.7	(2.8)	-18.7	(2.4)
	1981-84			-25.6	(1.3)						
Life cycle	Age	12.8	(0.8)	2.4	(0.6)	3.9	(1.1)	3.7	(1.3)	15.8	(1.4)
period	1971									-8.5	(0.8)
	1986			-5.5	(0.4)						
	1992					3.1	(0.6)				
	1995	6.9	(0.4)								
R^2		0.09		0.08		0.08		0.18		0.09	
(N)		(46,958)		(48,611)		(20,075)		(12,920)		(21,486)	

* Not statistically significant at the p < .05 level

General note: Regression models are designed to estimate simultaneously the effects of several independent variables on a dependent variable. The unstandardized regression coefficients (B) indicate the estimated effect for each independent variable (in this case, measured in minutes of reading time per day). The standard errors (SE) are used in calculating margins of error and determining whether results are statistically significant.

Notes on variable coding: Comparison birth cohort: 1920 and earlier. Age: 21 to 65, recoded on 0-1 scale. Analysis restricted to respondents 21 and over (except Canada, 2005, which is restricted to those 20 and over). In addition to weights provided by the original investigators, weights have also been applied so that each year represents equal numbers of respondents (except for Norway, where actual sample sizes for each year are roughly equal).

Source: Multinational Time Use Study, Version 5.5.2.

broader pattern of what was to follow, they take on a greater significance. It is among these cohorts born some eighty to ninety years ago that the long-term decline in newspaper reading seems to have begun.

The timing of these changes is consistent with the proposition that a drop in newspaper reading was a significant contributor to the decline in political knowledge among young people that became clearly evident by about 1980. At that time, those forming the twenty-one to twenty-nine age group were the 1951 to 1955 and 1956 to 1960 cohorts, who clearly spent less time than older cohorts sitting down with the daily paper. It is also plausible, given the timing of the initial decline in newspaper reading, to see the small but consistent knowledge gaps that existed in the earliest political knowledge data from the mid-1950s and start of the 1960s as manifestations of a smaller cohort effect among those who were aged twenty-one to twenty-nine at that time – in other words, people born in the latter half of the 1920s and the 1930s.

What is less clear is that the decline in newspaper reading can be incontrovertibly linked to the introduction and expansion of television. Again, timing is of the essence. In the US, for example, the drop in newspaper reading is clearly evident for those born between 1921 and 1925. People in this cohort were in their mid- to late-twenties when TV first started to make significant inroads in the US around 1950 and in their mid- to late-thirties by the time the technology had become nearly ubiquitous in 1960. The common adage is that those who "grew up" with television were the ones principally influenced by the new medium. Whether someone who experienced the introduction and expansion of television as they moved from their twenties into their thirties falls into this category is subject to debate. For the other countries, the first cohort to show signs of diminished newspaper reading was probably *older still* by the time TV made its mark on the social landscape. In Canada and the UK, this was the same birth cohort (1921 to 1925) as in the US, yet there was about a five-year lag in TV penetration in Canada and about a ten-year lag in the UK. In Norway and the Netherlands, it is the subsequent cohort, born between 1926 and 1930, that first shows signs of reduced newspaper reading, yet these countries were even further behind the US in their take-up of television. In 1960, for example, when the 1926 to 1930 cohort consisted of persons aged thirty to thirty-four, TV was present in only about 25 percent of Dutch households and 4 percent of Norwegian.

Perhaps the habit of newspaper reading was not sufficiently established in adults of this age so that they were in fact significantly affected as the new technology entered their homes and their lives. Or perhaps the impact of the change in media environment represented by the introduction of television has been overstated. It is the latter interpretation favoured here. This position is further developed and defended below, in considering a second essential component of news media attentiveness, following politics on television, and what it reveals about the broader phenomenon of waning political attentiveness among the young.

Attention to Politics on TV

The second element emphasized in media-oriented accounts of disengagement among the young is the reduced attention to politics and current affairs on television, TV news in particular. This change was allegedly precipitated by the proliferation of viewing choices attendant upon the widespread adoption of cable and related technologies. While the hypothesis has been widely circulated and seems plausible enough, definitive evidence seems to be lacking. Certainly, there are studies showing a marked gap between young and old in attention to TV news in various places in recent times. Missing are studies demonstrating a significant *change* in the viewing habits of young people subsequent to the widespread penetration of cable and the multiplication of viewing options. TV ratings data – akin to time-use studies in that respondents are asked to record the shows they watch over a given period rather than prompted in a general survey about whether or how often they watch TV news – would probably be the data source of choice for making the case. However, these numbers are difficult to come by for current periods, let alone thirty or forty years ago. Instead, survey data are more commonly used to track changing habits of attention to politics on TV over time. However, the election surveys that political scientists often draw on to study political behaviour, particularly earlier ones from the 1970s and before, often include no queries about TV news viewing, asking only about attention to specific election-related programming. Much of the relevant research on TV news viewing focuses on recent periods *postdating* the major technological innovations held responsible for declining attention to TV news (for example, a series of widely cited studies of American news consumption habits produced by the Pew Research Center since 1989). Previous work has also concentrated on the American case, failing to demonstrate that propositions about changing patterns of attention to politics on TV hold true in comparative longitudinal analysis.

Since beginning this study, a new book has appeared providing evidence that seems to fill some of these research gaps. Martin Wattenberg's study of voting and political attentiveness among young people (2008) covers similar ground to the material in this chapter, and includes comparative data on attentiveness to politics on television from early and recent periods for the US and, in lesser detail, Canada and various European countries. His interpretation of the numbers compiled is that they strongly support the case that young people in all these places have become decidedly less attentive to politics on television in the past thirty years, and that technological change affording greater viewer choice is the principal reason. The analysis presented here differs from Wattenberg's in both the sources consulted and some of the principal conclusions. In particular, the evidence presented below suggests the expansion of choice brought about by new technologies is not an adequate explanation for waning attentiveness to news and current affairs on television among younger generations. This difference in interpretation is important to our broader understanding of the origins of political inattentiveness among younger citizens and possible methods of addressing it.

The starting point in examining these issues is the national election studies, drawing on questions that have appeared down the years asking respondents whether they watched televised leaders' debates during election campaigns. As a measure of general attentiveness to politics on TV, the item is not ideal, as significant variation in the stakes of an election, the timing of the debate, and the total number of debates during a campaign can lead to significant fluctuations in the numbers tuning in. The advantage, on the other hand, is that questions about debate viewing afford a long-term perspective, since the earliest measurements date back to 1960 (for the US and Sweden). Table 3.7 displays full results for the five countries with available data (all but the UK, where election debates between party leaders have never been the norm). As in previous tables, cells display the difference between younger (twenty-one to twenty-nine) and older (fifty to sixty-five) groups in the percentage who reported watching either a specific debate or any one of the debates that took place during a given election campaign, followed in parentheses by the percentages for each group.[18]

Prior to 1979, the mean percentage point gap in debate viewing between younger and older respondents was –7.3, but this has since grown to –15.3. In the earlier period, the gap in the Anglo-American countries was smaller than in the Northern European countries (–3.3 versus –9.6), but now the two look about the same (–16.6 versus –13.9). These numbers provide some initial evidence of a growing gap between young and old in attention to politics on TV over the long haul across a range of different countries.

A preferable measure to watching election debates, less likely to be subject to intermittent fluctuation, is frequency of TV news viewing. While TV news covers more than politics, those who watch regularly cannot help but be exposed to a certain amount of political information. The drawback in analyzing age patterns for this measure is that the time frame that can be analyzed becomes more limited for most countries. One useful data source is the combined Eurobarometer polls, which have asked a consistent question about TV news viewing from time to time since 1970. This provides a number of measurement points for the UK and the Netherlands.[19] For the US, the national election studies from 1980 to 2004 have asked about frequency of TV news viewing, though inconsistency in question wording renders these far from ideal. For Canada, three polls with similar questions

Table 3.7

Age gap in election debate viewing in five countries, 1960-2004

Year	Canada	US	Netherlands	Norway	Sweden
1960		1 (71, 70)			-12 (63, 75)
1964					-6 (59, 65)
1965				-9 (48, 57)	
1968	-7 (57, 64)				
1969				-12 (44, 56)	
1976		-4 (82, 86)			
1977				-9 (55, 64)	
1979	-5 (46, 51)				-10 (65, 75)
1980		-13 (64, 77)			
1982					-19 (61, 80)
1984	-17 (52, 69)	-21 (55, 67)			
1985					-19 (57, 76)
1986			-6 (52, 58)		
1988	-21 (55, 76)				-12 (56, 68)
1989			-19 (40, 59)		
1991					-16 (61, 77)
1993	-20 (45, 65)				
1994					-14 (57, 71)
1996		-16 (53, 69)			
1997	-25 (35, 60)				
1998			-2 (65, 67)		-13 (56, 69)
2000	-24 (33, 57)	-13 (62, 75)			
2001				-23 (36, 59)	
2002					-14 (54, 68)
2004	-13 (42, 55)				
2006	-20 (26, 46)				

Note: Entries are the percentage viewing election debates among those aged 21 to 29, less the percentage among those aged 50 to 65, followed in parentheses by the percentage in each age group, respectively.

Sources: National election studies of each country.

on TV news viewing dating from 1962, 1977, and 2002 were identified (though the 1962 survey differs in asking only about the viewing of CBC news, at a time when the first private Canadian broadcaster, CTV, was just starting to provide news broadcasts in some Canadian cities). Finally, the Swedish election studies offer the most consistent and detailed series of questions, asking about the frequency of viewing each of the main news broadcasts on the air at different points from 1979 to 2002. These various sources provide some insight into patterns of TV news viewing for different age groups over time and place. Other sources are subsequently introduced that allow for further investigation of news viewing patterns in particular countries.

Table 3.8

Age gap in TV news viewing in five countries, 1962-2004

Year/period		Britain	Netherlands
1970			-21 (47, 68)
1980-86		-13 (67, 80)	-16 (60, 76)
1989-93		-19 (68, 87)	-25 (63, 88)
1995-98		-19 (67, 86)	-22 (63, 85)
1999-2001		-21 (60, 81)	-26 (60, 86)

Year	Canada	US	Sweden
1962	-17 (33, 50)		
1970			
1977	-29 (35, 64)		
1979			-27 (51, 78)
1980		-31 (18, 49)	
1982			-25 (52, 77)
1984		-37 (25, 63)	
1985			-23 (51, 74)
1988		-22 (44, 66)	-29 (45, 74)
1991			-31 (49, 80)
1992		-32 (29, 61)	
1994			
1996		-32 (8, 40)	-17 (53, 70)
1998		·	-15 (49, 64)
2000		-30 (9, 39)	
2002	-29 (53, 82)		-20 (45, 65)
2004		-26 (13, 39)	

Notes: Entries are the percentages of regular viewers of TV news among those aged 21 to 29, less the percentage among those aged 50 to 65, followed in parentheses by the percentage in each group, respectively. For Canada, 1962, the older age group consists of all respondents 50 and over.

Sources: Britain, Netherlands: Eurobarometer polls from the Mannheim Eurobarometer Trend File 1970-2002 (except Netherlands, 1970, which is the European Communities Study 1970); Canada, 1962: CIPO 299 (Gallup); Canada, 1977: Quality of Life: Social Change in Canada; Canada, 2002: Elections Canada 2002 Survey of Voters and Non-Voters; United States and Sweden: national election studies.

Results based on the percentage of regular news viewers in different age groups are presented in Table 3.8 (details about question wording and coding of "regular" TV news viewers are provided in Appendix B). As in previous tables, cells display the difference between younger (twenty-one to twenty-nine) and older respondents (fifty to sixty-five) in the percentage who report watching TV news regularly or daily, followed in parentheses by the percentages for each group. For the UK and Netherlands, results from several years of Eurobarometer polls are combined in order to increase sample size and produce more reliable estimates.

Some quirks in the results should first be acknowledged and explained. First, the relatively low level of TV news viewing for both younger and older persons in Canada in 1962 and the Netherlands in 1970 can be partly attributed to less than universal penetration of television at these dates – around 90 percent in Canada and around 80 percent in the Netherlands. This simple but important point is not always acknowledged when older data on TV news viewing are presented, leading to misleading conclusions about the propensity to watch TV news at early points (Wattenberg 2008, 51-52; Norris 2000, 81-84).[20] Secondly, the sharp fluctuations in TV news viewing in the US are largely a reflection of changes in question wording.[21] So too, in all likelihood, is the apparent jump among both young and old in regular news viewing in Canada from 1977 to 2002.[22]

These inconsistencies are unfortunate, but do not undermine the key observations. First, there are clearly large differences between young and old in TV news viewing that are consistent with the idea that lack of attention to TV news has been a contributing factor to the decline in political knowledge among young adults. At the point when lower levels of political knowledge were clearly evident around 1980, contemporaneous, and indeed earlier, measures of regular TV news viewing – in Canada (1962 and 1977), the US (1980), the Netherlands (1970), and Sweden (1979) – reveal significantly lower levels among those aged twenty-one to twenty-nine than among those fifty to sixty-five. On this point, there is no reason to quarrel with Wattenberg's conclusion that reduced attention to TV news among younger cohorts is part of the reason for their lower levels of political knowledge. While those who study the link between news media consumption and political knowledge have tended to conclude that newspaper reading is of greater benefit than TV news viewing, there has not been much consideration of the more marked effect that TV news probably has on those who spend relatively little time reading newspapers (Prior 2007, 72-84), whose numbers are greater among younger cohorts (Howe 2003b). Diminished attention to news in both print and electronic form is likely to have contributed to the diminished political knowledge of younger cohorts across multiple countries.

The second important observation, this directly counter to Wattenberg's conclusion, is that it is far from clear that lack of attention to TV news among younger citizens can be attributed to the significant increase in program choice and "narrowcasting" that accompanied the introduction of cable and related technologies. In all the countries considered, the earliest measurement of TV news viewing in Table 3.8 *precedes* the introduction or widespread penetration of cable and the attendant channel multiplication and fragmentation of the viewing audience. Viewing options were highly limited in countries such as the Netherlands and Sweden, where there were but two public channels prior to the late 1980s. They were not much more extensive

Figure 3.1

Viewership for national news broadcasts by age (Canada)

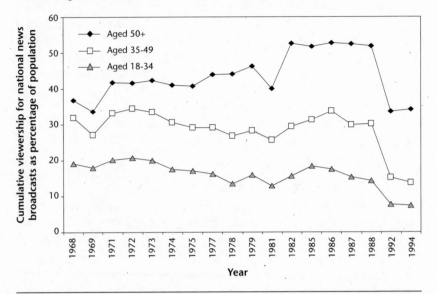

Source: BBM Television Network Program Reports.

in Canada and the US, where the simultaneous broadcasting of news programs on the major networks constrained viewer choice. Yet considerable
age differences in TV news viewing were evident everywhere pre-1980 and
have grown only modestly in subsequent years. That expanded choice in
viewing options has been the key precipitant of waning attention to TV
news is not evidenced by these results.

Further data from Canada provide additional detail on viewing patterns
in this country and reinforce this general conclusion. This added evidence
comes from a data source of a different type: TV ratings reports produced
by the Bureau of Broadcast Measurement.[23] As with the time-diary method
of capturing newspaper reading, there is reason to put greater faith in the
accuracy of these television ratings, as they are based on respondents recording their actual viewing choices as they occur, rather than responding to
survey questions about television news viewing in general. Figure 3.1 shows
results, based on the age categories provided in the BBM reports. Using
surveys conducted in the fall and winter months of each year, the lines in
the graph track average combined viewership (as a percentage of population)
for the main evening news broadcasts on the principal English and French
network channels – CBC, CTV, SRC, and TVA – through the 1968 to 1994

period (after which there are no further reports of this type available at the Toronto-based archive for BBM material).

The most striking pattern in the graph is the considerable gap in the percentage of older and younger viewers at every time point. Even back in the late 1960s, there were nearly twice as many news viewers in the fifty and over category as there were in the eighteen to thirty-four age bracket. The gap widened somewhat in the latter half of the 1970s and 1980s, but this was due principally to increased news viewing among the older group. The tendency of young people to refrain from watching TV news is again revealed to be longstanding, predating the changes to the electronic media environment that others suggest are principally responsible for this behavioural pattern. This is not to deny that the gap between younger and older viewers has widened somewhat over time: it is simply to observe that significant age differences in TV news viewing go further back than is commonly acknowledged.

The graph also reveals significant fluctuations in news viewing in Canada at certain points, though not all are in the downward direction, nor do they solely affect younger viewers. There is first an apparent increase in the percentage watching the news around 1982 across all age categories. A closer look at the numbers underlying the graph reveals that this was largely the result of a simple programming change: CBC moved its main news broadcast from eleven p.m. to ten p.m. (revamping it at the same time). This led to increased viewership for that program, but also for its main competitor, CTV news, which continued to show the news at 11:00 p.m. The jump in the graph could mean that a greater percentage of Canadians were watching the news, but it also probably reflects some double-counting, as those who wanted to could now watch both the CBC and CTV. More relevant to the issue of waning attentiveness over time is the sharp drop in 1992 in network news viewership, and the widening gap between young and old that opened up around that time. Again, a programming change explains some of the general drop-off: in 1992 CBC pushed its main news broadcast to nine p.m., a move that cost the public network viewers across all age groups and was reversed in 1994. But this was also the time that cable news was becoming a more prominent part of the TV landscape, a more enduring change that has shifted news-viewing patterns since that time and may have influenced the age gap in network news viewing. The first Canadian cable news networks, the English-language CBC Newsworld and the French-language RDI, were launched in 1989. Awareness of the cable news channels grew with their coverage of the dramatic last-ditch efforts to save the Meech Lake Accord in June 1990 (as well as CNN's coverage of the first Gulf War the same year). While these channels tend to have very low ratings at any given time, their cumulative viewership is considerable. According to recent CBC figures, some 6.2 million Canadians watch Newsworld in any given week, while another 2.5 million watch RDI, figures representing approximately one-third of the total adult population (CBC/Radio-Canada 2007, 46).

As these different options for keeping up with the news have emerged, the analytical focus must necessarily switch from how often people watch "the news" to how often they watch news of any sort. So we pick up the trail with another series of data on Canadian news-viewing habits, also based on data collected by BBM, but published by Statistics Canada. These reports provide information on Canadian TV viewing habits in general, including the percentage of viewing time that people spend watching "news and current affairs" programs. The one significant drawback is that the age breakdowns are rather limited. In a number of years, data are only available for all ages (both children and adults) combined; in other years, data are provided separately for teenagers aged twelve to seventeen. Presumably, however, if younger cohorts were drifting away from the news due to a surfeit of programming choice, this would show up in the viewing habits of the teenaged group. And over a sufficiently long period, this would also become manifest in the general population, as younger cohorts less inclined to watch news and current affairs would gradually pull down the overall average.

Figure 3.2 shows accumulated results for all available data points from 1986 to 2004.[24] Over this nearly twenty-year period, there is no evidence of a downward drift among either teenagers (twelve to seventeen) or the general population (aged two or over) in the percentage of viewing time spent on news and current affairs, reinforcing the conclusion that the proliferation of choice has not dramatically altered the news-viewing habits of younger generations.[25] Granted, there may be more subtle changes hidden from view in these aggregate numbers. Wattenberg suggests that younger viewers, more inclined towards entertainment programming, may have a greater penchant for "soft news" programs that have become more popular in recent times (2008, 59-60). The Statistics Canada reports provide no further breakdown on specific programs watched that might verify this proposition in the Canadian case. The reports do, however, provide information on another relevant distinction, the average number of hours spent watching TV by different age groups. These figures reveal a significant decline among young adults (eighteen to twenty-four) in the past ten to fifteen years (from about seventeen hours per week to about twelve), along with relatively stable levels for older age categories. So if the percentage of time spent watching news and current affairs has held steady among young Canadians, the actual number of hours of viewing time would have decreased nonetheless. In short, there probably have been some modest changes in the news consumption habits of young Canadians that are glossed over by the apparent consistency in the viewing of news and current events programs captured in Figure 3.2.

Figure 3.2

News and public affairs viewing time by age (Canada)

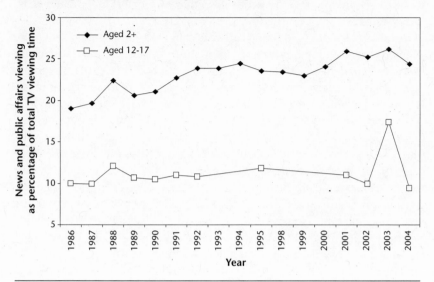

Sources: See text.

Yet none of this undermines the main point, which is not that there has been *no* decline in attentiveness to news and current affairs among younger cohorts as the electronic media environment has changed quite dramatically in the past thirty years. Rather, it is that any change that has taken place has been more gradual than abrupt and must be seen as part of a more long-standing pattern of this type of political inattentiveness among the young. One response to this line of argument might be to rework the media environment thesis by thinking afresh about the notion of programming choice in different eras. Perhaps the expansion of options that came with the introduction of cable and related technologies has been over-emphasized, and all that is needed for young people to eschew the news is some choice in viewing options, however limited. In both Sweden and the Netherlands, for example, there were only two public channels prior to the late 1980s. However, unlike private channels in competition with one another, they did not broadcast the news at the same time. If the news was appearing on one channel, there was always something else to watch on the other. The same was true in the UK, as BBC1, BBC2, and ITV all showed the news at different times. Canadians, for their part, could generally avoid watching the news by turning to another option on one of the American channels, as news programs south of the border were broadcast earlier in the evening. Ironically, given the lesser emphasis accorded news programming in countries where private networks predominate, perhaps the most captive audience pre-cable was to be found in the US. There, depending on the scheduling choices of local affiliates, news was the only viewing option for many viewers during the early evening time slot (Prior 2007, 64).

To address the possibility that early age gaps in news viewing reflect more limited forms of programming choice, we turn to Norway, the one country for which no data on TV news viewing have yet been presented. Norway is an especially instructive case because for many years there was only *one* channel available on Norwegian television (cable was introduced in 1982, though at first provided access to foreign channels only, as it was not until 1992 that a second Norwegian-based channel was introduced). In the one-channel era, the Norwegian public broadcaster, NRK, presented the main news program, *Dagsrevyen*, in the early evening for either an hour or half an hour, depending on the day of the week. Data collected by the Norwegian National Broadcasting System provide TV ratings for this news program by age group and offer a window into the news-viewing habits of young people in the absence of viewing choice.

Table 3.9 is based on aggregated data for multiple days in each of 1975 and 1983 (when cable was still very uncommon), and is based on the age categories provided in the Norwegian datasets. Clearly, news viewing in this period was less prevalent among younger than older Norwegians. Roughly one-third of those aged fifteen to twenty-four watched the news on any given evening in this period, just over half of those twenty-five to forty-four, and two-thirds or more in the two older age groups. Despite the near total absence of choice,[26] younger Norwegians in this period clearly were less inclined to watch TV news, suggesting deliberate avoidance rather than merely casual inattention in the presence of multiple viewing options. These

Table 3.9

TV news viewing, Norway, 1975 and 1983 (%)

	Age Categories			
Year	15-24	25-44	45-64	65-79
1975	36.1	51.1	65.6	70.9
(N)	(410)	(587)	(646)	(213)
1983	36.6	57.8	68.3	74.2
(N)	(355)	(672)	(565)	(299)

Notes: Entries are the average percentage who reported watching the evening news broadcast (*Dagsrevyen*) on a given day, based on aggregated data for seven days (1975) and eight days (1983). Calculations include those who reported watching no television over the relevant period, but exclude those who did not own a television.

Source: Norwegian National Broadcasting System viewer surveys.

data firmly establish, more than any other piece of evidence, that relative inattention to TV news among young people is *not* contingent on choice in programming options. That a pronounced age gap appears even at a time and place where there was no choice seriously weakens the case that changes in the electronic media environment are what have led young people to drift away from the news.

Taking stock of the findings, evidence has been marshalled of persistent and substantial age gaps in TV news viewing across different countries with different media environments at different points in time. There is also some suggestion – in the election debate numbers most patently, but also in the nuances in news-viewing habits in recent years – of a gradual erosion over the long haul in the relative propensity of young adults to pay attention to politics on TV. As with newspaper reading, there are different possibilities to consider when confronted with such findings. Sizable differences between young and old at early points could mean that there are life-cycle effects at work and that today's young adults stand to make up considerable ground in their TV news-viewing habits as they grow older.[27] But they could also reflect persistent differences between the cohorts comprising the younger and older age groups at those early points. Or, once again, it may be that both effects partly explain the news-viewing tendencies exhibited by young adults at different points in time.

Once again, a more structured cohort analysis is necessary to sort out properly life-cycle and cohort effects (again taking into account potential period effects). To assess the effects of aging versus birth year – i.e., whether cohorts change or stay the same as they grow older – measurements over a decent span of time are required. From this viewpoint, the election debate data have some advantages, as they go back to the 1960s. However, consistent measures, less likely to fluctuate for reasons extraneous to the analysis, are also desirable, so some of the time series on TV news viewing – particularly the ones that have been consistent in question formulation – are appealing. Based on these criteria, four measures were selected for a structured cohort analysis: election debate viewing in Canada; TV news viewing in the UK; and both election debate and TV news viewing in Sweden.[28]

The results of the analysis are presented in Table 3.10. The set-up is identical to that used for the cohort analysis of newspaper reading above, with all variables coded the same way. The one exception is that the comparison cohort is now those born in 1930 and earlier, rather than 1920 and earlier. The period effects that appear are for the most part readily explicable. In Sweden in 1960 and 1964, prior to the final leaders' debates, there were numerous lengthy and unmediated presentations by party leaders on radio and TV. Consequently, the final debate was not quite the singular event it was later to become, hence the negative period effect for those years. The 1991 Swedish election, on the other hand, was a landmark political event (the Socialists lost power after many years of electoral dominance) and seems to have garnered more public attention, judging by both the debate and TV news-viewing numbers from around that time. In Canada, there was just a single leaders' debate in 1979 (in English only), which led to fewer franco-phones tuning in and lower viewing numbers overall. In 1988, free trade with the US was the galvanizing issue in a campaign that generated more public attention than usual, leading to higher debate-viewing numbers. The 2006 Canadian election, on the other hand, was a less engrossing cam-paign, coming just eighteen months after the previous one, with the same leaders squaring off as in 2004. This perhaps accounts for the lower than expected viewership for these debates (there were actually two debates in each language for the first time, yet the number who reported seeing any one of these declined). The period effects for TV news viewing in the UK are not so readily explicable – 1980 in particular represents a large unexplained dip – but may simply reflect variations in the salience of the particular news stories making headlines during the periods the surveys were conducted.

Period effects aside, the other patterns revealed in Table 3.10 are quite illuminating. Age effects are generally small and only statistically significant in two of four cases (a small negative effect for TV news viewing in Sweden, and a slightly larger positive effect for debate viewing in that country). Again, it is the cohort effects that stand out more prominently. In all four instances, the decline in attention to debates and TV news among younger cohorts is considerable, creating gaps that will not be meaningfully reduced by aging processes. Yet the cohort effects are by no means limited to the young adults of today. Instead, there is evidence of diminished attentiveness to TV news and election debates beginning with cohorts born in the 1930s, with no sharp discontinuities that might be expected if the impact of new technolo-gies at particular points was truly decisive.

What the overall pattern most closely resembles is the cohort analysis of newspaper reading from before: a steady decline in attentiveness over many years and many cohorts rather than a decisive change at any particular point. This suggests it is probably more sensible to treat attentiveness to TV news and election debates as a reflection of the general inclination to follow political news and current events rather than emphasizing the particularities of the televised news medium; and to interpret the growing inattentiveness of rising cohorts as a reflection of waning attention to news media in general over a very long period rather than a decisive shift among any particular generation exposed to any specific media environment.

To round out this line of argument, some final figures offer evidence that the same pattern of longstanding cohort differences in attention to television news appears in the three other countries under consideration – the US, the Netherlands, and Norway. These numbers are based simply on age differences

Table 3.10

Cohort analysis of election debate and regular TV news viewing in three countries (OLS regression)

	Britain (TV news)		Canada (debates)		Sweden (debates)		Sweden (TV news)	
	B	*(SE)*	*B*	*(SE)*	*B*	*(SE)*	*B*	*(SE)*
Constant	95.8	(2.2)	67.0	(1.7)	82.9	(1.9)	71.6	(2.2)
Birth cohorts								
1931-35	-4.4	(1.1)	-1.8*	(1.4)	-7.0	(1.4)	-6.4	(1.4)
1936-40	-8.2	(1.2)	-3.6	(1.4)	-10.0	(1.4)	-8.6	(1.5)
1941-45	-9.5	(1.3)	-8.6	(1.4)	-12.3	(1.5)	-13.4	(1.5)
1946-50	-12.3	(1.4)	-14.3	(1.4)	-13.2	(1.6)	-18.0	(1.6)
1951-55	-17.2	(1.6)	-17.2	(1.4)	-19.3	(1.7)	-21.2	(1.9)
1956-60	-19.9	(1.8)	-17.8	(1.5)	-23.4	(1.9)	-20.4	(2.0)
1961-65	-24.2	(1.9)	-21.1	(1.7)	-27.8	(2.0)	-23.4	(2.1)
1966-70	-27.1	(2.1)	-25.0	(2.0)	-28.3	(2.2)	-23.0	(2.3)
1971-75	-31.7	(2.3)	-30.8	(2.2)	-25.7	(2.6)	-22.0	(2.8)
1976-80	-35.1	(2.8)	-29.1	(2.6)	-26.3	(3.4)	-27.3	(3.5)
1981-84			-32.7	(3.4)				
Life cycle								
Age	-3.3*	(1.9)	-0.1*	(1.5)	-4.8	(1.6)	7.3	(2.0)
Period								
1960-64					-12.0	(1.1)		
1979			-8.0	(1.1)				
1980	-27.4	(1.0)						
1988			12.0	(1.0)				
1991					5.6	(1.1)	6.7	(1.0)
1999	-3.5	(1.0)						
2000	-3.7	(1.0)						
2006			-7.6	(1.1)				
R^2	0.07		0.05		0.03		0.06	
(N)	(30,402)		(24,253)		(22,005)		(20,754)	

* *Not* statistically significant at the $p < .05$ level

Notes: The unstandardized regression coefficients (*B*) indicate the estimated effect for each independent variable (where the dependent variables are the percentage who are regular TV news viewers and the percentage who reported watching an election debate). The standard errors (*SE*) are used in calculating margins of error and determining whether results are statistically significant. Analysis restricted to respondents aged 21 and over.

Sources: Britain: Eurobarometer polls from the Mannheim Eurobarometer Trend File 1970-2002; Canada and Sweden: national election studies.

Table 3.11

Birth cohort comparisons of TV news viewing in three countries

	US (1996-2004)		Netherlands (1996-2001)		Norway (1991-95)	
	(%)	(N)	(%)	(N)	(%)	(N)
Regular TV news viewers in comparison cohort (1930 and earlier)	60.2	(643)	93.3 (1,078)		88.1 (1,943)	

Later birth cohorts	Cohort differences	(N)	Cohort differences	(N)	Cohort differences	(N)
1931-35	–13.8	(239)	–4.2	(616)	–4.6	(544)
1936-40	–11.8	(283)	–3.3	(622)	–7.6	(496)
1941-45	–17.5	(361)	–7.2	(605)	–11.9	(613)
1946-50	–24.4	(422)	–12.6	(821)	–16.9	(750)
1951-55	–32.3	(469)	–11.6	(920)	–20.2	(739)
1956-60	–37.2	(531)	–13.0	(980)	–27.7	(819)
1961-65	–42.2	(523)	–18.1	(1,096)	–26.8	(852)
1966-70	–44.7	(399)	–22.2	(968)	–33.3	(898)
1971-75	–47.6	(334)	–29.8	(937)	–40.7	(346)
1976-80	–45.0	(191)	–35.2	(494)		

Note: Analysis restricted to respondents aged 21 and over.

Sources: US: national election studies; Netherlands and Norway: Eurobarometer polls from the Mannheim Eurobarometer Trend File 1970-2002.

in TV news viewing at a single point in time (or, more precisely, several points in time grouped together in order to increase sample size). The assumption is that the finding from the cohort analysis above – that life-cycle effects for TV news viewing are weak – can be carried over, so that age differences appearing in cross-sectional data can be taken as principally reflective of cohort effects. Based on this assumption, the numbers are presented in this fashion in Table 3.11. The percentage of regular TV news viewers among the comparison cohort (1930 and earlier) is presented, followed by the differences with respect to this reference group for later birth cohorts. As before, in all three cases it is among those born in the 1930s that clear signs of reduced attention to TV news first appear, with the effects growing stronger for successive cohorts. This pattern, the accumulated evidence would suggest, exhibits considerable consistency across a diverse range of long-established democracies, countries that have not all marched at the same pace in their adoption of new media technologies. What might explain this pattern – quite different from that predicted by accounts that lay emphasis on the powerful impact of a changing media environment – is outlined in the concluding section.

Summary and Conclusion: Bringing Political Interest Back In

To recapitulate the findings of this investigation into political inattentiveness among the young, it was first found that a significant knowledge gap between young and old has gradually opened up in all six countries under consideration. Whereas forty years ago the knowledge gap was slight, today it is considerable. Political interest, on the other hand, has declined neither markedly nor consistently in these same jurisdictions. The patterns in the longitudinal data are more suggestive of a life-cycle pattern of lower interest at younger ages, apparent when survey measurements were first taken and continuing to this day. If young adults are less likely than their elders to find politics captivating, this is hardly truer today than it was forty years ago. Why young people would know less about politics nowadays thus remains an unresolved question.

A changing media environment giving rise to new patterns of news media use among younger cohorts appears to offer a persuasive answer, as it would seem to obviate the need to identify a motivational basis for why people turned away from the news – instead of turning away, young people, awash in media choice, simply drifted away. Parts of this account are consistent with the empirical findings. Certainly there have been long-term changes in both newspaper reading and attention to politics on TV that could explain declining levels of knowledge among the young. The cohort analysis of newspaper reading found a steady decline in time spent on this activity that began before lower knowledge levels became manifest. The gap between young and old in viewing election debates has also grown over time. These changes have taken place in both the Anglo-American and Northern European countries, suggesting that the latter, despite their richer media environments and greater stocks of civic literacy, have not been insulated against these important changes in political attentiveness among rising generations.

Yet there are also findings that are not congruent with this theoretical account. The timing of changes in media use does not really mesh with the environmental changes deemed responsible for young people's inattentiveness to news media. Cohort-driven decline in newspaper reading dates far back: people who had no exposure to TV when growing up were the first ones to show signs of diminished reading time. Early measures of TV news viewing, ranging from the early 1960s to around 1980, likewise reveal that gaps between young and old were already considerable before the expansion of channels and programming choice that came with the introduction of cable and related technologies. More formal cohort analysis suggests that the pattern of cohort decline for attention to politics on TV is similar in magnitude and timing to that for newspaper reading.

Stepping back from the details of the various measures, the patterns look less like decisive shifts precipitated by key changes in the media environment and more like a gradual ebbing of attentiveness to news media in general among rising cohorts from the 1920s to the present day. Changes to the media environment do not effectively explain the pattern. In order to understand the origins of political inattentiveness, it is necessary to grapple with the evolving motivational and behavioural dynamics that have shaped young people's engagement with politics in the established democracies over the long haul.

In part, this entails paying closer attention to the consistent life-cycle effects evident for various measures of political attentiveness. One of these is political interest: in all places and at all times considered, young adults indicated lower levels of general interest in politics, suggesting a persistent condition of early adulthood. Similar effects were apparent in other areas as well. For example, in the models above, newspaper reading – in addition to being less prevalent among younger cohorts – tended to increase with age. If there are important cohort effects giving rise to declining political attentiveness over the long haul, life-cycle patterns also crop up in different places and deserve closer attention.

Paying closer attention means more than simply identifying, measuring, and taking account of life-cycle effects in order to arrive at accurate estimates of cohort effects. It also means integrating these important features into our theoretical understandings of processes of change. The theoretical adjustment needed is to recognize that life-cycle effects can be implicated in cohort-driven change.

Mark Franklin's work on voter turnout exemplifies this style of reasoning (2004). Franklin identifies cohort-driven declines in voter turnout in six democracies in the postwar period. His explanation for the pattern is prosaic on the surface, focusing on what seems a mere technicality: the reduction in the voting age from twenty-one to eighteen in the late 1960s and early 1970s. The first-order effect was a simple shift down the life-cycle curve of participation: giving people their first opportunity to vote at a younger age led to more non-voting among first-time voters, because the typical eighteen-year-old is less likely to vote than the typical twenty-one-year-old. But because voting is a habitual behaviour, the second-order effect was more profound. Those whose first opportunity to vote (or first three opportunities, to be more precise) came at younger ages were less likely to develop into habitual voters. The dip in voter turnout among neophyte electors from the reduction in the voting age thus became a permanent dent.

In applying this style of reasoning to changing patterns of political attentiveness, the basic hypothesis is that an enduring life-cycle pattern of relative inattentiveness among the young may have gradually become more consequential owing to other changing social dynamics that have affected transitions from youth to adulthood (Kimberlee 2002; Environics 2003). Whereas previously the transition from inattentive youth to attentive adult was reliable and effective, it has gradually become more uncertain and imperfect. Connections between young and old – within the family, in society at large – are not as strong as they once were. Adolescents and young adults have their own distinct spheres of interaction that are highly insulated from the "mature" adult world. The change has been gradual and engendered by many background factors, such as the extended time spent in full-time education by young people and their slower integration into the workforce (Hooghe 2004, 336-37; Arnett 2005). In this context, a life-cycle pattern of relative inattention to politics in younger years has become more consequential and slowly given rise to cohort-driven decline in political attentiveness.

This theoretical terrain is explored at greater length in Chapter 9. Particular attention is given there to the period in the first half of the twentieth century when a more marked segregation of youth and adults became a permanent feature of society. At the same time, closer attention is given to earlier stages of the life cycle, in particular the developmental stages of adolescence. It becomes apparent that the modest life-cycle effects of early adulthood are the proverbial tip of the iceberg, signalling tremendous differences in attention to politics over the adolescence-young adult age range.

This alternative conception is more in keeping with the arc of long-term change revealed by the empirical analysis. Mapping out age differences in knowledge, interest, and media use reveals the longstanding and enduring nature of the problem of political inattentiveness among the young, including both life-cycle patterns of greater portent than first appearances might suggest and cohort effects of greater vintage than is normally acknowledged. If a lack of political attentiveness among younger citizens has only attracted close attention in recent times, there is nonetheless a longer history to the phenomenon that needs to be explored to better understand its origins.

4

Political Attentiveness in Canada: The Current Landscape

The previous chapter adopted a panoramic perspective, seeking to place recent observations about flagging levels of political attentiveness among young Canadians in a broad comparative and historical context. Longitudinal analysis reveals that certain aspects of political inattentiveness among younger adults have become decidedly more pronounced over time, while others seem to represent abiding qualities of early adulthood. Cross-national comparisons suggest that the patterns are similar across a range of long-established democracies, including ones where citizens are, on the whole, more politically attentive and engaged than those in Canada. The erosion of political attentiveness among rising generations is a widespread phenomenon that has significant implications for the democratic engagement of the citizenry, both now and in the future.

While this approach provides a panoramic view of the issue, breadth of analysis inevitably comes at the expense of depth. The current chapter reverses the emphasis, exploring in detail some of the more salient dimensions of political inattentiveness in Canada at the present time. The source for this analysis is a national telephone survey conducted in late 2007 and early 2008, the Canadian Citizen Engagement Survey (CCES), designed in part to tap aspects of political attentiveness less thoroughly explored in prior studies.

The general conclusion that emerges is twofold. A probing examination of different facets of current political attentiveness in Canada does not dispel concerns about the burgeoning inattentiveness of younger Canadians. It does, however, serve to clarify more precisely where the principal shortcomings lie, information potentially relevant to determining what measures might be taken to address the issue.

Political Knowledge
Tracking levels of political knowledge over time necessitated the use of a wide array of secondary survey data collected at different points. To ensure

a measure of consistency, the analysis of the previous chapter was limited to the most common type of political knowledge questions asked in the past, those designed to measure surveillance knowledge. It was further circumscribed by the fact that most such questions probe knowledge of mainstream electoral politics – political leaders, party policies, and so on – and ask for factual tidbits that might be considered of no great consequence to a citizen's capacity to be politically involved (Page and Shapiro 1992, 12). Thus one objective of the CCES was to pose a fuller range of political knowledge items in order to assess whether the gap between young and old extends beyond this narrow realm to knowledge domains of greater substance and consequence.

Some of the questions posed on the survey were designed to measure what might be termed *substantive* as opposed to trivial surveillance knowledge. The criterion distinguishing the two is whether a given piece of information might in itself be relevant to someone's political attitudes or behaviour (e.g., whether to vote, which party to support, or what stand to take on important issues of the day). If knowing the name of the leader of the Liberal Party can be seen as immaterial to the choice among political parties, knowing roughly what the Liberal Party stands for is not. So items akin to the latter were among the knowledge questions posed on the CCES.

A second type of question inquired about *emergent* political issues that have not traditionally been a focal point of mainstream politics. The claim is sometimes made that young people today are relatively indifferent to conventional electoral politics because their concerns lie in issue domains not easily or adequately addressed through standard political channels: globalization, human rights, the environment, and so forth. If what people care about affects what they know about, as many would reasonably argue, then enhanced knowledge among younger citizens of emergent political issues would be anticipated.

A third set of knowledge questions on the CCES was designed to assess *civics* or *institutional* knowledge. Such questions have appeared only occasionally in previous studies conducted in Canada. The Dominion Institute (now the Historica-Dominion Institute), best known for its annual surveys highlighting shortcomings in Canadians' historical knowledge, has sometimes included a handful of survey items pertaining to contemporary Canadian political institutions (Ipsos-Reid/Dominion Institute 2007). Henry Milner, extending his research on civic literacy, has reported results from twin surveys of Canadians and Americans conducted in 2007 that posed several civics-type questions (2007). While these previous studies have tended to confirm concerns about the impoverished state of political knowledge among Canadians, some of the specific questions used might be subject to the same criticism directed at measures of surveillance knowledge: they focus on civics trivia (e.g., naming three requirements that must be met to vote in a federal election) rather than assessing more general comprehension of the rules and principles governing our political institutions. The institutional knowledge questions included on the CCES were partly designed to address this concern, as most were aimed at assessing whether people had a grasp of certain basic structural features of Canadian democracy.

Finally a handful of typical surveillance questions – the names of three prominent political figures – were also included on the CCES. These serve as a benchmark for comparing this survey to others that have posed similar questions and allow for comparative assessment of results across knowledge domains.

Table 4.1 shows the results of this effort to produce a broad set of questions spanning diverse dimensions of political knowledge. While the aim was to devise questions that spoke to important and substantive matters, this had to be set against the need to pose questions with relatively unambiguous correct answers (the broader and more general the question, the more challenging this becomes). A balance was struck. In some cases, questions probed respondents' knowledge of issues or domains not well covered in previous research but were structured to require cut-and-dried responses. In other cases, questions were broader and allowed for multiple ways of articulating a correct response. For some questions, answers could be considered spot on or just roughly correct; variations in the precision of correct responses are reported in Table 4.1. Differences across age groups are the main focus of the table, but the results for the sample as a whole should also be acknowledged and absorbed in light of the earlier observation that Canadians generally

Table 4.1

Political knowledge by age group (percent giving correct response)

	Age					
	18-34	35-44	45-54	55-69	70+	Total
Surveillance (trivia)						
• Premier of own province	61	69	74	82	72	71
• Leader of Liberal Party (Dion)	32	42	46	63	53	46
• Minister of Finance (Flaherty)	8	13	14	23	20	15
Surveillance (substantive)						
• Federal party linked to unions/ supporting working class	29	47	51	59	49	46
• Federal party opposed to same-sex marriage	59	55	59	63	46	58
• Place with highest taxes	32	41	34	38	28	35
• Place with lowest taxes	45	57	54	51	36	49

▶

◀   *Table 4.1*

	Age					
	18-34	35-44	45-54	55-69	70+	Total
Emergent issues						
• Canada's commitment under Kyoto Accord						
Precise answer	10	11	11	14	10	11
Close answer	37	40	45	42	37	40
Total	47	51	56	56	47	51
• What WTO stands for						
Precise answer	45	51	46	44	25	44
Close answer	2	5	7	10	7	6
Total	47	56	53	54	32	50
• Issue Amnesty International focuses on						
Precise answer	26	35	42	43	27	35
Close answer	11	13	14	12	12	12
Total	37	48	56	55	39	47
• Number of Canadian soldiers killed in Afghanistan:						
Precise answer	19	24	35	50	52	34
Close answer	20	24	20	19	17	20
Total	39	48	55	69	69	54
Civics						
• Number of MPs in House of Commons						
Precise answer (290-320)	8	10	8	14	15	10
Close answer (200-400)	7	11	12	20	13	13
Total	15	21	20	34	28	23
• Level of government responsible for education	59	61	73	78	66	68
• How often free votes occur	44	51	62	69	66	57
• Positions appointed by PM						
One position named	15	17	22	24	18	19
Two positions named	12	24	27	35	23	24
Total	27	41	49	59	41	43
Summary (% correct)						
• Trivial surveillance	34	41	45	56	48	44
• Substantive surveillance	41	50	50	53	40	47
• Emergent issues	34	41	44	48	38	41
• Civics	31	39	45	53	43	42
• All knowledge items	35	42	46	52	42	43
(N)	(509)	(344)	(377)	(450)	(223)	(1,903)

Source: CCES 2007-08.

fare rather poorly in international comparisons of political attentiveness. People who follow politics closely would find their fellow citizens surprisingly ill-informed on a number of important issues, particularly considering that this sampling of the Canadian public, like virtually all surveys on political matters, probably over-represents those who are (relatively speaking) politically engaged.

For practical reasons, the age groups now used differ somewhat from those in the previous chapter. To ensure a reasonable sample size for the youngest category, the age brackets for this group are extended to create an eighteen to thirty-four age group. The change is largely immaterial: if political knowledge has been slowly ebbing in younger generations as part of a larger decline in political attentiveness, there is no compelling reason to focus attention on the under-thirty group or any other particular category of young adults. At the other end of the age spectrum, those seventy and over are separated out in recognition of a clear downward turn in knowledge scores among the oldest survey respondents. This is not an atypical finding – other surveys reveal a similar pattern – though it is one sometimes obscured when a broader upper-end age category is used (e.g., sixty and over). Interestingly, we will see below that this dip in knowledge is not accompanied by any decline in political interest or reduction in news media consumption among the oldest respondents. The reasons for the pattern are not entirely clear, though a reasonable conjecture would be that it reflects diminished recall abilities with advanced age (in other words, the information requested is known to respondents but is not quickly recalled in a telephone interview). In any event, for the purposes of age group comparisons, the analysis concentrates on those aged eighteen to thirty-four and the peak-knowledge group, those fifty-five to sixty-nine, with two intermediate groups (thirty-five to forty-four and forty-five to fifty-four) rounding out the age spectrum.

The first group of questions are typical surveillance items of the variety sometimes dismissed as mere trivia. Respondents were asked to name the premier of their province, the leader of the Liberal Party, and the current federal finance minister. The results mirror what has been found in recent election studies posing the same questions: overall levels of knowledge are surprisingly low and young people are considerably less likely to be familiar with these simple factual matters relating to mainstream electoral politics. Naming one's premier should have been facilitated by the longevity of most incumbents at the time the CCES was conducted in late 2007 and early 2008 (only Saskatchewan and Alberta had seen a new premier take office in the past twelve months). That only 61 percent of young adults in the CCES sample were able to provide the correct name is an arresting statistic, but is on par with the results of other recent surveys. The leader of the Liberal Party, Stéphane Dion, had assumed the position in December 2006, twelve months prior to the start of the survey, and after a quiet debut had been consistently in the public spotlight due to both election speculation in the fall of 2007 and concerns voiced about his leadership from within his own party. Despite this, and his intrinsic prominence as leader of the official opposition, fewer than half of those surveyed (46 percent) could come up with Dion's name, with a twofold difference between those under thirty-five (32 percent) and those fifty-five to sixty-nine (63 percent). The third politician, Finance Minister Jim Flaherty, was also a prominent public figure, having held this post since the Conservatives took office at the start of 2006, yet only 15 percent were able to recall his name. The question reveals another significant gap between those under thirty-five (8 percent) and the older comparison group (23 percent).

The second group of questions involved substantive surveillance items. Two sought to determine whether respondents were familiar with some of the basic orientations of the major political parties. Rather than ask people to position parties on the left or right of the political spectrum, unfamiliar concepts to many, more substantive policy orientations were cited. One question asked which federal political party has traditionally been most closely linked to the trade union movement and supported policies to help the working class. A second asked which party had been most strongly opposed to same-sex marriage in recent years. On the first question, just under half (46 percent) correctly named the NDP, on the second over half (58 percent) rightly identified the Conservative Party (a handful also mentioned its predecessor, the Canadian Alliance). The age gap on the first item is pronounced, the difference on the second question rather minimal. This undoubtedly reflects the nature of the questions. The first speaks as much to the NDP's history as its present policies and hence offers an advantage to those with a longer experience of Canadian electoral politics. The other focuses on a recent public debate, gay rights, which might be characterized as an emergent issue likely to be of greater salience to younger generations. The different results for the two questions probably offer some sense of the minimum and maximum differences between younger and older Canadians that one might expect to see from probes of this type.

Two further substantive surveillance questions asked about a basic background fact of general relevance to government spending and taxation policies. Respondents were asked, "Which country has the highest income taxes: the United States, Canada, or European countries like Sweden and Germany?" This was followed by, "And which has the lowest income taxes?" Only a third correctly selected the European examples as having the highest taxes, while 45 percent wrongly believed that it was Canada. On the followup question, just under half (49 percent) picked the US as the place with the lowest taxes.[1] Again, differences between younger and older respondents are apparent for both questions, but are not as significant as those seen for the more "trivial" surveillance items.

The emergent issue category also reveals a pattern of age differences less stark than that typically seen for surveillance trivia. One such question spoke to global warming, an issue on the periphery of public debate for many years, but which had rapidly become the most salient public issue in the twenty-four months prior to the survey. The question asked respondents about the Kyoto Accord, more specifically what Canada's commitment had been under the Accord. After coming to power in 2006, the Conservative government had abandoned any pretence (as they would have it) that Canada might seek to cut its greenhouse gas emissions by 30 percent below 1990 levels by 2012, a position that occasioned much public debate and attempts by the opposition parties to reverse the government's stand. To invite those unsure of the precise details of Canada's Kyoto commitment to offer a general response (e.g., cut greenhouse gases), the question asked whether respondents recalled "generally what [the] commitment was," with further instructions to interviewers to encourage hesitant respondents by saying, "I don't need a precise answer, just the general idea." The result: 11 percent provided a correct response with some measure of detail (e.g., the rough percentage of the cuts required), while another 40 percent gave a correct general answer. About the same percentage (41 percent) said they did not know, while 7 percent gave an incorrect answer (such as cutting "smog" or improving "the ozone layer"). To see if those in the "do not know" category were dissuaded from offering a response by their lack of familiarity with the precise details of Canada's commitment, a subsample of these respondents ($N = 435$) were posed an immediate follow-up question that asked simply whether they knew with what issue the Kyoto Accord was concerned. The vast majority either did not know (81 percent) or offered incorrect answers (5 percent). Thus, most of the 41 percent of the sample unfamiliar with Canada's commitment under Kyoto were also unfamiliar with the basic nature of the Accord, a sobering result, given the extraordinary attention afforded global warming in recent times. Differences between young and old are not exceptionally large on this question, though once again younger adults were less likely than the older comparison group to come up with a correct answer (47 percent versus 56 percent).

Further questions tapped into other emergent issues, all pertaining to developments in the international realm. The first noted that there have been protests in recent years at meetings of an organization called the WTO, and asked respondents if they knew what WTO stands for. If respondents came up with one or two words of the full title (World Trade Organization), this was considered a close response.[2] The second question asked what issue Amnesty International focuses its work on. Answers were considered precisely correct if they mentioned human rights or political rights (or gave a more specific example, such as freeing political prisoners), while close answers were those mentioning more general objectives such as supporting democracy or denouncing political oppression. On the WTO question, the age gap is rather small: indeed a difference only appears in the total row once close responses are factored in (48 percent versus 54 percent). The age difference on the Amnesty item is more substantial (total row, 37 percent versus 55 percent).

A third question relating to international developments concerned the Canadian military mission in Afghanistan. As a direct consequence of what is perhaps the defining event of the past decade, 9/11, the expectation would be that younger Canadians, if especially attuned to emergent issues, would see this deployment as highly consequential. Respondents were asked if they knew how many Canadian soldiers had lost their lives in the Afghan conflict, information potentially relevant to someone's opinion on Canada's continued presence and role in the country. Just over a third of respondents (34 percent) offered an accurate estimate (sixty-five to eighty, changed to seventy-five to eighty-five as the survey progressed to reflect the unfortunate reality unfolding in the field), while another 20 percent knew roughly the number killed (forty to one hundred). Others either gave incorrect answers (24 percent) or did not know (21 percent). Here the difference between younger and older respondents looms large, as only 39 percent of those under thirty-five had at least a rough sense of the number of Canadian casualties, compared to 69 percent of those fifty-five to sixty-nine. The focus on military losses may help explain the difference – older people perhaps pay greater attention to this aspect of armed conflict – but this seems, nonetheless, an important and relevant dimension of the larger debate on what role our military should be playing in the new, post-9/11 international context.

Finally, the fourth category of questions focused on civics knowledge. One was unabashed civics trivia, asking respondents if they knew the approximate number of MPs in the House of Commons in Ottawa. Only 10 percent came close to the right answer, providing a response in the 290 to 320 range. Included here are the 2 percent who volunteered the exact number, 308. Another 13 percent gave an answer outside this narrow range, but in the general ballpark (200 to 400). Of those who answered incorrectly (28 percent), the great majority significantly underestimated the true number (in other words, thought there were fewer than 200 MPs), while 48 percent said they did not know. The age difference on this question is very substantial, as only 15 percent of those under thirty-five were anywhere near the mark (in the 200 to 400 range) compared to 34 percent of those fifty-five to sixty-nine.

The other three civics questions spoke to more basic understanding of the rules and principles governing the exercise of power in Canadian government. One asked which level of government has primary responsibility for education: federal, provincial, or municipal? An issue of direct concern to many young adults was deliberately chosen in order to ensure that any advantage would fall to them. Yet those under thirty-five were still least likely to know that it is the provinces that hold primary responsibility for education. Another question described what a free vote is – when MPs vote how they think is best instead of voting with their party – and asked how often these occur in the House of Commons: often, about half the time, or only occasionally? Among all respondents combined, 17 percent gave an incorrect response (choosing "most of the time" or "about half the time") while 26 percent did not know, leaving a smallish majority (57 percent) who provided the correct answer. The age difference on the question is again considerable: only 44 percent of those under thirty-five knew that free votes are infrequent, compared to 69 percent of the older comparison group. Finally, respondents were informed that the Canadian prime minister chooses many of the people to fill important government positions and were then asked if they could name any of these positions, cabinet ministers aside. Interviewers probed for up to two responses. The most common answers given were senators, judges or Supreme Court judges, and the governor general, though virtually every possible position was mentioned by someone. The majority of those surveyed, however, could not name a single position, while only 24 percent could name two. The age gap, once again, is marked, as only 27 percent of those under thirty-five could identify at least one position correctly, compared to 59 percent in the older comparison group.

The final section of Table 4.1 summarizes results, showing the average percentage of correct answers within each of the four knowledge domains. Where there were definitive and less definitive answers to a given question, responses were scored as 1 and 0.5, respectively (a score of two was possible for the question about prime ministerial appointments). Having seen that for every single question asked, those under thirty-five were less likely to provide a correct response than those in the older comparison group, it is no surprise that average scores for the younger group are lower across the board. Nor is it surprising that there is some variation in the age gap across categories of knowledge, though, as we have seen, there is also considerable variation for individual questions within categories (obviously much depends on the specific questions asked). Two different spins can be put on the overall conclusion. The glass-half-full interpretation would focus on the fact that the knowledge gap is less pronounced in two domains – substantive surveillance and emergent political issues – though would have to acknowledge that civics knowledge is demonstrably lacking among younger Canadians, matching the age gap found for the surveillance trivia category. The glass-half-empty conclusion would be that the differences in political knowledge, if somewhat variable, are nonetheless persistent and non-negligible across all knowledge domains.

That the variation in results across knowledge domains is less noteworthy than the consistency is suggested by evidence of strong connections between the different types of political knowledge. A correlation matrix for the four knowledge domains, based on respondents of all ages, produces correlations no lower than 0.47 and as high as 0.59. Thus people familiar with the finer details of mainstream electoral politics – the names of political leaders and so on – tend also to know more about substantive matters and emergent issues, as well as having a better grasp of the functioning of Canadian political institutions. If the three-item index of surveillance trivia is measured against a combined index of the three other domains, the correlation coefficient climbs to 0.63. While there is some value in separating different domains of political knowledge for independent investigation, clearly they do form a cohesive cluster.

Two conclusions follow. First, if knowledge of surveillance trivia is highly correlated with other types of political knowledge, it can serve as a reasonable, if not ideal, proxy for political knowledge more generally. Hence, the earlier analysis of the evolution of surveillance knowledge across six countries can probably be taken as indicating a broader decline in political awareness and comprehension among younger citizens, rather than simply a growing disdain for political trivia. Second, strong correlations across knowledge domains suggest that aggregating all items to create a single composite index of political knowledge is a reasonable procedure.[3] Thus the final row of Table 4.1 shows overall scores for the entire set of knowledge questions on the study. The average percentage correct for those under thirty-five is 35 percent, for those fifty-five to sixty-nine, 52 percent. These translate into raw scores of 5.5 and 8.3 (out of 16), respectively. The gap in median scores for the two age categories is slightly larger – 5.0 versus 8.5 – reflecting the fact that the distribution among younger respondents involves greater clustering at the bottom end of the knowledge scale. Thus comparisons of the minimally informed reveal starker age differences still. For example, over one-third of those under thirty-five (35 percent) are able to answer at most three of the sixteen questions correctly, compared to only 15 percent of those aged fifty-five to sixty-nine.

These sizable differences on a fairly comprehensive index of political knowledge point to a deficit among young Canadians that is both broad and deep. There is undeniably some variation by subject matter, and if questions are chosen that are geared towards the perceived priorities of young people, age differences are reduced. Yet there is no evidence of any domain where young people are more knowledgeable than older Canadians, and the knowledge gaps in traditional realms of mainstream electoral politics and the functioning of political institutions are particularly gaping. If political knowledge of various kinds is important to the capacity of citizens to participate consistently and effectively – a theme examined more closely in the subsequent chapter – the knowledge deficit among younger generations cannot be considered inconsequential.

Patterns of News Media Use among Canadians

In probing the state of political knowledge among Canadians on the CCES, the primary objective was to extend the line of survey questioning to dimensions of political knowledge not much examined in previous Canadian research. The principal aim in devising questions about news media use, on the other hand, was to undertake a more fine-grained survey of well-canvassed terrain. Variegations in that terrain are readily apparent – news can be accessed via television, newspapers, radio, and the Internet, through a wide range of specific media outlets, on a more or less frequent basis, for brief or more extended periods – yet analysis of news media usage often focuses on only some of these dimensions, failing to assess whether shortfalls in one area might be made up by surpluses in another. In order to arrive at general conclusions about patterns of news media use among younger generations, it is necessary to measure media consumption in a comprehensive fashion.

The questions on the CCES were designed to provide a broad-based inventory of current patterns of news media use among Canadians. A series of fourteen questions was posed to respondents, beginning with queries about the frequency of following the news in different types of media: TV, newspapers, radio, and the Internet. Where respondents indicated at least occasional use, follow-up questions asked about the amount of time spent on a typical day in reading or listening to the news through that medium. Questions were also posed concerning which specific media outlet – which TV or radio station, which newspaper or website – respondents used most often. Viewers of Canadian network television news were asked if they watched local or national news more frequently. Finally, all respondents were asked a general question about how much attention they paid to stories about politics when reading or listening to the news. While hardly an exhaustive enumeration of all possible dimensions of news media exposure, these questions do cover a number of essential bases.

Results for frequency of news media use appear in Figure 4.1 (to keep the survey length manageable, media use questions were posed to a random subset of respondents, 1,103 in all). Some of the results are entirely predictable in light of the earlier analysis in Chapter 3. Among those under thirty-five, only 55 percent report watching TV news every day or several times a week, compared to 87 percent among older respondents (for consistency's sake, we continue to refer to the fifty-five to sixty-nine category as the older comparison group, though those seventy and older are generally the most avid news consumers). The age gap is similarly pronounced for regular

Figure 4.1

Regular news consumption by age

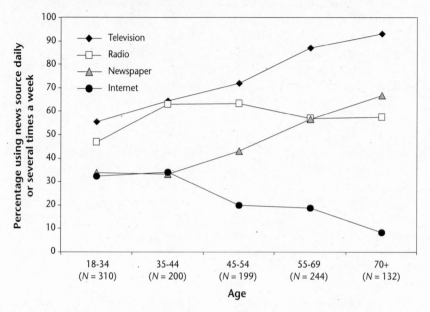

Source: CCES, 2007-08

newspaper reading: 34 percent versus 57 percent. Clearly many young Canadians eschew the two sources that have traditionally been considered the principal sources of political information – TV, because of its ubiquitous presence and widespread appeal; newspapers, because of the in-depth information and analysis they provide. Yet it may be the case that young Canadians simply prefer to get their news elsewhere.

Results for the other two news media, radio and Internet, are probably best described not as encouraging but less discouraging. As would be anticipated, it is the oldest respondents who are least likely to report reading news on the Internet on a regular basis.[4] The youngest group is more likely to use this medium, but does not stand out sharply from the pack: roughly the same proportion read Internet news regularly in the thirty-five to forty-four age group (one-third), while the rate in the forty-five to fifty-four and fifty-five to sixty-nine age categories is somewhat lower at around 20 percent. More than the age pattern, however, what stands out, a good decade after the Internet established itself as the information medium of choice among younger Canadians, is the generally low incidence of news consumption. The number who report daily use is particularly low: a mere 17 percent overall and only 22 percent in the eighteen to thirty-four age group. The age pattern for Internet news consumption may favour younger Canadians, but they do not make up much ground through this particular medium.

Probably more surprising than the Internet result is the pattern for radio news listening, as this is a traditional medium one might expect young people to eschew to the same degree as they do television news and newspapers. Yet the age pattern in this case is not nearly as sharp or consistent (indeed the highest rates of news listening are among those aged thirty-five to fifty-four). The result likely reflects the manner and circumstances in which radio news consumption takes place. First, use of the medium nowadays is largely limited to situations where it is a secondary activity serving as aural background to something else requiring primary attention – driving the car, preparing dinner, and so on. Secondly, on most radio stations, news programming is not the principal content but is instead featured in short, intermittent segments (e.g., news briefs every hour on the hour). Both features make it less likely that someone indifferent to the news will change stations or turn off the radio when the news is broadcast. The previous chapter expressed some scepticism about the "captive audience" argument when applied to television, suggesting that people still make choices about what or whether to watch even when there is limited or no choice in viewing options. However, the transmission of radio news occurs under conditions that probably render an individual's taste for the news largely immaterial to their exposure. Rather than "captive audience," the phrase "inadvertent audience" (Robinson 1976) might be more appropriate to this style of news listening.

It follows that news consumption via radio is rather different from the Internet, where people clearly make deliberate choices about which websites to visit and what material to read or view, leading to virtually no inadvertent news consumption. This, in turn, suggests two rather different processes underlying the flatter trend across age groups for Internet and radio news consumption: the Internet, because the greater appetite and aptitude of younger generations for the technology offsets their reduced inclination to follow the news; radio, because the medium is structured such that inclination to follow the news is largely immaterial to exposure.

If data on the frequency of consumption of different news media provide some initial insight into the news habits of young Canadians, statistics on the duration of use on a typical day are also revealing. It should first be noted that frequency of use and duration of use are highly correlated for all types of news media: those who read or listen only occasionally tend to do so for brief periods. This is partly why the age group patterns for frequency of use are largely replicated for duration of use. Thus, in the case of TV and newspapers, young viewers and readers report significantly shorter periods of use. Only 25 percent of those under thirty-five say they watch TV news for more

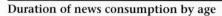

Figure 4.2

Duration of news consumption by age

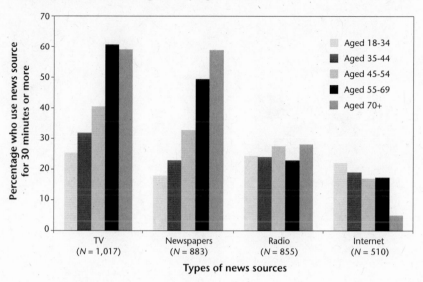

Source: CCES, 2007-08.

than half an hour on days when they watch, and only 18 percent read the newspaper for the same duration. These proportions climb steadily with increasing age, reaching 61 percent and 50 percent, respectively, in the fifty-five to sixty-nine age group (Figure 4.2). These patterns, however, are not solely a function of the fact that those who partake of the news less frequently do so for shorter periods. If the calculations are limited to those who use a given news medium every day, there remains a considerable age gap in duration of use. Among daily viewers of TV news, for example, 46 percent of those under thirty-five typically watch for more than half an hour, compared to 72 percent of those fifty-five to sixty-nine. For newspaper reading, the respective figures are 39 percent and 62 percent.

For radio and the Internet, where frequency of news consumption varies less with age, so too does duration. Younger and older Canadians who access news via radio or the Internet are roughly alike in the duration of time devoted to these activities on a given day (Figure 4.2). That duration, however, is considerably less than the time people spend watching TV news and reading newspapers. For radio, among all respondents combined, 25 percent report more than half an hour of news on a typical day; for the Internet only 19 percent. At the other end of the scale, approximately 50 percent in both cases report a typical duration of fifteen minutes or less, whereas for TV and newspapers, the respective figures are 18 percent and 25 percent.

Figure 4.3

Total news consumption estimates by age

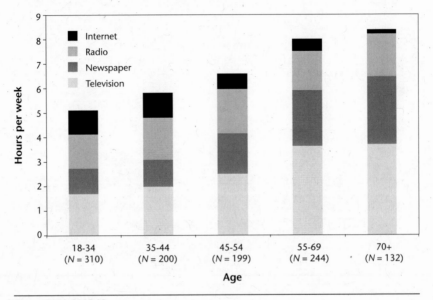

Source: CCES, 2007-08.

This difference is not surprising: radio news segments are typically brief and it is called surfing the Internet for a reason. So in a somewhat different way from TV and newspapers, these other media sources do contribute to the patchy news consumption habits of young Canadians. The two news sources for which young people show a relative preference are those that invite what is sometimes called "news grazing," a behaviour that limits the degree to which young people make up much ground through these media in their aggregate news consumption.

Clearly, duration of use is a valuable added dimension to consider in seeking to arrive at an overall assessment of news media use. With information on both frequency (approximate days per week) and duration (approximate minutes per day) of news media consumption, it is possible to produce aggregate estimates of news consumption. Figure 4.3 displays this summary information expressed in hours per week.[5] The overall difference across age groups is immediately apparent, as the aggregate mean for those under thirty-five is 5.1 hours per week, compared to eight hours for those aged fifty-five to sixty-nine.[6] These may seem like rather impressive totals, but it must be remembered that general questions about news media use invariably produce inflated estimates. However, it is not the absolute numbers as much as the difference across age categories that is of interest here. TV and newspapers account for most of the gap, for reasons, as we have seen, of both frequency and duration of use. Consumption of news via radio and the Internet has some equalizing effect, but the impact is limited, as frequency and duration of news consumption for these media are lower on the whole. For all age groups, the median value for news consumption per week is slightly lower than the mean, though the discrepancy is a bit larger for the youngest group (median = 4.5) for the same reason as before: a sizable block of young people clustered at the bottom end of the composite scale of news media consumption. The result is marked age disparities in the proportion who are decidedly inattentive to news media: a third of those under thirty-five (33 percent) report spending three hours or less per week reading, viewing, and listening to news compared to only 13 percent of those aged fifty-five to sixty-nine.

Beyond sheer time devoted to news consumption, another line of questioning on the CCES inquired about specific media sources favoured by respondents. Those who reported watching TV news at least occasionally were asked on which station they watch the news most frequently. For all questions on preferred media outlets, some initial collapsing of responses took place based on how politically informative each was believed to be, with an eye to later analysis of the relationship between patterns of news media use and political knowledge.[7] In the case of TV news, a distinction was drawn between those who watch the news on one of the Canadian public broadcasters, CBC and SRC, or one of the French or English all-news stations in Canada, and those who watch the shorter, more commercial-laden news broadcasts on CTV, Global, TVA, TQS, local channels (such as Citytv), or an American station. Those who watched one of the Canadian network channels were next asked whether they watched national or local news more often, the expectation being that political knowledge would be enhanced by a preference for national news. Newspaper readers were asked which paper they read most frequently, with a reasonably detailed listing of answers collapsed into a simpler classification: national newspapers (the *Globe and Mail*, the *National Post*, and *Le Devoir*) presumed to contain the greatest level of detailed political information and analysis; broadsheet publications in larger cities containing considerable political coverage (e.g., Canada's largest paper, the *Toronto Star*); and a mixed bag of less politically informative papers, including tabloid publications (e.g., the *Sun* chain of publications), free daily newspapers available in many larger cities such as *24 Hours* and *Metro*, and an "other" category, presumed to represent primarily smaller, local papers with relatively limited coverage of political news beyond the immediate region. Detailed responses were also collected from Internet news users about their favoured sites, with answers subsequently coded into those that are principally news sites, likely to be more politically informative, and those that are multipurpose sites. Finally, radio news users were asked their station of choice, with answers recorded simply as CBC/ SRC (public stations devoting much of their broadcasting time to news and current events) and other stations.

Results, limited to those who report using different forms of news media at least occasionally, are displayed in Table 4.2. Unlike other dimensions of news media use, in this case there is relatively little variation across age categories. The most notable age pattern is with respect to preferences for local and national TV news. The combined total watching national news (the more politically informative option) or national and local equally is 56 percent among those under thirty-five compared to 78 percent among those aged fifty-five to sixty-nine. Young people are also more likely than older Canadians to read the free daily newspapers, such as *24 Hours,* that have been making inroads in recent years, but the proportion indicating such as their paper of choice remains relatively small at this stage (13 percent). Beyond this, differences between younger and older Canadians are not particularly notable.

The absence of significant age differences on these questions indicates that young Canadians who use news media are just about as likely to favour higher-quality sources of information as older Canadians. So if the readership and audience for news media such as the *Globe and Mail* and CBC news are steadily greying, as we often hear, it is not, according to these numbers, because young people who read and watch the news are avoiding these sources. It is instead a reflection of the more general phenomenon of young people being less inclined to follow the news nowadays. That there has not been a marked deterioration in this respect is partly due to the fact that education is a powerful determinant of the quality of the news sources people favour (much more so than for sheer hours of use). The higher education levels of younger groups – those aged eighteen to thirty-four and those thirty-five to forty-four – partly explain their continued adherence to relatively informative media outlets.

The final question put to respondents in the news media series asked how much attention they paid to "stories about politics" when reading or listening to the news (Figure 4.4). Here, significant age differences emerge once again, as only 35 percent of those under thirty-five say "quite a bit" or "a great deal," significantly fewer than in the older comparison group (59 percent). Not surprisingly, responses to this question track very closely with responses to another question on the survey asking people about their general interest in politics ($r = 0.67$). Meanwhile, the correlation between general political interest and the number of hours spent using news media is significant but considerably lower ($r = 0.42$). There is consequently analytical value in maintaining a clear distinction between the behavioural tendency to spend time consuming news media – correlated with interest in politics but clearly not reducible to it – and the tendency to attend to political

Table 4.2

Preferred news media outlets by age group (%)

	Age					
	18-34	35-44	45-54	55-69	70+	Total
TV station (for news)						
Canadian public or all news	29	36	30	34	31	32
Canadian private	53	43	54	48	51	50
American	6	5	4	4	7	5
Other	12	16	11	14	12	13
(N)	(272)	(174)	(178)	(225)	(121)	(970)
National versus local news						
National	37	33	31	33	28	33
Both equally	19	33	40	45	55	36
Local	44	33	29	23	17	31
(N)	(186)	(117)	(135)	(159)	(87)	(684)
Newspaper						
National papers	7	9	9	8	7	8
Large-circulation broadsheets	34	40	38	38	45	38
Tabloids	19	20	20	19	14	19
Free dailies	13	8	7	7	1	8
Other	27	23	25	28	33	27
(N)	(245)	(148)	(161)	(211)	(112)	(877)
Radio						
CBC/SRC	21	25	22	26	24	24
Other, don't know	79	75	78	74	76	76
(N)	(237)	(170)	(167)	(196)	(98)	(868)
Internet						
News site	35	30	31	26	8	30
Multipurpose site, don't know	65	70	69	74	92	70
(N)	(192)	(122)	(96)	(90)	(24)	(524)

Source: CCES, 2007-08.

information when doing so, which is a more direct function of political interest (Chaffee and Schleuder 1986).

All of these numbers help in painting a relatively comprehensive and nuanced portrait of news media attentiveness among young Canadians. Significant differences between younger and older Canadians are evident for both the quantity of news media consumed (a function of both frequency and duration of use) and the attention given to politics when partaking of the news. Age differences are less conspicuous with respect to the quality of

Figure 4.4

Attention to political news stories by age

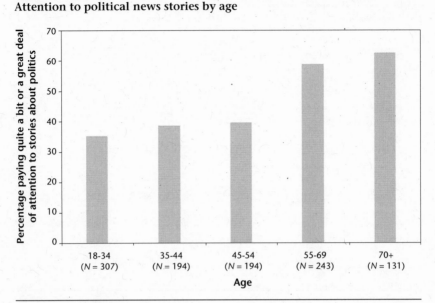

Source: CCES, 2007-08.

news sources consulted. Attending to these various dimensions helps to pinpoint more precisely where younger Canadians differ most sharply from older generations in their news media consumption habits.

News Media Use and Political Knowledge

Our consideration of political knowledge and news media use has thus far proceeded on parallel tracks, looking at one, then the other, to assess changes in political attentiveness over time in multiple countries and to examine more detailed patterns in Canada at present. While the link between the two facets of political attentiveness has been noted, it has not yet been demonstrated. The relatively rich measures of political knowledge and news media use on the CCES allow for investigation of this connection and consideration of the broader implications for political disengagement among young Canadians.

While the virtuous circle conception would suggest that there can be mutual influence between the two – that knowledge of politics can lead people to seek out political information, as much as exposure to political information can create informed citizens – the analysis that follows treats political knowledge as the dependent variable. This approach receives some support in recent research that has explicitly addressed the issue of causal direction between the two variables and found stronger evidence of news use influencing knowledge (Eveland et al. 2005). The concern that causation might partly run the other way serves as a general caveat to what follows, but is not repeated at every turn.

The analysis begins with bivariate results showing the relationship between various dimensions of news media use and political knowledge (based on mean scores out of sixteen). The results, for the most part, speak for themselves: across all types of news media, increased hours of use per week are associated with higher levels of political knowledge, as is the viewing of national rather than local news and a preference for higher-quality media sources (Table 4.3). The single most potent variable is the attention accorded to stories about politics when reading or listening to the news, underscoring the importance of taking into account how political interest guides people's use of news media at the point of exposure. Its overarching importance should not be exaggerated, however, as effects for other dimensions of news media use are divided among numerous variables. The cumulative impact for someone scoring high on a number of these variables would be very marked indeed.

With respect to sheer time spent accessing the news through different media, in all cases but television the impact on knowledge is greatest at the lower end of the news consumption scale, with smaller returns at the upper end. The same pattern is evident for all news media combined as the gains in knowledge from additional hours gradually diminish (the jump in the final category of "more than twelve hours per week" reflects the fact that this involves a larger increment in hours per week). This pattern makes a certain amount of sense: given that most of the knowledge questions posed on the CCES were relatively simple queries, it stands to reason that there would be diminishing returns from increased news media use. If the questions were more difficult, greater differences would likely appear at the upper end of the news consumption scale. But as we will see, the lower end of the spectrum is especially critical to understanding and potentially addressing some of the negative consequences associated with lack of political attentiveness.

These bivariate results offer a preliminary view of the connection between different dimensions of news media use and political knowledge, but further analysis is needed to arrive at firmer conclusions. After all, those who read a national newspaper frequently and at length also tend to watch TV news on public channels, listen to CBC radio, read news on the Internet, and pay relatively close attention to stories about politics when engaged in these activities. The influence of each variable net of the others remains to be determined through multivariate methods. Table 4.4 reports results of OLS regression to this end. Aside from determining how the bivariate results stand up in a multivariate context, the table serves other purposes as well: to assess the overall capacity of news media variables to explain variations

Table 4.3

Political knowledge scores by news media usage

Hours per week	TV	Newspapers	Radio	Internet	Hours per week	All news media
0	6.5	4.8	5.0	5.7	*0-2*	4.1
0.1-1	5.9	6.1	6.7	7.5	*2.1-4*	5.7
1.1-2	6.7	7.4	7.4	8.3	*4.1-6*	6.5
2.1-3	6.6	8.8	7.5	8.3	*6.1-8*	7.5
3+	7.6	8.5	8.0	9.3	*8.1-10*	8.1
(N)	(1,087)	(1,087)	(1,087)	(1,087)	*10.1-12*	8.4
					12+	9.5
					(N)	(1,058)

TV station		*Radio*	
Canadian public or all news	8.2	CBC/SRC	9.6
Canadian private	6.4	Other, don't know	6.6
American	7.2	*(N)*	(879)
Other	5.4		
(N)	(979)		

National versus local news		*Internet*	
National	8.2	News sites	9.2
Local	5.7	Multipurpose sites,	7.5
Both equally	7.3	don't know	
(N)	(691)	*(N)*	(529)

Newspaper		*Attention paid to political news items*	
National papers	11.0	None	2.1
Large-circulation broadsheets	8.1	Very little	3.7
Tabloids	5.9	Some	6.7
Free dailies	6.3	Quite a bit	8.0
Other	6.3	A great deal	9.6
(N)	(887)	*(N)*	(1,083)

Note: Entries are mean knowledge scores (out of 16).
Source: CCES, 2007-08.

in political knowledge, and to estimate the degree to which they help account for the sizable gap in political knowledge between younger and older Canadians, as well as differences by education level.

Given the latter objective, the necessary starting point is inclusion of only the two demographic variables in order to assess age and education effects on political knowledge before patterns of news media use are taken into account. In both cases, categorical variables are used and modelled with dummy variables (the omitted comparison categories are those aged fifty-five to sixty-nine and those with a university education). As the second model indicates, education is strongly linked to political knowledge – those with a high school education score nearly 5 points lower than the university-educated on the 0 to 16 knowledge scale – and its presence in the model slightly widens the gap between younger and older groups from Model 1 (since younger respondents are more educated on the whole). Subsequent models introduce successive blocks of news media variables. The third model adds hours spent reading or listening to the news in different media. For those media where the bivariate result suggested diminishing returns to political knowledge from extra hours of exposure, the natural log of the variable is used, an effective method of capturing this pattern. The fourth model adds variables representing preferred media outlets, distinguishing between higher- and lower-quality sources. The fifth incorporates the distinct dimension of attention paid to stories about politics when reading or listening to the news to create the most fully elaborated model. The sixth and final model bundles groups of variables together to create a simpler multivariate model of news media consumption and political knowledge. All independent variables are coded on a 0 to 1 scale, so that coefficients represent the estimated change in political knowledge scores across the full range of the variable.

In the penultimate model, many bivariate results remain intact, though some fade into insignificance. Time spent using news media certainly has a sizable effect on political knowledge. Newspaper and Internet reading are the most beneficial of the four by a fair degree; hours spent on radio and TV news have small positive effects, but these are not statistically significant. Yet the effects of time spent using news media are not as critical as might be imagined. The effects for particular news sources consulted are equally significant: reading one of the larger broadsheet publications, or better yet one of the national newspapers, listening to public radio, and reading Internet sites dedicated to news are all associated with higher levels of political knowledge (coefficients range from 0.97 to 1.68). In the case of television, watching news on a public station or all-news channel no longer has a significant effect on knowledge, but watching national news, or national and local equally, does. The latter effect partly explains the former non-effect: those who watch news on the CBC/SRC are much more likely to report watching national news compared to viewers of the private networks, which largely explains why choice of channel fails to register a significant effect in the full model.

Consistent with the bivariate results, the single most powerful variable in model 5 is attention to stories about politics when reading or listening to the news. However, when variables are combined in model 6, there is greater consistency of effects across different dimensions of news media use. The

Table 4.4

News media use and political knowledge, multivariate analysis (OLS regression)

	Model 1	Model 2	Model 3	Model 4	Model 5	Model 6
Age						
18-34	-2.28*	-2.68*	-1.96*	-1.89*	-1.57*	-1.51*
35-44	-1.40*	-2.05*	-1.49*	-1.41*	-1.04*	-1.02*
45-54	-0.69	-1.00*	-0.64	-0.68*	-0.34	-0.28
70+	-1.23*	-0.75	-0.84*	-0.82*	-0.89*	-0.87*
Education						
High school education		-4.67*	-3.99*	-2.94*	-2.64*	-2.95*
Other postsecondary		-2.68*	-2.44*	-1.65*	-1.56*	-1.75*
Quantity						
TV news hours			0.87*	0.82*	0.17	3.63*
Newspaper hours (log)			2.14*	1.71*	1.24*	
Radio hours (log)			1.37*	0.94*	0.40	
Internet hours (log)			2.66*	2.19*	1.59*	
Quality						
Watch TV news on public channel				0.23	0.05	3.24*
Watch national news more often				0.75*	0.54*	
Watch national and local news equally				0.63*	0.50*	
National newspaper				1.68*	1.58*	
Large-circulation broadsheet				0.97*	0.90*	
Listen to news on CBC/SRC				1.25*	1.00*	
Read news on news website				1.22*	0.99*	
Attentiveness						
Attention to political news items					4.17*	4.21*
Constant	8.08	10.99	8.14	6.67	4.87	4.66
R^2	0.04	0.25	0.36	0.42	0.48	0.46
(N)	(1,018)	(1,018)	(1,018)	(1,018)	(1,018)	(1,018)

* Statistically significant at the $p < .05$ level.

Notes: Entries are unstandardized regression coefficients (*B*) indicating the estimated effect for each independent variable. The dependent variable is the knowledge score measured on a 0 to 16 scale. All independent variables are coded on 0-1 interval. Comparison groups for categorical variables are: age group 55 to 69; university education; all other TV channels (Canadian private, American, other); watch local news more often; all other newspapers (tabloids, free dailies, other); all other radio stations; and read news on multipurpose site. For preferred news media outlets, comparison groups also include those who never use a given news medium (for example, those who never read the news on the Internet).

Source: CCES, 2007-08.

aggregate *quantity* of news media consumption, measured in hours per week across the four types of news media, produces a coefficient of 3.63 (again, all variables are scaled 0-1, so the coefficient represents the effect across the full range). The combined variable for *quality* of news sources yields a coefficient of 3.24. *Attentiveness* to political stories when using news media has a slightly greater effect of 4.21. The effects across these three broad dimensions are not only relatively consistent, but powerful as well. Summing up the coefficients, the model predicts that moving from the very bottom end of the news consumption ladder to the very top in all respects would be associated with an increase in political knowledge from 4.66 to 15.74 (on a scale from 0 to 16). The overall explanatory power of the news media variables is confirmed by the high R^2 value for the fully elaborated model (0.48).[8]

Another way to gauge the explanatory value of the model is to observe how demographic effects diminish as blocks of news media variables are added. This reduction can be taken as indicating the extent to which age and education effects can be explained by the news media habits of the relevant groups. In the second model, with demographic variables only, the coefficient for the eighteen to thirty-four age group is –2.68. In the final model, this is reduced to –1.51, or 56 percent of its original value. For the high-school-educated, the coefficient diminishes from –4.67 to –2.95, again 56 percent of the original value. Thus political knowledge differences associated with both variables reflect, in good part, variations in the news media habits of different socio-demographic groups. The specific media variables that help explain age and education effects are not one and the same, however. The first block of variables, hours spent reading and listening to the news, results in a considerable reduction in the age coefficients, but has relatively little impact on the education coefficients effect (Model 3). The next block of variables, distinguishing higher- and lower-quality news sources, has less impact on age coefficients and more on education (Model 4), consistent with the earlier observation that differences between young and old in preferred media sources are not profound, whereas differences across educational categories are greater. Attention to political stories when reading or listening to the news, for its part, has roughly equal effect in further reducing the age and education coefficients (Model 5).

The general conclusion is quite simple: the way people use news media is powerfully linked to their levels of political knowledge. This runs counter to another study of citizen engagement in Canada, which finds that people do not become significantly better informed about policy issues through their use of mass media (Gidengil et al. 2004, 93). Granted, the knowledge questions used in that study are rather different and not directly comparable, but the measures of media use employed are also more limited.[9] Both differences probably help explain the divergent result. The current analysis suggests that when political knowledge and news media use are comprehensively measured, there are powerful connections between the two. The linkage becomes stronger as the variegated dimensions of news media consumption are taken into account, underlining the importance of measuring media use in a fairly comprehensive fashion (de Vreese and Boomgaarden 2006). To consider, for example, only the number of days per week someone reports reading the paper and watching TV news – the two most commonly employed measures on election surveys – would produce much weaker effects than those seen here (see, for example, Hollander 1997).[10] It is possible that the current analysis could be taken further still, through more fine-tuned measurement of frequency and duration of media use, greater detail on specific sources consulted, as well as information on other media sources omitted here, such as news magazines and public affairs TV programs. The particular battery of questions used, however, does serve to establish the basic point that habits of news media use are in fact tightly linked to levels of political knowledge.

Conclusions of a practical orientation can also be teased from the results. Simply put, in seeking to enhance political knowledge by promoting attentiveness to news media, there is probably as much to be gained from enhancements in quality as increases in quantity. This speaks to the feasibility of effecting change. If persuading young people to spend a number of extra hours per week reading the newspaper or consulting other news media is likely to be a hard sell, a more viable approach may be to encourage greater use of certain media sources: national news broadcasts, CBC radio, national newspapers and broadsheets, Internet news sites. The quality of media sources favoured by young Canadians may not be a principal component of their lagging political attentiveness, but this does not mean that enhancing quality cannot be part of the solution, given the evident connection to political knowledge. There is also much to be gained from encouraging closer attention to political stories when reading and listening to the news. With respect to time spent using news media, large increases in hours are not needed to produce significant knowledge gains, especially at the lower end of the news consumption scale, where the returns to knowledge are greatest (Table 4.3). Persuading minimalist news users to become periodic consumers would probably have a considerable impact on their basic understanding of politics.

How such changes might be brought about, when and where the necessary blandishments might come into effect, is a separate matter taken up in Chapter 10. The point to emphasize is that a series of small qualitative changes in the news media habits of young Canadians could potentially have considerable impact on the political knowledge deficit and on levels of political engagement more generally.

Early Influences on Political Attentiveness

In analyzing the pace of declining newspaper reading and TV news viewing in the previous chapter and in seeking to pinpoint the timing of change, one central conclusion was that the changing media environment did not appear to be critical to waning attentiveness to news media and, by implication, political attentiveness more generally. This conclusion, however, was based on aggregate trends. It did not consider the relationship at the individual level between the media choices available to people in their own environment and the propensity to use different news media. Further questions posed on the CCES allow for this individual-level analysis necessary to shore up conclusions about environmental influences on attentiveness to news media.

The relevant CCES questions were predicated on an assumption borne out by the analysis in the previous chapter: there seems to be considerable stability in habits of news media attentiveness through the adult years (as evidenced by strong cohort effects), suggesting that media consumption habits tend to take root relatively early in life.[11] Thus the CCES questions asked respondents about the nature of the media environment in their own homes when they were adolescents to see how this might have affected their current news consumption patterns.[12] Only those under forty were asked the questions, in part because of concerns about the accuracy of recall for those far removed from their adolescent years, in part because all over forty would have had identical experiences in some important respects. The first question, in keeping with Wattenberg's emphasis on the impact of changes in television technology, was whether respondents had cable TV in their home when they were teenagers. A second tapped into a potentially pertinent aspect of the personal media environment less often invoked in the relevant literature, asking whether there was one TV in the respondent's household at that time, or more than one. Multi-TV households have become much more common in recent years (with additional sets often located in children's bedrooms), providing an alternative viewing option for youngsters when their parents insist on watching the news. A third question asked respondents if they had Internet access in the home when they were teenagers. It has been suggested, reasonably enough, that this more recent addition to the home media environment would have effects similar to cable, expanding the range of diversionary pursuits available to people and potentially undermining attention to news and current affairs (Prior 2007). Finally, respondents were asked if there was a daily newspaper in the home when they were teenagers, a factor anticipated to have a positive effect on newspaper reading and potential spin-off effects on other forms of news media consumption.

Further questions were included on the CCES that spoke to other dimensions of influence from the adolescent stage of life. One related to civics education. While scepticism was expressed above that waning political knowledge among younger generations can be linked to a decline in the teaching of civics, this does not mean civics courses have no bearing on processes of political attentiveness and might not serve as one avenue of renewal. Given that the relevant educational material is not always taught in courses with civics in the title, respondents were asked a more generic question: whether they had taken a course in high school where they learned about government and politics. Nearly two-thirds said they had (65 percent). Another relevant variable included on the CCES comes from the political socialization literature. There, the importance of the family setting rather than the media environment is often emphasized, in particular the influence of parents on offspring. To assess the degree to which parents might have helped orient their adolescent children towards the political world, a question was asked about the frequency of political discussion in the home when respondents were teenagers. Seventeen percent reported that their family discussed politics frequently, 54 percent occasionally, 29 percent never. While these latter questions are more apt than the media environment questions to suffer from recall bias – recollection of a civics course or political discussion in the family is more likely to be coloured by one's past or current level of political engagement than is recall concerning the presence of different media options in the home – they are nonetheless important variables to consider. Finally, two others variables, education level and age, are taken into account as basic controls.

While the immediate effects anticipated for the media environment variables are on news media consumption, the argument, as presented by Wattenberg and others, is that this then has knock-on effects on knowledge and interest, that is, influences political attentiveness more generally. Hence, all three dimensions of attentiveness are considered in the analysis, tracing connections between different experiences and circumstances of the adolescent years to see which are most strongly related to political attentiveness in adulthood. Bivariate results would be misleading, as the youngest respondents are distinctive with respect to both media environment variables in the teenage years (e.g., most had Internet access, most had multiple television sets in the home) and levels of political attentiveness, so we proceed directly to multivariate regression models.

In the first model (Table 4.5), the dependent variable is current hours per week spent using all news media: television, newspapers, radio, and Internet combined (a variable ranging from zero to twenty-one hours). Aside from age itself, the only significant variables in the model are frequent political discussion in the teenage years (1.55 additional hours of news media use per week compared to the no political discussion category) and exposure to civics education (0.90 extra hours per week). The effects for variables capturing the media environment of adolescence are considerably weaker, none

Table 4.5

Early influences on political attentiveness (OLS regression)

	Hours of media use per week (0-21 scale)	Political knowledge (0-16 scale)	Political interest (0-10 scale)
Age (in years, 18 = 0)	0.11*	0.09*	0.00
High school education	-0.38	-3.94*	-1.93*
Other postsecondary education	0.70	-2.10*	-0.69*
No cable television	0.16	-0.15	-0.12
One TV only	-0.33	0.06	0.20
Newspaper in household	0.50	-0.37	0.09
No Internet access	0.44	-0.23	0.04
Discussed politics occasionally	0.28	1.33*	0.97*
Discussed politics frequently	1.55*	2.50*	1.86*
Took course(s) on government and politics	0.90*	1.48*	1.08*
Constant	2.54	5.19	3.93
R^2	0.09	0.31	0.15
(N)	(377)	(648)	(648)

* Statistically significant at the $p < .05$ level.

Notes: Entries are unstandardized regression coefficients (*B*) indicating the estimated effect for each independent variable. All independent variables except age are coded on 0-1 interval. Comparison groups for categorical variables are: university education; had cable television when teenager; more than one TV in household when teenager; no newspaper in home when teenager; Internet access when teenager; never discussed politics with family; and did not take course on government and politics. Analysis is based on respondents aged 18 to 39 only.
Source: CCES, 2007-08.

achieving statistical significance. The largest coefficients are for the presence of a newspaper in the home (0.50) and the absence of Internet access (0.44). Further investigation reveals that the first largely reflects a slight increase in hours of newspaper reading per week (0.21) and reading news on the Internet (0.22) among respondents who grew up with a newspaper in the home, while the second largely reflects increased hours of TV news viewing (0.48) where Internet access was absent. In other words, these are effects of the type, if not the magnitude, proponents of the media environment thesis would expect to see. For political discussion and civics education, on the other hand, more detailed probing reveals positive effects for *all* forms of news media consumption for the political discussion variable (ranging from 0.21 for radio news to 0.69 for Internet news) and for three of four media for civics education (all but television news are in the 0.27 to 0.33 range). The latter variables thus do not necessarily have markedly stronger effects on consumption of specific types of news media, but the fact that they have effects *across the board* means that their cumulative impact is greater.

There is further evidence of the more sweeping influence of political discussion in the home and civics education in the models for political knowledge and interest. None of the media environment variables registers a significant effect on either political knowledge (the 0 to 16 scale from above) or political interest (based on a single general interest question with four categories, recoded to a 0 to 10 scale). Political discussion (both occasional and frequent) and civics education, on the other hand, show significant associations in both cases.

These results serve to confirm the earlier conclusion that media environment variables have a relatively minor impact on news media attentiveness and on political attentiveness more generally. The choices people make, the news media they consume, do not seem to be heavily conditioned by the degree of choice offered by new technologies that have entered their homes and lives over the years. More important are factors of general influence, including civics courses and political discussion with parents. The effects are more significant because they are more sweeping, influencing consumption of different news media, political knowledge, and political interest. Consistent with our earlier conclusions, there is more insight to be gained, more explanatory purchase to be found, in concentrating on variables relevant to political attentiveness in general rather than singling out factors that might influence the use of specific news media.

A number of detailed points extending the earlier analysis have been presented in this chapter, but the principal findings serve to reinforce prior conclusions. The political knowledge deficit among younger Canadians is substantial and cuts across different knowledge domains. Sporadic consumption of news media, on a variety of detailed measures and dimensions, is another distinguishing trait. There is a manifest connection between the two, as habits of news media consumption and levels of political knowledge are tightly linked, suggesting that modifying said habits is one way in which more robust levels of political attentiveness among younger Canadians might be achieved. It is therefore important to underline that changing patterns of news media consumption are not simply the product of a media environment abundant in choice that has inexorably reshaped the reading and viewing habits of younger generations – a pessimistic position implying there is little to be done to reverse the trend. Other factors more susceptible to purposeful tinkering, such as civics courses and political discussion, appear to be more important precipitants of political attentiveness and should receive greater attention.

5
Political Knowledge and Canadian Democracy

Having scrutinized current contours of political attentiveness in Canada, it remains to say something more about the consequences of the significant shortfall among younger Canadians. The particular focus will be on that aspect most intrinsic to exercising the full capacities of citizenship, political knowledge. As the cliché goes, knowledge is power, and political knowledge is a form of political power that underwrites virtually any democratic activity citizens might wish to undertake. Consequently, its effects on political engagement are manifold and could be explored at great length. As others have already done so (Delli Carpini and Keeter 1996; Althaus 2003; Gidengil et al. 2004), the present focus is on providing illustrative examples of some of the more fundamental areas of citizen engagement influenced by knowledge of politics: political participation, the capacity for critical judgment, and the formulation of sound political opinion. In addition to describing and documenting knowledge effects that others have previously identified, attention is also given to variations in those effects across the spectrum of political knowledge. This added dimension provides a more nuanced understanding of the way political knowledge influences democratic engagement, and also offers some practical benefit. Knowing where on the spectrum effects are concentrated can help in determining the optimal focal point (or points) for efforts to boost political attentiveness levels among young Canadians.

Voter Turnout

One important form of political involvement strongly connected to political knowledge is electoral participation. Knowing something about politics provides a foundation for political preferences, allowing the voter to make an informed choice at the ballot box. Knowledge thus encourages participation by lending meaning and consequence to the vote.

One voting question on the Canadian Citizen Engagement Survey (CCES) asked whether respondents had voted in all, most, some, or none of the federal elections that had taken place since they had become eligible to vote.

Figure 5.1

Voting and political knowledge in Canada

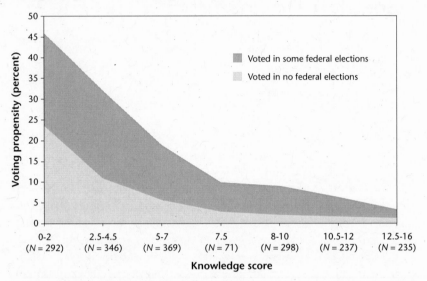

Source: CCES, 2007-08.

If respondents found the question difficult to answer due to a lack of prior opportunities to vote, interviewers were instructed to ask: "So do you think you are someone who would tend to vote in all federal elections, most, some, or none?" The distribution of responses suggests that the question, like others relating to voting, suffers from some inflationary bias. Over half (56 percent) of respondents say they have voted in all elections, 24 percent in most, and another 12 percent in some. If accurate, these figures would produce considerably higher turnout than the 60 to 75 percent range typical of Canadian federal elections in the past thirty years. Still, the question offers greater nuance than simply asking about participation in a single electoral contest.

Figure 5.1 captures the relationship between voting propensity and political knowledge (as measured by the sixteen-point scale on the CCES). There is clearly a sharp increase in electoral abstention as political knowledge decreases. At the top end of the knowledge scale, only 1 percent report voting in no elections and a further 2 percent in only some. At the bottom end of the scale, the combined total of the two groups is nearly 50 percent, as 24 percent admit to never voting in federal elections and another 22 percent say they voted in only some.

There is nothing particularly new or startling in this finding, as the simple fact of a strong relationship between political knowledge and electoral participation appears consistently in studies conducted in both Canada and elsewhere (Delli Carpini and Keeter 1996; Popkin and Dimock 1999; Rubenson et al. 2004; Howe 2006, 2007b). However, there is also evidence in Figure 5.1 of a more subtle point that has not been as frequently drawn out. The shape of the curve connecting voter participation and political knowledge is not a straightforward linear decline as knowledge decreases. Instead, the propensity to vote holds reasonably steady across the upper part of the knowledge spectrum, but falls precipitously below a certain point (Howe 2006). In the CCES, that threshold lies at roughly 7.5 on the knowledge scale, a point that roughly splits the survey sample in half (55 percent of respondents lie below this point). Given that the questions comprising this index include a fair number of relatively simple queries – the name of one's premier, the leader of the Liberal Party, which level of government is responsible for education, which federal party was most strongly opposed to same-sex marriage, how often free votes occur in the House of Commons, Canada's basic commitment under the Kyoto Accord, and so on – it is fair to say that the threshold below which electoral participation suffers markedly is, in absolute terms, quite low. It is only among those lacking relatively basic knowledge of the political world that electoral participation suffers markedly.

This observation is important to bear in mind, as it provides additional insight into other relevant patterns. First, it can help make sense of an interesting difference in the relationship between knowledge and voting in the six countries that formed part of our earlier comparative analysis. In the Anglo-American countries, there is a relatively strong connection between political knowledge and voter participation: the percentage point difference in turnout in recent national elections between those falling in the top and bottom quartiles of political knowledge is 29 to 41 points in Canada, Britain, and the US. In the Northern European cases considered earlier, the knowledge effect is not as pronounced, ranging from 17 to 22 percentage points (Figure 5.2).[1] The proposition that voting suffers most below a certain knowledge threshold, a relatively modest level in absolute terms, can help explain this difference. If the citizens of these Northern European states are more knowledgeable on the whole than those in the Anglo-American countries, fewer would lie below this threshold, and the effects of knowledge on voter participation would be weaker overall.[2]

A variety of evidence lends support to this proposition. Henry Milner draws direct comparisons of political knowledge across different countries in the course of making the case that the Anglo-American countries lag behind their Northern European counterparts in overall levels of civic literacy. Though pertinent cross-national surveys are relatively rare, Milner does cite a handful of scattered results suggesting that Swedes, Norwegians, and the Dutch (and other Northern Europeans) are more apt to know various facts

Figure 5.2

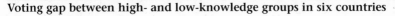

Voting gap between high- and low-knowledge groups in six countries

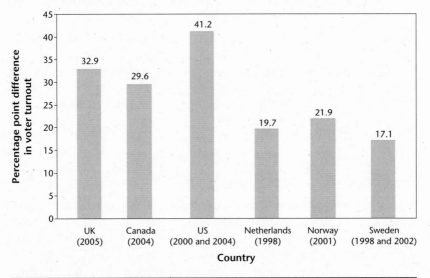

Note: N varies for different groups and countries. Minimum *N* = 423.
Sources: National election studies.

about international politics, such as the identity of the UN secretary-general. The 2002 National Geographic poll of young people mentioned above yields a similar result: Canadians, Americans, and Britons scored considerably lower on this wide-ranging test of geopolitical knowledge than the top-ranking Swedish respondents (RoperASW 2002, 17). However, one concern with attempts to draw comparisons across countries is the difficulty in devising an unbiased barometer of political knowledge for use in different countries. Asking about international issues is the easiest approach, but international politics is followed more closely in some countries than others, not just because citizens are more politically attentive, but for other reasons as well (for example, in smaller countries there is often greater interest in international events). Asking about a particular political office common to all countries – e.g., the name of the finance minister – would be another option, but the salience of the position and the prominence of the office-holder will vary considerably from one country to the next. It is difficult to think of any knowledge questions that might be posed across a broad range of countries that would be free of any such biases.

There is, however, an alternative approach (also adopted by Milner). Levels of news media consumption can be compared, since this is a powerful predictor of political knowledge and does not suffer from the same inherent

Figure 5.3

The inattentive public in six countries

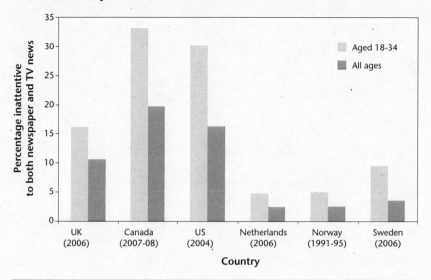

Note: Sample sizes vary. For all but Norway, *N* varies from 247 to 311 for the 18-34 age group, and from 944 to 1,091 for all ages. For Norway, *N* = 2,990 and 8,541, respectively.

Sources: Canada, CCES, 2007-08; US, 2004 election study; Norway, Mannheim Eurobarometer Trend File 1970-2002; other countries, Eurobarometer 65.2.

measurement difficulties. Given the objective of determining whether there are larger blocks of citizens in some countries falling below a modest knowledge threshold, the relevant comparative statistic is the percentage in each place whose attentiveness to news media is fairly minimal. Defining this as watching TV news and reading newspapers no more than once or twice per week, Figure 5.3 presents estimates of the inattentive public in each of the six countries, based on identical questions from the CCES and Eurobarometer studies, as well as similar questions from the 2004 American National Election Study.[3] The results reveal differences across countries that are very substantial, and consistent with expectations. There are exceedingly few in the Netherlands, Norway, and Sweden who could be considered profoundly inattentive to news media by this method of categorization – only 2 to 4 percent. While rates are higher among those under thirty-five, they remain below 10 percent in all three places. Substantially more fall into this category in the three Anglo-American countries. In Canada, the inattentive public, by this yardstick, constitutes nearly 20 percent of all adults and fully one-third of those aged eighteen to thirty-four.

These results are consistent with Milner's conclusions about the impoverished state of civic literacy in Canada and the Anglo-American countries

Figure 5.4

Voting gap between high- and low-knowledge groups in six countries, age categories compared

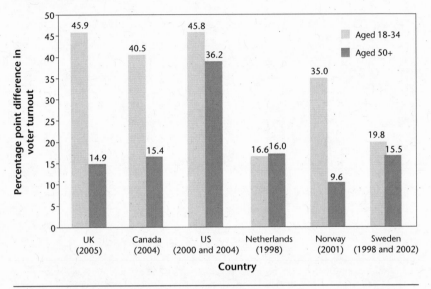

Note: N varies for different groups and countries. In all cases, *N* > 100, except for the 18-34 high-knowledge age group for the US (*N* = 96), Netherlands (*N* = 81), and Sweden (*N* = 65).
Sources: National election studies.

more generally, as well as his observation that deficiencies at the bottom end of the civic literacy spectrum are especially telling and damaging to political engagement (2001, 11-15; 2002, 61-62). Overall averages give some indication of salient cross-national differences, but comparison of the lower extremities reveals fivefold, even tenfold, differences in the proportion of citizens markedly inattentive to news media. Given the tight linkage found in the previous chapter between news media use and political knowledge, it is not a far stretch to posit that a higher percentage of citizens in the Anglo-American countries would lie below the knowledge threshold where voting is acutely affected. This would help to explain why the overall impact of knowledge on electoral participation is more pronounced in these countries (Howe 2006).[4]

Further consequences follow. In countries where overall political attentiveness levels are wanting, the decline in political knowledge among younger generations has seen relatively large numbers of young people falling below the knowledge threshold where participation effects are amplified. By contrast, in places where political attentiveness is more robust, knowledge among the young has not declined to the level where turnout is dramatically affected. Figure 5.4 captures this important difference. In Britain, Canada, and the US, the impact of political knowledge on voter turnout among those under thirty-five is profound, as a gap of 40 to 46 percentage points separates the most and least knowledgeable quartiles within this younger group. In the Northern European countries, variations in political knowledge among those aged eighteen to thirty-four do not have nearly as dramatic an effect. Indeed, in Sweden and the Netherlands the impact of knowledge on voting is virtually the same among those under thirty-five as it is among older adults. It is the heightened impact among younger generations in the Anglo-American countries that largely accounts for the greater overall effect of knowledge on voting, a pattern reflecting the relatively anemic state of political attentiveness in these places.

All of this serves as an important qualification to earlier comparisons between the Anglo-American and Northern European countries. The prior emphasis was on the surprising consistency in patterns of evolving political attentiveness. In all of these places, a significant generational decline in levels of political knowledge and attentiveness to news media was observed. For all that, we now see that it remains the case that citizens of the Northern European countries are on the whole more politically attentive. Most remain sufficiently attuned to engage in the most basic act of democratic citizenship, voting in elections. Thus, the consequences of a growing knowledge gap between young and old for voter participation have not been as dramatic as in Canada, the UK, and the US.

Participation beyond Voting

Other types of political and civic activities, typically seen as more selective forms of citizen involvement, are also strongly related to knowledge of political affairs. Figure 5.5 shows several examples of participatory actions seemingly influenced by political knowledge, drawn from two sources: volunteering for a federal political party and volunteering for a community group or a non-profit organization (from the 2006 Canadian election study), and contacting one's member of parliament and being a member of an interest group working for change on a social or political issue (from the 2004 Canadian election study). Since these questions are drawn from different sources, the political knowledge measures used to categorize respondents differ. In both cases, the survey sample is split into five knowledge categories with roughly equal proportions of respondents.

The impact of political knowledge on these various forms of public involvement is significant in all cases. The broad impact of political knowledge makes it a critical resource for citizens, facilitating diverse forms of public participation that afford people influence over issues of common concern. Inequalities in the distribution of political knowledge thus present significant normative concerns about the equality of political influence. It is noteworthy,

Figure 5.5

Other forms of participation and political knowledge

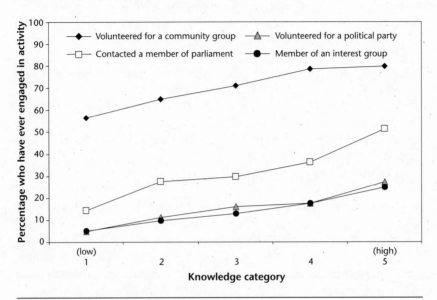

Source: 2004 and 2006 Canadian Election Studies.

too, that all lines in the graph move upwards in a steady, linear fashion, indicating that the effects of knowledge on these various forms of civic and political engagement hold across the full knowledge spectrum. Unlike voting, there is no threshold above which participation is largely unaffected by further increments of knowledge and below which effects are particularly acute.

Strategies to enhance political knowledge should be sensitive to these variations in the effects of knowledge at different points on the spectrum, and informed by normative concerns about democratic equality. Both considerations point to the importance of concentrating efforts to augment knowledge levels at the bottom end of the scale. From a practical perspective, improvements at the low end of the scale should boost voter turnout *and* generate involvement in more demanding forms of public engagement. At the upper end of the scale, effects would be limited to the latter activities, with no appreciable effects on voter participation. It might also be speculated that those near the bottom end of the knowledge spectrum are in greatest need of external stimulus in order to catalyze change. It seems unlikely that someone with essentially no knowledge of politics and no inclination to follow news in the media would find it within themselves to turn matters around. By contrast, someone further up the scale of political attentiveness, equipped with at least a modicum of political knowledge and some basic inclination to keep up with the news, is better positioned to make the changes necessary to become a more politically informed and engaged citizen, especially if noteworthy events transpire that serve to pique their political interest (Hyman and Sheatsley 1947; Bennett 1988). If there is a virtuous circle linking political knowledge, interest, and news media use, it is probably a bigger challenge to get the ball rolling in the first place than it is to impart added momentum once the ball is already in motion.

Mobilization

Other effects of political knowledge lie in a different realm of citizen engagement: interpersonal mobilization. Political scientists have paid considerable attention to the dynamics of mobilization, but have tended to focus on one side of the coin, evaluating people mainly as objects of persuasion and mobilization. The relevant research typically considers such questions as who responds most readily to mobilization efforts and what particular methods or messages are most effective in triggering political involvement. The motivations of the instigators of mobilization – be they political parties, the media, or fellow citizens – are often simply taken as a given. Closer examination of the factors that lead people to undertake mobilization of others can enhance our understanding of these dynamics.

The simplest form of mobilization is engaging others in political discussion. This can be conceptualized as an informal version of the much vaunted practice of deliberative democracy, allowing people to learn what others think, to voice their own opinions, and potentially to encourage heightened political interest on the part of participants (Mutz 2006). The informality of the action makes it a distinctive wellspring of political engagement, one emerging spontaneously out of everyday interactions and requiring little conscious effort or intent. For this reason, political talk is an element of citizen engagement that probably deserves closer attention (Bennett et al. 2000) A general question concerning political discussion on the CCES asked respondents how often they discuss political matters when they get together with friends. Most said occasionally (61 percent). The remaining responses were split roughly equally between frequently (17 percent) and never (22 percent).

Another form of mobilization is encouraging participation in specific political activities, including voting. A hypothetical question was posed on the CCES: if a friend of yours said they were not going to vote in an upcoming election, would you try to persuade them they should vote, or would you feel this is their decision to make? For one-third of respondents, "a friend of yours" was replaced with "someone you worked with," while the other third were asked about "someone in your family."[5] For all question wordings combined, just over half said they would try to persuade the person to vote (54 percent). The willingness to cajole others in this matter is only slightly greater for family members (60 percent) than for friends (50 percent)

Figure 5.6

Influencing others and political knowledge

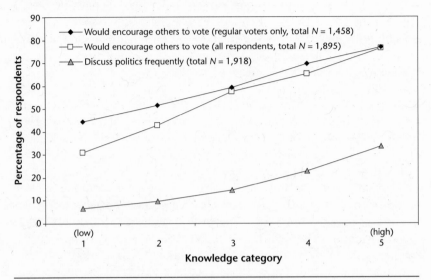

Source: CCES, 2007-08.

and co-workers (51 percent). This suggests that people do not limit themselves to exerting political influence only on those they know intimately. However, the fact that only a bare majority are thus inclined suggests scope for enlargement of the pool of citizens willing to act as advocates for voting. So too does another question that turned the tables by asking respondents if anyone had ever tried to persuade them to vote. Only 26 percent said someone had. The figure is higher among those tending not to vote, who are naturally more likely to be subject to such influence, but remains under 40 percent even for habitual non-voters. Many electoral abstainers apparently have never encountered anyone telling them they should vote.

Figure 5.6 displays connections between knowledge of politics and the propensity to engage in these two forms of interpersonal political influence. The results are predictable enough, but no less striking for that. Those who are knowledgeable about politics are much more likely to engage in political discussion. Frequent discussion rises from 7 percent to 34 percent in moving from one end of the knowledge spectrum to the other. If occasional discussion is included as well, the respective figures are 55 percent and 97 percent. The effects of knowledge are equally pronounced with respect to encouragement of electoral participation. Only 31 percent of the least knowledgeable would try to persuade a would-be abstainer to vote, compared to 76 percent of the most knowledgeable. Of course, the latter group are more likely to vote themselves, which partly explains why they are more willing to persuade others to do so. Yet even when the analysis is limited to respondents who themselves vote in most or all federal elections, knowledge has nearly as great an effect on the propensity to persuade others (Figure 5.6). Moreover, any effect that might be linked to one's personal penchant for voting should not be subtracted from the overall effect. Instead, this simply represents one mechanism – from knowledge, to voting, to the advocacy of voting – whereby the effect is realized.

As with some other forms of participation considered above, the effects of knowledge on interpersonal mobilization are more or less constant across the knowledge spectrum. Thus enhancements at any point would likely yield benefits of increased political interaction between citizens. The theme of interpersonal influence is revisited later, when the issue of social integration is taken up in the latter half of the book. There the case is made that societal fragmentation has made citizens more inclined to leave one another to their own devices and to eschew different forms of interpersonal mobilization. Also relevant to these changing social dynamics, the current results would suggest, is the individual disempowerment associated with political inattentiveness.

The Critical Capacities of Citizens

Further democratic desiderata linked to political knowledge can also be identified. Those who know a good deal about politics not only have a larger stockpile of information at their disposal, they are able to use that information to grasp nuance and shading in political discourse, to be discerning in their political judgments. Rather than relying on received wisdom, the politically knowledgeable are in a position to develop their own thoughts and opinions on issues. In short, their critical capacities are more highly developed. Citizens of this type not only benefit themselves, they also make an important contribution to the general welfare, helping to sustain a democracy where ideas and public policies are queried and criticized, debated, and refined, in a manner that typically leads to better ideas and better public policy.

Evidence of the discernment the politically knowledgeable bring to politics can be found in survey questions that tap into evaluations of different actors in the political system. One relevant question posed at different points has asked respondents whether they agree or disagree that "all federal political parties are basically the same; there isn't really a choice." When the question was asked on the 2000 Canadian election study, there were five parties represented in the House of Commons, two of them relative newcomers espousing highly distinctive political viewpoints – the Canadian Alliance, a more conservative party than any other, and the Bloc Québécois, an advocate of Quebec sovereignty. The other three included the two mainstream parties, the Liberals and Progressive Conservatives, and another of a socialist bent, the New Democratic Party. Given this diversity of political offerings, it is somewhat surprising that respondents split down the middle, roughly half agreeing that the parties are all the same, the other half disagreeing. The result becomes more sensible when the relationship between political knowledge and the tendency to see differences between political parties is considered (Figure 5.7). Among those with relatively little political knowledge, the percentage perceiving difference between the parties is relatively low (around 40 percent). As knowledge increases, so too does the ability to detect partisan shading (topping out at 80 percent).

This finding, on the one hand, bolsters the earlier reasoning on electoral participation: political knowledge allows people to understand the electoral choices before them and hence serves as an important motivational spring-board for this form of political participation (Prior 2007, 50). If young people know less about politics, they are less apt to have a preference to express at the polling booth. They are also less likely to develop more general partisan leanings. A decline in party identification, another important manifestation of changing patterns of democratic engagement, has been witnessed in numerous developed democracies. It is variously linked to changing citizen attitudes towards parties, the rise of special interest groups and issue-based social movements, and the more impersonal methods of political cam-paigning favoured by parties in recent times (Dalton and Wattenberg 2000). Given the trajectory of political knowledge over time and across generations, the trend also likely reflects growing incomprehension of what the parties stand for. Certainly knowledge and partisanship are tightly linked, as Figure 5.7 shows. Party identification in Canada climbs from 27 percent to 81 per-cent in moving from the lower to the upper end of the political knowledge scale. The age gap for party identification is not as severe – roughly a 15-point difference between those under thirty (49 percent) and those fifty and over (65 percent) on the 2000 Canadian election study – but then there are ways in which partisanship can be cultivated in the absence of personal engage-ment, most notably the traditional mechanism of family influence. For those who do not have this background experience, however, and who are more reliant on their own devices to navigate the political world, some basic degree of political knowledge would seem to be a necessary prerequisite for the development of party identification.

The poor powers of discernment displayed by less knowledgeable citizens not only affect their own political involvement, they also have broader implications for the political system (Delli Carpini and Keeter 1996, 267). If many potential voters are unable to distinguish political parties due to an inadequate knowledge base, there is an incentive for the parties to do what-ever it takes to make an impression on an inattentive electorate and set

Figure 5.7

Critical discernment and political knowledge

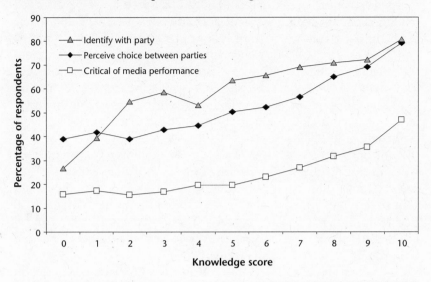

Source: 2000 Canadian Election Study.

themselves apart from their opponents. Invective directed at the policies of other parties, designed to sharpen the perception of difference in voters' minds is one option, but when parties take turns maligning one another's positions, voters can end up dazed and disoriented. Another approach is to forgo discussion of policy altogether and focus political campaigning on catchy slogans and the personalities of political leaders. As parties are drawn into a negative and superficial style of politics – and it is hard for any to stay above the fray if others do not, since such methods do seem to make an impression on the electorate – the average citizen can be forgiven for think- ing that there is little difference among them (though the more knowledge- able and discerning will remain cognizant of important differences in policy and ideological orientation). The possibility arises of a vicious circle wherein lack of political attentiveness on the part of citizens encourages parties to preen and bluster, while this style of politics reinforces citizen perceptions that the political parties are all alike, creating further incentive for the par- ties to resort to unsavoury methods of setting themselves apart (Howe 2001). In places where political knowledge is lacking, political discourse as a whole can come to suffer from a lack of civility and sophistication.

A further result suggesting marked difference in the critical capacities of more and less knowledgeable citizens involves asking whether the media did a good job in the same election campaign (2000) of "informing voters about the parties." The media, of course, are often criticized for contributing to the debasement of electoral politics through their reporting practices: training the spotlight on the party leaders and their personal foibles, freely recycling the gratuitous criticism the parties circulate, highlighting the horse-race aspect of election campaigns, and failing to inform voters about the issues (Taras 2001; Nadeau and Giasson 2005). A more charitable assessment would be that the media do succeed in conveying germane information in and among a certain amount of irrelevant jabber. There is room for debate on the matter, but one would anticipate that some citizens would see the shortcomings in the media's current approach to political journalism and that this might serve to generate pressure for improvement. And indeed some do, but they are again primarily concentrated among the politically conversant. Of those who know little about Canadian politics, only about 15 percent indicated dissatisfaction with the job the media did in the 2000 election campaign, compared to nearly 50 percent among the most knowledgeable (Figure 5.7). Again, political knowledge appears to serve as an important foundation for critical judgment.

This finding speaks to a potential criticism of an implicit assumption in much of the preceding analysis: that consumption of news media unequivocally empowers citizens. It might be argued that the assumption rests on a rather naïve understanding of the quality of the information and diversity of the perspectives offered by mainstream media. Rather than being empowered, citizens who faithfully "follow the news" will instead be imbued with conventional wisdom and be less capable of adopting a critical and independent viewpoint on important issues. The negative assessments of media performance offered by the politically knowledgeable suggest otherwise. Though they use news media more heavily, these politically aware citizens remain more dubious of its value. Some presumably would be inclined to seek alternative media sources or the political viewpoints of others, while most would be likely to take what they hear with a grain of salt, drawing on a deeper knowledge base to derive their own conclusions on important issues. By this reasoning, information garnered from mainstream media is a reasonable starting point for the critical citizen to engage in personal reflection likely to lead to independent judgment.

To highlight an important connection between political knowledge and the critical capacities of citizens is to imply that these capacities would have diminished over time as the knowledge base of the Canadian polity has eroded due to waning knowledge levels among younger generations. Such a position runs counter to the viewpoint of others who believe the critical faculties of citizens have grown more acute over time. Books with titles like *Critical Citizens* (Norris 1999) and *Citizen Politics* (Dalton 2006) contend that the democracies of the developed world have been reshaped for the better by rising education levels among citizens, ever-expanding information resources available to them, and their newfound willingness to challenge authority. It is important, however, to distinguish between capabilities and temperament. Certainly, it would seem true that citizens nowadays have a critical mindset and are more disposed to take an independent stand on a wide range of issues. Distrust of government, for example, is probably a reflection of this as much as it is of changes in the trustworthiness of government. However, this does not necessarily mean citizens have the knowledge base to criticize effectively or constructively.[6] The vacuity of political discontent in the absence of political knowledge is revealed quite starkly when people are asked their views on specific issues related to the functioning of Canadian democracy. Whether it is the fairness of the electoral system (2000 Canadian election study), new political finance laws (2004 election study), the merits of minority government (2004 and 2006), or Senate reform (2004), anywhere from 50 percent to 85 percent of Canadians who know little about politics say they have no opinion on these matters (compared to roughly 5 percent to 15 percent of the most knowledgeable citizens). Yet ask people whether government cares "what people like me think" or whether they are satisfied with Canadian democracy (questions also appearing on recent election studies), and nearly everyone has an opinion, often a negative one.[7] Rather than sharp and reasoned dissent, criticism issuing from the politically uninformed often amounts to little more than amorphous discontent, a genuine enough sentiment, but not one that points to obvious prescriptive action. The constructive impact of political discontent – giving voice to distinctive viewpoints and reform alternatives that might help guide corrective action by government – is significantly diminished in the absence of a broadly knowledgeable citizenry.

Thinking in more practical terms about the relationship between citizen knowledge and critical judgment, it is important to note that the linkage is strongest at the upper end of the political knowledge scale for two of the three measures in Figure 5.7. There is only a slight increase in the percentage who detect differences between the political parties or express critical attitudes towards the media as political knowledge climbs from 0 to 5 – representing, in this case, slightly under half of the respondents – and much more as knowledge increases from 5 to 10. This pattern represents the reverse of the knowledge-voting relationship, where effects were concentrated in the bottom half of the scale, suggesting a caveat to earlier statements about preferred approaches to enhancing political attentiveness among the Canadian citizenry. If exclusive emphasis were placed on improvements at the lower end, the final result might be higher levels of political participation without much enhancement of the critical capacities of citizens, a less than ideal outcome. Greater participation is desirable, but so too is participation by citizens who can think for themselves. This entails a twofold strategy, one aim of which is to bring about greater political equality by ensuring a minimum level of political attentiveness on the part of the greatest possible number. The other is to seek improvements at other points on the spectrum in order to realize the fullest benefits of a more politically attentive citizenry.

Informed Opinion and Policy Preferences

If political knowledge facilitates broad-based political participation and strengthens the critical capacities of citizens, it is also essential to the development of sound judgment on important policy issues of the day. Again the effect is pervasive, as knowledge of relevant factual background has the potential to influence opinion across many different areas. One example worth considering is the plight of Aboriginal peoples, whose struggle to overcome past injustices and present inequities has led many to judge this the most pressing issue of social inequality in contemporary Canada. Most Canadians are far removed from the realities of daily life for Aboriginal peoples. It is, therefore, reasonable to ask if their understanding of Aboriginals' sometimes dire circumstances is accurate and whether this in turn has any bearing on their attitudes towards policies that might help ameliorate the situation.

A question concerning the condition of life for Aboriginals was posed in the 2000 Canadian election study and produced results that many with even passing familiarity with the realities of Aboriginal life would consider surprising. The question asked: "In general would you say Canada's Aboriginal peoples are better off, worse off, or about the same as other Canadians?" The results are not much different from what one would expect if the facts of the matter were actually in dispute: 26 percent said better off, 29 percent about the same, and 39 percent worse off, while 6 percent did not know. This pattern of responses, difficult to fathom at first blush, may partly reflect the fact that the question is open-ended in its wording (not specifying what is meant by better or worse off) and is therefore subject to interpretation. This allows considerations other than a respondent's knowledge of the realities of Aboriginal life to influence the response given. One such consideration, it would appear, is respondents' political ideology. Those who expressed conservative sentiments in response to varied questions about minorities, immigrants, and the welfare state were significantly more likely to say that Aboriginals are better off.[8] In other words, some people appear to give politically coloured responses (whether intentionally or subconsciously) to what is meant to be a matter of factual knowledge. This renders it a less than ideal question for demonstrating knowledge effects on opinion towards Aboriginal policy (Gidengil et al. 2004, 90-97).

To see the results that would obtain if this ideological inflection were removed, a modified question designed to ensure that respondents were focusing on the economic realities of Aboriginal life was posed on the CCES: "Thinking about Canada's Aboriginal peoples, do you think their average incomes are higher or lower than those of other Canadians, or are they just about equal?" Concentrating respondents' attention on this more specific factual proposition does substantially reduce the number of incorrect answers. Only 7 percent say Aboriginal incomes are higher, 15 percent think they are equal, and 74 percent say they are lower (5 percent do not know). Responses to this question also track closely with overall knowledge levels: among the most knowledgeable decile on the CCES, 97 percent correctly respond that Aboriginal incomes are lower (whereas only 69 percent of the most knowledgeable on the 2000 election study correctly responded that Aboriginals are "worse off"). The new question also reveals the age pattern anticipated in light of the abiding political knowledge deficit among the young. Among those under thirty-five, over a third (35 percent) give an incorrect response or do not know, versus only 18 percent of those aged fifty-five to sixty-nine (on the election study question, there are no such age differences). In short, the more focused question on the CCES does seem to be a more unbiased measure of knowledge, revealing the problem of misunderstanding about Aboriginal economic circumstances to be less widespread, but still considerable.

To see if knowledge of those realities is linked to opinion on related policy, a general question was put to respondents: Should government be doing more to help Aboriginal people or is enough being done already? Respondents on the CCES were just about evenly split. Of those who expressed an opinion, 53 percent said more should be done, 47 percent indicated enough is being done already. Moreover, opinion on the matter is closely tied to knowledge of Aboriginal income levels. Those who know that incomes are lower supported doing more by a ratio of six to four, whereas those who feel incomes are higher stood in opposition to such a policy by a ratio of eight to two (Figure 5.8). Though the misinformed are not especially numerous, their strong opposition serves to shift overall opinion from a solid majority in favour of doing more for Aboriginals to a public more or less split down the middle. The higher incidence of misinformation among young Canadians also has consequences for their views: only 49 percent of those aged eighteen to thirty-four want to see more done for Aboriginals compared to 59 percent of those aged fifty-five to sixty-nine, the most knowledgeable age category. This is, then, an example of misinformation with serious consequences, which, if corrected, might well lead to stronger public support for more decisive government action on this front (such as the initiatives outlined in the Kelowna Accord of 2005, cancelled by the Harper government in 2007 with little outcry from anyone other than Aboriginal peoples themselves).

Figure 5.8

Opinion on Aboriginal policy by knowledge of Aboriginal income levels

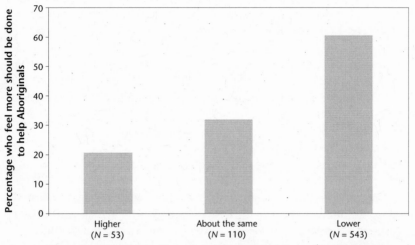

Perception of Aboriginal income levels relative to those of other Canadians

Source: CCES, 2007-08.

As the example demonstrates, political knowledge is important not only to recognizing one's own interests in order to support the policies and parties that will serve them best, it is also an essential prerequisite to fully appreciating the interests and rightful demands of others.

The example of Aboriginal peoples is just one of many where knowledge appears to have a significant influence on public opinion and where it is likely a more informed public would hold different aggregate policy preferences. This general theme is examined at length in the work of Scott Althaus (2003). Other Canadian examples, in areas such as welfare spending, environmental protection, and electoral reform have been provided by other scholars (Gidengil et al. 2004, 72-101; Cutler and Fournier 2007). The point is well established that those who hold factually incorrect views, or simply do not know much about a given issue, are less likely to arrive at judgments consistent with their own values, preferences, and interests (Kam 2005). Recalling some of the knowledge questions described above, some reasonable extrapolations would include: that people who do not know what Canada's commitment was under the Kyoto Accord will be less able to assess whether it matters that we did not make good on those commitments or what our environmental policies should be moving forward; that those who do not know roughly how many Canadian soldiers have died in Afghanistan will be less likely to hold an informed opinion on whether Canada should stay in the country and, if so, whether we should continue in a combat role; that those mistaken about how Canadian tax rates compare to those of other countries may hold inappropriate views on tax policy and levels of government spending; and that people unfamiliar with the prime minister's power of appointment and the extent of party discipline in the House of Commons are less likely to be exercised about the concentration of political power in Canada or to have a well-formed opinion on democratic reform.

The general conclusion from these and earlier examples of the effects of political knowledge is clear: an inattentive citizenry has numerous detrimental consequences both for citizens individually and society collectively. The knowledge deficit among young Canadians, and the larger political attentiveness deficit of which it is part, is a critical facet of their disengagement from politics, and has broad implications for the quality of Canadian democracy.

Part 3
Social Integration

6
Community Attachments

Attentiveness to public affairs is an essential ingredient in political engagement, and the growing gap between young and old in this regard helps explain lower levels of political involvement among young Canadians. Evidence of a strong relationship between attention to politics and political engagement is hardly startling. However, concentrated analysis on the political inattentiveness of young Canadians provides a useful window of exploration into different aspects of the phenomenon and a more refined understanding of the challenges faced in seeking to reverse current trends. A second critical factor giving rise to disengagement among young Canadians is less self-evident because of its pervasiveness and attendant elusiveness: lower levels of social integration among the young. The two key manifestations of the phenomenon explored in this section of the book are the relatively weak attachments to community and the more pronounced individualism that exist among young Canadians. Both have important consequences for the participatory dispositions of the Canadian citizenry and the general nature of Canadian democracy.

Some relevant questions in assessing the state of social integration among younger Canadians were outlined in the introductory sections. These include conceptual matters: elucidation of the concepts of community and individualism, articulation of the linkages between the two, as well as reflection on the potential normative implications of their decline or ascendance over time. There are also empirical questions to address, most obviously (for the purposes of this study) consideration of the dimensions of community attachment and individualism on which younger and older Canadians differ most starkly, and assessment of the relative significance of cohort and life-cycle effects in explaining such age gaps. As will be seen below, there are broad similarities in the pattern of results with those observed above for political inattentiveness: to some extent, weaker social integration among the young appears to represent an abiding feature of the earlier stages of adult life, but in other important ways it seems to reflect distinctive dispositions among birth cohorts coming of age in more recent times. There are finally the democratic implications to consider, entailing an examination of the connections between social integration and civic and political engagement, as well as some consideration of additional consequences relevant to assessing the good and the bad in the changing nature of social integration among younger generations.

These questions are addressed across three chapters: Chapter 6 focuses on the concept of community, Chapter 7 on individualism, and Chapter 8 on political and social consequences, though the separation of subject matter is not entirely strict as effective exposition is better served by some degree of overlapping analysis. The starting point is an account of the evolving state of community attachments among young Canadians. That the bonds of community have gradually weakened down the years is an idea frequently voiced in academic studies and public discourse both in Canada and other places. Background perspective on the issue is provided by reviewing the most prominent such account of recent times, a study of the changing nature of American society, which serves as an illustrative counterpoint to the interpretation of the phenomenon developed here.

Social Capital and Community

The most acclaimed work of recent times on the decline of community is Robert Putnam's *Bowling Alone*. The core of the book is a wide-ranging analysis of trends in participation in social activities, civic and voluntary associations, and public affairs in the US over the past forty years, along with changing social attitudes and norms over the same period. Based on his findings, Putnam concludes that Americans have withdrawn from community life to a disconcerting degree. Most conspicuously absent from the public square are younger Americans, who have failed to follow in the participatory footsteps of earlier generations. While based on strictly American trends, the substance and tenor of Putnam's analysis resonate with the experience of other countries that have been grappling with the problem of democratic disengagement. Academics and public officials in many places have taken note of Putnam's work, using it to shape research agendas and fashion public policy initiatives. Here in Canada, the federal government has launched wide-ranging research programs building on the core ideas set out in *Bowling Alone* (Policy Research Initiative 2005). It is fair to say that Putnam's study has become the benchmark for understanding the social dynamics underpinning democratic disengagement and shaping the policy prescriptions deemed necessary to stem the apparent erosion of community uncovered in his research.

Bowling Alone, as the review in the *Economist* enthused, is a prodigious book. Over the course of more than 500 densely packed pages, Putnam offers an abundance of evidence documenting the changing dynamics of social connectedness in the US, wrapped in a theoretical framework that is intuitively compelling, language that is engaging and persuasive, and backed by methods of analysis that are thorough and rigorous. Yet despite its impressive sweep and undeniable insights, *Bowling Alone* fails to provide a comprehensive framework for understanding the decline of community and its connection to public disengagement.

One reason for this is that the book does not actually spend much time discussing the concept of community, despite its being heralded by the subtitle on the front cover – *The Collapse and Revival of American Community*. The text, however, immediately turns its focus to "social capital," a term coined by scholars early in the twentieth century and revived in recent years to denote social connectedness in action and thought. As Putnam defines it, "social capital refers to connections among individuals – social networks and the norms of reciprocity and trustworthiness that arise from them" (2000, 19). Early sections of *Bowling Alone* focus on the postwar evolution of social capital in the US across diverse arenas of social interaction – in community associations and volunteer organizations, in the workplace, in churches, in the political realm – while later sections trace the causes and consequences of declining social capital and recommendations to reverse the downward trend. The term "community" appears infrequently, resurfacing mainly towards the end, where findings about social capital turn into conclusions about community. Synthesizing in the final chapter, Putnam speaks of the "ebbing of community over the last several decades" (2000, 402) and the importance of a broad-based effort aimed at "restoring American community" (2000, 413).

That a book notionally about community speaks mainly about social capital underlines an important assumption: for Putnam, social capital *is* the essential marrow of community. People feel connected to their community when they are actively involved with those around them: family, friends, neighbours, co-workers, bowling league acquaintances, co-volunteers, fellow congregants, and so on. Out of these social connections, norms of cooperation, trust, and reciprocity emerge, which reinforce the propensity to be socially engaged. This idea, that interpersonal connection fosters positive social norms and vice versa, is a venerable one in the social sciences. Referred to, in other contexts, as the "contact hypothesis," it is a proposition entirely consistent with common sense: contact with others helps us come to know and understand them, to develop empathy and shared understandings. Multiplied in a diffuse manner across many individuals, the result is a web of social connectivity that rightly deserves the name community. But there are other ideas, not quite as self-evident, about how people develop communal bonds. An exploration of social capital, however extensive, will not succeed in capturing the full range of ways that people come to feel connected to one another.

The exclusive emphasis on social capital as the wellspring of community reflects a particular understanding favoured in *Bowling Alone*. When Putnam speaks of community, he is referring to community of a generic variety – a sense of trust in and goodwill towards people in general, of no particular range or shape. If Putnam sometimes places emphasis on local *interactions* – at various points he speaks of the importance of face-to-face interaction, which for all but the most jet-setting among us means knowing and engaging with those in our local area – this is not to be taken as a statement in favour of local *sentiment*. Instead, interaction with those in our immediate surroundings is important because it involves real human contact, a more effective way of fostering understanding and shared norms than impersonal ties across longer distances. The type of community sentiment Putnam has in mind is probably best captured by a question about trust frequently posed on social surveys and treated as an important measure of social capital in *Bowling Alone*: "Generally speaking would you say most people can be trusted or you cannot be too careful in dealing with people?" Certainly, others have taken this to be the key attitudinal measure of social capital, using survey respondents' feelings about the trustworthiness of people in general to draw conclusions about the state of community in various places.

This is one reasonable way to think about of the concept of community, but there are others as well. Instead of general community spirit, community is sometimes used to refer to specific groups of people who share a sense of belonging, commitment, and trust. One obvious example, of considerable importance to world history, is the attachment people feel to national communities: their commitment and affinity towards fellow Canadians, Americans, and so on. People in particular regions or provinces also sometimes exhibit strong feelings of mutual attachment that merit the designation community, as do ethno-cultural groups that sometimes demonstrate the strength of their shared commitment by seeking political autonomy or outright independence. The kinds of survey questions that tap into these attachments are more pointed and specific: How attached do you feel to Canada? Do you tend to think of yourself as an Albertan? How important is being Québécois to your personal identity? While citing a vast array of survey data, no cognate questions relating to the US are invoked in *Bowling Alone*. Instead, all measures of community sentiment are questions tapping people's general attitudes towards generic others. Thus the subtitle of the book, *The Collapse and Revival of American Community*, is properly read as the collapse of community spirit in contemporary America, not collapse in attachment to the American national community or other more strictly defined communities within the US.

In considering the place of social capital in the writings of those who have sought to understand the nature and origins of the attachments people have to specific communities, particular large-scale loyalties to nation, region, or ethno-cultural group, it is the absence of any references to the concept (or similar concepts that predate that term's widespread adoption in the early 1990s) that is most notable. The one scholar who perhaps came closest to developing a "social capital" account of national attachment was Karl Deutsch, an early exponent of the behaviouralist approach in political science. First presented in his book *Nationalism and Social Communication* in the early 1950s, Deutsch's theory treated national sentiment as a function of effective communication between individuals, positing that "membership in a people ... consists in the ability to communicate more effectively, and over a wider range of subjects, with members of one large group than with outsiders" (1969, 97). This ability, the theory held, was cultivated through personal interactions among community members, or what Deutsch described as "intensive communication among contemporaries" (1969, 120). Applying his ideas in the 1960s to a case of "incipient community formation" (1967, 228), he argued that continued progress in integrating the six member states of the then fledgling European Economic Community was dependent upon the flow of communications between the people of Europe, measured through such concrete indicators of social and economic interaction as "trade, travel, postal correspondence and the exchange of students" (1967, 219). This research agenda never really took off, however, as this way of thinking about the basis of large-scale communal attachments came to be superseded by new understandings of what these communities are and how their members come to feel connected to one another.

The key insight, articulated in various ways by different thinkers, is that attachments to large-scale communities do not emerge solely from lived experience but instead reflect an abstract feeling of connectedness among their members generated by a shared sense of themselves as a people. As Benedict Anderson, the most celebrated exponent of the idea, puts it, "the members of even the smallest nation will never know most of their fellow-members, meet them, or even hear of them, yet in the minds of each lives the image of their communion" (1991, 6). Anderson uses an evocative phrase to capture this quintessential quality of nations, describing them as "imagined communities." Understanding national attachments, by this account, entails plumbing the imagining process that sustains a sense of community in the hearts and minds of millions of far-flung strangers. The accounts that have emerged from previous reflection on the matter are many and varied, partly because on this interpretation national attachments are more ideational than tangible, and therefore rather subjective and elusive, and partly because the answer depends on the historical period and particular nations considered. Anderson, in the first part of his wide-ranging work, seeks to uncover the earliest origins of nations and develops an innovative argument suggesting that the invention of the printing press was a critical development because it allowed for the development of standardized languages in place of the motley oral dialects that were the principal form of communication in earlier times. It became easier for individuals spread across a large geographic expanse to imagine themselves as one people when they shared a common written (and eventually spoken) language. For others interested in understanding the powerful consolidation of nationalist sentiment in the nineteenth century, the role of schools (backed by the power of the modernizing state) in implanting feelings of national belonging in the young is often emphasized (Weber 1976, 332-38; Hobsbawm 1990, 91-96). Quebec political scientist Louis Balthazar, on the other hand, offers a twentieth-century application of Anderson's thesis about how ideas of community are transmitted through new media, suggesting that the introduction of television and the establishment of a French public network in Canada in the 1950s meant that Quebecers were henceforth exposed on a daily basis to "a mirror of themselves forming a nation" (1993, 8). This greatly contributed to the emergence of a more defined sense of Quebec identity in that decade. Thus have various scholars sought to understand the myriad ways in which peoples in different places and at different times have come to feel a sense of attachment and commitment to millions of nameless, faceless others. It is rare to find any who would suggest such sentiment is mainly a function of the types of social interaction and connectedness – joining associations, volunteering, having dinner with neighbours, bowling in leagues – that underwrite the generic community feeling Putnam stresses in *Bowling Alone*.

Recognizing this other category opens up new ways of thinking about the decline of community and its relationship to disengagement. If community encompasses Putnam's amorphous community spirit, with its origins in tangible social connectedness, *and* attachments to specific large-scale communities based on connections as much imagined as real, then an examination of the erosion of community and its effects on disengagement among younger generations must include both. So too must the search for solutions predicated on the idea of reinvigorating community. There may well be merit in seeking to strengthen particular attachments rather than simply encouraging social connectedness and community spirit in general – in promoting a reinvigorated Canadian identity, to be unambiguous, rather than simply building social capital among Canadians.[1]

The merits of this alternative strategy may not be immediately obvious. One of the attractive features of the generic conception of community implicit in Putnam's work is precisely that it is amorphous, radiating outward from community-spirited individuals in a diffuse and undiscriminating manner. Perhaps it dissipates with distance (Putnam doesn't really specify), but it presumably has no fixed point at which it is disappears completely because it involves no principled distinctions between insiders and outsiders. In contrast, specific communities – whether national, regional, provincial, or ethno-cultural – are predicated on a clear demarcation of those inside and outside the fold (Howe 2005). In the case of the Canadian national community, for example, the radius of belonging emanates outward in an undiscriminating manner – the stranger in Port Alberni, British Columbia, is as much a fellow Canadian to me as the stranger in nearby Moncton – but stops short at clearly marked borders. The bond felt to fellow Canadians, wherever they may reside, is stronger than the attachment to those living just across the border in Bangor, Maine. All particularist communities, be they geopolitical, ethno-cultural, or otherwise, have these conceptual and real-world borders that mark some as part of the community and others as outsiders. Some are more easily traversed by outsiders than others: Canada does admit new citizens who come to feel as Canadian as the next person; people do move between regions of the country and experience a change in regional allegiance; Quebec nationalists try their level best to bring cultural minorities into the Québécois fold. Yet none is as permeable as Putnam's more nebulous aura of community spirit. In a world where the distinction between insiders and outsiders, between those of my kind and those not, has been a major source of enmity and strife, why push for the continuation of such distinctions? Even if some dividing lines are less invidious than others – that between Canadians and Americans, for example – the exclusiveness intrinsic to specific community attachments is not something we should be actively promoting. The wiser course is to foster community spirit in general and downplay particular communal loyalties that have the effect of undermining more indiscriminate comity.

As an abstract ideal, there is something to be said for this argument, but as a practical approach to contending with weakening bonds of community and the impact on public engagement it fails to take account of important realities. The strict demarcation of insiders and outsiders that can be seen as a disconcerting feature of our attachments to nations, provinces, and the like also has a positive side. These perimeters of community serve, in many cases, as borders presided over by governments that have the power to effect significant change. In such instances, a strong communal identity becomes an important resource allowing government to move forcefully in many realms as it acts on behalf of a people with a sense of shared commitment and common purpose. It is this sort of reasoning that has been invoked by philosopher David Miller, a defender of nationalism in moderation, when he suggests that national sentiment is what underwrites support for the welfare state: we willingly contribute to the maintenance of universal social programs because we feel a strong sense of obligation to other members of our national community (1995, 92-96). It is not clear that a more nebulous sense of goodwill and trust towards others would produce the same willingness to sacrifice on behalf of strangers. Equally important is the connection running from government action back to community: if a cohesive national identity can empower governments to act with purpose and conviction, so too can decisive government action to positive ends strengthen national identity and civic commitment (Mettler 2007). Thus government itself is potentially an important vehicle for reinforcing the bonds of community. Nor do these dynamics between community and government have to revolve exclusively around inward-looking sentiment and action. A strong sense of national identity is entirely consistent with initiatives designed to help those in other parts of the world through mechanisms such as foreign aid, support for human rights, mutually fruitful economic exchange, and/or forceful intervention on behalf of the oppressed. The argument has been made that a renewed emphasis on making a real difference in the world on these lines would be entirely in keeping with the history and values of the Canadian people (Cohen 2003; Byers 2007). And actions of this sort, if carried out with conviction and success, would almost certainly serve to reinforce our sense of national community. The reality is that the attachments we hold to specific communities – nation, but also sometimes region or province – are closely bound to government-led action and the achievement of important social and political goals.

This is not to say that social capital is without practical benefit, but the manner of its contribution is less closely tied to activity in the public realm. Across the wide range of positive consequences enumerated by Putnam, the consistent focus is on the benefits social capital provides over and above what public action alone is able to accomplish. Thus Putnam suggests that social capital leads to healthier populations not because people who feel part of a strong community demand high-quality health care services for one and all, but because people who are socially connected enjoy support networks that offer practical and psychological benefits conducive to well-being (2000, 326-35). Likewise, economic prosperity results not from individuals committed to their community's well-being insisting on public support for high-quality education or economic development strategies in the general interest, but from the lubrication of commercial networks linking self-interested economic actors (2000, 319-25). In fairness, this emphasis on what society does for itself through the mechanisms of social capital, rather than what society achieves collectively through the vehicle of government, is deliberate. Putnam's intent, his key insight many might say, is to demonstrate the significant and independent contribution of social dynamics to fair and effective public policy. But to the extent social capital is treated as the sum and substance of community, this insight runs the danger of limiting our understanding of the ways that community, good governance, and public commitment are linked. It entirely leaves aside that category of community most intimately connected to the public realm, which remains a critical arena for the realization of social progress and citizen engagement.

There is, then, reason to avoid wholesale adoption of the analytical framework of community implicit in *Bowling Alone*. In the dense thicket of statistics, analysis, and anecdote presented by Putnam, it is easy to lose sight of the book's omission of a category of community that is an integral part of how people feel connected to one another in the modern world, which is closely tied to purposeful public policy, and which may have considerable relevance to the apparent weakening of community bonds among younger generations. Alongside social connectedness and generic community spirit, consideration must be given to the particular community attachments that structure our conception of the public realm and lend meaning and motivation to engagement in public affairs. A broader analysis of this sort is more likely to produce fruitful analysis of the current state of community attachment among young Canadians and ideas about how we might go about strengthening any eroding connectivity.

Social Capital and Community Attachments in Canada

An ideal source for exploring these ideas further is the 2003 General Social Survey on social engagement carried out by Statistics Canada. This is the same study used in Chapters 1 and 2 to explore patterns of participation among younger and older Canadians. Three questions from that survey served to signal at the outset the importance of weak community attachments to processes of disengagement among young Canadians. All, it might be noted, were questions about *specific* community attachments: how strongly attached respondents felt to their local community, to their province, and to Canada. The latter two are clearly directed towards defined populations, while the first, though not defining local to mean any specific group or geographic locale, would presumably conjure up such a setting in each respondent's mind – their own town, village, city, or area within a large metropolitan area, along with the denizens thereof. Combined into a single index, these community attachments were shown to be considerably weaker among younger Canadians and to have considerable influence on different sorts of public involvement, political and otherwise. Other questions from the survey probe trust in others, the key indicator of generic community sentiment emphasized by Putnam and others. The Statistics Canada study also measured some key behavioural indicators of social capital. Three that are typically considered integral in the social capital literature are used in the analysis below: the number of organized groups in which people are involved, whether they volunteer, and how many people in their neighbourhood they know. The first two were also part of the preliminary analysis in Part 1 of the book, used in assessing the degree to which young Canadians are engaged in civic activities beyond the manifestly political. They now are conceptualized slightly differently, as key markers of social connectedness as articulated by Putnam. That all these questions appear together in a single study allows for comparative evaluation of different interpretations of the decline of community thesis as it applies to Canada.

The principal method of pursuing this analysis is to take a closer look at age differences with respect to these various measures of community and social capital. In doing so, we remain sensitive to the critical distinction between life-cycle and cohort effects. Where younger Canadians show signs of weaker community attachments, diminished levels of trust, or lower levels of social connectedness than older Canadians, should this be seen as a temporary condition reflecting their stage of life, or an abiding characteristic reflecting something distinctive about the cohorts to which they belong? And where life-cycle and cohort effects appear, what are the underlying processes that might be giving rise to these patterns? In considering these questions, it is worth recalling Putnam's conclusion that generational differences are the single most important source of declining social capital in the US. Starting with the youth of the early 1960s, successive cohorts of young people have been less socially connected and involved than those who preceded them. This has resulted in a significant ebbing of social capital that is set to continue into the future should nothing be done, as socially disengaged generations come to constitute ever more of the American population. If community and social capital can be equated, as Putnam implies, this translates into a pronounced and ongoing erosion of community. Should the same empirical trends appear in Canada (and if we accept the conceptual assumptions), there would be merit in pursuing the social capital-building strategies outlined by Putnam and others inspired by his work.

Before turning to age patterns, however, the starting point is to take note of important differences in the relationship between the key behavioural elements of social connectedness – group involvements, volunteering, and knowing one's neighbours – and different categories of community sentiment. Despite the centrality to his overall thesis of the idea that various forms of social involvement and (generic) community sentiments are linked, there is not much empirical analysis of these relationships in Putnam's study. Particular elements of social capital are instead analyzed serially, the relationship between them mentioned only sporadically and in passing (2000, 151).

To examine these connections in the Canadian case, Figure 6.1 brings together the three social connectedness measures – group involvements, volunteering, and knowing neighbours – in a single scale, running from 0 to 9 along the horizontal axis. Those at the low end of the scale (4.1 percent of the population) are involved in no groups,[2] do not volunteer,[3] and report knowing nobody in their neighbourhood. Those at the high end (2.9 percent of the population) belong to three or more groups, volunteer at least one hour per month, and know "most" of the people in their neighbourhood. Between these two extremes are people who are involved in social networks and connected to those around them in varying degrees.

Figure 6.1

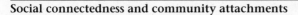

Social connectedness and community attachments

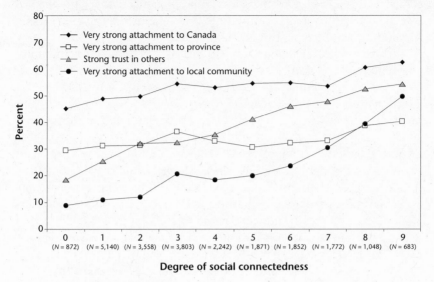

Source: Statistics Canada, GSS 17 (2003).

The lines on the graph trace the relationship between this index of social connectedness on the one hand, and community sentiments, as conceptualized and measured in various ways, on the other. Consider first social trust, the key attitudinal barometer in Putnam's conception of community. The two questions from the Statistics Canada survey that ask about trust in generic others are combined to create a single trust scale.[4] Figure 6.1 shows the percentage scoring at the upper end of this scale at different levels of social connectedness. Trust in others rises sharply in moving across the graph, climbing from 18 percent among the most socially atomized individuals to 54 percent among those most connected to others through group involvement, volunteering activity, and neighbourly acquaintance. This central assumption of Putnam's, that social connectedness is strongly linked to community spirit as gauged by social trust, is strongly supported in these Canadian figures.

Set against this robust relationship, the associations between social connectedness and specific community attachments – in particular those to province and country – are rather flat. Among those at the bottom end of the social connectedness scale, 29 percent report a very strong attachment to their province. Moving across the graph the figure climbs slowly, reaching 40 percent among those at the top end of the scale. Attachment to Canada shows a slightly stronger relationship, rising from 45 percent to 62 percent. But again, this does not match the powerful connection between social connectedness and trust in others. The proposition that social connectedness is less critical to particular community attachments than it is to generic community sentiment is strongly supported.

Yet there is one exception to this pattern. The trend for *local* community attachments slopes sharply upward across the spectrum of social connectedness. The starting point at the left side of the graph is relatively low – local attachments are generally not as strong as those to province or country – but the upward slope across the page is steep. Whereas only 9 percent of the most socially disconnected Canadians say they have a very strong attachment to their local community, fully 50 percent of the most connected do so. At first blush, this result might seem a simple matter of common sense. People involved in groups, volunteering, and getting to know neighbours are directly brought in touch with those in their local community, so naturally there would be a strong connection to feelings of belonging to that community. But this way of stating the matter actually presumes a great deal. After all, doesn't being involved in groups, volunteering, and knowing one's neighbours also serve to bring people directly in touch with fellow Canadians? And with fellow members of their provincial community? It does, of course, but the critical point is that we do not tend to *think* about it this way. It is this that is revealed in the relatively weak relationship between social connectedness and national and provincial attachments, as well as in the natural presumption that activities taking us out of our homes to interact with others nearby serve to bring us in touch with the local community, but not the provincial or national.[5]

If not social connectedness, then something else must help explain our feelings of attachment to (and detachment from) province and nation, of which more below. First, however, a further look at the relationship between age and these various measures reveals more clues about the general contours of community attachments in Canada and the nature of the "decline of community" that may be contributing to disengagement among the young. Figure 6.2 displays the relationship between age and the three measures of social connectedness (groups, volunteering, and knowing neighbours). The Statistics Canada survey here affords two significant advantages. First, because nearly 25,000 Canadians were surveyed; narrow age categories can be considered without undermining the reliability of the results (though we are limited to the categories provided in the dataset). Second, the inclusion of those as young as fifteen allows for examination of a somewhat greater span of the adolescent and young adulthood years than would typically be the case.

The patterns revealed are both striking and consistent. The most socially connected Canadians are the very youngest ones on the survey, teens aged

Figure 6.2

Social connectedness by age

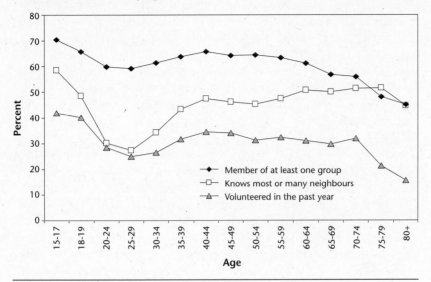

Note: Total *N* = 24,525, minimum *N* = 754.
Source: Statistics Canada, GSS 17 (2003).

fifteen to seventeen. From this high point of mid-adolescence, social engagement drops rapidly through to the late twenties. The importance of a fine-
grained analysis is clear. If everyone under thirty were grouped together,
those in their twenties would outnumber the adolescents and drag down
the overall average. This would lead to the misleading conclusion that young
Canadians on the whole are less socially connected than older adults and
obscure the substantial change taking place across the teen and early adult
years. Nor are gaps in social involvement between different groups of younger
Canadians the only differences of note. The low point of the late twenties
is followed by a considerable increase in social connectedness from the early
thirties through to middle age, followed by a levelling off until the golden
years and then a final drop, sharpest in the case of volunteering, around age
seventy-five.

These peaks and valleys point clearly towards a powerful *life-cycle* pattern
of social connectedness. With the topography mapped out, the reasons
behind the pattern are not hard to discern. Life-cycle variation in knowing
neighbours is the most straightforward. Many teenagers, still at home with
parents, have lived in the same place for a reasonably long period and consequently know many in their neighbourhood. When they move out of the
family home in their twenties and become more mobile for a number of

years, often living in neighbourhoods where others are equally itinerant, familiarity with neighbours decreases substantially. At a certain point, often not until their thirties nowadays, most settle in a particular place for a longer period and consequently are more likely to know their neighbours from that point forward – until old age produces physical and other challenges that make it more difficult for some to stay acquainted with those living nearby. Patterns of involvement with groups and volunteering can similarly be traced to life circumstances prevailing at different points. Residential stability probably contributes to both types of social involvement, so adolescents are advantaged over young adults in this way. Virtually all teenagers are still in school as well, where opportunities to become engaged in certain activities are considerable. Indeed, sometimes these are opportunities students can't refuse: forty hours of volunteering was a requirement for graduation in Ontario high schools at the time of the Statistics Canada survey in 2003 (and has since become a requirement in British Columbia and Newfoundland, as well as all three territories). But volunteering among teens is not simply a reflection of involuntary enlistment – with Ontario respondents excluded, there is still a sharp decline in volunteering rates from adolescence (35 percent) to the late twenties (24 percent). The diminished involvement of early adulthood likely reflects new circumstances of that stage of life: mobility limits opportunities for volunteering and group involvement, while preoccupation with personal priorities – pursuing postsecondary education, starting a career, meeting a life partner – reduces the time and inclination to be involved in these ways. Once settled into their adult lives, however, people gradually become more active in groups and volunteering, until advanced age limits the ability of some to participate and contribute to the extent they once did.

To say there is clearly a life-cycle pattern underlying social connectedness in these Canadian data is not to discount the possibility of cohort effects. One survey from one point in time can provide fairly compelling evidence of life-cycle dynamics, if distinctive patterns that can be sensibly traced to different life stages are uncovered, but it cannot rule out the presence of cohort effects that might *also* be at play. Cohort effects in this instance would mean that young people today are starting off at a different point on measures of social connectedness than young Canadians of the past – a lower point, presumably, if Putnam's findings about the US do indeed carry over to Canada – and even as they move through the ups and downs of the life cycle, they will remain at a different level at each stage of life from those who went before them. But while this possibility cannot be ruled out definitively, neither is it supported in any way by this single survey snapshot. What is clear is that on some basic benchmarks, measures that Putnam considers important indicators of social capital, there is a manifest life-cycle logic that explains at least some of the differences between age groups in Canada. While this account is acknowledged as a possibility in Putnam's study, his analysis of age differences concentrates heavily on cohort effects, his conclusions on the attendant spectre of a steady erosion of the social underpinnings of community in the US. The fact that Canadian data affording a detailed look at age-based variations in social connectedness point to rather different conclusions suggests that the study of social capital in the US might benefit from renewed scrutiny of life-cycle patterns. On that note, at least two American studies (both using relatively fine-grained age categories and including respondents as young as fifteen) find evidence of life course variations similar to those detected here for both composite measures of civic engagement (Zukin et al. 2006, 66) and volunteering (Wattenberg 2008, 181).

These first two findings provide initial insight into the contours of community in the Canadian context and relevant variations across age groups. First, some community sentiments (general trust in others and local community attachments) are closely linked to social connectedness, while others (provincial and national attachments) are not. Second, the relationship between age and basic measures of social connectedness reveals clear life-cycle effects. From these two results, a third would be anticipated: that those community sentiments most closely linked to social connectedness will show a similar rhythm of change as people move through different stages of life, while the others will not necessarily do so.

This is in fact the case. Figure 6.3 starts by considering changes in trust over the life cycle.[6] Since trust is significantly influenced not only by age but also by education, and since age groups differ considerably in their average levels of educational attainment (adolescent respondents are still in high school, while young adults are more likely to have university degrees than older adults), it is necessary to look at age patterns within four different groups: those with less than a high school education, those with a high school diploma, those with a technical or community college education, and those with a university education. The youngest respondents are dropped from the graph for the postsecondary education categories that they are too young to have entered or completed.[7] The figure reveals that the age patterns for social connectedness are broadly mirrored in levels of social trust. For the two lower educational categories, there is evidence of a sharp decline in trust as people move from adolescence into their twenties, followed by steady growth thereafter. For the two postsecondary education categories, the same steady increase from early to later adulthood is apparent, as is a downward turn in trust among the oldest respondents. As expected, changing patterns of social connectedness over the life cycle do seem to engender variation in levels of social trust.

Figure 6.3

Social trust by age and education

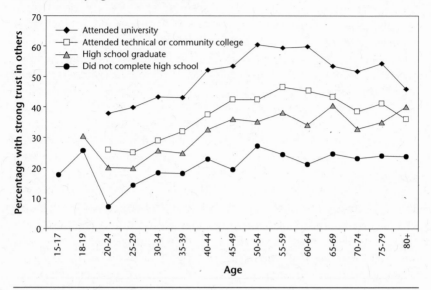

Note: Total *N* = 22,460, minimum *N* = 80.
Source: Statistics Canada, GSS 17 (2003).

Turning to the other important form of community sentiment, feelings of belonging to specific communities, Figure 6.4 displays the pattern of local, provincial, and national attachments across age groups (since education has little effect on these attachments, there is no need to look at educational categories separately). Two lines are drawn for local attachments, one showing the percentage who have "very strong" attachments to their local community, the other those who have either "very" or "somewhat" strong attachments. A fairly clear picture emerges: feelings of local belonging, shown above to be closely associated with social connectedness, follow the familiar life-cycle pattern. This is most apparent for the upper line showing those with strong or somewhat strong attachments. From a relatively high starting point among teens, attachments to local community drop sharply as people move into their twenties, then rise steadily until reaching a peak among those in their early seventies, only to dip once again in the twilight years of life.

Set against these results, the age patterns for provincial and Canadian attachments are at once distinctive and disconcerting. The ups and downs that mark trust in others and local community attachments, and which are seemingly tied to changing life circumstances over the lifespan, are nowhere

Figure 6.4

Community attachments by age

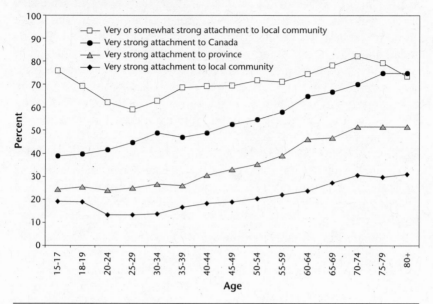

Note: Total *N* = 24,281, minimum *N* = 735.
Source: Statistics Canada, GSS 17 (2003).

to be seen. Instead, there is a consistent rise in provincial and national attachments in moving across the graph from young to old, which is to say, a consistent decline in moving backwards from old to young. This conclusion is barely altered when Quebec is omitted from the calculations, on the suspicion that these results might be influenced by the atypical mix of loyalties to province and country among those of a sovereigntist bent: strong provincial attachments among non-Quebecers fall from 52 percent among the oldest respondents to 21 percent among the youngest, strong Canadian attachments from 78 percent to 44 percent.

Conceivably, such differences across the adult lifespan could represent life-cycle effects, meaning that attachments to province and country start off weak but strengthen gradually and steadily as people age (Stolle and Cruz 2005, 90). Life-cycle patterns can take different shapes depending on the underlying factors giving rise to them. There is a general tendency, however, for such change to be curvilinear, that is to say, greatest in early adulthood and more modest later on. In part, this is because the major life events thought to give rise to attitudinal change (embarking upon a career, marriage, residential stability) are concentrated in these earlier years; in part, it is because people tend to become more set in their ideas and sentiments at a certain point. Such attitudinal crystallization is not evident here, however, as differences in attachment to Canada are essentially constant across age groups, while the greatest movement in provincial attachments lies in the thirty-five to sixty-five age range. Moreover, it is difficult to imagine what underlying mechanism would give rise to relatively consistent changes in feelings of belonging to province and country across the *entire* age spectrum of adulthood. What life events or experiences would continue to generate steady increments in community attachment as people move from early adulthood to their middle years and on through the later stages of life? As others have argued (Norris 2003), the more plausible interpretation of this type of trend is that life-cycle change is not in fact a principal source of age differences. Instead, cohort effects are responsible: something made older generations feel a strong sense of attachment to province and country, and something has been steadily sapping those attachments among rising generations. Herein lies the disconcerting element, since a pattern of abiding cohort differences portends continued erosion in aggregate levels of attachment to province and country as time moves on. If this interpretation is correct, this is an important trend deserving greater attention than it has hitherto received, for it is here that the "decline of community" is most manifest in Canada.

These conclusions about the life-cycle and cohort effects embodied in age differences in community attachments and social connectedness can be bolstered by other evidence. If the supposition is correct that age differences in social connectedness and interpersonal trust are primarily a reflection of life course variation, they should exhibit relatively little aggregate change over time, for only cohort effects produce such change. To determine if this is so, there is not much Canadian material to draw on, certainly nothing that matches the rich body of survey data that Putnam draws on for his longitudinal analysis of social capital trends in the US. However, a few relevant comparisons of past and present can be drawn by utilizing questions posed on the Canadian Citizen Engagement Survey (CCES). These items were replicated from a study conducted thirty years earlier, the Social Change in Canada study carried out by researchers at York University, which involved three national surveys conducted in 1977, 1979, and 1981.[8] Figure 6.5 displays comparisons for questions asking about working with others in the community in the past five years to solve some community problem;[9] feeling part of the neighbourhood in which one lives; the number of neighbours known by name; and the standard interpersonal trust question (the more current comparison for this last question comes from Statistics Canada's 2003 General Social Survey, as this particular item was not included in the CCES).[10] These measures are taken to be indicators of community "on the ground," the tangible connections and sentiments that link us to those in

Figure 6.5

Social capital in Canada, past and present

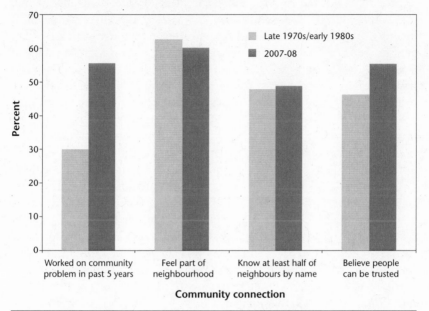

Sources: Social Change in Canada, 1977 and 1981; Statistics Canada, GSS 17 (2003); CCES, 2007-08.

our immediate vicinity. It is evident from Figure 6.5 that none has suffered any sharp aggregate decline in recent decades. Involvement with community problems has jumped significantly, trust in others has increased moderately, while manifestations of neighbourliness, both knowing neighbours and feeling part of the neighbourhood, have held steady over time. The first of these trends can also be seen in the US, where researchers have compiled data showing that working with others on community problems has increased by about 10 percentage points since the late 1960s (Wattenberg 2008, 186). The apparent increase in trust among Canadians, on the other hand, stands in contrast to Putnam's findings for the US, which reveal a decrease from about the 55 percent level to the 35 percent level over the period stretching from 1960 to 1999 (Putnam 2000, 140). Granted, the sharpest decline in the US occurred between the late 1960s and early 1980s, so the starting point for the Canadian data (1977) may postdate changes that had already taken place in this country. Nonetheless, it is reassuring that there has been upward movement in levels of social trust since that time, at least as measured on the General Social Survey of 2003.

If the absence of aggregate change over time is consistent with a life-cycle interpretation of lower levels of social capital among young adults, the contrary expectation for national and provincial attachments is that some gradual erosion should have occurred, as younger cohorts less committed to province and country have taken the place of older generations more deeply imbued with these sentiments. Evidence to this effect is difficult to uncover, however. There are, to my knowledge, no surveys from earlier periods using "attachment" questions akin to those on the 2003 General Social Survey. Cognate questions asking about pride in Canada, meanwhile, have produced contradictory results. On the World Values Survey, the percentage saying they are "very proud" to be Canadian moved from 62.2 percent in 1981, to 60.2 percent in 1990, to 67.1 percent in 2000. However, this series is compromised by the fact that in 2000 a series of earlier questions on the survey asked respondents about national achievements in different areas (e.g., cultural, economic, political, sporting) that made them proud of Canada, a design liable to produce upward bias in responses to the general national pride question. Another longitudinal comparison based on questions asking about pride in Canada reports a sharp drop in the percentage feeling very proud to be Canadian from 80 percent in 1985 to 61 percent in 2004. Outside Quebec, the decline was smaller, but still considerable, from 85 percent to 71 percent (Geddes 2006).[11] This result suggests a change in the expected direction, though evidence based on just one item from two time points is clearly rather limited.

In this analysis, there lies some querying of Putnam's assumptions and conclusions regarding the American case, including his conceptual understanding of community and the contribution of life-cycle variation to age differences in social capital. Further research and analysis of the American case would be needed to buttress this critique. For the Canadian case, the conclusions, if not definitive, are more solidly grounded in empirical evidence. The decline of community in this country does not appear to reflect significant erosion in social connectedness and allied sentiments of trust and local belonging. Instead, the empirical evidence at hand suggests the decline primarily reflects the weakening attachment among younger Canadians to large-scale communities, both provincial and national.

The following section offers a theoretical interpretation of these trends with a twofold purpose. The first is to provide an explanation of why a gradual decline in attachments to large-scale community would have occurred among younger generations of Canadians. The second is to bolster the empirical case by demonstrating how such attachments can be seen as part and parcel of broader social changes of the postwar period that are generally conceded to be generational in nature.

Imagined Communities in Current Times
Understanding the apparent erosion of large-scale community attachments among younger generations of Canadians requires further consideration of

the origins of these sentiments. Social connectedness is of limited value here, as it simply does not appear to have much bearing on identities of this sort. There is more insight to be gained from reflecting on Benedict Anderson's observation that the puzzle of national attachments is that they wed us deeply to millions of people we do not know and never will. Nations are, in this sense, imagined communities requiring some sort of imagining process to come into being and remain vital over time. Two questions arise: what are the key elements of the imagining process – in general and in the Canadian case specifically – and what might be weakening their influence among younger generations?

The imagining process Anderson describes as the origin of nations – a reconceptualization of the horizons of community in the age of the printing press that is partly an account of how the very idea of nations came into being and partly an account of how the earliest nations moved from a state of oblivion to self-awareness – is far removed from the Canadian experience. Canada is a nation that came into being much later in history, at a point when the idea of nations was firmly established, numerous nations existed already, and the creation of new ones had become a relatively conscious and deliberate process. Yet for all the strategic manipulation involved, there was also imagination at play – political vision and a willingness to transcend past loyalties in favour of a new conception of national community – in the developments that saw Canada take shape out of its colonial roots in the nineteenth century (Saul 1998). The efforts of Louis Lafontaine and Robert Baldwin in the 1840s to bridge the French-English divide that had defined Canada for nearly a century and to work together in wresting control of Canada's domestic affairs from appointed British governors were bold endeavours that laid the groundwork for the formation of the new country. Likewise Confederation, for all the complex and sometimes nefarious motives involved, required political vision and leadership to transcend provincial interests in favour of a new national frame of mind (LaSelva 1996). This is not to suggest that everyone was enthusiastic about the project, for clearly there were objections to Canadian unity at the time and have been ever since. It is simply to outline the type of process that gave rise to the idea of Canada and its subsequent (imperfect) realization.

The initial act of envisioning a group of diverse colonies as something potentially greater than the sum of its parts is one part of the imagining process relevant to Canada's existence, but its significance to our sense of national belonging has diminished over time. For once a national vision assumes concrete form – a defined territory and government, the symbols and trappings of nationhood, policies involving the pooling of resources, and efforts to support common national endeavours – it enjoys a certain self-sustaining presence that obviates the need for wilful imagining. So whereas some have emphasized the necessity of constant reaffirmation to sustain national bonds over time – nineteenth-century French philosopher Ernest Renan's famous essay describing the nation as a "daily plebiscite" comes to mind (1996) – this exaggerates the degree of conscious effort required. Once established, nations assume a pervasive presence in people's lives and are principally maintained in an unconscious manner through processes of social conditioning and reinforcement (Billig 1995). Children are imbued by family and society with a sense of national identity from the earliest age: as studies of political socialization have shown, awareness of national identity is one of their first cognitions with respect to the political world (Hess and Torney 1968, 30-37). Perhaps part of this can be attributed to engaging the imagination of the young through enlightenment about the origins of the nation – teaching them the history of its incipient struggles, underscoring that it might never have come into being but for the foresight and courage of their forebears. But the more dominant mechanism, at work before children ever set foot in a classroom, let alone experience a history lesson, is the etching of the national idea upon their fledgling social and political consciousness. The bottom line is that once nations are established, there is (somewhat ironically) little imagination required on the part of individuals, just acceptance of a pervasive social idea that treats membership in the nation as an attribute inherited at birth.

Yet national attachment is not quite as simple and automatic as this. There is a third, more dynamic element beyond the establishment and basic sustenance of the national idea: the potential *re-imagining* of the nation at later points that can lend national sentiments fresh vitality and meaning over time. This is the sort of process described by Louis Balthazar when he suggests that the introduction of television and the production of Québécois programming in the 1950s allowed Quebecers to see themselves in a way they never had before, energizing and transforming a pre-existing sense of community. Other developments aside from new media of communication, discussed below, can also breathe fresh life into national communities, imparting a sense of common purpose and commitment that goes beyond mere acceptance of a social given.

How then to conceptualize attachment to Canada in contemporary times? In part, it represents an inherited identity based on processes of socialization that inexorably impart the idea of Canada to each new generation. In part, it embodies a more dynamic and vibrant element that is contingent on the reinvention of what Canada means over time. From this, two factors likely to have contributed to the erosion of Canadian identity can be identified. The first relates to the socialization dimension. It is not that the process has broken down, that younger generations are somehow failing to take on board the idea that they are Canadian. Identity as a Canadian remains an entrenched part of the self-conception of virtually every Canadian, young and old. The point, however, is that insofar as it is nothing more than this, it fails to resonate with younger Canadians for the simple reason that *inherited identities are less meaningful to younger generations*. This renders the second buttress of national attachment all the more critical. As the inherited dimension of Canadian identity has receded, the strength of national attachment among younger generations has come to be more dependent on processes of reinvention to lend it greater meaning and substance. However, *the process of reinvention has faltered* in recent times. National identity, diminished due to the compromised state of inherited attachments, has not been revitalized with anything new.

To elaborate on these arguments: the first, that inherited identities are less meaningful to younger generations, should be seen not as an isolated phenomenon but instead as part of a broader set of changes that have seen shifts in the basic values and dispositions of younger generations over the past several decades. The felicitous phrase Neil Nevitte uses to describe the changing temper of the times is the "decline of deference" (1996). Younger generations have come of age at a time when authority and tradition are viewed with suspicion. They have been taught from an early age to be independent in their thinking, to be discerning in their judgments, to pursue their own dreams and ideals without excessive regard for social expectation. In short, they reject the idea that that which is handed down from the past or on high must be accepted without question. To the extent Canadian identity is one such given, it too will be subject to critical scrutiny by younger generations. Don't just tell me that my Canadian identity is important, today's twenty-somethings will respond if questioned about their loyalty to their home and native land. Tell me *why* I should consider it important in ways that matter to *me*.

Evidence of a connection between the weakening of certain forms of community attachment among younger generations and the decline of deference can be found in a couple of sources. One is an older study conducted in 1989, part of a series of surveys on the social values of Canadians carried out by Environics and its Quebec partner firm, CROP (CROP Socio-Cultural Survey, 1989). The survey asked Canadians how important it was to them that "law and order are respected." It also inquired about the importance they attached to feeling "part of a community that shares a common history and a set of values." The two attitudes were intimately connected: among those declaring it very important to feel part of a community sharing a common history, 78 percent also felt it very important that law and order be respected. Among those indicating this type of community attachment was not important to them, only 28 percent attached high importance to respect for law and order. The shared connection to generational change is found in the fact that younger cohorts were much less likely to assign importance to either proposition (Figure 6.6).

Figure 6.6

Attitudes by age towards law and order and feeling part of a community with common history

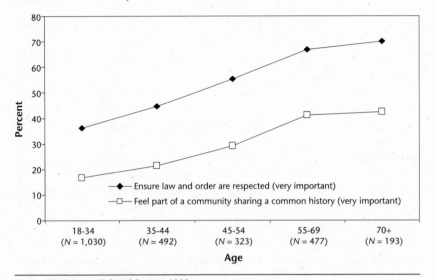

Source: CROP Socio-Cultural Survey, 1989.

A second source of evidence concerning the broader cultural shift in which changing dispositions towards community are embedded is more current. The 2007-08 CCES posed two questions relevant to the decline of deference thesis: one asked respondents whether "we need to strengthen respect and obedience for authority" or "there is sufficient respect for authority in today's society," the other whether they "prefer people who, whatever happens, do their duty or people who pursue their own happiness." The survey also replicated the Statistics Canada question about the strength of one's attachment to Canada. Again, there is evidence of a relationship between deferential attitudes and depth of national attachment (Figure 6.7). Among those who reject both deferential options – responding that there is sufficient respect for authority and that people should pursue their own happiness – only 45 percent indicate a strong attachment to Canada. In the intermediate category of respondents (those selecting one deferential response), this figure climbs to 51 percent. Among those opting for the deferential response to both items, strong national attachment reaches 62 percent.

The assessment that our large-scale loyalties are suffering from generational erosion due to a generalized scepticism towards the "givens" of social life is bolstered by the interesting counter-example of local identities. As we saw earlier (Figure 6.4), Canadian and provincial identities seem to be ebbing among younger cohorts, whereas the age pattern for local attachments reveals

Figure 6.7

National attachment and deferential attitudes

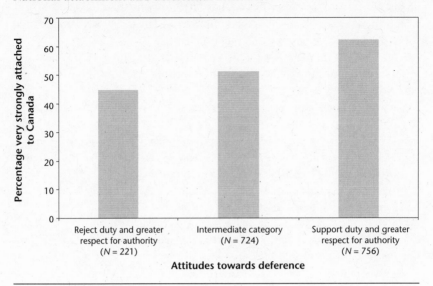

Source: CCES, 2007-08.

life-cycle undulation that can be more readily tied to conditions prevailing at different stages of life. Furthermore, while local identities are weaker on the whole than provincial or national ones, the gap between local attachments and the other two is significantly smaller for younger Canadians. Thus, the relative significance of local attachments seems to be growing among younger generations. In short, local identities do not seem to be implicated to nearly the same degree in the questioning of social givens engendered by the decline of deference. This makes eminent sense, however, when we reflect on the nature of those identities. For local identities are not inherited to the same degree as provincial and national ones due to the simple fact of geographic mobility. Over the course of their lives, many people move at least once from one local community to another. If that move occurs any time after they are old enough to engage in what might be termed autonomous personal development – an age hard to pinpoint, but certainly from the mid-teens on – then the attachment that develops to the new local community (and, in many cases, the choice of community itself) will be partly based on conscious decision and action on the part of the individual. In this way, local identity is typically something that individuals cultivate for themselves rather than something they simply accept, or are expected to accept, as a birthright.[12] It is, as we have already seen, deeply rooted in the lived experience of individuals, in the social connections they establish through activities such as volunteering, involvement in groups, and getting to know their neighbours. For this reason, local identities will have greater *personal* meaning for most people than attachments on a larger scale and would therefore not have been markedly affected by the scepticism towards social givens implied by the decline of deference.

To the extent that the weakening of national attachment in Canada is a product of the decline of deference, it is not something easily reversed. As Nevitte argues, the latter is a deeply entrenched feature of our contemporary social and political culture unlikely to fade away. The next chapter returns to this theme, broadening the decline of deference concept by subsuming it under the more general rubric of individualism, but retaining the idea that this culture shift is here to stay, and along with it relative indifference towards inherited identities. Strengthening national identities thus requires a different tack. It entails making our large-scale attachments more akin to local identities by giving them greater meaning and resonance in present-day activity. This brings us back to the second argument about why national ties have been weakening: the process of *re-imagining the nation* that can lend new meaning to national identity as time wears on has been faltering in recent times and has been inadequate to compensate for the diminished salience of the inherited component of Canadian attachment.

To understand that faltering, it is instructive to consider earlier successes – those processes and developments of the past that helped Canadians re-think their common ties and revitalize their shared commitments. The most important have been projects carried out collectively, meaning, as it does for most large-scale communities, actions and programs carried out by government in our name. Those most relevant to national reinvention and regeneration have been ones broadly supported by the Canadian public that made a real difference in the world, whether within Canada or without, and which provided us with a new sense of ourselves – the defining nature of our society or our place in the world. Thus Canada's contribution to the First World War is typically seen as a decisive turning point in our history, the event that marked our coming of age as an independent country, when we began to see ourselves as distinctly Canadian rather than a mere adjunct of the British Empire. The interwar period and the Canadian contribution to the Second World War cemented this understanding, while the postwar period saw us making new strides as a player in world affairs, promoting and advancing newly inscribed principles of international law and multilateralism. Our contributions to international institutions and practices, such as the United Nations and peacekeeping, came to be tightly woven into the fabric of an evolving Canadian identity. Domestically, the postwar period saw other collective achievements in the creation of the welfare state and its centrepiece, a publicly funded health care system, the program most often cited as our mark of distinction from the US. The 1960s saw Canada entering a new period of self-examination and reinvention as we confronted our French-English duality and broader cultural diversity. Out of this emerged new pillars of Canadian identity: official bilingualism, multiculturalism, and a policy of open immigration to people from all parts of the world. All of these have changed the face of Canada dramatically in the years since their implementation. These features of post-1960s Canada were enshrined in Pierre Trudeau's crowning achievement, the Charter of Rights, a document that also established a new collective tenet – rigorous protection of individual rights – in a manner respectful of the complexity and diversity of modern Canadian society (Weinrib 2001).

In breezing through these milestones and turning points, it is not to be assumed that periodic re-imagining of the Canadian nation has gained the universal approval of Canadians. Quebecers in particular have looked askance at some of these undertakings. It is simply to note the type of government-led contributions and projects that can invest a national community with renewed meaning and vitality as time goes on. That many Quebecers have distanced themselves from these Canadian processes of reinvention is partly due to interesting parallel developments in the province. While Balthazar notes how television helped inspire a new Québécois consciousness in the 1950s, he also observes that the 1960s were a decade of more overt national-ist mobilization within the province. In seeking to understand the passion and zealotry of that period, a common interpretation in English Canada at the time was that it was a flare-up of ethnic nationalism, that the French in Quebec were revealing themselves to be a people too deeply rooted in the inherited ties of history and culture. A more sympathetic interpretation is that this period witnessed a profound re-imagining of the nation, involving both shifting horizons of community – no longer French-Canadian, but Québécois – and government-led projects to transform society that invested that new identity with substance and meaning (Balthazar 1993, 9). The vibrancy of the Québécois identity in the 1960s was intimately connected to the provincial government's efforts to modernize the education system, to take greater control of the province's economy on behalf of the French-speaking majority, and to develop policies designed to preserve the French language and culture. This process of government-led transformation was eventually taken further across most sectors by the Parti Québécois when it came to power in the mid-1970s. Particularly noteworthy throughout this period is the prominent role of young people, those under age thirty, as both instigators and supporters of reform. It is they who were at the forefront of this movement of social change and national redefinition, as members and supporters of both the Liberal Party and later the PQ (Hamilton and Pinard 1976), the smaller sovereigntist parties that predated the PQ (Howe 1998, 359-60), and the diverse range of social and political movements springing up in those early years. The feelings of collective belonging within the generation coming of age in those years were greatly intensified by the sense of meaning and purpose imparted by concerted public action.

More recent developments in Quebec are also instructive, as the dramatic process of national re-imagining that began half a century ago seems to have run its course, leaving national attachments intact and yet diminished, especially among today's younger generation. This became evident when three elected members of the PQ travelled about the province in 2004 to find out why young Quebecers were no longer joining the party. The main issue they reported encountering was a desire to know what present purpose sovereignty was meant to serve (Bourdeau et al. 2004, 11-12). It was reminiscent of the sentiment expressed a decade earlier when public hearings were held to discuss sovereignty prior to the 1995 referendum in Quebec: many who approached the microphone were less interested in discussing separation per se than in asking what was to be the *"projet de société"* for an independent Quebec? No satisfactory answer was forthcoming, then or now. While some might cite the Quiet Revolution as evidence of the changes that can be achieved when Quebecers take charge of their own future, for today's young Quebecers these accomplishments are a *fait accompli* far removed from contemporary experience. Their disposition towards the national collectivity seems analogous to that of young Canadians in other parts of the country: their Québécois identity is not in question for the most part, but as an identity impressed upon them from birth it is not especially meaningful in itself. Nor are they willing to accept its overarching significance simply because their elders or certain political elites expect them to. In the absence of a sense of collective purpose to lend this inherited identity greater significance, it remains rather inert, their support for sovereignty, though reasonably high in sheer percentage terms, relatively equivocal and devoid of the fervour of those who came of age during the Quiet Revolution. The result has been a shake-up of the Quebec political landscape, with many young Quebecers turning to newly formed political parties in search of fresh ideas, or simply disengaging from politics altogether.

In Canada outside Quebec, we have come to a similar pass, as there are no contemporary collective accomplishments to inspire today's younger Canadians. The most recent of any note was the patriation of the Constitution and the introduction of the Charter of Rights in 1982. Free trade, the focal point of the 1988 election, inspired passionate debate about the meaning of Canada, but was an issue bearing on Canadian identity for opponents only, not advocates. The latter, sensitive to this concern, downplayed the agreement's significance ("a commercial document that's cancellable on six months' notice" in Brian Mulroney's words [Watson 1998, 5]). This assessment garnered enough support to win the Conservatives the election and now seems to predominate in public perceptions of the pact. Constitutional negotiations, starting with agreement among the first ministers at Meech Lake in 1987 and ending with the referendum on the Charlottetown Accord in October 1992, were more direct exercises in national reconstitution, but also for this reason more divisive than earlier endeavours, where national reinvention was a by-product of collective action rather than the explicit focus. In the final analysis, they fell far short of the broad consensus needed to inspire any sense of national regeneration. The experience of the years of constitutional turmoil has made most politicians wary of Canadian *projets de sociétés* and attention has since turned to more mundane matters such as getting the government's financial house in order. But no matter how much achievements in this area are dressed up in florid prose – slaying the deficit, and so on – people are rarely inspired by sound fiscal management. A sense of Canadian pride can still be called forth by victory in international hockey tournaments and the like, but the larger undertakings of government that have historically underwritten more sustained and enduring national cama-raderie have been absent from Canadian politics for a quarter century. The end result is that even as we have been prospering economically, we have been languishing as a national collectivity. Critical commentators suggest that Canada has become little more than a glorified hotel (Bliss 2003), pro-viding comfortable accommodation for its residents as they go about the business of their daily lives, but little else.

Those content with the current state of affairs would point to a country that is prosperous and peaceful, knit together by shared democratic and liberal values, in need of only a steady hand to oversee the affairs of state, not any grander ambition. This sanguine view would be consistent with Francis Fukuyama's "end of history" argument, in which the American scholar, writing in 1989, took the impending demise of communism to represent the final triumph of liberal democracy, which left nothing of any great consequence to achieve. While there were still parts of the world where liberal democracy was absent, its status as the presumptive ideal was now ubiquitous, Fukuyama argued. And in places where it had been achieved, government would henceforth be limited to "perpetual care taking," "the endless solving of technical problems," and the "satisfaction of sophisticated consumer demands" (1989, 18) – not unlike the mandate of managers at the finer hotels. But the problem with living at the end of history (or thinking we live at the end of history) is that people do not want just to inherit his-tory. They want to make history – not necessarily as individuals, not neces-sarily in grandiose ways, but as members of a collectivity that is contributing to the ongoing and positive progression of human affairs. In the absence of any collective orientation of this sort, the natural inclination is to concentrate on personal priorities, pursuing our own ambitions and desires, with weaker regard for the public realm (Taylor 1991; Griffiths 2009, 46).[13]

What Is to Be Done?

The prescriptive dimension of this study is for the most part left until Chapter 10, where the accumulated analysis is drawn upon to outline a series of potential strategies and actions for encouraging democratic engagement among younger Canadians. The analysis in this chapter, however, merits more immediate and extended discussion of the general approach required to address the challenges identified through this examination of the state of community attachments among younger generations of Canadians.

Most importantly, for those who believe in the importance of an engaged citizenry and the value of collective focal points to anchor this engagement, there is a need to identify public projects that have the potential to serve this purpose (Kersh 2007). Similar advice has recently been dispensed by Rudyard Griffiths in *Who We Are?*, an insightful essay on Canadian identity. In it, he cautions against the embrace of a "post-national concept of nationhood," calling instead for a new "great imagining" of Canada grounded in an "overarching idea for the country ... based on the lessons of our history and the convictions that define us as a people" (2009, 73 and 97).

Past successes in the realm of national re-imagining have involved projects broadly supported by Canadians that made a real difference to our own society or the larger world. Some have represented new areas of endeavour, while others have been newly emphasized priorities consistent with past achievements. Three come to mind as viable avenues to pursue at present. First, Canada could strive, in these times of cultural strife both globally and domestically, to be a model multicultural society. Precisely what this entails is subject to debate, but it likely means moving beyond mere tolerance to genuine acceptance of those hailing from elsewhere (Bissoondath 2002), as well as striving for more effective socioeconomic integration of newcomers into Canadian society. Second, Canada could play an important role in bringing about robust environmental policies to address the global warming crisis, a position that would be in keeping with the stated priorities of most Canadians. Third, as a number of writers have suggested in the past few years (Cohen 2003; Welsh 2004; Byers 2007), Canada could make itself a more forceful presence in the international arena. This could occur on various fronts – with a more generous foreign aid policy, in support of international efforts to stop human rights abuse, through the example provided to others by the way we order our domestic affairs (successful management of cultural and ethnic diversity again being one key element).

In all of these areas of national re-imagining, offered only as illustrative examples, there is scope for grassroots involvement. This is an important consideration, for if the aim is to make sentiments of national belonging more akin to local attachments by investing them with greater personal and contemporary significance, then opportunities must be provided for at least some Canadians to play an active part in these projects. Actions in the international realm are perhaps the most challenging in this regard, posing certain practical limits to broad-based citizen involvement, and the main effect of a new Canadian internationalism would be the national pride engendered as others carry out worthwhile actions in Canada's name. There is, however, considerable scope for public input in the shaping of our foreign policy, as well as room for greater government sponsorship of initiatives that provide opportunities for young people to work or volunteer abroad, activity currently organized mainly under the auspices of non-governmental organizations. A reaffirmed multiculturalism can more readily involve Canadians at large in helping to make stated government policy a social reality: through individuals extending respect and cordiality to neighbours and acquaintances, by employers providing work opportunities to immigrants with less familiar credentials, by people taking the time and effort to appreciate the cultural backgrounds of others in their community. The same is true of a more robust environmental policy. Stringent federal regulations and a forceful stand in international negotiations on greenhouse gas emissions can be complemented by the efforts of Canadians on the ground: changing lightbulbs, retrofitting homes, working together in their local communities to adopt greener policies. Such activities are more likely to flourish if seen as part of a meaningful national effort to make genuine progress on this front. In this way, certain projects likely to strengthen bonds of attachment to fellow Canadians through collective government action can also build social capital on the ground. Critically, however, this will be social capital with a purpose, indeed social capital with a public purpose, a more focused form of citizen involvement than the myriad forms of social connectedness enumerated and advocated by Putnam.

This prescriptive approach points to a different assessment of the relative roles of government and citizens in effecting the changes needed to revitalize community and foster public engagement. Putnam ostensibly finds this issue a distraction, suggesting that the top-down/bottom-up distinction – government-led change versus grassroots revival – is a "false debate." Yet he seems to take a fairly strong stand on this debate just a half-page later in submitting that "institutional reform will not work ... unless you and I, along with our fellow citizens, resolve to become reconnected with our friends and neighbors" (2000, 413-14). If the aim is to encourage indiscriminate social capital and community of the generic variety, Putnam may be right that reconnecting with one another in manifold ways is what matters most, and the onus is on citizens to reach out to one another. If the objective, on the other hand, is to strengthen community attachments that lead to public commitment, then government has the lead role to play in overseeing projects that people will see as theirs, strengthening feelings of national belonging, and building purposive social capital in the process. The only real nod in this direction from Putnam is his passing observation that a crisis such as war or natural disaster would serve as a galvanizing event that would see government springing into action along with citizens, hardly a desirable method of catalyzing change. There is, by the light of the current argument, merit in reflecting on what action government might undertake to instil a sense of common purpose before crisis forces it upon us (McLean 2006, 163).

The use of government in this formulation focuses on the agency ultimately responsible for effecting public policy, but this is not to suggest it is for government alone to define and develop such plans. A broader class of actors must be involved in shaping the objectives that might provide renewed direction for our national community. There is first a role for political leaders of different stripes, in conjunction with their parties and other sources of potential guidance, to articulate ideas about pillars of Canadian policy that can provide us with a renewed sense of national purpose. Rather than focusing only on short-term priorities and promises, it is incumbent on political leaders to outline long-term ideals, identifying where Canada should be twenty years from now, not just four. The standard venues of day-to-day politics are not particularly conducive to this undertaking. Even election campaigns, as short-lived Prime Minister Kim Campbell mused during the 1993 federal campaign, are not the most propitious time for debating serious issues (nor, as Ms. Campbell was shortly to discover, for musing). There is a need for forums where leaders *can* offer up ideas meant for rumination and reflection, not immediate application. One possibility would be an annual party leaders' debate, similar to those held during election campaigns, where the participants would focus on general and long-term public priorities. For this to succeed, political leaders would require the courage to set forth ideas that might be at odds with the status quo, but this in turn would depend on the willingness of Canadians (and media pundits) to receive these ideas in an open spirit. In adopting a mindset open to reflection, we would do well to remember that many ideas that eventually come to seem perfectly reasonable, even unimpeachable, start off as jarring notions, taking time to mature and gain widespread public acceptance. Some of Trudeau's long-term initiatives, such as the Charter of Rights, exemplify the long period sometimes required for new plans and conceptions to gain general acceptance and come to fruition.

If stronger political leadership is needed to articulate possible focal points for more purposeful public policy, other changes are required to help shape these ideas into broadly agreed agendas for public action. Most importantly, a more consensual approach to political decision making is required, a sensible idea on democratic grounds, but also important for formulating projects that enjoy broad public backing and can serve as touchstones of national identity. Royal commissions have sometimes served this purpose in the past, removing important issues from the arena of partisan debate to allow for more in-depth and wide-ranging reflection on public issues of broad significance and producing recommendations that have served as the basis for important new initiatives: the creation of a public radio network in the 1930s, the wartime introduction of a national program of unemployment insurance, the development of Canadian cultural agencies in the 1950s, the establishment of official bilingualism in the late 1960s. These will continue to have their place in Canadian public life, but must, in recognition of contemporary sensibilities, be complemented by other forms of deliberation that allow for greater public involvement. An electoral system based on proportional representation would encourage greater cooperation between political parties, particularly those likely to come together in coalition governments. Supporters of those parties would feel better represented in the processes of negotiation and compromise that are part of any policy deliberation. Alternatively, greater cooperation across party lines in the House of Commons, facilitated by a loosening of party discipline, would be another way that broad support could coalesce around widely backed policy ideas. In conjunction with this, MPs with a freer hand in parliament could do more to reach out to citizens in their ridings and, through regular local consultations, bring them into the processes of public deliberation. On a larger scale, citizens' assemblies, already used to make recommendations on electoral reform in British Columbia and Ontario, are another promising possibility, and go furthest in removing public deliberation from the divisive realm of partisan politics. This is an especially important feature, for while democratic reforms are normally evaluated for their potential to address declining confidence and trust in government, they can also be an important means of overcoming sectionalism and thereby facilitating the sort of consensus building necessary for processes of national regeneration. This may in fact be the more important criterion of the two. For whereas distrust in government does at least inspire some to become politically involved in order to rectify perceived shortcomings, weak attachments to community are more predictably linked to public disengagement and withdrawal.

Thus, changes to the way ideas are introduced, debated, and fleshed out in the public arena are a necessary part of developing broad consensual agendas that can instil a greater sense of national purpose and thereby strengthen weakening attachments to the national community among younger generations of Canadians. Three constituencies might object to efforts to enhance public engagement through such means. The first is Quebec, or many within Quebec who are committed to another national vision and would see promotion of projects embodying putative Canadian ideals as intrusive and presumptuous. In recognition of these sensitivities, it is important that national re-imagining on the Canadian level proceed in an unintrusive manner. One basic proviso is to avoid issues that touch directly on Canadian unity: thus no constitutional debates or discussions of language politics. Instead, the focus should be on other focal points – such as multiculturalism, environmentalism, or internationalism – around which Canadians can potentially rally and strengthen our sense of common commitment. Admittedly, multiculturalism touches on important sensitivities in Quebec, but there is surely a common need to devise suitable immigration and integration policies to support our shared commitment to social cohesion coupled with cultural diversity. Subtle political marketing is needed as well: success in common endeavours should not be trumpeted too loudly nor treated as evidence of the indissolubility of Canada. Better to simply take note of what Canadians can achieve when we work together, and let the results speak for themselves. In short, what is required is an approach to national regeneration that is meaningful yet unassuming. At the same time, it has to be accepted that parallel efforts promoting provincial attachments will continue to be part of the mix. The Quebec government was especially active in instilling a sense of Québécois pride during the Quiet Revolution, and continues to sponsor initiatives that in both form and substance seem designed to further that end. These include the Estates-General on the Reform of Democratic Institutions, a 2001 initiative involving many groups within Quebec society in the most far-reaching deliberation on democratic reform undertaken by any provincial government (and which might have had a real effect on Quebecers' sense of common purpose had any democratic reform actually come of it). Similarly, Quebec commissions on language politics and cultural relations in recent years have taken the form of broad-based public deliberations designed to establish fresh direction for the nation by forging new common understandings in contentious areas of public life. Other provincial governments, if not always with the same deliberate intent, also engage in activity from time to time that is likely to strengthen provincial attachments among citizens. Considered in their own right, such actions can have salutary effects on public engagement, giving citizens in a particular province a stronger sense of common purpose and mutual connection. Set in the larger context, there are obvious complications that can arise when efforts are made to strengthen provincial attachments while similar Canadian initiatives are underway. But the potential for conflict among citizens, as opposed to governments, should not be overstated, for the fact of the matter is that Canadian and provincial attachments are positively correlated – those who are strongly attached to Canada are, in good part, the *same* people who are strongly attached to their province.[14] This suggests these sentiments partly reflect a single underlying affinity for large-scale public commitment and engagement that manifests itself on both a provincial and a pan-Canadian scale. This holds even in Quebec,[15] evidence of the old saw that what Quebecers really want, some at least, is a strong Quebec within a united Canada. Without denying the complications of loyalties in a federal state, there is evidence that community-building efforts

on different levels can peacefully coexist, making distinct yet complement-
ary contributions to citizen comity and engagement.

A second constituency that might find reason to object to efforts to
strengthen Canadian attachments through the promotion of common
projects and ideals are small "c" conservatives, whose preference is for a state
that creates the conditions that allow people to pursue their own dreams
and ambitions, not one that imposes common objectives on the public.
Theirs is the ideology most consistent with the end-of-history prescription
that government in a liberal democracy should limit itself to managing the
practical affairs of state. This ideology, however, is not widespread in Canada
and instead reflects a current of thinking that holds more sway in the US.
Conservatism in Canada has traditionally been a more communitarian creed
and retains this colouring, despite the inroads of a neo-conservative philosophy more focused on the individual. The apparent erosion of national
attachment among young Canadians is something that would arouse concern among many latter-day conservatives if brought to their attention.
Furthermore, the methods suggested for defining new national objectives
should not cause undue consternation to those wary of government intervention, as these consist in opening avenues of public reflection and debate,
not inviting government to impose its agenda on the country. If it turned
out that Canadians, when given proper opportunity to reflect on where we
stand as a people and where we wish to go in the future, decided their preference was for maximal individual freedom and minimal common endeavour, it would be hard to argue against this. But anyone familiar with Canadian
history and political culture will recognize this as an unlikely outcome.

The third constituency that might resist efforts at national reinvention
around shared national projects are those who see themselves as marginalized from society by virtue of their race, gender, sexual orientation, or some
other analogous quality. These groups and their academic defenders sometimes see the appeal for renewal of community as a veiled method of seeking
to undermine, indeed delegitimize, opposition and conflict as a means of
effecting much-needed social reform. This is an important critique that has
been directed at Putnam's calls for the revitalization of social capital (Arneil
2006) and the same charges might apply to the idea of strengthening national and provincial bonds through broadly supported public projects. The
objection loses force, however, when considered carefully against the arguments and stipulations outlined above. The promotion of common endeavours designed to make collective identities more meaningful does not imply
unanimous support from all Canadians, nor does it entail agreement in
other areas of public life. All that is envisaged are a few key rallying points
that can serve to instil a greater sense of comity and shared purpose. Moreover, those on the margins would arguably be better served by a renewal of

national ties along these lines. Where community is weak, the claims of the marginalized are more likely to be dismissed as the griping of outsiders who don't really belong, or simply ignored altogether by those too wrapped up in their own concerns to pay attention to the public realm. Where community is strong, citizens are more likely to be attuned to public life and to treat the claims of those on the margins as grievances of fellow community members that deserve a fair hearing. While some communities can be restrictive and oppressive, others can be open and generous in a way that enhances public sympathy for those who feel their interests are not being served, their concerns not being heard. Suggestive evidence for this view lies in the greater sensitivity to issues of social equality in the small, tight-knit nations of Northern Europe compared to larger, more fractious countries (the US being one evident example).

In sum, the national re-imagining process, properly understood and executed, is consistent with the democratic, inclusive, and unassuming governance practices favoured by most Canadians and should trigger no deep resentment from any quarter. It is, moreover, an important dimension of public engagement that can help reconnect Canadians to the public realm, particularly younger Canadians whose attachments to both country and province are considerably weaker than those of older generations. If the decline of deference has undermined the strength of the involuntary attachments inherited at birth, the meaning of national belonging depends more than ever on processes of reinvention that have previously succeeded in giving greater contemporary meaning and authenticity to our shared identities. It is this strategy, more than any built around Putnam's analysis of declining social capital in the US, that holds significant promise of stemming the erosion of community in Canada and which must be part of any serious effort to re-engage young Canadians in the public life of our country.

7
Ascendant Individualism

The waning of community attachment among younger Canadians is one important aspect of the shifting foundations of social integration with broad implications for social and political engagement. Yet it is too blunt a description to characterize this simply as a "decline in community," for the change has involved a more complex shift in the nature of communal commitments among rising generations. One way to understand this evolution is through the lens of the decline of deference thesis: young Canadians, more sceptical of the givens of social and political life than preceding generations, are less inclined to embrace identities of an inherited nature, instead placing greater emphasis on attachments that involve greater personal choice and authenticity. This line of analysis can be taken further, for the decline of deference can be seen as but one component of a larger social process that has slowly unfolded down the years. That larger process is the heightened individualism of younger generations.

The significance of individualism to changing patterns of social integration is not fully recognized in much of the relevant literature. Putnam, for example, styles his work as an investigation into the "strange disappearance" of social capital.[1] That it may be the *appearance*, or more judiciously phrased, the *increased presence*, of individualism that is responsible for evolving patterns of social connectedness in the US is not a theme much considered in his work.[2]

Another recent work does shift the focus from what's gone missing from the social landscape to what has taken its place. *Generation Me*, by American social psychologist Jean Twenge, argues forcefully that individualism is the new guiding ethos of contemporary times that can explain a good deal about the personal and social priorities of younger generations. Like *Bowling Alone*, the book is geared towards a wide audience and has received considerable attention both within and without the US. *Generation Me* offers a wide-ranging exposition of the nature of individualism, and many examples of its current manifestations in popular culture and the personal, social, and political attitudes of young Americans. While much of the evidence is anecdotal, the book is based on a solid body of academic research built on analysis of large-scale psychological profiling from the past and present, which finds evidence of marked increases in individualistic attitudes among young Americans over the past several decades. Though set in the American context, the Canadian reader finds much in *Generation Me* that resonates with common experience and general social trends north of the forty-ninth parallel.

The broad sweep of Twenge's analysis of individualism, encompassing a wide array of social and psychological phenomena, highlights the complexity of the concept, or perhaps more accurately, its multidimensionality. Recognizing this, an essential first step in seeking to investigate individualism and its possible relationship to political disengagement among younger generations is to define the concept and elaborate on its various dimensions. While the temptation might be to work towards a definition of individualism specific to the realm of politics, this would be an unduly resstrictive approach, for the value of Twenge's work lies precisely in her characterization of rising individualism as a sea change affecting a broad swath of contemporary life: the social and the cultural, the personal and the political. There is also merit in her conceptualization of individualism less as an explicit ideology – a transparent set of values to which people subscribe – and more as an implicit ethos rooted in personal qualities and dispositions that have grown increasingly prevalent over time. Adopting a similarly catholic approach allows for a more searching consideration of the topics taken up in this and subsequent chapters: the nature of the individualism exhibited by younger generations in Canada; the implications for social integration and different facets of political engagement; and the origins of the ascendant individualism that has gradually reconfigured the social and political landscape in Canada and other countries.

The Meanings of Individualism

While offering many telling examples of the phenomenon, *Generation Me* does not set out a precise definition or systematic typology of individualism. In seeking to flesh out the concept, there are various places one might turn to for guidance. One is political theory literature, in particular that branch that addresses individualism as a guiding philosophy (Avineri and de-Shalit, 1992). This would include the voluminous literature on liberalism, the political ideology that places the individual at the heart of political life. The real world of politics is also a possible source of insight into meanings of the term, as individualism, and an attendant emphasis on individual rights and prerogatives of some description or other, are an integral part of contemporary political discourse. The empirically oriented literature in political science, in particular that branch which examines attitudes and behaviours of the population at large through survey research, is another place to turn, though many pertinent works do not speak explicitly of individualism, instead using other terms to describe roughly equivalent concepts. When Nevitte demonstrates, for example, that there has been a decline in deference among younger generations of Canadians, who question the dictates of authority and tradition (1996), I take him to mean that we have become more individualistic in a certain sense of the term. Explicit use of the term individualism in the empirical study of population traits and attitudes is more common in the fields of sociology and psychology. Relevant works, those of Twenge and others, can provide further guidance in elucidating a concept that the political behaviour literature has not addressed as explicitly.

Before turning to the definitions and distinctions to be found in these various fields, it is helpful to set out some elementary observations. The simplest observation is that individualism involves emphasis on the individual, that is to say accords value and significance to the self. Different dimensions of the self are variously emphasized, leading to distinct strands of individualism. Four descriptors would seem to cover much of the conceptual terrain. Arranged in accordance with the relative emphasis typically accorded them by those on the left of the political spectrum and those on the right, they are: self-direction, self-confidence, self-reliance, and self-regard.

These faces of individualism appear in different guises across the diverse intellectual and political arenas in which individualism is assessed and analyzed. Self-direction – or more simply, liberty or freedom – for the purpose of allowing for the fullest development and expression of the self is a cornerstone of much liberal philosophy. That this has become a more important priority for many in the established democracies is implicit in a number of works that examine the changing values of citizens over time. The decline of deference, for example, reflects a heightened emphasis on self-direction, that is to say, personal autonomy and freedom from social constraint. In developing this thesis, Nevitte draws heavily on the post-materialist framework developed by Ronald Inglehart, which highlights the increasing priority younger generations in various countries have come to place on higher-order values such as "self-actualization" in the postwar period (1990, 1997). As a political force, this form of individualism came into its own in the 1960s, principally in movements of the new left that combined traditional demands for social equality and justice with a new emphasis on personal liberty and expression of the self. As Twenge underlines, such attitudes have diffused widely since that time, infusing day-to-day life and popular culture, leading to heightened emphasis on individual choice and judgment across many spheres: careers, life partners, music, fashion, personal scruples. Other psychologists, whose work focuses on human personality, which we will revisit below, have identified "openness to experience" as a key dimension of the self closely allied to the desire for self-direction. Those temperamentally inclined to seek novel experiences and engage new ideas naturally crave personal autonomy and resist social restrictions. The terminology thus varies across different fields and subfields, but the underlying concept and insistence on its relevance to the general workings of contemporary society is consistent.

The second dimension of individualism, self-confidence, likewise surfaces in a variety of contexts. Within the political behaviour literature, the concept of "cognitive mobilization" is often invoked in tandem with post-materialism, the supposition being that respect for authority, tradition, and other social bulwarks has been undermined not only because of a preference for self-direction on the part of citizens, but also because of newfound confidence in their own capacity to contribute to democratic governance. Bringing this into the personal realm, Twenge wryly notes the blithe endorsement of self-confidence in the "you can be anything you want to be" bromide commonly dispensed to young people nowadays. She likewise points to the emphasis currently placed on self-esteem, offering a range of examples from pop songs opining that "learning to love yourself" is "the greatest love of all" to the prevalence of self-help books designed to bolster belief in oneself. The concept of self-esteem involves a slight shift in emphasis to a more inward-focused variant of self-confidence, reflecting the individual's estimation of his or her own personal worth. In this, there is a connection to the position of those liberal philosophers who have taken a sense of self-respect to be of singular importance to individual well-being. The work of Canadian scholar Charles Taylor (and others such as Will Kymlicka) on the politics of recognition in culturally diverse societies, for example, is largely predicated on the presumption that respect for one's beliefs and culture, and the sense of self-worth thereby instilled, are of paramount importance (Kymlicka 1989; Taylor 1992).

If self-direction and self-confidence are emphasized in some contexts where individualism is invoked, in others there is greater emphasis placed on self-reliance and self-regard. Both were important precepts underlying the neo-conservative political movements that rose to prominence and power in a number of Western democracies from the 1980s on: the ideologies of Thatcherism and Reaganism and political parties such as Canada's Reform Party. Of the two, self-reliance is the quality more openly espoused as a virtue by neo-conservatives. Standing on your own two feet, refusing the charity of others, and cognate qualities are seen as reflections of personal empowerment and resilience by advocates. Twenge, on the other hand, does not emphasize self-reliance in her account of individualism among young Americans. Indeed, in assessing the consequences of the indulgent parenting practices that she believes have contributed to the entrenchment of individualism among young Americans, she describes offspring who are self-absorbed in many respects but not obviously self-reliant (2006, 74-77).

Others, however, do see this quality as part of the fabric of American individualism. *Habits of the Heart,* an earlier influential work assessing the impact of the individualist ethos on contemporary society, describes individualism as "the first language in which Americans tend to think about their lives," an ethos that values "independence and self-reliance above all else" (Bellah et al. 1996, viii).

The other salient dimension of individualism prevalent in neo-conservative thought is self-regard: the habit of caring mainly for one's own well-being with little regard for the interest or concerns of others. That this practice is a virtue is typically not expressed openly in neo-conservative discourse, but critics would say this is only because it is too callous a proposition for public espousal. If explicitly defended, it is more often as a tolerable rather than laudatory principle. That there is merit in self-regard is a more transparent position in the work of the classical economists that neo-conservatives favour. From Adam Smith on, the pursuit of self-interest in the economic realm has been treated as a righteous form of personal behaviour that leads, through the workings of the invisible hand, to socially beneficent outcomes. Psychologists, usually not quite so sanguine about the end result, apply other terms to those whose habit it is to put themselves first: egocentric to describe those unwilling or incapable of seeing matters from any perspective other than their own; narcissistic to describe those who hold themselves in excessively high regard and place inordinate emphasis on their own well-being. Twenge's *Generation Me* (and her more recent work with Keith Campbell [2009]) is replete with examples of such behavioural and attitudinal tendencies on the part of young Americans.

If all of these examples represent manifestations or statements of individualism, the concept is clearly a multifarious one. Delineating four dimensions of the self that are variously emphasized in different contexts helps lend some order and structure to the concept. So too does the observation that the term "individualism" is used in two distinct ways in different bodies of literature. In some instances, "individualism" refers to a philosophy – a set of principled and coherent beliefs that lay emphasis on the self or some dimension of the self. This is, not surprisingly, most clearly the case in philosophical treatments of individualism, whether sympathetic or hostile to the doctrine. In other cases, "individualism" is simply a descriptive term denoting behaviours and attributes of an individualistic nature. This usage is typical of the psychology literature, where individualism is commonly assessed on the basis of questionnaires that probe individuals' personal views and behavioural predilections.

The distinction between the two usages is critical, as there are implications for both the measurement of individualism and its broader ramifications as an organizing principle for modern society. For one of the defining elements of a philosophy, any philosophy, is that it is meant to be for general application. A philosophy is not just a set of beliefs and principles that I find appealing, but a system of thought and action held to produce desirable outcomes when applied to society as a whole. For this reason, philosophical inquiry and belief, by its very nature, presses the individual to be mindful of the interests and concerns of others. This is most clearly evident in the initial precepts underlying liberal philosophical inquiry. When John Rawls, for example, presents his influential liberal theory of justice, the initial conceit is a "veil of ignorance" serving to shroud personal interest in favour of the impartial consideration of the interests of all concerned (Rawls 1999). Ronald Dworkin's insightful observation on this point is that the fundamental precept of liberalism, contrary to much common belief, is not liberty but equality – the shared presumption that in developing principles of justice, all must be treated with "equal concern and respect," to quote his succinct and influential formulation (1985).

In brief, whether stated directly or merely implied, within philosophies of individualism there is intrinsic mitigation of that individualism by virtue of the fact that philosophy is an inherently other-regarding enterprise. The same, however, is not necessarily true of individualism in the descriptive sense of the term. People who themselves are self-directing, self-confident, self-reliant, and/or self-regarding do not necessarily think of these as prescriptive norms that should be applied to society as a whole. That said, some might: individualism, as practised by the individual, *can* involve the application of principled belief to the self and others, rather than mere personal predilection. It follows that people can be individualistic in two rather different ways: as bearers of individualistic traits and behaviours or as adherents to an individualist philosophy, tendencies that might respectively be termed personal and principled individualism. Empirical investigation of individualism – whether in psychology, sociology, or political science – has not generally been sufficiently sensitive to this important distinction.[3]

Applying the distinction to the dimensions of individualism outlined above – self-direction, self-confidence, self-reliance, and self-regard – results in a more nuanced, if complex, typology. Table 7.1 is the result. The personal variant of self-direction is the desire to develop and pursue one's own preferences and ideas. It is akin to, but distinct from, the principled belief that everyone should be afforded the same opportunity to pursue their preferred life goals. Likewise, the personal quality of self-confidence is to be distinguished from the principled belief that people in general are capable and competent agents. The personal tendency to be self-reliant is distinct from principled belief in the virtue of self-reliance. So too is the manifest self-absorption of putting one's own interests first distinct from the principled stand in favour of people generally being permitted to concentrate on their own self-interest. The addition of this division creates a more nuanced framework that can better capture the complex shadings of individualism

Table 7.1

Individualism, personal and principled

	Personal trait	Principled belief
Self-direction	Desire to develop and pursue own preferences and ideas	Belief in the value of people pursuing own preferences and ideas
Self-confidence	Confidence in own capabilities	Belief in the capabilities of people in general
Self-reliance	Preference for taking care of oneself, not relying on others	Belief in value of people being self-reliant
Self-regard	Tendency to put own interests first	Belief in the right of people to focus on own self-interest

appearing in contemporary society – both the personal qualities that quietly guide people in their daily lives and the more explicit public values they sometimes espouse.

The categories in the table are not, of course, mutually exclusive. Any given individual can be individualistic in more than one sense of the term. Furthermore, the personal and the principled will tend to cohere, as personal practice can inform the principles one adheres to and principled belief normally influences personal behaviour. But clearly the personal and the principled are not one and the same and some slippage is to be anticipated. Indeed, in moving down the table, the marriage of the personal and the principled seems increasingly tenuous. If it is easy enough to imagine someone being both protective of their own autonomy and mindful of the wider norm of self-direction for one and all, it is harder to conceive of someone remaining loyal to a general principle of self-regard when the guiding maxim in their personal life is to look out for number one. The disregard for others embedded in the personal way of being will inevitably undermine the disinterested manner of thinking necessary to respect the principled belief. Eventually the principle will be pinched from within by the very behaviours and attitudes it sanctions (Waterman 1984, 71-82).

It is perhaps in recognition of this dynamic that others have suggested that a supplemental source of respect for others is necessary in order to sustain a public philosophy of self-regard. Alexis de Tocqueville, the French observer of nineteenth century American society, was much taken with the republic's social and political cohesion, which he believed to be rooted in wide adherence to the precept of "self-interest properly understood" (1969, 525-28). Tempering self-interest with small but steady sacrifices for the common good, the doctrine provided the grounding for a society of "orderly, temperate, moderate, careful and self-controlled citizens" (1969, 527). But Tocqueville also recognized that the philosophical principle did not stand alone. The cohesion of early America was also underwritten by widespread and powerful religious convictions that served to keep unvarnished self-interest in check (1969, 294-301, 442-49). A pithy summation of the later evolution of American society would be that "self-interest properly understood," forced to stand on its own as a public philosophy as religious commitment has waned over time, has been slowly revealed as incoherent. In the contemporary US, the universal pursuit of self-interest is still held up as a viable ideal, but the realities of self-regarding excess on the ground – whether in the economic, social, or political realm – often seem at odds with the fundamental value of equal respect and concern for others that must form the foundation of any sustainable public philosophy.

An analysis of the contemporary social landscape consistent with these assessments appears in Michael Adams's comparative investigation of social values in the US and Canada in his 2003 book *Fire and Ice*. Drawing on a wide-ranging set of survey data, Adams identifies individualism as a key dimension of social values in both countries, but draws important distinctions between two variants. In one corner are those whose overarching goal is personal "fulfillment" and who place heavy emphasis on autonomy and idealism. Theirs is not a "self-obsessed" individualism. Instead, they are sensitive to the aspirations of others because, reasons Adams, "if one wants the freedom to adopt a lifestyle and philosophy of one's own choosing, it is only reasonable to embrace the principle that everyone should be accorded the same freedom" (2003, 31-32). The other type of individualism is oriented towards "survival" broadly conceived. Adherents of this creed exhibit animosity towards others, social alienation, and anomie. Adams detects in their outlook "very little ... in the way of spiritual, social or ethical direction. Their law is the law of the jungle" (2003, 33).

These two clusters of individualist values, and differences in their basic character, are consistent with the interpretation of the dimensions of individualism offered above. Also noteworthy is Adams's assessment of Canadian-American differences in this regard, as well as generational change in the two countries. While finding that individualism in both places is markedly stronger among younger age groups, Adams observes that attitudes among younger Americans lean more towards the survival side of the spectrum, whereas individualism among younger Canadians tilts more towards the fulfillment pole. The values of older adults, though less individualistic as a rule, reveal the same Canadian-American difference. These findings serve as the basis for Adams's optimism that Canadian values remain distinct, that there is, contrary to popular opinion, no inexorable Americanization taking place. He also reports, however, some movement in the direction of survivalist values among Canadians under age thirty (2003, 89). This is not to the point of their drawing even with their American counterparts, who are following the same trajectory of change, but potentially a signal of common dynamics in the two countries and a harbinger of further changes to come.

Adams's work thus reinforces our conceptual reasoning and gives an initial sense of what might be expected in examining patterns of individualism in the Canadian case. To recapitulate, sensitivity to the complexity of individualism is necessary on two fronts. From the perspective of empirical measurement, it is useful to see the concept as an overarching construct that weaves together a number of distinct strands that should, for some purposes at least, be kept analytically distinct. From a normative standpoint, it is important to underline that some forms of individualism are more agreeable than others, because the behaviours and attitudes they sanction are consistent with the maintenance of a coherent and sustainable public philosophy. And the latter is important – if the implication was not already clear – as a key ingredient in social integration, in turn a critical underpinning of citizen engagement in public affairs. These general considerations are to be borne in mind in turning to take a closer look at the contours of individualism in the Canadian population.

Assessing Individualism

Having mapped out a typology of individualism to help guide normative and empirical exploration of the phenomenon, the aim now is to assess individualism in the current Canadian context. The main data source used is the Canadian Citizen Engagement Survey (CCES), which included a number of questions designed to evaluate different dimensions of individualism. Some were developed independently and were deliberately broad, aimed at encapsulating particular categories of individualism captured in Table 7.1 above, in both their personal and principled guises. Others were modelled on questions asked elsewhere, including the extensive social values surveys conducted by Adams and his colleagues over the years, which provide the data used in the exploration of Canadian and American values presented in *Fire and Ice*. Those same surveys are directly consulted in certain places below to supplement the data available in the CCES.

Age differences are the principal focus of the analysis. Where such differences appear, there follows some reflection on the relative importance of life-cycle and cohort effects. Given that the CCES is a single cross-sectional survey, there is no possibility of tracing levels of individualism within cohorts over time to assess the question in a definitive manner, so other forms of evidence and reasoning are required. One simple method is the demarcation of an eighteen to twenty-four age category. Where attitudes in this young adult group deviate sharply from the general age trend – as they do at several points – a life-cycle effect is suggested. At the same time, it is worth bearing in mind that the more common interpretation in the relevant literature is that individualism among today's young adults is primarily a reflection of cohort effects. Twenge argues that those who came of age in the 1960s were pioneering purveyors of the ethos and that subsequent cohorts have faithfully followed in their footsteps ever since. Adams also conceptualizes the very significant age differences uncovered in his analysis as reflections of cohort differences. The later analysis in Chapter 9 is consistent with these assessments, developing a theoretical interpretation as to why individualism would have increased slowly and steadily over the long haul in rising generations. It also, however, weaves salient life course variation in individualistic attributes into that same account, arguing that the more pronounced individualism of the early years of life – and in particular, the traits and qualities associated with personal individualism – is implicated in these broader generational changes.

The general approach is thus to keep an open mind by considering age differences closely before ascribing them exclusively to one or the other demographic effect and acknowledging that both may be present in some instances. The analysis begins with those facets of individualism that do not reveal significant age differences and require briefer attention, before moving on to those that do show sizable differences and merit more extensive discussion.

Self-Reliance

In Twenge's account of a rising focus on the self among young Americans, the one manifestation of individualism that receives relatively little attention is self-reliance. Her sole allusion is that indulgent parenting practices of recent decades may have rendered younger generations less self-reliant than those of the past, not more. Two questions were posed on the CCES to gauge the relative emphasis placed on this form of individualism by different age groups in Canada. One item spoke to the significance of self-reliance as a personal quality, the other to its importance as a social principle. Both were designed to cut to the chase, conceptually speaking, by presenting respondents with relatively broad statements with which they could agree or disagree (either "somewhat" or "totally"): "I prefer to take care of things myself and not rely too much on the help of others"; and "People today are not as self-reliant as they should be."

The results indicate that, on these broad-based measures, younger Canadians are less likely than older respondents to acknowledge the merits of self-reliance.[4] The percentage indicating total agreement with statements in support of self-reliance climbs steadily with increasing age (Figure 7.1). Education controls weaken the age pattern slightly, as less educated respondents are more inclined to affirm the merits of self-reliance. But the effect of

Figure 7.1

Self-reliance, personal and principled, by age

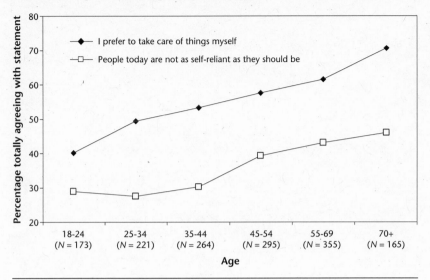

Source: CCES, 2007-08.

education is not sufficiently powerful to diminish the age differences significantly. Using these general survey measures, then, a belief in the virtues of self-reliance does not appear to be a salient component of heightened individualism among younger Canadians.

Self-Confidence

If there was not a strong expectation of finding accentuated self-reliance among young Canadians, the same is not true of self-confidence. In Twenge's analysis, self-confidence, in the guise of self-esteem, represents an important component of the broader individualist ethos she sees all around her in contemporary American society, particularly among younger generations, who have been taught to believe in themselves and their own abilities from the earliest age. Within the political science literature, a broadly related argument is made by those advancing the "cognitive mobilization" thesis. Authors in Canada (Kanji 2002) and elsewhere (Dalton 2006) contend that citizens, mainly due to rising education levels, have gradually grown more confident in their own capacity to contribute to democratic deliberation and decision making. The political implications are generally held to be positive, as the development promises to enrich democracy by engendering new forms of political activism and engagement requiring more substantive contributions from individual citizens.

Figure 7.2

Confidence in self and others by age

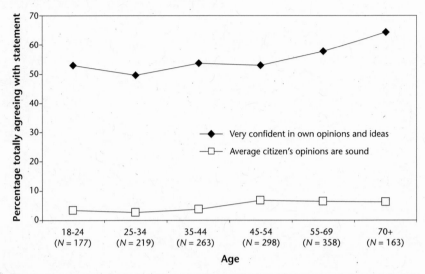

Source: CCES, 2007-08.

Two questions posed on the CCES do not, however, bear out the expectation of heightened self-confidence among younger Canadians. In response to the statement, "I generally feel very confident about my own opinions and ideas," younger respondents are less likely to indicate total agreement than older individuals, particularly those fifty-five and over (Figure 7.2). Nor do younger people exhibit greater-than-average confidence in the wisdom of others. The proportion in total agreement with the statement, "The average citizen's opinion on issues is generally sound and carefully considered," is roughly equivalent – and rather minimal – across all age groups.[5] In these broad assessments of individual competence, young Canadians do not appear exceptionally individualistic in either the personal or principled sense of the term.

Relevant to this result, given the higher education levels of younger respondents, is the fact that education does not boost confidence in individual capabilities to the extent that might be expected. This is despite the fact that education has a powerful effect on political knowledge and presumably *does* render individuals more capable of forming sound ideas and opinions, objectively speaking. But subjective assessments do not appear to track closely with objective capabilities. Of those with, at most, a high school degree, 59 percent totally agree that they feel very confident in their own opinions and ideas, compared to only 49 percent of those with a university education.[6]

The university-educated are also slightly less likely to believe that the views of the "average" citizen are "sound and carefully considered," though it is probably less surprising that those with more education would be less inclined to put faith in the opinions of the "average" citizen.

The general conclusion again is that individualism in the guise of self-confidence – of both the personal and principled variety – is not obviously elevated among younger Canadians. If there is a pattern of increasing individualism, burgeoning self-confidence and principled belief in the reasoning capacities of "the individual" are not among its salient features.

Self-Regard

In Twenge's account of ascendant individualism in the US, emphasis on self-regard among younger generations is implicit in many of the examples cited. Michael Adams also recognizes this as an important dimension of individualism. While arguing forcefully that self-regard is generally not as prominent among Canadians as Americans, he does allow that there has been some movement in this direction among the youngest Canadians in his surveys (now conducted some time ago, in 1992, 1996, and 2000). To investigate the matter further, the CCES asked respondents whether they agreed with two broad statements aimed at encapsulating self-regard of the personal and principled varieties: "Generally speaking, I tend to focus on my own concerns and not worry too much about other people"; and "In today's society, it is reasonable for people to look out mainly for themselves."

Age differences on these items are not particularly significant. However, if attention is focused on those who "totally disagree" with the statements, a pattern appears mildly suggestive of increasing self-regard among the young, as younger respondents are slightly less likely to categorically reject these statements in support of self-regard (Figure 7.3). In considering this result, education is again a factor to be borne in mind. Self-regarding tendencies, as gauged by these particular measures, are markedly stronger among those with lower levels of formal education. Whereas only 30 percent of those with less than a high school education disagree with both statements, 58 percent of those with a postgraduate degree do so. Since younger groups have higher education levels on the whole, the introduction of education controls has a mild amplifying effect on the differences between age groups. Overall then, based on these CCES questions, there are hints of heightened self-regard among younger Canadians, along with some suggestion that this tendency may have been partly held in check by their higher educational levels, but there is no compelling evidence of a powerful trend.

Of course, the survey measures used may not be ideal. There is, in this case, the particular challenge that self-regard, whatever inroads it may have made over time, is still widely viewed as an undesirable quality – something that people might practise but shy from openly espousing. It is not surprising

Figure 7.3

Self-regard, personal and principled, by age

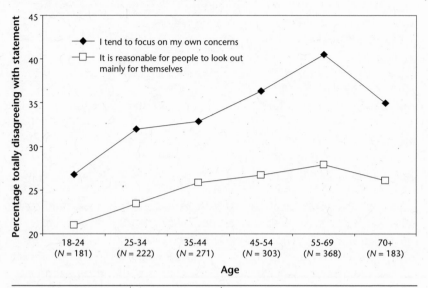

Source: CCES, 2007-08.

that fully three-quarters (76 percent) of all CCES respondents declare themselves opposed to the proposition that they tend to focus on their "own concerns" and don't "worry too much about other people." Other data sources point to a sharper pattern of rising self-regard among younger generations of Canadians. Adams's work draws on much more extensive survey measurements of Canadians' values, though the precise mix that underlies his "survivalist" conception of individualism is somewhat obscured by the relatively complex methods of aggregation of multiple survey questions that are not entirely transparent (2003). However, the datasets he uses – based on surveys conducted by Environics and its partner firm, the Quebec-based CROP – are available for secondary analysis. Perusing the items in those datasets, there is one that stands out as a simple and clear statement of personal self-regard: how important respondents feel it is to "make more money and be better off than most people around me." The mention of money gives the question a materialist tinge, but the question also clearly conveys the idea of putting oneself before others. Other researchers have conceptualized similar questions involving materialistic orientations as useful barometers of individualism: Putnam in his brief discussion of individualistic values among younger generations in the US (2000, 273) and other American researchers in more extensive longitudinal analysis of the changing personal values of young Americans (Rahn and Transue 1998).

Figure 7.4

Emphasis on personal material well-being by age

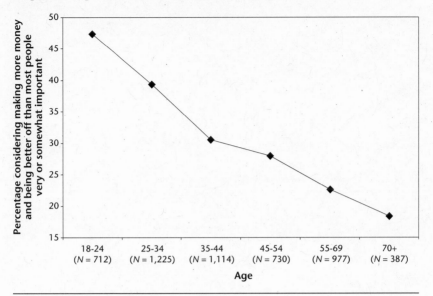

Source: CROP Socio-Cultural Surveys, 1989 and 1996.

Combining results for the two CROP surveys where the question appears (conducted in 1989 and 1996) reveals a clear age pattern, as young Canadians are considerably more likely than older respondents to assign importance to having more money than others (Figure 7.4).[7] The differences extend across the entire age span, suggesting (in the absence of any compelling explanation as to why personal self-regard would slowly ebb from early adulthood right through to the twilight years) that there is generational change occurring on this count, a conclusion consistent with the results of American research looking at similar survey items (Rahn and Transue 1998, 552-53). There may, however, also be a life-cycle component at play, as the gaps separating age groups are somewhat larger at the younger end of the spectrum: 8 or 9 points compared to 3 or 4 points. The result suggests that Canada has not entirely escaped the burgeoning self-regard among younger generations that Twenge and Adams have both detected in their studies of trends in the US, but that life-cycle patterns may also contribute to heightened self-regard among the young.

Self-Direction

Alongside self-regard, the other quality emphasized most heavily in Twenge's rendering of individualism is self-direction – the desire and determination to pursue one's own dreams, ideas, and ambitions. The same

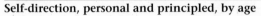

Figure 7.5

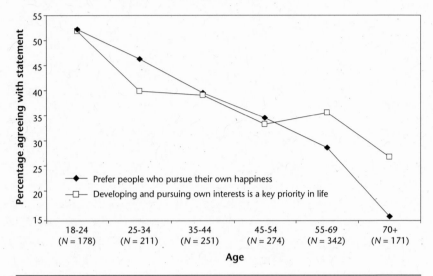

Self-direction, personal and principled, by age

Source: CCES, 2007-08.

theme underwrites Nevitte's analysis of declining deference among younger generations in Canada and elsewhere. An emphasis on self-direction is closely allied to a growing penchant for self-expression and self-discovery, or what the post-materialist literature describes as self-actualization – found in various studies to be a greater priority among younger, postwar generations. Consistent with these findings, Adams also highlights the attraction of younger cohorts of Canadians to the "fulfillment" dimension of individualism, which encompasses many of the same features. There are thus numerous overlapping accounts leading us to anticipate a greater emphasis on self-direction and allied qualities among young Canadians.

Two items on the CCES spoke to personal and principled dimensions of self-direction. The personal item asked whether respondents agreed or disagreed that "developing and pursuing my own individual interests is a key priority in my life." The principled item asked about the life priorities of others, asking respondents whether they preferred people "who, whatever happens, do their duty" or those "who pursue their own happiness." Figure 7.5 reveals a clear pattern of rising support for self-directing values among younger Canadians. As with other measures of individualism, the pattern of steady change across the entire age spectrum is suggestive of cohort effects. For the personal item, however, there is also a sharp rise in the incidence

Figure 7.6

Tolerance of group difference by age

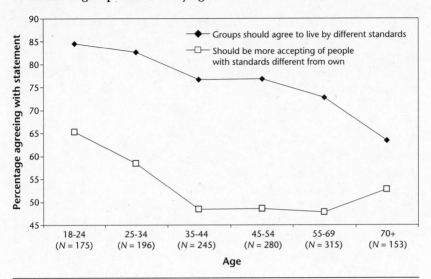

Source: CCES, 2007-08.

of total agreement among those aged eighteen to twenty-four – a jump of 12 percentage points from the adjacent age category – suggesting again that there may also be a life course component that helps to explain greater emphasis on self-direction in the younger years of life.

Other items relating to self-direction were also included on the CCES to allow for further examination of this important dimension of individualism. As intimated in the typology of individualism presented in Table 7.1 above – and as others have also suggested – the principled variant of self-direction involves respecting the right of others to pursue their own preferences and ideas, which implies support for values of tolerance and permissiveness. Two questions on the CCES spoke to general dispositions in this regard. One asked respondents which came closer to their own view: "We should be more accepting of people with different standards from our own" or "There is adequate acceptance in today's society of groups with different standards." The second followed up by asking: "If two groups of people living in the same country have very different standards should they try to persuade one another to change their ways, or should they just agree to live by different standards?" The responses to these questions reveal high levels of tolerance across the board. However, they are especially elevated among younger Canadians (Figure 7.6), confirming a pattern of heightened tolerance among younger generations found in most studies of the topic, whether in Canada (Nevitte 1996, 233; Howe and Fletcher 2002) or elsewhere (Zukin et al. 2006, 166-69).

Three other questions on the CCES focused on another distinct dimension of self-direction. These particular items were included for two reasons. First, they were modelled on questions posed in the Environics/CROP values surveys (with small modifications), thus permitting some useful linkages in the analysis to this other rich data source. The more substantive reason for their inclusion is that the three items are akin to some that appear in the large battery of items used by psychologists to measure an important dimension of personality termed "openness to experience" (part of a larger typology involving four other broad dimensions of personality: conscientiousness, extraversion, agreeableness, and neuroticism). They are, for this reason, relevant to the thesis alluded to above: the notion that the rising emphasis on individualism identified by Twenge, Adams, and others might be conceptualized not just as a reflection of changing values, but perhaps more fundamentally as a manifestation of evolving personality dispositions – in other words, changes not just in what we believe but in who we are. That rising individualism might be interpreted in this manner is an idea pursued at greater length in Chapter 9, which looks more deeply into the social origins of the phenomenon. Here the focus is simply on establishing the basic age pattern. The three items tapping into openness to experience are:

- I like to experience new emotions every day.
- As soon as I see an opportunity to try something new, I do it.
- I enjoy being able to explore aspects of my personality I don't usually express in everyday life.[8]

Responses to the three items (agree/disagree scales) were combined into an additive index. Figure 7.7 displays the percentage in each age group falling into the upper tier of this index. Results are displayed for both the relatively current CCES data and the older Environics/CROP data, the latter representing five combined surveys from 1992 to 1996. The question texts were the same in both cases, but response options varied on the Environics/CROP studies, whereas these were rendered consistent on the CCES. Thus the indices from the two points in time are similar, but not identical.

In both instances, there is evidence of heightened openness to experience among younger sections of the Canadian population, though the pattern is sharper and more consistent in the Environics/CROP data, which draws on a much larger sample for each age category. In the latter data, the pattern of age differences – a steady diminution of openness to experience across the entire age spectrum – is suggestive of cohort effects. Yet there is also, as with other measures from before, a strong signal of life course variation in

Figure 7.7

Openness to experience by age

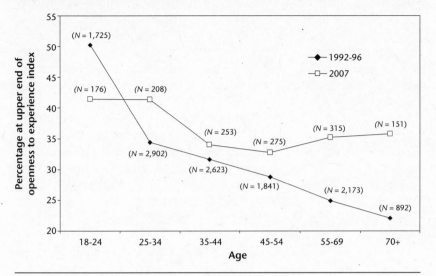

Source: CROP Socio-Cultural Surveys, 1992-96; CCES, 2007-08.

the sharply elevated levels of openness to experience among the eighteen to twenty-four age group.

Overall, these varied questions from different data sources confirm the view that a heightened emphasis on principles and predilections associated with self-direction is an important facet of rising individualism among younger groups in Canada. This gradual transformation encompasses changing values of both a personal and principled nature, that is to say, the desire to be free to pursue one's own desires and goals, along with respect for the right of others to do likewise. It also extends, the evidence would suggest, to differences across age groups in basic dispositions relating to the dimension of personality closely associated with self-directing values, openness to experience.

Conclusion

This chapter has explored conceptual and empirical terrain important to gaining a catholic understanding of the nature of social integration in current times and the degree to which it has been undermined by rising individualism – large themes but necessary background to making sense of political disengagement among rising generations. The principal conclusions are that the main manifestations of individualism among younger Canadians are elevated levels of self-regard and more marked emphasis on self-direction. In both cases, the relevant age patterns would suggest that cohort effects partly underlie the differences between age groups, auguring further change as time wears on. However, life course patterns are also evident in some of the distinctive attitudes and dispositions of young adults under age twenty-five, particularly for those measures capturing what we have termed personal (as opposed to principled) individualism. The empirical conclusions are similar to those derived from the longitudinal analysis of political attentiveness in an earlier chapter: that generational change is part of the story behind substantial age differences on relevant measures, but life-cycle effects play a part as well.

The empirical assessment of these matters is admittedly far from definitive. The questions posed on the CCES are somewhat limited and could be refined and expanded. In some instances, alternative sources have been used to strengthen the case that age differences exist in certain domains. But the objective is as much conceptual as empirical: to place trends in the political realm in their more general social and cultural context by bringing together facets of changing citizen attitudes and dispositions emphasized by various political science accounts under the broader tent of individualism. The purpose, in part, is to underline that rising individualism should be seen not only as a shift in explicitly held values, but also as a change in underlying qualities and dispositions of a more personal and implicit nature.

The next chapter sharpens the focus by considering the effects of changing patterns of social integration on political engagement. A more expansive approach is adopted once again in Chapter 9. There, we endeavour to make sense of the mix of life-cycle and cohort patterns encountered across the study and thereby shed light on the root origins of ascendant individualism that, combined with other forces, has gradually reshaped patterns of citizen engagement in contemporary Canadian democracy.

8

Social Integration and Political Engagement

The decline of community and the rise of individualism cannot but have significant repercussions for citizen engagement. If these changes to the social fabric are more nuanced and complex than simple summary statements typically allow, there are nonetheless changes abroad in Canadian society with potentially negative consequences. The broadest repercussion, outlined already, is a general weakening of commitment to the public realm. Erosion of the pillars of social integration threatens to undermine support for public endeavour of various kinds and to weaken the other-regarding dispositions necessary for the maintenance of an equitable and cohesive social order.

This chapter narrows the focus to standard indicators of political engagement, to consider how changing patterns of social integration influence particular forms of political involvement. The simplest summary is that the erosion of certain forms of community attachment and the ascendancy of individualism have led to a more individualized approach to politics (Delli Carpini 2000, 346; O'Neill 2007; Stolle and Hooghe 2005, 162). Concern for the community interest and an attendant sense of obligation to be involved in political affairs have weakened. So too have the affective connections to community that can generate political engagement. Participation is instead more contingent on individual interest in the dual sense of the word: that which affects me (the self-regarding dimension) and that which intrigues me (the self-directing dimension). Political involvement is thus more selective, more contingent, and in the case of those detached from community and unmoved by personal interest of either variety, absent altogether.

One manner in which these influences manifest themselves is with respect to personal engagement in politics. This is apparent in the relative weight of different motivations in sustaining political involvement. But another distinct way in which the shifting sands of social integration affect political engagement is by altering the dynamics of interpersonal mobilization – the processes whereby people persuade and cajole one another, whether consciously or unconsciously, to be politically attuned and involved. In a society marked by weak attachments to community and heightened individualism, such mobilization becomes less widespread and less robust. Declining engagement is thus a product of combined effects of the personal and the interpersonal, both of which reflect gradual changes in the general realm of social integration.

Personal Motivations for Political Engagement

To explore personal motivations for political involvement, two different tacks are adopted. The first is the more direct method. A set of questions was posed on the Canadian Citizen Engagement Survey (CCES) that asked respondents about the personal importance they attach to various reasons for engaging in two forms of political activity: voting and following the news and current affairs. Reservations were expressed earlier about this method of identifying motivational wellsprings, as the influence of a particular factor may not always be apparent to respondents themselves, especially if it is not an immediate precipitant of the behaviour in question but instead exerts more subtle and remote causal influence. Those reservations remain, and these self-professed reasons behind political engagement should be seen only as partial statements of reality. The second method of analysis complements the first by drawing linkages between separate and distinct measures of motivational cause and behavioural effect in order to capture less self-evident motivations.

Motivations for Engagement: Direct Queries

Respondents on the CCES were asked about the importance they personally would assign to four different reasons for voting and four analogous reasons for following the news and current affairs. Two were expected to reflect the reasoning of socially integrated respondents – one citing the notion of civic duty or responsibility (to vote or follow the news), the other citing the sense of community connection engendered by the activity. The other two were expected to resonate with those more individualistic in their approach to political involvement: participating in order to look out for one's own interests (self-regarding reasoning) and engaging in activities in which one takes an interest (self-directed reasoning).

As a preliminary caveat, responses to both sets of questions are heavily influenced by the behaviours about which they inquire: those who vote regularly and those who follow the news consistently assign greater importance to each cited reason. The perceived importance of the action in general seems to colour opinions about the importance of specific reasons for undertaking it. This is partly why older age groups, more apt to vote and to follow the news regularly, tend to assign greater importance to all of the reasons proffered. One way to compensate for this would be to control for respondents' propensity to vote or their tendency to follow the news in analyzing

Figure 8.1

Relative importance of reasons for voting by age

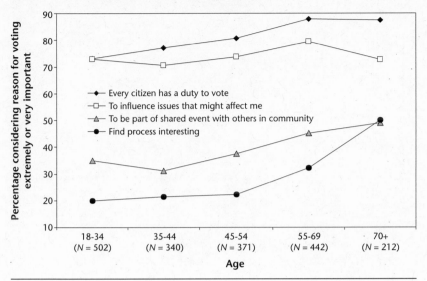

Source: CCES, 2007-08.

the strength of different motivational factors. Another method, followed here, is the simpler one of concentrating attention on the *relative importance* assigned to different motivational factors by respondents and variations in the pattern of salience across age groups.

The overall pattern of responses first bears comment (Figures 8.1 and 8.2). In the case of voting, two motivations are most significant in respondents' minds: the perceived duty to vote, reflecting a social conception of the voting, and the desire to influence issues of personal concern, an individualistic rationale. Between 70 percent and 90 percent of respondents in all age groups consider these "very" or "extremely" important reasons why they vote (Figure 8.1). The other two reasons – that voting provides an opportunity to be part of a shared event with others in the community and interest in the voting process itself – do not resonate to nearly the same degree. Across all age categories, fewer than 50 percent (substantially fewer for most age groups) consider these reasons to be very or extremely important motivations for voting in elections. This overall ranking of reasons is not terribly surprising, given the dominant arguments on behalf of electoral participation advanced in public discourse: the importance of doing one's civic duty and the opportunity that elections provide to make one's voice heard. The communal nature of the event and the intrinsic appeal of the voting process are rarely cited explicitly.

Figure 8.2

Relative importance of reasons for following the news by age

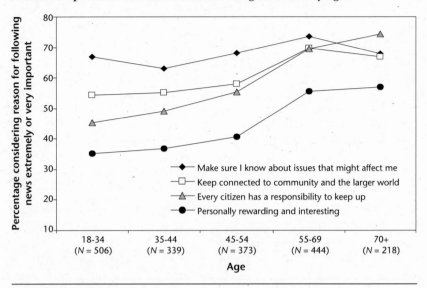

Source: CCES, 2007-08.

The desire for community connection and the personal appeal of activities undertaken are more evident as motivational wellsprings of one key background activity that has previously been shown to exert a powerful influence on political participation: following news and current affairs. Responses to the four items probing motivations for engaging in this activity cluster more closely (Figure 8.2). A sense of citizen responsibility and the desire to know about issues potentially of personal relevance remain important motivators, but are less critical determinants than in the case of voting. The idea of keeping up with the news in order to feel connected to one's "community and the larger world" (a phrasing chosen to avoid exclusive focus on the local community) is of equal significance. The personal appeal of following the news – believing the activity to be "rewarding and interesting" – is less significant to respondents but not exceptionally so. In short, all four factors have some bearing on important manifestations of political engagement, though some are more immediately apparent to respondents themselves, particularly in the case of voting.

Turning to the age patterns revealed in the two figures, a greater focus on individualistic motivations among younger respondents can be detected in some, but not all, of the trend lines. Of the two most salient reasons for voting, the civic duty motivation is less compelling to younger respondents, while the self-interested rationale of looking out for one's interests is more consistently supported across age groups. Thus the latter is relatively more important to the young than the old. The discrepancy is not all that great, however, partly due to the generally strong emphasis placed on voting as a civic duty: this social norm, if not quite as entrenched today as it once was, still holds considerable sway. The same is not so true with respect to keeping up with the news – citizen duty is less commonly cited in public discourse as a reason people should keep abreast of public affairs – and in this case the relative importance of obligation and self-interest diverges more sharply between young and old. Among the eighteen to thirty-four age group, the percentage citing self-interest as an important factor is 22 points higher than the percentage citing citizen responsibility (67 percent versus 45 percent). This gap decreases steadily with increasing age, until among the seventy and over the relative importance of the two reasons is reversed (68 percent versus 74 percent).

The age patterns with respect to community connection are similar to those for duty or responsibility in both graphs. Younger respondents are less inclined to consider this a salient reason for voting and following the news, a result consistent with the proposition that reasons relating to social connection or obligation matter less to the young. However, results for the final item, undertaking activities with personal appeal, are not consistent with expectations. Rather than being of greater significance, this self-directing rationale appears to be considerably weaker among younger respondents. Thus, the individualistic motivation for democratic involvement that appears to stand out in the minds of young Canadians is the pursuit of self-interest – looking out for one's own interests by keeping up with the news and participating in elections.

Motivations for Engagement: Indirect Evidence

Direct queries are one way of accessing motivational origins of behaviour, but they do not reveal all. Not only do they tend to disclose only the most immediate motivations, they also tend to bundle too much into a single survey question – in this case, the importance of the act itself and the importance of the specific reason for engaging in the act. The other method of assessing motivational underpinnings, which avoids some of these problems, is examining the empirical linkages between independent measures of respondent attributes and reported behaviour.

In the direct queries about reasons for voting and following the news, an individualistic orientation was apparent in the greater tendency of younger respondents to cite self-regarding motivations, but not in any notable preference for self-directed activity. The latter characteristic is evident, however, when more indirect methods of investigation are used. Figure 8.3 shows how the influence of political interest on following the news varies across age brackets. Among the youngest group, those aged eighteen to thirty-four,

Figure 8.3

Following politics daily: the influence of political interest by age

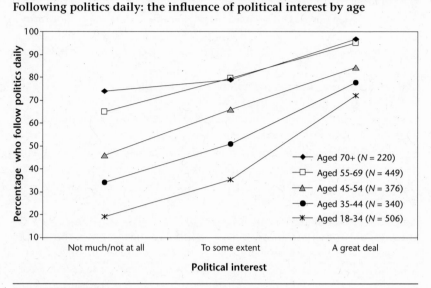

Source: CCES, 2007-08.

the percentage who follow the news daily moves from 20 percent among those least interested in politics to 70 percent among the most interested – a jump of 50 percentage points. With increasing age, the effects of political interest on following the news grow weaker, so that there is only a 23 point gap separating the least and most politically interested respondents seventy and over. The differential effects of political interest on following the news are consistent with the broader notion that younger generations are more inclined to be guided in their actions by personal preferences and interests, rather than simply adopting socially prescribed behaviour.

Figure 8.4 provides more direct evidence of the role of individualistic values in producing this result. Again, the figure displays the relationship between political interest and following the news. Now, however, instead of looking at variation in the relationship across age groups, the focus is on differences associated with the relative emphasis placed on self-directing values (specifically the CCES questions asking about the importance of developing and pursuing one's own interests; and one's preference for people who do their duty or those who pursue their own happiness – see Figure 7.5). The contrasts are not as stark as they are across age groups, but the anticipated pattern does appear. Among those who place the greatest emphasis on self-direction, political interest has a powerful impact on whether or not they choose to follow the news each day – 60 percentage points separate the most and least politically interested respondents (33 percent versus

Figure 8.4

Following politics daily: the influence of political interest by self-direction

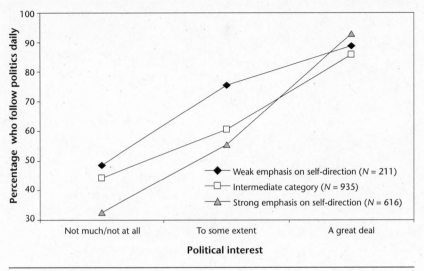

Source: CCES, 2007-08.

93 percent). The effect of political interest among those assigning the least importance to self-direction, though still considerable, is somewhat weaker at 40 percentage points (49 percent versus 89 percent). Dispositions on this important dimension of individualism seem to influence the degree to which personal interest in politics guides attentiveness to public affairs.

Also rendered more intelligible by taking into account the individualistic predilections of younger Canadians are demographic patterns with respect to voter participation. Rather than political interest, the individual attribute considered in this case is political knowledge. The supposition is that political interest is less important than knowledge to the act of voting per se. While strongly linked to various background behaviours, such as following the news on a regular basis, that help put someone in a position to vote, at the moment of voting (or staying home) interest is not as critical since the activity requires relatively little effort or motivational energy. Consistent with this reasoning, we have seen that few Canadians cite the intrinsic interest of the voting process as a reason for participating. At the point of voting or abstaining, it is more individual capability – a function of knowledge and the capacity to make reasoned electoral choices – than interest that tips the scales in favour of participation or abstention.

Figure 8.5 captures the relationship between political knowledge and electoral participation across age groups. There are clear differences in this

Figure 8.5

Voting in federal elections: the influence of political knowledge by age

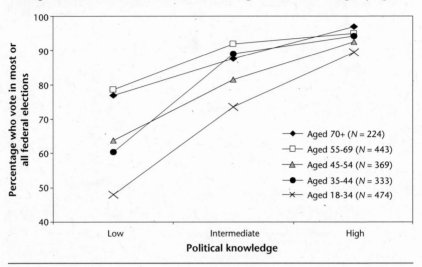

Source: CCES, 2007-08.

relationship, as the tendency to vote in elections is more sharply influenced by political knowledge among younger Canadians. The differences are of a similar magnitude to those seen for political interest in Figure 8.3 above. Among the youngest group, the percentage voting in most or all federal elections climbs from 48 percent in the low-knowledge category to 89 percent in the high-knowledge group – a difference of 41 percentage points. The participation gap between the low- and high-knowledge categories declines steadily with increasing age, falling to 20 percentage points or less in the two upper age brackets.[1]

More direct evidence that this pattern reflects the individualistic propensities of younger Canadians is presented in Figure 8.6. The figure displays the relationship between voting propensity and knowledge, this time as a function of the importance respondents assign to duty as a reason for voting. Among those who place relatively little emphasis on duty, political knowledge has a very sizable impact on whether or not they participate in elections (the gap between low- and high-knowledge categories is 44 percentage points). As the perceived importance of duty increases, the influence of knowledge on the propensity to vote decreases (falling to 17 percentage points among those placing the greatest weight on duty). Thus the fact that political knowledge has a greater impact on voting among younger Canadians partly reflects their diminished sense of civic duty, which in turn reflects the larger syndrome of weakened social integration and rising individualism among

Figure 8.6

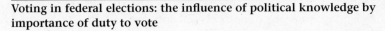

Voting in federal elections: the influence of political knowledge by importance of duty to vote

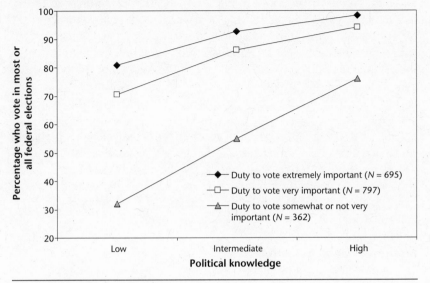

Source: CCES, 2007-08.

younger generations. Without duty as a buttress for electoral participation, personal knowledge of politics looms larger in the voting decision.[2]

In these various results lies a reasonably consistent story about the motivational wellsprings behind engagement in public life across different generations of Canadians. Among older generations, keeping up with the news and voting in elections are firmly rooted in motives associated with a high level of social integration, including a sense of obligation to be involved and feelings of community attachment. They are not immune to individualistic considerations by any means, but these personal reasons for participating are reinforced by powerful sentiments of social connectedness. This is why in the absence of political interest, older Canadians are still generally inclined to follow the news on a regular basis. It is also why older Canadians who know relatively little about politics and may have some trouble discerning the appropriate electoral choice, vote nonetheless. A blend of social and individual motivations for involvement leads to relatively high levels of democratic engagement.

For younger Canadians, the individualistic rationale stands more on its own, without the same backing of social connection and obligation. When asked directly about their motives for voting and following the news, the most distinctive feature of their responses is the heightened emphasis on looking out for one's own interests, suggesting the application of a self-regarding lens to decisions about political involvement. A self-directing rationale, on the other hand, is implicit in the marked variation in attentiveness to news and current affairs associated with the personal political interest of younger Canadians. Likewise, differences in voter participation associated with political knowledge – an important individual resource permitting the formulation of appropriate electoral choices – suggest a more individualized approach to political involvement. When social motivations are weaker, engagement becomes more contingent on a blend of individual interests and capabilities.

Thus, couching analysis of political attentiveness and electoral participation in a framework of broader social change helps to make sense of important generational differences in political involvement. As social integration weakens, individualistic motivations come to the fore, leading to more contingency and variation in political engagement and lower levels of involvement overall.

Interpersonal Mobilization

The more dominant approach to studying political involvement is to focus on the qualities of individual citizens that influence their ability and desire to be involved – their interest and knowledge in politics, their sense of civic duty, their desire to be connected to their community. But another important stream of research looks at the forces and factors that precipitate involvement on the part of citizens. Rather than assessing why citizens elect to become involved, this entails considering how they are mobilized into politics. The prism of broader cultural change can be fruitfully applied to this area of investigation as well, to consider how mobilization dynamics have been influenced by the changing patterns of social integration and ascendant norms of individualism. We begin with a brief overview of some of the relevant political mobilization literature and then focus on one particularly important form of mobilization – interpersonal inducement – apt to be affected by broader cultural change.

The Personal Touch

In assessing the external forces that engender citizen participation in politics, one line of research has focused on the mobilization efforts of political parties, particularly in the area of electoral participation. Given their abiding interest in persuading supporters to turn up at the polls on election day, parties are natural vehicles for this type of political mobilization. Some of this involves impersonal techniques such as television advertising and direct mail campaigns, but the most effective way of getting people to vote, leading proponents of the thesis contend, is traditional grassroots mobilization involving personal contact with citizens. Based on an extensive analysis of one particular item that has appeared on the American National Election Studies – "Did anyone from one of the political parties call you up or come around and talk to you about the campaign?" – Rosenstone and Hansen conclude that the personal touch embodied in direct contact is the most effective means of encouraging voter involvement (2003, 161-77, 231-34).

In the past decade or so, researchers have turned to other methods of determining the effects of different mobilization methods. The use of field experiments – randomly assigning individuals to either receive or not receive some inducement to vote in the context of actual elections – has been an important innovation in this area of research, allowing for more precise estimates of the effects of different methods of voter contact and persuasion on electoral participation. One of the central insights has been to confirm the earlier conclusion that the personal touch makes a considerable difference. "Mobilizing voters is rather like inviting them to a social occasion. Personal invitations convey the most warmth and work best" (Green and Gerber 2004, 92).

In the numerous field experiments conducted to date, the personal touch has typically consisted of strangers enjoining people in a personalized manner to participate by knocking on doors or by telephone canvassing using personalized appeals rather than reading from a script. But those involved in this area of research have suggested that truly personal appeals and pressures – those coming from people we actually know – would likely have greater effects on political involvement (Green and Gerber 2004, 93). This proposition is confirmed by their more recent experimental work, which involved exposing people to social pressures to vote by mailing out information (during a 2006 primary election) concerning their own and neighbours' records of electoral participation. This experimental manipulation was unusually effective in boosting turnout compared to a control group receiving no such inducements (Gerber et al. 2008). It is also supported by other research, using non-experimental methods, which focuses not only on electoral participation but a broader range of political and civic activity: working on election campaigns, contacting public officials, attending protests, being involved in community activity. Based on a national survey in the US, Sidney Verba and his colleagues have found that the majority of requests to be involved in such activities come from people we know personally, and that people are more likely to agree to participate when the request comes from someone in that category (1995, 139-44). Likewise, research on party members in Canada finds that people (young people especially) often report joining because they were asked by someone they know personally, most commonly a family member, but in other cases a friend or acquaintance. Party representatives, on the other hand, are "seldom the ones issuing the invitation" (Cross and Young 2007, 12). This focus on informal acts of persuasion between individuals, rather than formal contact from political organizations (see also Beck et al. 2002), represents a return to one of the important themes of the earliest years of political behaviour research. As the seminal study of voting behaviour concluded, "In the last analysis, more than anything else people can move other people" (Lazarsfeld et al. 1968, 158).

This seems to be especially true, scattered evidence would suggest, for those relatively unlikely to participate. One study reports that the effects on individual electoral participation of living in a household where *others vote* are strongest among groups that typically have lower voter turnout: those under forty-five, those with lower levels of education, and non-partisans (Gray 2003, 119-20). Another study focusing on the effects of election campaigns on the intention to vote finds that persuasion by a personal acquaintance (to vote for a particular candidate) has a greater impact on those initially inclined not to vote. For more formal methods of mobilization, by contrast, the finding is reversed: the effects on participation of contact by a political party are greater for those with a prior intention to vote (Hillygus 2005). The same finding is confirmed in numerous field experiments utilizing formal methods of voter contact in which mobilization effects are generally found to be greatest among those who have a prior history of voting (Green and Gerber 2004, 37-38; Niven 2001, 2002, 2004). Recalling our earlier distinction between intermittent and habitual non-voting, the suggestion in these various findings is that those with a prior inclination to participate are more readily reached by formal methods of mobilization, whereas those without any such inclination – the habitually disengaged – are more effectively mobilized through informal inveigling by those they know personally. The latter dynamic may therefore be of particular importance to understanding and potentially addressing the phenomenon of chronic disengagement among younger generations.

The considerable potential of interpersonal mobilization to engender greater political participation, especially among the deeply disengaged, is thus strongly suggested by prior research. Two findings from Canadian sources offer some sense of the potential magnitude of these effects. The first is based on Statistics Canada's General Social Survey of 2003, the study used to investigate patterns of voting and other forms of public engagement among Canadians in earlier chapters. The survey asked people about their living arrangements in reasonable detail, making it possible to distinguish those living with other adults in the household (typically a spouse or parents) and those living alone or with children but no adults. This basic demographic variable is associated with significant differences in electoral participation. Among those living with other adults, the rate of habitual voting – defined as having voted in the most recent federal, provincial, and municipal elections – is 61.5 percent. Among those living on their own or with children only, the figure drops to 50.3 percent.[3] When controls are introduced for age, education, and sex, potentially relevant confounding factors, the gap is undiminished (indeed it becomes slightly greater at 12.4 percentage points).

If there is a substantial increase in habitual voting associated with simply living with other adults, the effects from living with others who are politically active are, of course, likely to be greater still. The potential avenues of influence are numerous. Someone who votes, for example, can bring someone they live with along to the polling station, can serve as a civic example to others in the household, or can, in the run-up to an election, engage others in the household in discussion about the campaign. Whatever the precise mechanism(s), a second Canadian research finding suggests how potent such influences can be. A survey conducted in Manitoba in December 2003 asked respondents whether they had voted in the June 2003 provincial election and whether others in their household had participated.[4] The basic finding speaking to interpersonal influence is striking: "About three-quarters of respondents, whether they were voters or non-voters, report that their households contain other eligible voters. However, only one-quarter of non-voters report that all other eligible members of their household voted. This compares with some 9 in 10 voters" (Prairie Research Associates 2004, 4). Even allowing for some inaccuracy in reported voting, for oneself or other household members, this vast discrepancy suggests very powerful mechanisms of interpersonal influence on voter participation. Large differences associated with the voting behaviour of other household members have also been reported in studies of both British and American voters (Zuckerman and Kotler-Berkowitz, 1998, 474; Gray 2003, 119), and a more recent study, based on rigorous experimental techniques, has confirmed a powerful "contagion" effect of voting within households (Nickerson 2008).

In short, there is considerable evidence from various sources to suggest that interpersonal influence is a significant catalyst of political engagement, and, in particular, a potentially important way of reaching those whose disengagement runs deep. There is, then, reason to examine interpersonal dynamics more closely in order to understand variation in political involvement – from one person to the next, from one place to the next, and, if change has taken place in the mechanisms of interpersonal influence over time, from one period to the next.

Who Influences Others?

If there is a fairly compelling stockpile of evidence that interpersonal influence has considerable bearing on political participation, there is also a significant gap in this body of research. The principal focus is on mobilization as an independent variable – how the influence of others encourages and facilitates political participation. There has been relatively little consideration of interpersonal influence as a dependent variable, that is, of the factors that make people inclined to influence others. Where the question has been considered, the focus is typically limited to the demographic characteristics of those apt to engage in acts of mobilization, rather than relevant attitudinal or behavioural qualities (Verba et al. 1995, 149-55).[5]

The question of what leads people to influence others was briefly broached in Chapter 5 in the analysis of the manifold effects of political attentiveness on political behaviour. There, the rather obvious but not inconsequential point was made that those who are politically engaged themselves, as gauged by their knowledge of politics, are more apt to undertake forms of behaviour that involve influencing or mobilizing others: engaging people in political discussion and persuading others to vote when the occasion arises. Political attentiveness thus has both a personal and interpersonal impact, affecting not only individual engagement but also broader social dynamics of political mobilization. At this point, we turn to consider how individualistic norms also have some bearing on these same processes.

With an eye to linking this analysis to the ultimate question of generational differences in political engagement, it is first necessary to establish how interpersonal mobilization varies between younger and older Canadians. Figure 8.7 displays the trend across age categories for the measures of interpersonal influence employed earlier – political discussion with friends and whether, if someone said they were not going to vote in an upcoming election, one would try to persuade that person to vote. Control variables are also introduced by looking separately at committed voters only (for the vote persuasion question) and the most knowledgeable third of voters (for the political discussion question). In all cases, younger age groups are less inclined to engage in acts of political influence. Whereas over 60 percent of older respondents say they would persuade a would-be abstainer to vote, only 44 percent of young adults would do likewise. Similarly, the reported rate of frequent political discussion is substantially higher – about twice the rate – among older adults. The control variables do weaken the age relationships (the gap between young and old on the two measures is smaller among regular voters and more knowledgeable respondents) but this should not be taken as indicating that the age relationship is partly spurious. Instead, the controls are more properly seen as intervening variables that help explain *why* young people are less inclined to engage in acts of interpersonal influence. Less likely to be regular voters themselves and less likely to have substantial knowledge of politics, young adults are, for these reasons, less likely to seek to influence others in political matters. At the same time, the fact that there remain differences between age categories with the controls in place suggests that other relevant variables remain to be identified to more fully explain why young people are less apt to mobilize others.

Figure 8.7

Influencing others by age

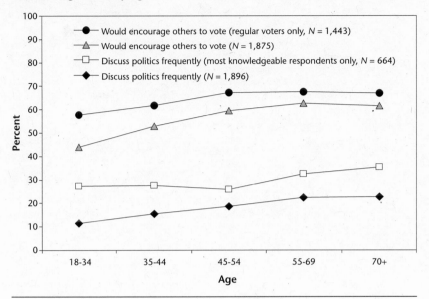

Source: CCES, 2007-08.

One set of pertinent variables are those capturing individualistic norms. Figure 8.8 shows how the propensity to engage others varies in accordance with the emphasis respondents place on background dimensions of individualism – self-regard and self-direction – along with the importance they place on duty-based norms for voting and following politics.[6] In almost all instances, as individualism increases (or sense of duty/responsibility decreases), the propensity to engage others in political matters declines. The question asking respondents about convincing someone else to vote (the top set of lines in Figure 8.8) is a more direct statement of interpersonal persuasion and it is this item that shows the strongest relationship to individualistic norms. For control purposes, the analysis is limited to regular voters only. Among those who score low on the scale of self-regard, nearly three-quarters (73 percent) say they would seek to persuade a potential abstainer to vote, whereas at the high end of the self-regard scale this drops to just over half (54 percent). For self-directing norms, there is likewise a reduced proclivity to persuade others to vote (from 69 to 57 percent) with increasing individualism. The relationship is substantially stronger when a norm specifically linked to voting is invoked: among those who cite duty as an "extremely important" reason for why they personally vote (on the left side of

Figure 8.8

Influencing others by individualist norms

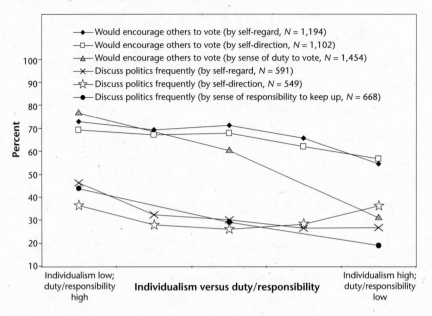

Legend:
- —◆— Would encourage others to vote (by self-regard, *N* = 1,194)
- —□— Would encourage others to vote (by self-direction, *N* = 1,102)
- —△— Would encourage others to vote (by sense of duty to vote, *N* = 1,454)
- —✕— Discuss politics frequently (by self-regard, *N* = 591)
- —☆— Discuss politics frequently (by self-direction, *N* = 549)
- —●— Discuss politics frequently (by sense of responsibility to keep up, *N* = 668)

X-axis: **Individualism versus duty/responsibility**

Individualism low; duty/responsibility high — Individualism high; duty/responsibility low

Source: CCES, 2007-08.

the figure), 77 percent would try to persuade another to do likewise, whereas only 31 percent of self-guided voters – those who consider duty either "not very" or only "somewhat" important to their own voting behaviour – would do so.

The effects of individualistic norms on political discussion (the bottom set of lines in Figure 8.8) are somewhat weaker and less consistent, but then this measure speaks more to engaging others than persuading them to change their stripes and is for that reason perhaps less unpalatable to ardent individualists. Still, there is evidence of a decline in political discussion with heightened individualism. The analysis in this case is limited to the most knowledgeable third of respondents only. Within this relatively conversant and loquacious group, the incidence of frequent political discussion falls from 46 to 27 percent as emphasis on self-regarding norms increases. Similarly, it falls from 44 to 19 percent as respondents put less stock in the notion that citizens have a responsibility to keep up with current events. The one null result is for self-directing norms. In this case, there is no evidence of reduced political discussion with increased emphasis on this dimension of individualism.

Implicit in this set of results is an alternative proposition about declining political participation rooted in propositions about changing dynamics of mobilization over time. The most widely circulated hypothesis on these lines is Rosenstone and Hansen's argument that changes to party mobilization techniques – decreased emphasis on personal techniques of door-to-door contact in favour of impersonal methods of mass advertising and media events – have put a significant dent in electoral participation. Designed to explain declining turnout in the US, the argument has been invoked elsewhere as parties everywhere have adopted similar campaigning strategies. In Canada, the fact that young people are less likely to report being contacted by a political party has been cited as one reason their participation levels have declined (Blais et al. 2002, 57; Rubenson et al. 2004, 413-14). An additional Canadian twist is the suggestion that the change to a permanent voters list in 1997 exacerbated turnout decline, partly due to registration problems, but also due to the loss of "direct contact with eligible voters" by enumerators during election campaigns (Black 2005, 218). While Rosenstone and Hansen recognize that mobilization effects are not limited to official political organizations, that people can and do influence people as well, their contention is that changes in the degree of social integration over time can account for only a small proportion of the decline in turnout (2003, 217).[7] An emphasis on the changing strategies of political organizations in precipitating turnout decline also emerges from the more recent body of research using innovative experimental methods (Green and Gerber 2004, 108-9).

A greater emphasis on decline over time in the interpersonal relationships that can help sustain political involvement is evident in other works. One central contribution, of course, is Putnam's *Bowling Alone*: the book's overarching thesis is that social connections of varied types have slowly atrophied with wide-ranging consequences for participation in public life (2000). If Rosenstone and Hansen might be criticized for offering a rather limited analysis of changes in social connectedness over time (they base their assessment only on whether people live near where they were born and whether they attend religious services regularly), Putnam more than fills the gap with a welter of evidence documenting declining involvement in social and civic life in recent decades. But we have already voiced significant scepticism about the applicability of Putnam's findings to the Canadian case. Earlier analysis of Canadian patterns did not reveal significant change over time in basic measures of social connectedness, such as the number of neighbours known by name, whether people feel part of their neighbourhood, and the level of trust in others. Nor did close examination of age trends for other measures of civic participation and social connectedness reveal anything more than readily explicable life-cycle undulations.

If it is not obvious that Canadians are less socially connected nowadays than in the past, an alternative hypothesis is that rather than a decline in the quantity of social connections over time, it is perhaps the *quality* of those relations that has gradually changed (Wolfe 1998, 261). As individualistic norms have gathered force, the degree to which political influence and persuasion are present in interpersonal relations has diminished. Those embracing self-regarding and self-directing norms are inclined to focus on their own interests and priorities and leave others to their own devices. Younger generations are more imbued with these norms than older generations and for this reason less likely to cajole, persuade, and mobilize others. If this is true in general, the political manifestations include a reluctance to persuade others to vote or to engage people in political discussion. Individualism is not the only source of a generational divide on this count: declining democratic engagement among younger citizens itself contributes to a reduced inclination to mobilize others, as those who do not vote or know much about politics are less likely to seek to influence, engage, and persuade others (Cassel and Hill 1981, 193; Nickerson 2008, 55). The process as a whole might be characterized as a vicious circle – political disengagement eroding mechanisms of interpersonal mobilization, thereby engendering further disengagement – exacerbated by the gradual ascendance of individualistic norms.

Putting a precise estimate on the overall magnitude of the effects associated with these interactive processes is an unrealistic goal, but more imprecise conclusions seem reasonable. If is widely accepted that an important factor in determining whether someone is politically involved is whether or not they are subject to mobilization influences, then changes to party mobilization techniques are one possible source of declining engagement over time. Another, however, is the rise in individualistic norms that has rendered citizens themselves less apt to influence others around them. The more subtle arena of changing interpersonal relations is an important site to consider in seeking to understand evolving trends in political engagement.

Tolerance: The Silver Lining?

Changing social norms thus affect political involvement through various channels, both altering the array of individual motivations that give rise to participation and weakening the inclination to engage with or persuade others in political matters. Some who concede such effects on citizen engagement, nonetheless contend that that there may be as much good as bad in the changes. If the weakening of community and the ascendance of individualism have produced a more disengaged society, these changes have also ushered in a more liberal and less conformist social order. One proponent of the position, Michael Schudson, argues: "The trade-off between community and individualism is also a trade-off between hierarchy and egalitarianism, between authoritarian codes and democratic ones, between unitary, rigid ways of living and pluralistic ones, between imposition and individual choice" (Schudson 1998, 304). That there are such benefits was implicitly acknowledged earlier when it was observed that one strand of the individualist ethos – the principled belief in self-direction – effectively equates to respect for difference and diversity, i.e., tolerance. Canadians might take particular solace in this interpretation, reasoning that if we are (perhaps always have been) a relatively disengaged people lacking a strong sense of community and solidarity, we are also one of the world's more tolerant societies – a place where differences of ethnicity and culture, of religious and political belief, of sexual orientation, and so forth have been accepted and accommodated earlier and more readily than elsewhere.

Certainly others have taken the view that tolerance is an indispensable democratic virtue that must be given proper acknowledgment in assessing the evolutionary arc of contemporary democracy. Russell Dalton, in various scholarly contributions, has consistently offered more sympathetic accounts of citizen engagement than others such as Putnam and Wattenberg. In his most recent work, *The Good Citizen* (2008), he highlights how the younger generation in the US is more tolerant and empathetic towards others than older cohorts. Dalton would not subscribe to the view that this comes at the expense of engagement, for he also contends that the political energies of the younger generation are simply channelled into different activities, such as attending demonstrations and boycotting products, yet another manifestation of their engaged citizenship. But the greater emphasis in *The Good Citizen* is on citizenship norms – beliefs and attitudes rather than action – of which tolerance is an integral component.

There is certainly something to the idea that tolerance is a positive by-product of the rising tide of individualism, but the proposition requires qualification. There is first the need to reflect on the diverse wellsprings of tolerance. The purest source is respect for the right of others to cleave to their own preferences and values and pursue their own conception of happiness – what was previously termed a principled belief in self-direction. But other manifestations of individualism can also contribute to a more diffuse "live and let live" attitude. The principled variant of self-regard, for example, involves respecting the right of others to pursue their own self-interest. If less emphatic about the merits of difference and diversity, the principle nonetheless implies a certain forbearance towards others. The personal variant of self-regard can lead to a similar outcome grounded more in indifference than in respect for others, as those focused on their own concerns may simply tend to leave others to their own devices. Dalton seems to assume the best of young Americans, arguing that they are distinct by virtue of their staunch belief in "autonomy and social solidarity" (2008, 170) and rejecting the characterization of young Americans as "self-centered" or "selfish" (2008, 165). He is, on this point, explicitly critical of Twenge for suggesting that heightened self-regard might be part of a broader individualist ethos prevalent among younger generations, suggesting she "is obviously talking to different people" from those interviewed in his surveys (2008, 169). But rather than different people, it is more likely a matter of different survey questions being consulted by Twenge, questions that more fully disclose the subtleties and complexities of individualism that are present among the younger generation and which contribute to different shadings of a relatively broad and nebulous live-and-let-live philosophy.

Further reason to be cautious about celebrating tolerance as a by-product of individualism lies in the effects of the latter on attentiveness to public affairs. For the value of political attentiveness extends beyond individual empowerment and the capacity to identify issues relevant to one's own personal interests. A broad knowledge of public affairs also underwrites enhanced understanding of others, including knowledge of the circumstances and challenges facing diverse groups within society (Griffiths 2009, 47). Recall the example from earlier concerning Aboriginal peoples: a fair number of respondents on the CCES, including a disproportionate number of young adults, were unaware that average income levels among Aboriginals are lower than those of other Canadians and this simple piece of information seemed to be linked to attitudes concerning whether government should be doing more to help Aboriginal peoples. Tolerance is not really at issue here: people unaware of the social and economic conditions facing Aboriginal communities do not necessarily wish them ill or harbour sentiments of cultural antipathy. What is at stake is basic understanding of the realities of Aboriginal life, including the material circumstances that render the preservation of viable Aboriginal communities exceedingly difficult. Tolerance is an easy virtue in that it does not require much understanding or knowledge of others: it can, in theory, thrive in conditions of complete ignorance. A more substantive respect and regard for others – especially those who are distant from us, geographically, culturally, or socially – requires greater effort and solicitousness.

Those inclined to see more good than bad in the current condition of citizenship struggle somewhat in reconciling the realities of deficient political awareness with their otherwise optimistic appraisal. In his defence of the younger generation in the US, Dalton simply does not address the matter. Young Americans, he asserts, are more apt to express sympathy for the "worst off" in America and in the world and to emphasize the importance of understanding others (2008, 27, 38). But he offers no evidence that young Americans actually have any meaningful or comprehensive understanding of the challenges and barriers facing others far removed from their own place and circumstances. The omission weakens his contention that young people in the US are "good" citizens with a different set of democratic virtues from previous generations. Others acknowledge the importance of political attentiveness, but seek to lower the bar, suggesting an archetype of the attentive citizen consistent with practices of the current age. Schudson, for example, argues that the "monitorial citizen" is a more fitting ideal for contemporary times than the "informed citizen" of earlier periods. The monitorial citizen is passive yet alert, keeping an eye on the political landscape and seeking more information on issues and events as it becomes necessary. But the examples Schudson offers of information that might penetrate the ken of the monitorial citizen are telling:

> [Monitorial citizens] may learn that a product they own has been recalled; that a drought will make produce more expensive in a few weeks (and they might want to buy that lettuce or those blueberries now while they still have a chance); that the road they normally drive home on is tied up with traffic and they should take an alternate route; that an earthquake has made it impossible to contact friends in Los Angeles directly so they should stay tuned for further information; that right-wing militia are far more numerous and serious than they had thought so the context in which they understand the dangers or possibilities in current politics has to be altered. (1998, 310)

Most of these examples embody an individualistic logic, similar to that captured in the survey wording used on the CCES to inquire about self-interested motivations for following the news: "to make sure I know about issues that might affect *me*." They are instances of what Pippa Norris – another scholar who defends today's citizens against the charge that they are lacking in relevant knowledge of public affairs – labels as practical as opposed to abstract knowledge (2000, 213-14). But practical knowledge, as the examples attest, typically means knowledge that is of direct personal relevance. When the information gleaned pertains to matters such as whether to stock up on blueberries, it is clearly far removed from the larger social issues that citizens might attend to. If this is the type of information gathering most likely to flourish in an individualistic society, the depth and breadth of our understanding of others, an important underpinning of compassionate public policy, is likely to suffer.

On this interpretation, if tolerance is rightly seen as a corollary of rising individualism, optimism about the net benefits for democratic citizenship should not be overemphasized. Scratching beneath the surface, the tolerance engendered by individualistic attitudes can be rather minimalist, rooted not so much in principled respect for difference and diversity as in simple indifference towards others borne of a focus on the self. Moreover, tolerance alone is not always enough: groups in need of public succour sometimes require not just forbearance but active understanding. And this entails a degree of attentiveness to public affairs on the part of the average citizen that is unlikely to obtain in a highly individualistic society. It is, then, not enough for Canadians to console themselves that if we have become relatively disengaged from our politics and from one another, we are by the same token a highly tolerant people willing to allow one another the freedom to pursue our own ideas, values, and way of life. It is possible to retain and strengthen the virtue of regard and respect for others, including the right to be different, even as community is strengthened. It is a matter of strengthening social integration and engagement in public life through methods and mechanisms respectful of the widely felt desire for individual autonomy and authenticity. Suggestions for achieving this balance as we move forward follow in Chapter 10. But first we peer backward in Chapter 9 to further probe the early origins of the changing dynamics of citizen engagement over the long haul.

Part 4
Looking Back, Looking Forward

9
Political Culture in the Age of Adolescence

This study has adopted a catholic approach to the exploration of political disengagement in Canada, taking the position that the issue can best be understood through an expansive consideration of different facets of political and social behaviour informed by theories of general applicability. In investigating longitudinal patterns, the time horizon adopted has been considerable, as has the range of countries brought into the analysis in certain places. While some topics examined are explicitly political – patterns of political participation, trends in political attentiveness – others are more social and cultural in nature, including the nature and strength of community attachments and the contours of ascendant individualism. The influence of these factors has been invoked to help explain motivational underpinnings and processes of social mobilization bearing on the political engagement of younger generations. That these same evolutionary changes have probably contributed to greater levels of tolerance in Canadian society is the silver lining (subject to caveats previously noted) in this account.

While the different elements stand on their own as independent factors relevant to disengagement, they also can be seen as an interactive set of changes that have worked together to reshape the nature of Canadian democracy over the long haul. This chapter further explores this common ground, in part to offer a more general synthesis, but also as a means of distilling essentials that can help shape an agenda designed to tackle the problem of disengagement at its roots. The specific aim is to identify a common source, a shared point of origin, for various long-term social and political trends identified in the study.

One common denominator encountered throughout is the proposition that generational change is the driving force behind different facets of a changing political culture. This reflects a widely agreed understanding that political culture consists of deeply seated assumptions and dispositions that are "largely unconscious" and therefore unlikely to be abandoned by the individual once crystallized (Elkins and Simeon 1979, 131). Hence, it is the malleability of rising generations that allows new ways of thinking and acting to emerge. Thus Wattenberg, Putnam, Twenge, and Dalton, though concentrating on different phenomena, all concur that it is distinctive qualities of younger cohorts that have reshaped the political and social landscape in either the US or the developed democracies more broadly. The analysis offered here is consistent with this view, providing either concrete evidence (where feasible) or plausible conjecture in support of the proposition that cohort effects account for much of the age gap evident across a wide range of relevant characteristics and behaviours, including political partici-pation, attentiveness to politics, community attachments, individualism, and tolerance.

There is less common ground, however, when attention turns to the forces and influences behind generational change – that is to say, the root causes of long-term transformation of the social and political landscape. Wattenberg sees the media environment as quite critical, especially changes of the past thirty years that have greatly expanded the choice of viewing and listening options in the realm of electronic media. Putnam traces generational change further back, and suggests two principal reasons for civic disengagement and the weakening of social connectedness among younger cohorts: the introduction of television and the absence of any unifying external threats since the Second World War. Studies of tolerance, on the other hand, Dalton's among them, typically attribute the rise in support for this democratic virtue to the marked increase in levels of education over time (Dalton 2008, 88-90). As one study notes, persons exposed to higher education "learn about diverse points of view and ways of experiencing life, thus becoming less dogmatic, even if they had a tendency toward closed-mindedness before achieving a high level of education" (Sullivan et al. 1981, 100). Across these different accounts, many of the major features of the postwar period – technological advances, unprecedented peace and prosperity, a more educated citizenry – are invoked. This has made for a complex array of possible explanations, raising the question whether there might be some further commonality beyond the mechanics of generational turnover that would help explain assorted dimensions of social, cultural, and political change.

Twenge, for her part, does not probe as deeply as the others into the origins of the changes she identifies, but the fragments she offers raise a question worth pursuing. In accounting for the rise of individualism, the extent of her analysis is the suggestion that the baby boom generation, lacking guid-ance from the past, had to discover individualism for itself, had to "reinvent their way of thinking" (2006, 49). In contrast, the next generation, Genera-tion Me, "entered a world where things had already changed and ... soaked it up like little sponges" (2006, 191). The argument seems strangely incon-sistent in presuming that one generation (or some members thereof) had the presence of mind to consciously fashion a new cultural ethos, whereas the subsequent, sponge-like generation simply absorbed what was handed down to them. As an account of socialization processes, this does not really suffice. However, it does raise the question whether a more satisfactory account of socialization dynamics, the processes whereby extant ideas and beliefs are imparted to new generations, might offer any insight into processes of political culture change.

Other theories likewise do not offer much on this front. Having identified an important development as the key precipitant of change – be it new media technologies, education, or extended peace – the analysis typically proceeds to demonstrate that younger cohorts are the ones who have absorbed the effects, while older ones have proven largely resistant. Little is noted about the endogenous dimension of transmission, the imparting of attitudes and behavioural dispositions from older generations to younger ones, and how this might alter or mediate exogenously induced change. At most, it is perhaps implicitly assumed that the socialization process will serve as a brake on change, hence explaining why change emerges only gradually in rising cohorts – a bit of change in one cohort, a bit more in the next – rather than abruptly. But there also seems to be the further presumption that this is ultimately inconsequential, as the external forces of change will eventually overcome whatever inertia is imposed by socialization dynamics.

This chapter considers more closely the role of socialization processes in inducing and mediating political and social change. The theory is general in its application, addressing changes that in some measure appear to have affected all of the developed democracies and could equally impinge on other countries that experience a similar social evolution. The general approach is to consider changing dynamics of socialization over time and how these have contributed to the evolution of various facets of political culture. The specific argument advanced is that the emergence of adolescence as a discrete stage in the life cycle in the early years of the twentieth century was a critical development, leading to a marked shift in the relative influence of adults and adolescent peers in the formative years of life. With this shift, adolescent dispositions became more deeply entrenched, gradually diffusing upwards into adult society. Adolescence has been an important wellspring of change, planting the seeds of new attitudes, values, and ways of behaving that have slowly germinated and matured to become established elements of the social and political landscape. The case presented is largely circumstantial, but rests on assumptions and empirical evidence that point towards its plausibility.

Linking Life-Cycle and Cohort Effects

One way of framing this inquiry is as an investigation into changing processes of socialization that have given rise to new ways of thinking and acting among rising generations in the developed democracies. Another way is to conceptualize it as an attempt to rethink the linkages between life-cycle and cohort effects, the technical distinction applied in the analysis of longitudinal data that has been invoked regularly throughout this study. The conceptual connection lies first in recognizing that socialization research and life-cycle analysis deal with the same subject matter, focusing on developmental processes over the life course. Life-cycle research (in the field of political science at any rate) normally adopts as its starting point age eighteen, the youngest age for inclusion in many survey samples. This is also the point where political socialization research typically takes its leave, bidding Godspeed to its young research subjects as they leave adolescence behind to join the adult electorate. That researchers pass the baton in their study of these matters should not obscure the underlying continuity of the life course processes involved.

To examine changing processes of political socialization and how these have contributed to a changing political culture among postwar generations is, then, to consider alterations in life-cycle patterns and how these might have given rise to distinct attitudes and behaviours among rising birth cohorts. This represents a modification of the typical strategy in cohort analysis. The standard approach, particularly in quantitative studies, where simplifying assumptions must be made, is to assume an unchanging life-cycle trajectory over time. This has the merit of allowing for the unencumbered specification of cohort effects, which are typically the subject of greatest interest since these are what produce aggregate change over time. But this method of proceeding also precludes more complex ways of thinking about the relationship between life-cycle and cohort effects.

An example of a more nuanced approach can be found in Mark Franklin's work on declining voter participation (2004). It is not the specifics of the argument, but rather the conceptual scaffolding that is relevant for present purposes. Franklin takes his lead from Eric Plutzer's innovative approach to studying voter participation. In brief, Plutzer argues that voting in elections is a stable behaviour once established. Thus, to understand why some people vote more than others we must examine processes that lead to the development of the voting habit, which lie in the developmental stages of early adulthood (2002). Whereas Plutzer applies this developmental model to analyze individual-level variation in voter participation, Franklin uses it to explain long-term aggregate change in voter participation rates. In brief, Franklin suggests that the developmental process that leads people to become (or fail to become) habitual voters was significantly *altered* when the voting age was lowered from twenty-one to eighteen. The change, innocent enough in its conception, had significant repercussions. One feature of life course patterns is that the typical eighteen-year-old is at a more unsettled stage of life than the typical twenty-one-year-old and, for this reason, less likely to vote at the first opportunity. In turn, failing to vote at the first opportunity (or first three, to be precise) hinders development of the voting habit. So, those who came of age after the reduction in voting age were less likely to become habitual voters. Thus a small perturbation in the life-cycle pattern of political development, induced by the reduction in voting age, gave rise to a substantial and enduring pattern of behaviour among new cohorts of voters. The result has been consistently lower levels of voter turnout among younger cohorts in a number of established democracies.

This is an insightful way of thinking about the origins of cohort effects that has wider application. For there most certainly have been *other* significant changes in life course dynamics over time that could have altered the development of behaviours and attitudes that subsequently exhibit considerable persistence. This includes not only life course developments from age eighteen on, but also the earlier stages that have traditionally fallen within the purview of political socialization research. The general lesson we can take from Franklin's research is the importance of an expansive consideration of the formative influences that could potentially give rise to cohort effects. These can include not only the most commonly cited overt influences that shape different generations – new technologies, social change (e.g., education), historical events (e.g., war or its absence), or the usually nebulous, and often tautological, "spirit of the times" – but also the more subtle impact of distinctive life course patterns that guide particular generations down different paths on the road to mature adulthood. It is from this conceptual starting point that we turn to consider the impact of adolescence on the long-term evolution of political culture in the developed democracies.

The Impact of Adolescence

The most significant change in life course patterns over the past hundred years has been the consolidation of adolescence as a distinct life stage, a feature of modern, industrial society that is historically unprecedented. The critical consequence of this development is that it enhanced peer influence relative to adult influence at a critical juncture in the life course. Political science has long recognized the importance of social context and interpersonal influence for individual political behaviour, a theme receiving renewed emphasis in recent years (Beck et al. 2002; Nickerson 2008; Zuckerman 2005) and discussed at some length in the previous chapter. There has been recent encouragement to focus on adolescence in particular, as it is "an especially significant period of the life span for the internalization of social norms" (Campbell 2006, 163; see also Stolle and Hooghe 2004). In light of this recognition, the historic change to the social context of youth produced by the consolidation of the adolescent stage of life is potentially of great significance.

The importance of adolescence as a feature of modern life is remarked upon in various contexts and numerous disciplines, most notably psychology and sociology. There are two general characteristics of the treatment of adolescence in these literatures. The first is that they focus on the impact of adolescence on adolescents. Less often considered is the impact of adolescence on adults – that is to say, on the adults that adolescents eventually become. The second general feature is the considerable emphasis given to the problems and pathologies associated with wayward adolescents (e.g., drug use, juvenile delinquency), rather than the more benign and universal tendencies of this stage of life. The theory offered here is atypical on both counts, considering how immersion in the social context of adolescence affects people beyond their adolescent years, and focusing on traits typical of the adolescent character that have relevance to the changing political culture of the developed democracies. To the extent adolescent attitudes are distinct from those of adults, and to the extent adolescence is an impressionable period during which many basic attitudes and behavioural dispositions take shape, a shift towards heightened peer influence in adolescence will represent an important change in the formative experiences of young people likely to give rise to eventual change in the adult population.

If this is a novel way of conceptualizing the origins of culture change in the developed democracies, there is a more specific articulation of the argument that is commonplace, which can be summed up in the phrase "the sixties generation." It is widely held that those who came of age in the 1960s, a time when youth were numerically preponderant and youth culture was especially vibrant, became a distinctive group as a result of their early experiences and have remained so as they have aged (Fendrich and Lovoy 1988; Marwell et al. 1987). If the idealism and hedonism that marked the decade of their formation have become muted over time, a residue of these qualities has remained even as they have aged. Their youth experience remains an abiding influence that continues to affect both their conduct in their personal lives and their political inclinations.

The sixties generation example invites further clarification of the more broadly gauged argument we are seeking to make. First, the youthful foment of the 1960s encompassed not just adolescents, but young adults as well, in their early twenties or older still. The inclusion of a wider range of ages in the adolescent category is certainly a reasonable amendment for this period. Adolescence is meant to be a flexible term designating those who have moved beyond childhood to a more independent stage of life, but who have not yet fully entered or embraced the adult world. The ages bracketing this period are not fixed and stable, but are subject to change over time. At an early point, however, back in the day when the typical life path involved entry into the workforce directly from high school, the period of heightened peer influence would have been adolescence proper, that is to say, ages fourteen to eighteen (approximately) spent in the high school setting. A second point of clarification also arises from consideration of the 1960s example, as this period can give the misleading impression that, in order for young people to be shaped by their peers, there must be an identifiable "youth culture" that conditions their outlook. The literature on social context suggests that the influence of others can be more personal and subtle, yet potent nonetheless, operating through the casual and intimate contacts an individual has on a day-to-day basis with those in his or her immediate surroundings (Dey 1997; Klofstad 2005). This type of peer influence, of individual youth on individual youth, would certainly have been in play prior to the 1960s, and would have continued to shape the adolescent experience subsequent to that that colourful decade. In short, the youth movement of the 1960s is just one manifestation, albeit a relatively prominent and transparent one, of a more subtle and longstanding process of heightened peer influence for those coming of age in the age of adolescence.

Specifying a precise starting point for this process is impossible. However, the key development, alluded to already, would have been the expansion of secondary education that started to take place around the turn of the twentieth century and culminated in near-universal enrolment by the 1950s, or in some countries, the 1960s. Rather than leaving school at age twelve or thirteen to join the adult workforce, young people now continued for several more years in the company of peers. As the proportion attending secondary school increased over the decades, so too did the significance of the adolescent stage of life for the socialization process. Other structural changes were relevant as well – urbanization, for example, not only facilitated regular attendance at school but also allowed for greater socializing among teenagers outside the school setting. But for those who subscribe to the notion that adolescence is a product of the modern age, extension of the period of full-time education is typically seen as the critical development (Fasick 1994).

Earlier authors recognized that the impact of this development on the life of adolescents was profound. A classic sociological study of the 1920s, *Middletown*, conveyed the essential features of the distinctive social setting provided by secondary education in a small American town:

> The high school, with its athletics, clubs, sororities and fraternities, dances and parties, and other "extracurricular activities," is a fairly complete social cosmos in itself, and about this city within a city the social life of the intermediate generation centers ... The school is taking over more and more of the child's waking life ... [it] is becoming not a place to which children go from their homes for a few hours daily but a place from which they go home to eat and sleep. (Lynd and Lynd 1929, 211)

The potentially negative consequences of this social setting were later highlighted by sociologist James Coleman: "The child of high-school age ... is 'cut off' from the rest of society, forced inward toward his own age group, made to carry out his whole social life with others his own age. With his fellows, he comes to constitute a small society, one that has most of its important interactions within itself, and maintains only a few threads of connection with the outside adult world" (1961, 3). More recently, political scientist David Campbell has taken a more positive view of the potential of the peer environment in the high school community to foster "civic inclinations," and has offered compelling evidence of variation between schools in the extent to which students emerge predisposed to participate in political and civic life (2006, 147-79). But the more general effect of the high school setting has been to immerse all teenagers in what Coleman called "adolescent society," a very different milieu from the blended adolescent-adult settings that characterized the workplace and social life in earlier times.

Some would say that postwar developments have deepened and extended the adolescent stage of life. Again, the principal reason for the change has been expanded opportunities to remain longer in full-time education, now at the postsecondary level. This development is identified as one of the key factors responsible for the crystallization of a stage of life sometimes labelled "emerging adulthood," referring to the period from roughly ages eighteen to twenty-five when young people continue to live in social enclaves somewhat disconnected from the adult world (Arnett 2004, 2005). Others, of the view that this new stage of delayed development may have more in common with adolescence than adulthood, might prefer the term "extended adolescence." Regardless, there is general agreement that the period of life during which young people are embedded in social settings where peer influence is substantial has grown longer in the past fifty years. However, the effects of this postwar extension are more uncertain, as it is does not apply to young people universally and would depend on whether (and in what ways) peers in one's twenties provide a social context markedly different from that which would be encountered in "adult" society.

That these changes in life course patterns have been gradual is one reason the impact of adolescence on adult attitudes has been slow to materialize. A second reason lies in the intrinsic inertia of the socialization process. The field, after all, is largely built on the assumption that the weight of existing opinion and disposition, exerted by various socialization agents in the adult world, is considerable, steering young people, in the absence of any countervailing force, towards acceptance of existing norms. Considered in the abstract, it is possible to imagine periods when the weight from above would be sufficient to forestall any change whatsoever on the part of rising generations. In such periods of stability, adolescents might well differ from adults, but socialization pressures combined with natural maturation processes would result in their eventually becoming just like the adults who preceded them, and from there taking their turn to steer the next generation of adolescents towards the same outcome.

The emergence of adolescence as a distinct stage of life, assuming greater significance in the formative experiences of young people, would upset this state of equilibrium, but only gradually. The first cohort of adolescents to experience adolescence – an abstract rather than empirically identifiable group – would display small, subtle changes, as socialization pressures from the adult world would continue to exert considerable influence, mitigating the effects of enhanced peer influence. The initial impact would be minimal, the distinctiveness of the first cohort consisting perhaps less in an explicit commitment to adolescent ideals and more in mild ambivalence towards adult norms. This faint residue, however, would be sufficient to set the stage for further change, as the first cohort, once part of the adult world, would alter the socialization context of the next cohort of adolescents, rendering it more amenable to adolescent predilections and enabling the subsequent cohort to take the process of change one step further, tilting it more strongly in favour of adolescent norms. The influence of adolescence on the adult world would thus occur in gradual waves, manifesting itself in changing attitudes and behavioural tendencies among rising birth cohorts over a long period.

In a nutshell, the argument is that there are certain deep and abiding tendencies of adolescence that were stifled historically by the socialization pressures of the adult world and which have gradually been permitted freer expression in the age of adolescence. Presumably, the process of social change implied by the theory could eventually exhaust itself. Successive waves of change producing adults ever more reflective of adolescent tendencies might at some point generate a new equilibrium where vertical socialization pressures and horizontal peer influences would balance out, leading once again to simple reproduction of extant norms in rising generations. The differences between adolescents and adults in this end stage would necessarily be smaller than they were at the onset of the process, as the relative weight of adult socialization influence would be smaller relative to the impact of peer influence in adolescence. Whether we have already arrived at this point is difficult to say, though certainly there is anecdotal evidence of some convergence of adolescent and adult sensibilities in recent times (von Hahn 2007).

To sum up: the emergence of adolescence as a distinct life stage, first and foremost a consequence of extended time in full-time education, has generated a gradual process of social change, which we will argue below is a significant factor in the political culture changes that have occurred in the developed democracies. In the twentieth century, young people increasingly found themselves in a social context where peer influence was considerable, but the effects of the change were slow to appear. The principal structural change giving rise to this development, expanded educational participation of greater duration, was slow to unfold. Equally drawn out were the changes in socialization outcomes echoing from this development. Over the long haul, however, major changes have occurred and can be seen in some of the basic dispositions and behavioural tendencies prevalent in modern society that have important implications for the political realm.

Making the Case

The central prediction flowing from this argument is that with the entrenchment of adolescence, traits distinctive of the adolescent character will become more prominent in the adult population over time. When this will happen is difficult to predict with any precision, first because there is no single point at which adolescence became a discrete stage of life, and second because the effects will have appeared incrementally over multiple generations. Eventually, however, persistent life course patterns associated with adolescence will generate cohort effects that see adolescent predilections becoming more prevalent in rising cohorts.

Embedded in this account are three separate claims in need of verification to substantiate the argument:

1   The influence of peers in the adolescent stage of life – as gauged by factors such as the amount of time spent in their company and exposure and receptiveness to their ideas and values – has increased over time.
2   Adolescents differ from adults in ways pertinent to political culture: core ideas, values, and dispositions broadly relevant to politics. Propositions 1 and 2 together entail that adolescents, in the age of adolescence, have been exposed to distinct ideas and patterns of behaviour, thus altering their formative experiences compared to those who came before.
3   This element of young people's formative experiences, though not the sole influence on adult outcomes, nonetheless has had a lasting effect that is evident in identifiable cohort patterns that have gradually emerged over time and have reshaped the political culture of the developed democracies.

It would be difficult to make a watertight case in support of all three propositions. The first is the most challenging to verify empirically. From the account offered above, it would follow that the greatest changes in peer influence for youth would have come with the full-scale introduction of compulsory secondary education, since this was a development affecting the core of the adolescent years that was universal in its impact. Assessing the change in peer influence attendant upon this development would require comparable measurements prior to and after the change, a tall order. For this reason, a rigorous assessment is unlikely. Changes in the degree of peer influence in more recent decades, for which data might be more readily available, are apt to be less dramatic. It is not obvious, for example, that the teenager of the 1990s would be subject to significantly greater peer influence than the teenager of the 1960s. But then again dramatic changes in recent decades are not required by the current theory, which posits that the repercussions of enhanced peer influence in adolescence will continue to echo through a process of gradual inter-generational change long after the initial perturbation has occurred.

That said, the idea that there would have been a sharp increase in peer influence with the onset of the age of adolescence seems incontrovertible. It is hard to imagine that young people spending the bulk of their days in educational settings surrounded by peers would not be subject to greater peer influence than young people who had left school behind to take their place manning the plough, helping to run the household, or toiling in the factories, mines, or office towers of the adult world. Robert Epstein, whose recent book *The Case against Adolescence* rails against the extended period of social confinement that is modern adolescence, estimates that American teenagers probably spend sixty hours a week more time together than teens in preindustrial society (2007, 92). Other academic research confirms that the intensity of peer bonds grows stronger in the adolescent years as the influence of parents and other adult figures wanes (Andersson 1979). Such observations are consistent with the common wisdom that the social environment of the modern teen is heavily tilted towards peer influence.

There is likewise no investigation undertaken of the third claim, the proposition that adolescent characteristics have appeared in adult society in the form of gradually emerging cohort effects which have reshaped the political culture of the developed democracies. For this proposition, existing research and earlier parts of the book provide ample evidence for at least the second part of the statement (that cohort effects have reshaped political culture) if not the first (that these represent a manifestation of adolescent tendencies). Whether it is Wattenberg on political attentiveness, Twenge on individualism, or Dalton on tolerance, there is an abundance of evidence that various facets of the political culture of the developed democracies have been slowly reconfigured by gradual processes of inter-generational change.

It is, then, the second proposition that claims our full attention: that there are abiding differences between adolescents and adults that can help explain these cohort-driven changes in political culture. Naturally, in seeking to build this case, the outcome to be explained orientates the investigation, so that the objective becomes to identify distinctive tendencies of adolescence that correspond to the various elements of cohort-driven change in social and political values and dispositions. One approach to identifying such adolescent tendencies is to draw on the insights of theoretical models of life course development, drawn principally from works of developmental psychology. Another method involves empirical assessment of adolescent-adult differences on relevant measures. Both are used below.

For the empirical method, the age span examined should not be too great, otherwise the standard difficulty arises of distinguishing life-cycle from cohort effects. Of course, the theory posited here anticipates the presence of both – that life course patterns associated with adolescence will have generated identifiable cohort effects – but for verification purposes, the two must be considered separately. One simple way to isolate the life course pattern is to focus on a relatively narrow age span: to look for differences not just between adolescents and adults but between adolescents and young adults. As we will see below, the differences that appear are typically too large to plausibly represent emergent cohort effects. When fifteen-year-olds differ substantially from twenty-one-year-olds, it is unlikely to be a reflection of anything distinctive about those born a mere six years apart. A more likely explanation is that this age range represents a section of the life cycle marked by significant change.

By the reasoning of the current theory, the time period examined is not a critical variable, as the life course effects giving rise to cohort change are conceptualized as abiding differences between adolescents and adults. Such differences would exist in a period of equilibrium, when socialization pressures and maturation processes are sufficient to bring adolescents in line with existing adult norms as they age. Such differences would also exist at a time of emergent cohort effects, as adolescents would continue to change as they aged, but would simply not finish up at quite the same point as those who went before them. Of course, evidence of the persistence of adolescent-adult differences over time is desirable, and where available is provided below. At other points, however, this consistency is simply assumed, thereby justifying the use of a slightly unorthodox procedure: cross-sectional surveys from different points in time are aggregated and treated as a single cross-sectional swath as a means of bringing together sufficient numbers of cases to accurately capture the trajectory of attitudes and dispositions over short spans of the life cycle.[1]

The sections that follow examine different elements of adolescent-adult differences, concentrating on two that are fundamental to the broader arguments of the book: political inattentiveness and individualism. In both cases, the distinctiveness of adolescents lends credence to the notion that adolescence is a likely wellspring – not the only source, but certainly a significant one – of long-term inter-generational change in attitudes and dispositions of considerable consequence to the political culture of the developed democracies.

Political Inattentiveness

To assess whether the adolescent years are marked by distinctive levels of political attentiveness, the Eurobarometer dataset combining all studies from 1970 to 2002 is used. The value of this combined dataset is twofold: the use of consistent questions has generated an exceptionally large N for certain measures when multiplied across the various EU countries and the numerous years the questions have been administered; and the surveys include respondents as young as fifteen, the minimum age of eligibility for the surveys. These two features allow for close scrutiny of differences between adolescents and young adults that would be impossible to capture with most datasets.

Two measures of political attentiveness are considered: political interest and political discussion. Both have been encountered in earlier chapters aimed at understanding different facets of political attentiveness. In the six-nation comparison of longitudinal trends in Chapter 3, a life-cycle pattern across the adult years was observed for political interest: that is to say, a consistent, if modest, gap in political interest between younger and older adults. It was suggested that this should not be dismissed as inconsequential, as it might represent the proverbial tip of the iceberg, signalling even lower levels of political interest at younger ages still. Political discussion was not considered in this longitudinal analysis, but entered the mix when considering precipitants of political attentiveness in the adolescent years in Chapter 4. There it was demonstrated that political discussion in the family home is strongly linked to different measures of political attentiveness in adult life. While most obviously a finding in support of the significance of parental influence, the results can also be taken as more broadly indicative of the significance of interpersonal dynamics in the adolescent years to processes of political attentiveness – dynamics which should encompass peer as well as parental influence. In both instances, then, the prior analysis points towards the potential significance of political interest and political discussion in the adolescent years to developmental processes of political attentiveness (for a similar argument, see Mindich 2005, 64-66).

Figures 9.1 and 9.2, derived from the combined Eurobarometer 1970-2002 dataset, demonstrate the distinctiveness of adolescents by displaying age trends with respect to political interest and political discussion, controlling for other relevant variables. The figures are based on predicted values generated by OLS regression models. For those under age thirty, each specific age in years was captured by a dummy variable, with those thirty years old serving as the excluded comparison category. Those over thirty were grouped into ten-year intervals, the results plotted at the mid-point of those intervals. In both models, controls are in place for country and survey year (coded continuously); for political discussion, it is feasible to include birth year (coded continuously) as a control variable as well.[2] Using these results, the graphs present the level of political interest and discussion for the "average"

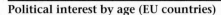

Figure 9.1

Political interest by age (EU countries)

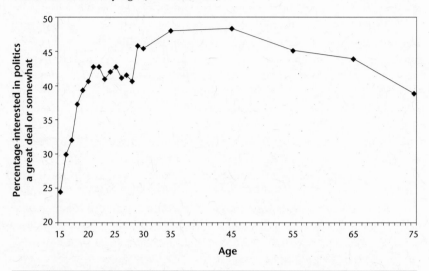

Source: Mannheim Eurobarometer Trend File, 1970-2002. N = 106,150 (seven surveys between 1983 and 1994).

thirty-year-old (average with respect to other variables – country, year, and birth year),[3] alongside estimates for other ages comparable in other respects to this average thirty-year-old. In other words, the graphs present adjusted figures that take into account potential confounding factors to isolate the early life course trajectory for measures of political attentiveness.

An argument might be made for introducing education controls as well, since the youngest respondents, still in school for the most part, would generally have less education than older respondents, which might help explain their lower levels of political interest and discussion (education being strongly associated with both dependent variables). However, this seems unnecessary. Educational differences might help explain *why* adolescents are less politically attentive than young adults, but would not alter the fact that they are less attentive, which is the principal point to be established here.[4] Later in the chapter, we will invoke education as an important variable to be included in seeking a broader understanding of the long-term evolution of political attentiveness, but for the purpose of establishing adolescent-young adult differences, education controls are not necessary.

Turning to Figures 9.1 and 9.2, it is clear that the differences in political attentiveness across the adolescent-young adult span are considerable. The proportion interested in politics ("a great deal" or "to some extent") sits at a mere 24 percent among those fifteen years of age but climbs sharply to

Figure 9.2

Political discussion by age (EU countries)

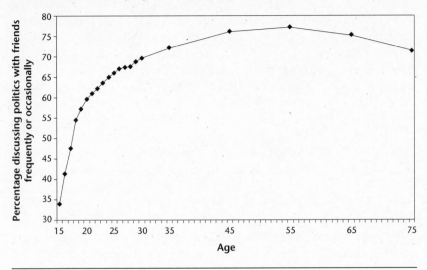

Source: Mannheim Eurobarometer Trend File, 1970-2002. *N* = 768,363 (sixty-three surveys between 1973 and 2002).

40 percent by age twenty-one, after which it levels out and increases at a much slower pace.[5] In the case of political discussion with friends, the adolescent difference is equally dramatic, the trend line smoother due to the exceptionally large sample size: the incidence of political discussion (frequent or occasional), only 34 percent among fifteen-year-olds, climbs sharply to reach 60 percent among twenty-one-year-olds, increasing much more slowly thereafter.

Why there would be such significant differences between adolescents and young adults does not require deep theoretical reflection. It is probably best accounted for by simply extending the common sense reasoning used to explain why young adults are less politically attentive than older adults: less invested in society, unburdened by adult concerns, preoccupied with other matters, politics simply does not hold that much appeal for younger people (Jowell and Park 1998, 2, 17). And yet the fact that there are differences of this magnitude in levels of political attentiveness across this short section of the life cycle has not been well documented (see, however, Park 2005, 30). This is partly due to how life course patterns have been studied in political science. While political socialization research has examined patterns of development across both childhood and adolescence, early influential studies suggested there was much more change in the former stage than the latter, leading some to conclude that adolescence was probably best conceptualized as the starting point of a long adult period involving only gradual change (Hess and Torney 1968, 10-11; Greenstein 1969, 75-84). Others queried this assumption, but tended to pick up their investigation at the tail end of adolescence, including some working in the political socialization tradition (Jennings and Niemi 1974, 251-83) and others in the political behaviour field. The latter, with its particular emphasis on voting behaviour, tended to produce datasets, and consequently analysis, including only eligible voters eighteen and over (or twenty-one and over prior to the change in voting age in the late 1960s). While such studies have consistently identified moderate increases in political engagement through the adult years, by virtue of their starting point they have failed to detect the more striking changes occurring between mid-adolescence and early adulthood. More recent calls to concentrate attention on the adolescent-to-young adult period (Niemi and Hepburn 1995; Niemi 1999; Stolle and Hooghe 2004) have yet to yield much empirical work documenting development over this period (one exception is Watts 1999).[6]

The rapid changes in political attentiveness between adolescence and early adulthood are the obvious trend that stands out in Figures 9.1 and 9.2, but it is important not to lose sight of the larger argument the analysis is intended to support. After all, in the absence of further commentary, these results could simply be taken as demonstrating the ephemeral and inconsequential nature of adolescent indifference to politics. The aim, it will be recalled, is not simply to highlight an important life course pattern, but to reflect on the implication of that pattern for the political attitudes and behaviours that exhibit cohort-driven change over time. From that perspective, the key observation is that adolescents differ greatly from adults in their levels of political attentiveness and it is therefore eminently plausible that the enhanced peer influence associated with modern adolescence – consisting, in this case, of relative inattentiveness to politics – would have some impact on the attitudes and behaviours that young people carry forward into the adult world. Clearly that impact is far from determinative: politically indifferent adolescents do still go on to become more attentive and engaged adults. But given all we know about the importance of social context, it seems plausible to conjecture that adolescence might leave a residual effect, an adolescent imprint that would gradually manifest itself in a slow and steady ebbing of attentiveness among successive birth cohorts.[7]

Individualism

The same method of analysis can be applied to individualism, leading to the same result and conclusion: adolescence is a period of life in which individualism is especially pronounced; consequently the consolidation of this stage of life in the first half of the twentieth century helps to account for the gradual ascendance of individualistic norms over time. Arriving at that conclusion is a bit more involved, however, because individualism is a multidimensional concept. To be considered first is the earlier distinction between strands of individualism that emphasize different dimensions of the self: self-direction, self-confidence, self-reliance, and self-regard. While there may be something to be said about the effects of adolescence on the qualities of self-confidence and self-reliance, we retain the earlier focus on the two dimensions of individualism that seem to have gained the greatest foothold among younger generations over time, self-regard and self-direction. Some attention must also be given to the further distinction between individualism as a personal trait and individualism as a principled belief. For reasons explained below, the individualism exhibited by adolescents tends more towards the personal than the principled. This is not to suggest, however, that the age of adolescence has had no bearing on the ascendance of principled individualism, since personal preference does inform principled belief, particularly when abetted by other factors as elucidated below.

Personal Individualism: Self-Regard

That adolescents are self-regarding, not as a matter of philosophical conviction but in their reflexive attitudes and behaviour, is an abiding theme in the developmental psychology literature. One influential writer on the subject forthrightly states: "Now it is well known that the young adolescent ... is primarily concerned with himself" (Elkind 1998, 94). The crux of this egocentrism, in Elkind's view, is that adolescents suffer from the illusion that others are as preoccupied with them as much as they are with themselves, a cognitive misapprehension that generates such acknowledged proclivities of adolescence as excessive self-consciousness, self-criticism, and self-admiration. Jeffrey Arnett, a leading scholar of emerging adulthood, likewise emphasizes how greatly teens differ in their understanding of others from those just a few years older. In his interviews of adolescents and emerging adults (those aged eighteen to twenty-five), Arnett reports being "struck by how much less egocentric emerging adults are, compared with adolescents. Emerging adults are more considerate of other people's feelings and better at understanding others' point of view" (Arnett 2005, 10).

Empirical evidence that allows for assessment of these differences on a broader scale is harder to locate. As suggested earlier, devising questions that ask directly about self-regard on survey questionnaires is challenging, since the trait is generally seen as socially undesirable. It is more common to encounter survey items where self-regard is implied but is not the direct focus of inquiry. A handful of questions fitting this description have appeared on the CROP/Environics surveys used by Michael Adams in his various investigations of Canadian social values in the past ten years (1998, 2003). These surveys have certain important merits: relatively large sample sizes (especially when several are combined), the inclusion of respondents as young as fifteen,

Figure 9.3

Self-regarding attitudes by age (Canada)

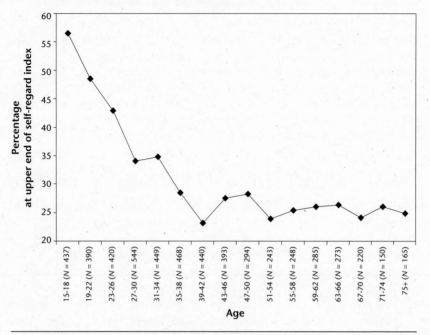

Source: CROP Socio-Cultural Surveys, 1989 and 1996.

and availability for secondary analysis. Relevant items that speak to self-regard (while also tapping into materialistic values) are as follows:

- to make more money and be better off than most people around me (how important)
- to spend, to buy myself something new, is for me one of the greatest pleasures in life (agree/disagree)
- to take advantage without restraint of the good things in life (how important).

All three questions appeared together on the 1989 CROP survey, the first two on the 1996 survey. Using these questions, respondents from these two years are classified according to their score on a simple additive index (based on three and two questions, respectively) and categorized by whether they fall in the upper tier of this index. Displayed in Figure 9.3 is the percentage in each age group in this upper range (four-year groupings are used to ensure adequate sample sizes). The distinctiveness of adolescents is abundantly clear: the tendency to concur with self-regarding propositions is sharply elevated among those aged fifteen to eighteen and drops rapidly through early adulthood, until stabilizing in the late twenties.

Evidence bearing more directly on self-regard and egocentrism in the realm of politics comes from an older study that sought to evaluate how adolescents' "sense of community" influences their thinking on political matters and how this influence varies between younger adolescents and those on the cusp of adulthood. Seeking to capture deep-seated patterns of thinking rather than specific issue preferences, Adelson and O'Neil devised an abstract situation (1,000 men and women on an island in the Pacific seeking to establish a new government and laws) that provided the backdrop for a number of concrete scenarios pitting individual rights and preferences against the community interest. Questions designed to elicit reactions to these scenarios were posed to 120 adolescents ranging from age eleven to eighteen. The results reinforce the notion that adolescence is a period marked by an intractable self-regard. The youngest students, aged eleven, were decidedly "egocentric" in their responses and could not "transcend a purely personal approach to matters which require a sociocentric perspective" (1966, 297). When confronted with conflicts between individuals and their island society, they exhibited "a failure to understand that political decisions have social as well as personal consequences, and that the political realm encompasses not merely the individual citizen, but the community as a whole" (1966, 297). This tendency steadily diminished across the four ages included in the study (eleven, thirteen, fifteen, and eighteen), as older adolescents revealed themselves to be "increasingly sensitive to the fact of community and its claims upon the citizen" (1966, 301). The trend captured in this study across the adolescent years is similar to the pattern found above. If it can safely be assumed that sensitivity towards the "community and its claims upon the citizen" remains intact beyond age eighteen, perhaps continuing to climb (if at a slower pace), it follows that adolescence on the whole represents a phase of life where a focus on the self is significantly elevated.

The dominant interpretation of such patterns in the psychology literature is that egocentrism is an intrinsic developmental feature of adolescence that diminishes in a predictable manner with age and maturation – in other words, is a life course pattern only. But as Twenge forcefully argues, self-regard can equally be seen as a social or cultural phenomenon, subject to change and variation over time and place, which has become increasingly prevalent over the years (at least in the younger cohorts of Americans Twenge has studied). Linking these interpretations involves hypothesizing that intrinsic qualities of adolescence, when allowed relatively unfettered expression, can be carried forward to adulthood, albeit in modified form (and perhaps relabelled as "values" or "attitudes" rather than personality traits). In the age of adolescence, teenagers have been immersed in social settings where their own tendency towards egocentrism is reflected in the self-regarding propensities of those around them, leading to validation and reinforcement of the attitude and attendant behaviours. As one psychological study of adolescent development suggests, "feedback from friendships and the peer group provides not only support but also a mirror for the self" (Kroger 2007, 78). Self-regard in this setting appears as a normal and un-objectionable manner of thinking and behaving. As adolescents become adults, natural developmental processes mitigate this egocentrism, but the experience of the formative years leaves a lingering residue, which slowly accumulates in society at large to appear most prominently in aggregate social change down the generations.

Contrary to these thoughts, there is the viewpoint that the rise of self-regard among younger generations of Canadians has been relatively muted. Michael Adams, based on a fuller analysis of the CROP survey items, suggests that the norm in Western democracies, the US excepted, is for individualism among the young to lean towards the fulfillment end of his individualism spectrum (akin to self-direction and self-expression) rather than the survival pole (closer to self-regard). That self-regard has not emerged as a stronger force may reflect the countervailing impact of another important influence on self-regarding propensities, education. On the items cited above in Figure 9.3, those with higher education levels do tend to be less self-regarding, though the differences on these particular items are relatively modest (about a 10 percentage point difference between those who have not finished high school and those with a university degree). In analyzing individualism in Chapter 7, alternative survey questions appearing on the CCES were intro-duced. These items, more patent in their espousal of self-regard, reveal stronger differences by education level. For example, when asked whether they agree with the two statements, "Generally speaking, I tend to focus on my own concerns and not worry too much about other people" and "In today's society it is reasonable for people to look out mainly for themselves," 42 percent of those who failed to finish high school agree with both, com-pared to only 11 percent of those with a graduate or professional degree. Since education levels have increased steadily from the start of the twentieth century to the present day (the same period in which adolescence has made its impact felt), the dampening effects of educational attainment on self-regard could have served to hold in check the amplifying influence of ado-lescent disposition. The need to consider the joint effects of adolescence and education is important to bear in mind and something we return to at later points in the chapter.

Personal Individualism: Self-Direction

Another dimension of individualism emphasized in the adolescent years is self-direction. Like self-regard, this can be conceptualized as a funda-mental feature of the adolescent character reflecting intrinsic developmental processes. A classic statement consistent with this proposition comes again from the developmental psychology literature. Erik Erikson's seminal work on adolescent development identified the search for an independent identity as a critical priority of this stage of life, as the young person leaves childhood behind and engages in a process of exploration in attempting to forge his or her own personal identity (1968). This "search for something and somebody to be true to" inevitably entails "shifting devotion" and "test[ing] extremes" (1968, 235), that is to say, a strong emphasis on personal exploration and self-direction.

Other psychologists have identified a particular cluster of personality traits that one would expect to appear among those for whom self-discovery is an overarching priority: openness to experience. Openness to experience refers to both amenability to external encounters – the opportunity to explore new experiences – as well a penchant for inner exploration – getting in touch with one's own feelings and ideas. Previous research in this area is fairly extensive and has, among other things, examined how different dimensions of personality, such as openness to experience, evolve over the life cycle. The finding, replicated across a number of countries, has been that young adults tend to score higher on measures of openness to experience than older persons (McCrae et al. 1999). While typically interpreted as evidence of life course patterns in the evolution of personality – the default assumption of developmental psychology – a social psychologist like Twenge less wedded to invariant developmental models would presumably look at these results and query whether such age differences might partly represent generational change in the societies concerned. The question also arises whether the extension of this life course research to the pre-adult years might reveal any sharp distinctiveness of the adolescent personality, potentially, by the light of the current theory, an important source of generational change.

The battery of questions used by psychologists to measure openness to experience and other dimensions of personality is extensive – the long version has over 300 questions, the short version 60 (Costa and McCrae 1992) – and it therefore tends to be deployed only in research contexts where the main focus is personality evaluation. I am not aware of any datasets resulting from such research that would allow for examination of changes over the adolescent-young adult span and which are available for secondary analysis. However, a handful of cognate measures, similar in wording to those normally used to measure openness to experience, have appeared on the Environics social values surveys. Three relevant items, seen before in Chapter 7, appeared consistently on the surveys from 1992 to 1996. These are as follows:

- As soon as I see an opportunity to try something new I do it.
- I like being able to explore aspects of my personality that I don't usually express in everyday life.

• I should like to experience new emotions every day.

A simple additive index of "openness to experience" was created based on these three items. Respondents were then categorized according to whether they fell in the upper tier of this scale. The resulting age pattern (Figure 9.4) is very similar to that for self-regard. Adolescents and those in their early twenties score exceptionally high on this scale, with a sharp decline taking place until stabilization occurs in the late twenties.[8]

Unlike prior results above, education shows no relationship to this measure of openness to experience. The implication is that the growth of openness to experience and a preference for self-direction over the long haul has not been abetted by rising education levels over time, but neither has it been inhibited. In other words, unlike self-regard, there is no reason to think that an adolescent infusion of self-direction and self-expression might have been held in check by countervailing effects due to increased education levels. This perhaps helps explain Michael Adams's observation that the more dominant strain of rising individualism over time has been an increased emphasis on fulfillment – akin to self-expression and self-direction – rather than survival.

Figure 9.4

Openness to experience by age (Canada)

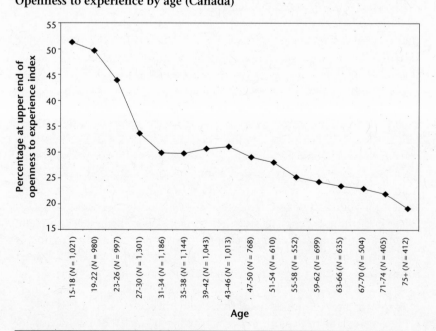

Source: CROP Socio-Cultural Surveys, 1992-96.

Principled Self-Direction (or Tolerance)

One further dimension of our changing social and political culture subject to the gradual influence of adolescence on adult disposition is tolerance, a quality that some authors emphasize must not be overlooked in taking stock of the current state of democracy. While some scepticism was expressed in the previous chapter about thin forms of tolerance that involve little genuine empathy or understanding of others, the merits of tolerance as a political virtue should not be discounted.

Demonstrating that adolescence has contributed to rising tolerance over the years is partly just a matter of pointing to the strong linkage that has been established between openness to experience and attitudes of social and political tolerance. This finding has emerged from different quarters. Psychologists whose main focus is the measurement of personality have observed that openness to experience is the dimension of personality most strongly linked to social and political phenomena such as aversion to authoritarianism (McCrae 1996), while political scientists whose principal focus is the wellsprings of tolerance have identified openness to experience as one of the more powerful personal predispositions conducive to tolerant attitudes (Marcus et al. 1995, 164-77).

The CROP studies on social values bear out these prior findings. Scores on the three-item index of openness to experience show strong connections to attitudes reflecting social and political tolerance. One question probes tolerance on a personal and immediate level, asking respondents whether they "prefer people who act like everybody else, without trying to stand out or people who do not always feel obliged to be like everybody else and who show some originality in their dress or behaviour." A second reflects socially liberal attitudes, asking whether "society should regard people who live together without being married as being a family." A third question probes one of the more salient areas of social tolerance in recent times, gay rights, asking whether "society should regard people of the same sex who live together as being the same as a married couple." In all three cases, tolerance rises steadily with increasing openness to experience (Figure 9.5). To the extent adolescence has contributed to long-term changes in personal qualities reflecting openness to experience, it has by extension contributed to rising levels of tolerance.

Yet despite this, adolescent respondents on the CROP surveys are not exceptionally tolerant or liberal on these same measures. This is not to say they are exceptionally intolerant either, but simply that their sharp distinctiveness vis-à-vis young adults vanishes when queried directly about personal conformity, common-law relationships, and gay marriage (Figure 9.6). In other words, taking into account their elevated levels of openness to experience, adolescents display less tolerant attitudes than would be anticipated.

Figure 9.5

Openness to experience and tolerance (Canada)

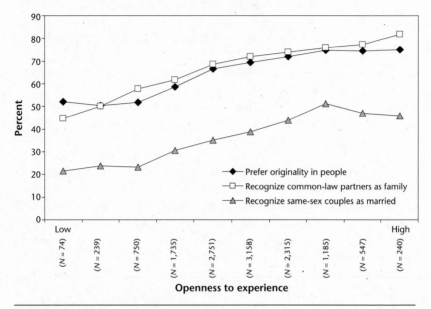

Source: CROP Socio-Cultural Surveys, 1992-96.

There are a couple of reasons for this. One is the influence of education, cited in most accounts as the single most critical factor engendering rising levels of tolerance over time. Adolescents, still in high school, have lower education levels than young adults. With education controlled, adolescents do move up on the graph, especially in the case of preferring originality in others, though the gap separating the youngest respondents from young adults remains less substantial than might be anticipated. A second factor that likely hinders the translation of openness to experience into attitudes of social tolerance among the youngest respondents comes from an earlier result: the self-regarding proclivities of adolescents. For tolerance does not follow directly from openness to experience: instead it requires that a personal preference for new experiences and free development of the self be applied to others in an even-handed manner, granting them the same latitude coveted for oneself. Until the egocentricity of adolescence starts to be transcended, this application of personal preference to others is less likely to occur: as one author puts it, "perspective-taking ability" is critical to the development of tolerance (Mutz 2006, 80-81). Personal preference and principled belief come to be more closely aligned only as a result of maturation processes associated with aging and the curtailment of self-regard. Thus the passage from adolescence to early adulthood enhances

Figure 9.6

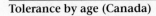

Tolerance by age (Canada)

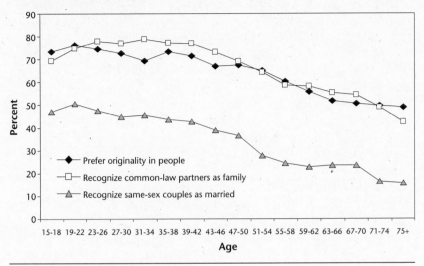

Source: CROP Socio-Cultural Surveys, 1992-96.

tolerance in two ways – one through psychological processes that diminish egocentricity and improve perspective-taking ability, the other through educational experiences that facilitate understanding of others and appreciation of diversity.

These further observations serve simply to establish that the overarching thesis is not compromised by the unexceptional levels of tolerance displayed by adolescents: adolescence, by virtue of the intrinsic importance of openness to experience during those years of life, has contributed to rising tolerance over time just as it has helped produce other long-term changes in political culture. This contribution is slightly obscured, however, by other features of the adolescent period that suppress the fullest expression of the tolerance associated with openness to experience.

Discussion and Conclusion

The case has been made that political inattentiveness, individualism, and tolerance, salient elements of the current social and political landscape in Canada and other established democracies, are of a piece, representing different facets of the adolescent character that have insinuated their way into the broader culture through a gradual process of altered formative experiences and inter-generational change. The case is circumstantial, but draws on a blend of reasoned assumptions and empirical evidence that suggest its plausibility.

To identify a common wellspring for these changes is not to discount the influence of factors highlighted in other theories of long-term social and political change. The evolution of political culture can hardly be reduced to a single determining factor: those emphasized by other observers, including peace, prosperity and new technologies, have surely influenced the assumptions and behavioural tendencies that shape political attitudes and behaviour today. Moreover, there would likely be value in investigating interactions between these factors and the social dynamics of the age of adolescence. The effects of television on people's attitudes and behaviours, for example, are surely influenced by a social structure that affords adolescents the opportunity to develop in relative isolation from adult society. The main aim has been to identify an important explanatory strand that has hitherto been overlooked.

The other factor that we have been most sensitive to is education, making reference to the fact that education is also implicated in attitudinal and behavioural qualities relevant to political and social engagement. Education must be considered as a contributing factor in its own right to political culture change over the long haul. At the same time, however, we must recognize its intrinsic linkage to the "age of adolescence" thesis, since it was the extension of the period of full-time education in the twentieth century that was principally responsible for creating a clearly defined adolescent stage of life. Recognizing the intertwining of adolescent development and educational experience, it is helpful to step back and review the broader consequences of their joint effects on the evolution of different facets of political culture. In particular, we might consider the implications of the twin processes that unfolded simultaneously over the course of the twentieth century: the infusion of adolescent sensibilities engendered by the age of adolescence and vast increases in average education levels over the same period. In the case of attitudes and dispositions where the effects of education work *in concert with* adolescent influence, the direction of change will be predictable and the degree of change considerable. The evolution of tolerance conforms to this scenario, as the two factors have jointly served to generate more tolerant attitudes in rising generations over time (adolescent disposition producing greater emphasis on self-direction and openness to experience, education providing enhanced appreciation for democratic values and greater awareness of difference and diversity). Where education promotes change *counter* to adolescent influence, it is uncertain which factor will prove more influential and what the overall direction and magnitude of change will be. Political attentiveness is one important example here, as enhanced adolescent influence would have served to counter the positive effects of increasing education levels over time, eventually, we would contend, overwhelming those positive effects and helping to produce the decline in political attentiveness evident in any number of countries over the last three or four decades. Self-regard can perhaps also be seen in this light, a negative feature of adolescence held in check for some time by rising education levels, but starting to manifest itself more fully in changing attitudes and norms of the past twenty-five years (the period in which neo-conservative values have become more prevalent in many countries).

This interpretation provides responses to a couple of puzzles about the general evolution of political culture others have pondered. First, this reading offers a different account from others of the seemingly inconsistent effects of enhanced education in the postwar period: why tolerance has increased surely and steadily as one would expect in a more educated populace, whereas engagement in politics has not (Nie et al. 1996). The gradually escalating impact of adolescent influence, aiding and abetting the first development while undermining the second, helps explain this conundrum. This resolution of the puzzle also points to a considerable irony, for it is not simply the case that higher education levels and enhanced adolescent influence happen to have emerged contemporaneously, but rather that extended time in full-time education is the principal reason behind the entrenchment of the adolescent stage of life. In this sense, with respect to political engagement at least, the vast expansion of educational opportunity in the twentieth century has generated two distinct effects that have been working at cross purposes.[9] This is all the more ironic considering that part of the rationale for extending educational opportunity to one and all was to enable citizens to participate in democracy on an equal footing.

The interplay of adolescent influence and education effects also offers a response to a puzzle raised by Putnam. In the course of arguing against the view that tolerance and civic disengagement can be seen as different sides of the same coin – with an eye to refuting the idea that tolerance might be seen as the silver lining in civic disengagement – Putnam points out that the timing of developments is inconsistent with this proposition, since increases in levels of tolerance clearly predate the decline in civic engagement. Citing the generational patterns that have given rise to change over time, he notes that "something in the *first* half of the twentieth century made successive cohorts of Americans more tolerant ... By contrast, something happened in America in the *second* half of the twentieth century to make people less civically engaged" (2000, 357). The "something" of the postwar period that led to declining civic engagement lies at the heart of Putnam's analysis; the main explanatory factors invoked are the introduction of television and the absence of war. But the mysterious something of the first half of the century that helped generate increased levels of tolerance remains unidentified. The current theory proposes a different resolution of the mystery, suggesting first that tolerance and civic disengagement are more closely linked than Putnam allows, in their common origins in the predilections of adolescents, and second, providing a reason why, despite this common origin, a rise in tolerance would have occurred earlier than a decline in civic engagement. Where education and adolescent influence work in concert to produce change in the same direction, change will come more rapidly and therefore earlier – in the case of tolerance, prior to the Second World War. Where educational effects and adolescent influence are at odds, the direction of change is uncertain and it will almost certainly take longer to appear – in the case of civic disengagement, well into the postwar era.

In short, recognition of the importance of the adolescent stage of life can provide a deeper understanding of the evolution of different social and political trends relevant to the democratic dispositions of the contemporary citizenry. Curiously, that recognition, if largely absent from theoretical accounts, is often present (at least implicitly) in practical efforts undertaken to tackle those elements of current political culture considered undesirable, including both civic disengagement and an excess of self-regard. A consistent theme in that respect is the importance of engaging young people in their formative years by drawing them out of their adolescent enclaves to interact with the larger society – for example, in the emphasis and high hopes placed on community service as a means of catalyzing civic engagement and instilling values of empathy and concern for others. It is likely this emphasis emerges from recognition that the external factors implicated in political culture change lie beyond our control (there is no turning back the clock on television, for example) and/or offer substantial benefits that clearly outweigh any attendant costs (e.g., the absence of war). Appropriate guidance and direction for adolescents as they develop into adults, however, is something that can be structured through conscious design and promises more uniformly positive effects in the political realm and other areas of social life. This, then, is one of the central matters considered in the final chapter, which looks at how we might go about fostering greater democratic engagement on the part of the citizens of tomorrow.

10
Engendering Engagement among Young Canadians: A Holistic Approach

Were there a simple solution to the problem of democratic disengagement among young Canadians, it would have already been suggested and put into effect. But the problem is not so readily resolved. Shaping current patterns of political and civic participation are larger tides of social and cultural change that have slowly altered basic norms, dispositions, and habits of behaviour among younger generations. Addressing the problem requires a holistic approach that is sensitive to the depth and breadth of the underlying dynamics responsible for the phenomenon. Such are the presumptions informing the policy agenda presented below, which builds on the central findings of this study and the normative positions articulated and defended at various points. To recapitulate, the principal conclusions are as follows.

- The problem of political disengagement among today's young Canadians is most clearly revealed by examining patterns of habitual or chronic disengagement. Today's young Canadians, compared to those of the past, are much more apt to be habitual rather than intermittent non-voters. These young habitual non-voters are also disinclined to be involved in other forms of public engagement – volunteering, community groups, and other political activities. The fact that non-participation carries over from election to election, and from voting to other forms of political and civic involvement, suggests that chronic disengagement is rooted in abiding dispositions of the individual, which points to the importance of the formative years in moulding habits of engagement. Putting the spotlight on chronic disengagement also raises doubts about the wisdom of certain approaches to encouraging participation. Easy fixes – those that only facilitate rather than induce participation – are more likely to have an effect on the intermittently active than the chronically disengaged. But the latter group, by virtue of its consistent lack of input into democratic governance procedures, should be of greater concern.

- Socioeconomic differences in habitual non-voting are starker among younger generations of Canadians. Left unaddressed, these threaten to skew public policy in favour of the interests of well-heeled, better-educated citizens. In the interests of democratic (and thereby social and economic) equality, policy initiatives should be designed to close these gaps by encouraging at least minimal participation by the chronically disengaged. Increased participation among those already interested and engaged does, however, promise other distinct benefits, in that it is only at higher levels of engagement that citizens seem to develop a significant capacity for independent and critical judgment – qualities essential to a robust democracy. Thus, enhancing engagement at all points on the spectrum of involvement is desirable, as long as enhanced equality of participation is not compromised.
- Two underlying factors help explain diminished engagement among younger generations of Canadians: political inattentiveness (as manifested by low levels of political knowledge, political interest, and news media consumption) and the weakening of social integration (evident in ebbing attachments to community and stronger adherence to individualistic norms). Both attentiveness and social integration exert broad influence on electoral participation and other forms of political and civic involvement.
- The long-term evolution of political attentiveness – political knowledge, political interest, and news media use – in both Canada and other countries reveals generationally based change across a variety of geographic settings. While these results are generally consistent with Martin Wattenberg's emphasis on the importance of political attentiveness to long-term changes in political engagement, the timing of the changes revealed through cohort analysis undermines Wattenberg's explanation for the phenomenon: that extensive media choice, resulting from technological developments such as cable TV, is principally to blame. Doubts about Wattenberg's thesis are confirmed in a separate piece of analysis that asks under-forty respondents in a nationwide Canadian survey about conditions prevailing during their formative years of adolescence. The results suggest that political attentiveness is little influenced by media choice in the household when growing up. Instead, civics education and political discussion within the family have considerably greater effects. The latter is taken to be indicative of the general importance of interpersonal influence in the developing years to processes of political attentiveness.
- The thesis of weakening social integration in Canada is likewise akin to a prominent existing account but differs in critical details. Robert Putnam's *Bowling Alone* contends that social capital – forms of social connectedness and norms of trust and reciprocity – has suffered substantial intergenerational decline in the US over the past forty years. That there has

been such erosion in Canada is far from clear. If there are age differences on basic benchmarks of social capital, they are most readily explained by life course dynamics: a downward arc from the teen years to early adulthood, a gradual ascent throughout most of adulthood, and a final dip in the twilight years. Where there does appear to be a marked generation gap is in a form of social connection not considered by Putnam, attachment to large-scale communities of province and nation. Thus, it is not, the available evidence would suggest, tangible connections to fellow citizens that have atrophied in Canada, but rather abstract feelings of belonging to what Benedict Anderson calls imagined communities.

- These observations lead to an interpretation of "the decline of community" quite different from Putnam's assessment. The weakening of attachments to province and nation can be attributed to a changing political culture – captured by Neil Nevitte's phrase the "decline of deference" – that has seen younger generations more apt to question social givens across a wide variety of contexts. Among these social givens is national identity, an attachment the individual normally inherits at birth rather than consciously adopts. Preferring that which they choose and fashion for themselves, younger generations are more drawn towards those forms of community consistent with individual choice and self-development. Local community often fits the bill, helping explain why there has been no obvious generational decline in local community attachments (the age variations that appear look more like life-cycle undulations than cohort decline). Communities beyond the local face a greater challenge in engendering a sense of personal involvement and authenticity. That said, the task is not insurmountable, but dependent on the degree to which a sense of purpose is created through meaningful common endeavour, a task that requires both political leadership and public involvement. In recent times, there has been too little of both: Canada's politicians and parties have focused on managerial governance, failing to give us a reason to believe in Canada beyond the creature comforts it provides, while Canadians keen to be part of meaningful collective projects have drifted off in other directions.

- While the decline of deference is one felicitous way of describing the change in political culture that has rendered younger generations more questioning of social givens, among them inherited community attachments, the more encompassing concept that describes these changes is the growth of individualism. In reviewing definitions and understandings of individualism in the fields of psychology, political science, and philosophy, distinct emphases are apparent in which individualism is variously conceptualized as self-direction, self-confidence, self-reliance, and self-regard. Empirical assessment of these dimensions suggests the more prominent aspects of individualism among younger Canadians are self-direction (a corollary of the decline of deference) and self-regard.

- Heightened emphasis on self-direction and self-regard has tended to undermine political engagement among younger generations. Both contribute to weaker regard among the young for relevant social norms that have sustained participation in the past – the sense of obligation to keep up with current events, the belief in a civic duty to vote in elections, the desire to be connected to one's community by being engaged in these ways. Political behaviour has instead come to be more closely guided by personal interest, meaning both that which affects me (self-regard) and that which intrigues me (self-direction). These motives influence processes of personal engagement (why and whether I might get involved) as well as dynamics of interpersonal mobilization (why and whether I might encourage others to be involved).
- The contention throughout is that these varied influences on democratic engagement among younger Canadians have their origins in generational changes that started to manifest themselves long ago. The theory of political culture change developed to account for these patterns, which are not unique to Canada, points to the entrenchment of the adolescent stage of life in the first half of the twentieth century as a critical development. This alteration in the social structure, attendant on the extension of secondary education from a minority of young people to one and all, created a very different social context for teens in their critical developmental years. The key change was the strengthening of peer influence, which gave freer rein and expression to adolescent disposition – including relative indifference to politics and conspicuous individualism. The effects were seen, so the argument runs, not only in adolescents, but also, due to the abiding influence of the formative years, in the adults that adolescents eventually became. In other words, the entrenchment of adolescence produced not just distinctive life course patterns, but also long-term generational change. Adolescence has thus been an important wellspring of key changes in political culture that have influenced the nature of democratic life in the modern period.
- The expression of adolescent tendencies has been influenced by another important development intrinsically linked to the entrenchment of the adolescent stage of life: rising education levels over time. In some cases, educational effects run counter to, and inhibit the full expression of, adolescent tendencies. In other cases, education effects augment or complement adolescent qualities, leading to their amplification. Taking account of the joint effects of the infusion of adolescent sensibilities and increased education levels over time sheds new light on different dimensions of political culture change in the developed democracies.

These conclusions speak to both academic research on the political disengagement of young Canadians and broader debates in the wider literature regarding the long-term arc of modern democracy. But there is also a policy agenda to be derived from these findings. It involves two distinct, yet inter-related, components. One focuses on adolescents and is informed by two essential principles: planting the seeds of democratic engagement in the formative years and doing so in a universal fashion in order to promote equality of democratic participation. Specific proposals relate to rethinking and restructuring important elements of the adolescent stage of life, along with school-based initiatives such as enhanced civics education. The second policy agenda has a more diffuse focus. It involves encouraging changes in attitude and behaviour on the part of citizens more generally as well as political leaders, and reforming the political system itself. This latter set of measures is partly aimed at enhancing democratic engagement among those who have already come of age. But it is also designed to help create a sup-portive social and political environment that will assist in sustaining positive effects achieved through interventions among the adolescent population. In comparison to other recent prescriptive works (such as Macedo et al. 2005), and in keeping with the general approach throughout, less emphasis is given to institutional and administrative remedies and more to measures aimed at effecting a general reorientation of young people in favour of a deeper involvement in politics and civic life.

From Adolescence to Adulthood

The theory of adolescent influence developed above points to both a process and an outcome: an altered socialization process involving enhanced peer influence in the teenage years has resulted in significant changes to political culture in society at large over an extended period. Adults have not become indistinguishable from adolescents, but the adult world has gradually become more reflective of adolescent sensibilities and dispositions. Altering this outcome – a gradual process, inevitably – involves targeting the underlying mechanism of change by altering the balance between peer and adult influ-ence in the adolescent years to allow adult sensibilities greater sway.

In concrete terms, this means reversing the longstanding tendency towards adolescent segregation and encouraging greater interaction with the adult world at an earlier stage. It does not entail the forceful inculcation of specific adult qualities, nor does it mean exclusively promoting civic engagement per se. Instead, the strategy is partly based on the assumption that interaction without specific intent will naturally result in the imparting of adult sens-ibilities and dispositions from which more specific proclivities, including civic and political involvement, will emerge. It also reflects the view that the problems associated with adolescent segregation appear across other domains that have not been touched on in this study – social, cultural, economic – so that there are other benefits aside from civic engagement to be derived from the reconfiguration of adolescent life. These broader benefits might be invoked in seeking to generate support for changes that might be seen as rather far-reaching if intended only to enhance democratic engagement.

The most sweeping assessment of the problem and how it should be addressed comes from those who propose a full-blown paradigm shift in which the idea of adolescence and attendant social practices of enforcement would be discarded altogether. Robert Epstein's recent book, *The Case against Adolescence*, suggests that adolescents have been infantilized without evident justification by a raft of social and legal restrictions placed on them since the advent of the industrial age in the nineteenth century (2007). His most radical suggestion for dismantling this constrictive framework is to make competency rather than age the basis for the attainment of a host of adult rights and privileges. Instead of a voting age, for example, he recommends a test for voting competency open to all applicants of all ages (2007, 335). Epstein is confident that many adolescents would seize such opportunities if presented with them and take up many "adult" activities in a responsible and productive manner.

Epstein's proposals are intriguing, his emphasis on the scope of the problem enlightening. But the complete abandonment of age-based restrictions on adult activity seems unlikely. More realistic than calls for the abandonment of adolescence is the proposition that we should endeavour to create more meaningful connections between adolescents and the adult world with the objective of instilling – or, to follow Epstein, allowing for the natural development of – a sense of competence, agency, and maturity at earlier stages. Responsibility and empowerment should be extended to teenagers in a measured manner across diverse settings: by parents, by schools, in workplaces, in volunteer settings.

This advice is consistent with the parenting philosophy which holds that the cosseting has gone too far and that youngsters should instead be given more responsibility and opportunity – flip sides of the same coin – at a younger age. While there is the contrary viewpoint that the lives of children have become overly programmed to the detriment of carefree play and exploration, this tends to be an argument invoked in defence of unstructured space in the lives of pre-adolescent children (Honoré 2008). The prescription of adult interaction and orientation is aimed at adolescents ready for the challenge, and places as much emphasis on opportunity as obligation.

Parents are in a position to effect such changes within the home environment through the expectations they impose on their adolescent offspring and the opportunities and leeway they extend them. But parenting practices are not the most tractable domain for public policy intervention. Schools are a more likely place where specific programs encouraging and enabling adolescents to step out of their adolescent enclaves to interact with society at large can be more readily put into effect. These already exist in the form of community service programs in place in many schools. A recent review, based on interviews with high school graduates in Ontario, reveals that community service in that province currently involves a sundry assortment of activities in diverse settings: in the community (volunteering with seniors, at daycare centres, as youth counsellors); at one-off events (helping with "community fairs, picnics and parades" or with fundraising events such as golf tournaments); in schools (on yearbook committees, in the school office or library, assisting with athletic events); or in churches (working with children, helping with renovations) and sports clubs (as referees, as judges) to which students already belong (Brown et al. 2007b, 19-20). While in a number of provinces such service is mandatory, an important shortcoming is that the requirements tend to be minimal – the forty hours of community service required for high school graduation in Ontario is currently the most stringent (Brown et al. 2007a). For most, community service is an isolated episode rather than a more integrated part of their high school experience. The impact of community service could be bolstered considerably by extending these requirements (Niemi et al. 2000), which could probably best be achieved by making them a more integrated part of the school curriculum (e.g., part of a social studies or civics course), something rarely done in Canada at present (Brown et al. 2007a).

Taking this a step further might involve the establishment of programs for young people that entail taking a year off from their schooling to pursue some form of community service, most likely in the year after graduating from high school. Again, limited opportunities along these lines do already exist. Katimavik, established in 1976, offers about 1,000 Canadians aged seventeen to twenty-one the chance each year to participate in community service in different parts of the country for a nine-month period. The question arises whether programs of this type might be further developed to increase the annual intake or whether participation might even be made compulsory in order to vastly extend their reach. It is an idea that has been previously proposed in the US (Barber 2003, 298-303; Dionne et al. 2003; Macedo et al. 2005, 152) and is receiving renewed consideration and discussion under President Obama, but has received relatively little attention in Canada. The notion, if somewhat foreign, is not outrageous: in countries where military service is compulsory, there is sometimes an alternative public service option for those who would rather not serve in the military. If the premise is accepted that adolescent segregation is a formidable social barrier impeding effective transitions to adulthood, which has deep implications not only for teenagers but for the adults that teenagers eventually become, bold measures are worth considering. A requirement for public service would allow all young Canadians to spend a year in a relatively diverse social setting before moving on to the largely age-segregated environment of university or college, or into the working world where personal preoccupations can quickly become predominant and the possibilities for self-development become more limited.

In his recent book *Who We Are*, also an inquiry into the present state of civic engagement and national belonging in Canada, Rudyard Griffiths likewise proposes the idea of mandatory service for young Canadians. He offers some practical suggestions that might enhance the feasibility of such a program (2009, 167-71). One is that only some young people, chosen through a random national lottery, should be selected for mandatory service (he suggests one in four or about 100,000 individuals per year). Another is that a significant incentive, in the form of a financial subsidy to cover the cost of three years of further education at an institution of their choice, should be provided to participants. Some modification of these ideas might be in order. In particular, if the program is not universal yet offers substantial financial benefits, it is likely mechanisms would need to be in place to allow those keen to be included to participate and those adamantly opposed to opt out. In addition, the viability and attractiveness of a large-scale service program could be further enhanced if Canadian universities were to provide their own incentive for participation by placing greater weight on community service as a criterion for admission and by encouraging the newly admitted to defer their studies for a year to pursue such opportunities. Currently in Canada, there is little encouragement to delay postsecondary education (Baxter 2003), whereas in Britain the practice referred to as taking a "gap year" is viewed much more favourably. Different attitudes and practices with respect to university entry would not only facilitate the establishment of extended community service programs, they might also benefit universities struggling with burgeoning problems of academic disengagement and attrition at the undergraduate level (Côté and Allahar 2007): students taking a gap year to undertake community service would begin their postsecondary studies with greater life experience and maturity. These potential benefits appear to have some intuitive appeal to Canadians. In a 2008 survey commissioned by Katimavik, 69 percent agreed with the idea of "young Canadians taking a year between high school and post-secondary education to travel and take part in a structured full time national volunteer program, as a means of gaining life and work skills, while learning about themselves and the country" (Ekos Research Associates 2008, 11).

Whether community service programs are obligatory or not, and whatever their precise duration and scope, there are other features of such programs that should be in place to produce desired effects. A broad choice of options is important if community service is to be seen as more of an opportunity than an obligation (and, under a large-scale or mandatory service program, if placements are to be found for a small army of young people each year). Personal interests must play a significant role in determining what specific activity a young person will undertake, in order to enhance the prospects of the "positive experience[s]" that researchers have identified as necessary to a successful outcome (Brown et al. 2007b). Furthermore, community service programs should be designed to avoid the re-creation of adolescent enclaves – clusters of young people working in relative isolation – and instead promote age-integrated activity (Kusiek 2007). This might mean interaction of adults and adolescents, but it can also mean interaction of adolescents and children, in which adolescents assume the role of mentor – a concept becoming more popular in education circles under the rubric of "peer teaching." One program in place in some Canadian schools is the Healthy Buddies program, which involves older students educating younger ones about different aspects of healthy living. The success of the program has been apparent not only in the altered attitudes and behaviours of younger charges (Stock et al. 2007), but also (anecdotally at least) in the sense of agency and empowerment engendered in the older students (Mick 2007). Other Canadian examples include programs that see varsity athletes visiting elementary schools and reading to students in order to promote literacy, and an Alberta initiative that allows high school students to develop and teach social studies material to local grade 2 students as part of their own social studies class. One teacher involved in the latter initiative reports that students gain self-esteem through the process, as they "like to call themselves teachers and take pride in and ownership of their work."[1] Allowing young people just out of high school to serve in various support capacities at different levels of the school system – as tutors, as classroom assistants, as coaching aides for sports teams – would be one way of significantly extending this mentoring approach. If a handful of suitably inclined young people were offered such positions in each of Canada's thousands of schools each year, many opportunities for meaningful and beneficial community service would be opened up.

There is also considerable benefit to be gained from designing programs that are not strictly local in scope but are instead integrated into broader public initiatives. One of the findings from research on the effects of community service is that students may come away with a new understanding of the benefits and value of volunteering, and perhaps the intention to do so again in the future, but do not show consistent enhancement of qualities relating to citizen engagement. The activity undertaken teaches the young participant what he or she can personally do for others, but does not necessarily generate awareness of the larger possibilities that emerge when people work jointly to bring about change in society (Walker 2000; Barber 1992). A further limitation is suggested by our earlier analysis of social connectedness and community attachments: being involved with others in myriad ways serves to enhance feelings of attachment to local community, but has limited effects on people's sense of provincial or national belonging. But it is the latter attachments that seem to be suffering from generational erosion and which stand in greatest need of reinforcement.

A different type of community service designed to address these shortcomings would be to offer young people the opportunity to participate in local endeavours expressly linked to provincial or national public projects. For example, a national environmental plan to tackle greenhouse gas emissions through various policy measures – carbon taxes, promotion of new technologies, restrictions on emissions – could include a citizen-based component allowing for a variety of local projects designed to support national objectives. Young people with a keen interest in environmental issues could choose to be part of such a project for their mandatory community service. Another possible example, in these times of global cultural strife, would be a renewed national commitment to Canadian multiculturalism, a commitment that could take shape on the ground through citizen-led projects designed to build bridges between different ethnic and cultural groups. Consistent with this approach, Katimavik, in addition to its general service program, has now started to offer three thematic options for its young participants under the headings of "cultural discovery and civic engagement," "eco-citizenship and active living," and "second language and cultural diversity."[2] Over 700 community partner organizations are reportedly involved at present in providing opportunities for young Canadians to work on these issues of broad public relevance.

There presumably would be other groups involved in such issues that could offer further avenues for young people to pursue meaningful service activity, particularly if placement opportunities are not limited to groups in the narrowly defined voluntary sector. Community service for young people could include working for an advocacy group with a clear purpose and mission to change public policy in a given issue area. It might also include working for a political party or an individual elected official. Just as there are currently internship programs for university graduates who can spend a year working for a member of parliament in Ottawa, those finishing high school might be given the chance to work in the local constituency offices of federal and provincial elected members. There, they would receive a hands-on education in the functioning of government, the role of the local elected member in providing constituency service, and general exposure to a range of public policy issues.

These suggestions for a revamped approach to community service hearken back to our earlier critique of Putnam's endorsement of unqualified social capital, his implicit view that it matters less what brings people together than the fact that they come together to work, to volunteer, to bowl, to pray

in concert. There is greater value from the viewpoint of democratic engagement in seeking to build social capital with a purpose, indeed social capital
with a public purpose (Riedel 2002; Boyte and Farr 1997) on a scale beyond
the merely local. There is a clear role here for government not only to design
suitable community service programs, but also to develop public projects
that embody a sense of collective purpose and which allow for small-scale
citizen contributions, thus permitting young people and others to feel part
of something larger and more lasting in its effects than simply lending a
helping hand to those in need in their immediate vicinity.

Alongside these suggestions for greater emphasis on, and greater coherence
in, community service requirements, there are other methods of orienting
adolescents to the adult world that focus more directly on electoral involvement. One is related to an idea proposed on previous occasions with respect
to voter registration: that Canadians should be allowed to register to vote
at age sixteen, two years before becoming eligible to vote at age eighteen
(Elections BC 2001, 14; Archer 2003; Howe 2006, 32). In other places where
early registration is permitted – the UK (at age sixteen) and Australia (at age
seventeen) – the main rationale is practical exigency, a consideration that
applies in Canada as well. A lag between registration and voting eligibility
allows extra time to ensure young people are added to the voters list before
an election occurs. Canada has been experiencing problems in this area,
especially since the door-to-door enumeration method of assembling the
voters list at each election was abandoned with the adoption of a permanent
register in 1997. Now, newly eligible electors, upon turning eighteen, receive
an invitation by mail to have their names added to the permanent voters
list, but many fail to respond. As a result, they are not registered when an
election is called, do not receive information about when and where to vote,
and often fail to rectify the situation before voting day arrives. If young
people could be registered at age sixteen, there would be extra time to address these matters. Registration at age sixteen could also, in theory, be
coordinated through high schools, perhaps as part of a civics or social studies
course. As a further practical expedient, if online registration were permitted
– as it now is in British Columbia, with Elections Canada seeking to follow
suit at the federal level – registration in high school civics classes would be
even more straightforward and effective (Archer 2003). A similar set of proposals has been developed by the American organization, Fair Vote, to address
the more pronounced problem of deficient registration levels among young
Americans (Richie 2007).

These ideas are aimed at producing practical benefits. But there are also
ways that voter registration at age sixteen could be turned into a symbolic
milestone designed to connect adolescents to the adult world they are on
the cusp of entering. The potential value of this is suggested by a 2004

Australian survey of senior high school students that invokes the idea of rites of passage to adulthood. The study found that voting in an election was *not* looked upon as a significant milestone by young Australians: the more significant markers of adulthood were turning eighteen, getting a driver's licence, and being permitted to drink (Print et al. 2004, 16-18). While negative or indifferent attitudes towards political participation may be one reason for this, the lack of enthusiasm may also reflect the absence of any fanfare associated with electoral initiation. The first-time voter is accorded no special recognition, simply going off to the polling station and casting a ballot along with everyone else (Eisner 2003). If voter registration at age sixteen were introduced and coordinated through high schools here in Canada, it would be possible to fill this gap by organizing an annual ceremony within each school to mark this electoral coming of age. The member of parliament or another local dignitary could preside over the event, offering her or his thoughts on the significance of democratic participation, and congratulating students on their new status as registered electors. Such an event would serve as the youth equivalent of citizenship ceremonies for immigrants, an emotionally resonant milestone for most inductees. As a further symbolic measure, consideration could be given to designing a new permanent voter identification card (for pros and cons, see Archer 2008) to be awarded to each student on the occasion. This would serve as acceptable identification for voting in elections (and, on a further practical note, would outline the action to be taken to update one's voter registration status in the event of moving).

In suggesting that the age of eligibility for voter registration be lowered to sixteen for reasons of both expediency and symbolic initiation into the electorate, the question arises whether the voting age itself might likewise be reduced. In my view, the time is not ripe for this. While others have argued that it would be better to initiate voting at an age younger than eighteen when adolescents are at a more settled stage of life and more likely to take advantage of the opportunity (Franklin 2004, 213-14; Milner 2005, 15-16), other factors would militate against participation and the end result could be disappointing. The analysis in the previous chapter of age differences in political interest and political discussion revealed marked change between mid-adolescence and the early twenties: at this stage of life, two or three years makes a very considerable difference to levels of political awareness. Furthermore, there are not currently the necessary supports in the school system and within homes to ensure that sixteen-year-olds will receive sufficient encouragement to vote. It is possible that other changes designed to foster democratic interest and engagement among adolescents, including those noted above and below, could eventually change this situation and make a lower voting age worthy of consideration. The clearest sign will be when sixteen-year-olds themselves start agitating for the vote. Until then, we are better off conceptualizing adolescence as a time for democratic apprenticeship and initiation.

Civics Plus

In outlining ways that adolescents can be better connected to the adult world, the role of schools – in facilitating community involvement, in playing host to electoral induction ceremonies – has been underlined because of the capacity of these institutions to effect significant change that touches all young people. Schools are also the site for another initiative that must be part of any attempt to stem disengagement among young Canadians, enhanced civics education. To many observers, this is the single most important change required to address the problem.

The changes to current practice needed to make significant strides in this area are considerable. In recognition of the growing concerns about the engagement of young citizens, some provinces have moved ahead with new curriculum initiatives in recent years. In Ontario, students are now required to take a half-year civics course in grade 10, the only such mandatory course in the country. In BC, an optional course, Civics Studies 11, was introduced in the fall of 2005. There also exists in a number of provinces, such as BC and Alberta, a commitment on paper to consistent civics instruction throughout the social studies curriculum. But as one recent review suggests, "[l]ooking beyond the rhetoric ... exposes the extraordinarily weak commitment of educational jurisdictions in Canada to implementing strong programs in the area" (Hughes and Sears 2008). The problems include lack of curriculum materials, the absence of clear teaching objectives, and a failure to provide adequate training for teachers. Others have rightly suggested that, despite provincial jurisdiction over education, there is a strong case for federal leadership to advance the civics agenda more forcefully (MacKinnon et al. 2007, 21). Other countries, including both unitary (UK) and federal states (Australia), have seen the central government jump-start the process, coordinating efforts across jurisdictions and providing necessary resources for effective civics teaching. Australian efforts in this area are particularly exemplary. They include electoral education centres in four cities that are visited by about 100,000 students each year; a dedicated staff person at the Australian Electoral Commission for teacher training; and the presence of three permanent staff members in each of the country's 150 constituencies, among them a district returning officer, available to provide education sessions in schools upon request (Howe 2006, 28-29). The Canadian federal government cannot unilaterally impose itself in this field but should seek to cooperate with the provinces (through the interprovincial Council of Ministers of Education) to establish civics education as a genuine priority in schools throughout the country.

Research on the types of curricular content and pedagogical practice that produce the best results in civics education has flourished in recent years. It is generally acknowledged that there is much that can be done beyond simply offering a standard civics course that teaches students the basics of how government works and leaves it at that (Kahne and Sporte 2007, 22-23). Experiential learning has been found to be highly effective, including simulations and debates within the classroom and visits to the classroom by community leaders and activists (Kahne et al. 2006). Getting students out of the classroom is also an effective learning tool, allowing students to become involved in a project, typically at the local level, to address an issue they consider important (Kahne et al. 2006). In the civics education literature, the emphasis tends to be on motivational benefits (caring about politics and social issues) and educational outcomes (learning how change is achieved) of such activity (Niemi et al. 2000, 48). To this must be added the benefit emphasized above, the social dividend of leavening adolescent segregation through connections with the broader community. Thus there are multiple reasons to make community service – broadly understood to mean volunteering or something more akin to community activism, involving wide-ranging opportunities, including some connected to projects that are provincial or national in scope – an integrated part of civics instruction. The teaching of civics in Canada largely fails to incorporate such activities into the curriculum and would benefit from adapting models developed elsewhere, such as the Public Achievement program pioneered by the Center for Democracy and Citizenship at the University of Minnesota (Kunkel et al. 2001). The closest current example is the requirement to "implement a plan for action on a selected local, provincial, national, or international civic issue" for students enrolled in BC's Civics Studies 11 course (British Columbia Ministry of Education 2005, 23), though the form this requirement has taken in practice is not well documented.

A further pedagogical objective that must be emphasized, given earlier conclusions about the importance of political attentiveness to democratic engagement, is the promotion of media literacy. Young people today pay relatively little attention to traditional forms of news media – newspapers and television – and do not make up the balance through news consumption via the radio and Internet. This inattentiveness to news media is strongly linked to shortfalls in political knowledge, including not only awareness of what might be considered political trivia – the names of party leaders and so on – but also basic understanding of more enduring political issues and the fundamental workings of government. As part of an enhanced civics curriculum, students should be required to become regular consumers of news media, with a particular focus on the high-quality sources that seem to produce the greatest enhancements to political knowledge – in particular, national newspapers and Internet sites that offer detailed news coverage and analysis. Woven into the curriculum, this attention to current events via news media would also serve as a natural focal point for the discussion-and-debate pedagogical techniques that contribute to better outcomes in civics teaching.

Another beneficial form of experiential learning linked to the real world of politics is mock elections. These, of course, are already in operation in Canada. Beginning with the Ontario provincial election of 2003, mock elections have now been organized for several provincial elections and three federal elections under the auspices of Student Vote, an independent organization that coordinates and oversees the procedure with logistical support from elections agencies in each jurisdiction. Advocates of mock elections tend to emphasize two principal effects on students: familiarity with the act of voting so that it is not seen as a foreign activity undertaken only by others; and related activities around mock elections, such as debates and classroom discussion, that pique student interest in politics and enhance their understanding of the democratic process. A third benefit that should also be underlined is the potential of mock elections to concentrate student attention, for a limited period at least, on the provincial or national scene and to impart some sense of community attachment from the process of being involved in the electoral deliberations of province or nation.

While there has been no detailed research in Canada on the supporting activities that do take place within schools around mock elections or the tangible impact on students, they are a natural fit with an enhanced civics curriculum and to my mind should be taken further. Two ideas for extending the practice come from the UK. First, the custom there is for students to serve as candidates for the various parties in mock elections. This allows for school-based activities such as debates in which student candidates can represent different parties. It might also lend itself to the involvement of larger groups of students, who could band together behind their favoured candidate to support his or her campaign, thereby creating the spirited atmosphere of a real political campaign (without the vitriol, one hopes) within the schools.

The other British innovation worth importing is the effort to encourage mock elections on an annual basis, rather than only when an actual election is taking place, an initiative designed to increase students' exposure to the experience. Here in Canada, high school students would typically have one, perhaps two, opportunities to participate in a mock election during their high school years (depending on whether their province is one where mock elections are organized). An annual event would raise this to at least five opportunities.

The question that naturally arises is what might serve as the occasion for mock elections throughout the country's schools when no actual election is taking place. One answer, to return to a suggestion from an earlier chapter, is an annual debate between the leaders of the federal political parties. This could take place at a fixed time each year, early fall being the most sensible in order to align the timing, in those years when a real election is occurring, with the fixed election date now established (ostensibly at least) for the third Monday in October. The debate would be presented to Canadians at large, but would naturally serve as a focal point for students involved in mock elections in their schools. The stipulation would also apply that an annual debate, particularly outside election years, should be expansive in its deliberations, focusing less on the finer details of policy and more on the grander goals for Canada envisaged by each leader and how these might be achieved in the coming years. The sniping and strategizing that characterize much political discourse, including election debates, has undermined public confidence in political parties, which has fallen to very low levels indeed among both younger and older Canadians. More inspirational messages designed to appeal to the younger generation might help some see in particular leaders or parties a philosophy that resonates, thereby enhancing perceptions of politics in general and improving the prospects of future party and electoral involvement.

As part of their civics instruction, students would be required to watch this annual leaders' debate, though naturally it would also be available on the Internet for later viewing, perhaps in the classroom setting. An Internet site could also provide areas for comments to be posted, allowing for broader public discussion involving contributions from Canadians across the country, young and old. Within schools, subsequent to the event, there would be further opportunity for student candidates to continue the debate. If the leaders' debate were to take place on a Monday, the mock vote in schools could be scheduled for the Friday, allowing a few intervening days for follow-up activities. The week might be given an official designation, a title akin to the "Celebrating Democracy Week" that occurs each fall in Australian schools.

To inaugurate annual leaders' debates along these lines would be relatively straightforward. Election debates are currently organized by a consortium of television networks. If that consortium decided to hold a leaders' debate on an annual basis, the opposition leaders would presumably jump at the chance for enhanced public exposure and the prime minister would have little choice but to join in the fun. If the private networks are not interested in sponsoring such an exercise, the CBC should take the lead, pushing ahead without the participation of other networks. Ensuring a certain tone and focus for the debate is also easily achieved, by tying debate questions – whether formulated by journalists or chosen from among those suggested by Canadians – to general priorities and visions for the future.

While mock elections in the absence of an election might be dismissed as an empty and contrived exercise, there is reason to think they might take on some significance. Since the mock election results would be the only ones available to gauge public reaction to the annual leaders' debate, there could well be public interest in the results (just as there is in by-election results). And while student voting patterns are unlikely to reflect the electoral preferences of Canadians at large, *changes* in the student vote from one year to the next would be more meaningful and might well reflect changing political sentiment within the country. The results would likely receive some play in the media, giving young people the feeling that their views were having an impact on real-world politics – an additional benefit, alongside enhanced familiarity with the voting process and opportunities for related school-based activities.

Annual mock elections would be a significant undertaking and adequate resources are again essential to the task. Student Vote has sometimes struggled to find the resources to organize mock elections at each electoral opportunity and would need significant public funding to take the lead on this project. It again comes down to priorities. If we are serious about stemming demo-cratic disengagement among the young, a significant investment in mock elections, conceptualized as an integral part of an enhanced civics curricu-lum, could deliver considerable dividends.

All of the foregoing focuses on civics education at the high school level. Previously, I have voiced the opinion that mandatory courses in introductory politics at the university level might be worthwhile (Howe 2001, 23), a tenta-tive suggestion predicated on the assumption that not much was likely to change at the secondary level. My inclination now is to insist that tackling the problem at the high school level is the only sensible solution, as it would simultaneously advance two distinct goals: enhancing democratic equality by engendering wider participation in elections and other forms of political activity; and enlarging the pool of citizens deeply engaged in politics whose discerning judgment and critical faculties serve a vital role in sustaining vibrant and productive democratic debate. The latter effect would be a natural by-product of the former, as enhanced civics education for one and all would presumably increase the number who would graduate to a life of self-directed engagement, which might include postsecondary study in the social sciences, continued involvement in various civic activities, close attentiveness to public affairs, and so forth. Thus civics education at the secondary level would effectively serve the twin goals of encouraging rudimentary engage-ment by the largest number possible and promoting more intensive engage-ment on the part of a smaller subset of self-selected citizens.

Advocating for Politics

A policy agenda aimed at adolescents is one element needed to bring about greater democratic engagement among young Canadians. Adolescence and adulthood can be brought into closer contact through greater emphasis on community involvement, along with adult responsibility and opportunity, at earlier ages; civics education and related undertakings can give young people the tools, experience, and motivational disposition to be involved in elections, in local community projects, and in larger public undertakings. But the effects of these changes might prove disappointing if young people continue to come of age in a society that is not particularly supportive or enthusiastic about democratic engagement. To bolster and reinforce the adolescent agenda, changes of more general effect are required.

One broader initiative that would serve this end is promotion of the concept of interpersonal mobilization. Flagging engagement in current times, it was argued above, is partly attributable to the reluctance of Canadians to press one another into political and civic action. Younger generations in particular are not inclined to encourage others to be involved, though the tendency is not limited to this group. The tremendous potential that can be unleashed when people not only become personally committed but transmit their enthusiasm to others was revealed by Barack Obama's campaign for the Democratic presidential nomination in 2008 (Von Drehle 2008). Interpersonal mobilization, most notably from one young person to the next, accounted for much of the momentum that led to his successful nomination bid and eventual election.

But waiting for a charismatic leader to spark a similar process in Canada is not the recommended course of action, or rather inaction. Interpersonal mobilization needs to be cultivated so that it becomes a natural reflex embedded in norms of social conduct. A British study on electoral disengagement uses an apposite phrase to describe the type of citizens needed to make this a reality: "advocates for voting," or indeed advocates for politics more generally (Johnson and Marshall 2004, 17). It is not enough for citizens to be politically engaged themselves. They, or at least some among them, must take it upon themselves to encourage participation by others, whether by voting in elections, keeping up with politics, or being engaged in other ways.

If this seems a tall order, I am optimistic it is a norm that could take root and spread of its own accord if deliberately sown. One method of disseminating the idea would be through media advertising by elections agencies during campaigns. Recent efforts by Elections Canada to encourage voting have directly targeted those who do not vote – young people in particular. An alternative approach to electoral incitement is to target those who do vote and encourage them to get others involved: slogans might include "Bring a friend to vote" or "Why vote alone?" Advertisements could depict people encouraging others to be electorally engaged in a variety of ways: discussing campaign literature, watching a televised debate together, speaking together with a candidate on the doorstep. The image of an older person, hand on the shoulder of a young adult as they head into the polling station, would plant the idea of the most likely conduit of personal influence on the youngest voters, parental persuasion. A key benefit of this approach is that it would target those most likely to hear the message and respond positively: those who do pay attention to TV news and election ads, who probably vote themselves, and who, by virtue of their less individualistic tendencies, would be relatively receptive to the idea of becoming an advocate for politics.

Political parties could also make more concerted efforts to promote interpersonal mobilization, not only by returning to the traditional face-to-face canvassing techniques that have been proven to be more effective in bringing voters to the polls (Macedo et al. 2005, 59), but also as a means of recruiting new party members. This is, after all, the principal mechanism whereby young people are currently brought into party politics: they are asked to join by family, friends, and acquaintances. While the parties can probably do little to promote greater mobilization within families, they can seek to ensure vibrant organizations and ample opportunity for interpersonal contact in places where youth congregate, particularly on university and college campuses, by generously supporting the social and political activities of student party organizations (Cross and Young 2007, 26).

There is also value in more generally promoting "advocating for politics" as an important conceptual element of democratic citizenship. One place this can be done is in the civics education classroom. That citizens can do their part and exert influence not only by participating themselves but also by persuading others to do likewise is a valuable lesson to communicate to young people. Rather than being couched as a responsibility of the good citizen, there is an instrumental argument to be made that would appeal to those individualistic in their thinking: that while the individual's personal participation in politics may have little effect, more can be achieved by encouraging others to participate as well, particularly if those individuals in turn persuade others to be involved – what might be styled the multiplier effect of interpersonal mobilization. Elections, it might be pointed out, are rarely won by a single vote, but they are often won by 100 or 200 votes, a margin of victory that can sometimes be attributed to a handful of people – perhaps even just one – who have made a dedicated effort to "get out the vote." The possibility of ripple effects effectively counters the "my vote makes no difference" lament and obviously applies to forms of political and civic involvement besides voting. In virtually any area of public activity, getting others involved produces more significant results than individual effort alone.

Seeking to enhance processes of interpersonal mobilization is a strategy very much designed to work in conjunction with other initiatives aimed at engendering greater democratic engagement among young Canadians. Community service requirements, enhanced civics instruction, annual mock elections, and other initiatives can lay the groundwork for active citizenship, but the effects of such initiatives will almost certainly be rendered more permanent if those primed for participation are subject to ongoing encouragement and persuasion by the peers and adults in their lives (Shea and Harris 2006). To focus on young people exclusively would be to overlook other changes that are needed as part of a more holistic response to the problem of political disengagement among younger Canadians.

The Political Realm

Mindful of the larger picture, there is finally the realm of politics to consider for its potential contribution to the project of re-engaging young Canadians. The general conclusion is presaged in things already said: there is a need to create a greater sense of common purpose among Canadians through broad-based public projects that combine government action with contributions from Canadians on the ground. Such initiatives could emerge at either the provincial or federal level, or both. I personally would be reluctant to see the provinces alone taking the bull by the horns, while the federal government fades from public prominence. But if federal and provincial initiatives proceed in tandem, developing parallel projects that strengthen the attachment of Canadians to both province and nation, so much the better.

The call for concerted public endeavour to strengthen civic commitments has something in common with the idea that engaging or dramatic events are an effective way to capture young people's attention and get them thinking about public affairs. In simple terms, people need something to care about. After 9/11, for example, political scientists were curious to see whether this defining event of the new millennium would trigger a surge in interest in public affairs and civic engagement among members of the American public. There was indeed such a spike (Putnam 2002), though the most notable changes were more attitudinal than behavioural (Skocpol 2002). The upswing was also short-lived among most sections of the population, though it does seem to have been more enduring among those who were adolescents at the time of the attacks (Putnam 2008; Pryor et al. 2006, 3). However, relying on rare and devastating events to trigger interest in public affairs is hardly an adequate solution. A more relevant American example is the civil rights movement of the 1960s. In this instance, purposeful action by government in the form of new laws, directives, and social programs, was joined by the efforts and actions of those active on the ground – in marches, sit-ins, voter registration drives, and so on. It was not, of course, a wholly consensual endeavour, as many in the South were deeply opposed to the changes. But for those who did rally to the cause, the combination of shared moral purpose and individual contribution left a deep personal imprint that has been carried forward through their adult lives (McAdam 1988; Verba et al. 2005, 108-9).

Outside of wartime, one cannot really point to an analogous Canadian experience where decisive government action on behalf of a particular issue has been wedded to popular mobilization designed to further the cause. The only example, to my mind, would be the 1960s period in Quebec, when the Quiet Revolution and the sovereignty movement together generated a good deal of grassroots activism aimed at modernizing the politics and economy of Quebec and improving the position of the francophone majority. At the Canadian level, the achievements that have shaped our sense of national identity have tended to be government-inspired and government-executed from start to finish (e.g., medicare, official bilingualism and multicultural-ism, the introduction of the Charter of Rights). If these served the purpose well enough in earlier times, in current circumstances where the desire for personal involvement and authenticity is keenly felt, projects that allow Canadians to play their part are sure to have greater effect. What is needed, then, are meaningful public projects that rally Canadians to a common cause and provide opportunities for the practical involvement of citizens.

To achieve this goal, which requires both the articulation of suitable pro-jects and effective execution, political leadership is indispensable (Kersh 2007, 607-8). However, it is important to recognize that political leadership is not strictly a function of the qualities individual leaders possess, but also of the environment in which they operate. The critical reflex of media and citizens towards the political class is not without justification and does serve some useful purpose. However, it must also be recognized that it has the effect of closing the door on bold or innovative ideas. Creating space for these to be voiced requires providing venues where this can occur – an an-nual leaders' debate, for example – and a frame of mind on the part of media and polity alike that permits occasional blue-sky reflection by politicians.

In conjunction with political leadership, changes to political structures are also needed that will facilitate consensual decision making in order to rally broad support behind ideas for collective action that resonate. Demo-cratic reform initiatives should bear this proviso in mind. An electoral system based on proportional representation would encourage cooperation between like minded political parties and the formation of governments enjoying the support of true majorities of the population. Within parliament, reducing party discipline and allowing individual MPs greater sway would also have the potential to enhance consensual dynamics, though such changes should not be taken too far, for we do not want to create an assembly of free spirits unable to work in concert. Also of considerable moral force are extra-parliamentary devices – Royal Commissions, Quebec's Estates-General model, citizen assemblies – that allow for the transcendence of partisan divisions and the articulation of new directions for the country. The over-arching principle is that democratic reform, in seeking to give Canadians greater say in government, should not disperse power excessively, for this can lead to citizen disempowerment as much as the excessive concentration of power. A balance must be struck that allows Canadians to have democratic input in a manner that permits resolution of differences and the fashioning of general consensus.

Whatever the precise institutional mechanisms might be, what is needed, in the final analysis, is a political system that allows for *projets de sociétés* to emerge that we feel are truly ours. To bring about the necessary institutional changes partly entails putting our finger on what is wrong. The indifference and discontent towards politics currently evident in Canada is not just a reflection of a dysfunctional political system that requires some technical fixes, but of a system that seems to present a distorted image of who we are and who we would like to be – which many therefore choose to disparage or ignore. A sense of collective ownership of our political institutions, sorely lacking under the current dispensation, can best be engendered by restructuring the system to allow for the emergence of some sense of shared public purpose amid the inevitable cacophony of day-to-day politics.

Catalyzing Change

Whether any or all of this agenda for change might actually come about is difficult to say. Different players in officialdom have their part to play in initiating change: education ministers, the media, election officials, political parties, and elected members, premiers, and the prime minister. These potential agents of change will act to the extent they are persuaded by compelling arguments and pressured by engaged Canadians concerned about the current state of our democracy. In other words, in order to build a society where citizen engagement and political leadership can jointly flourish, the necessary prerequisites are pressure from engaged citizens and political leadership. This is the conundrum we face, making it an uphill battle that will not necessarily be won.

The agenda could certainly be advanced more quickly from above, if the issue were identified as an overarching priority by a prime minister or a serious aspirant to the position. To date, the disengagement of young Canadians has been a matter of secondary importance, remarked upon by most politicians at one point or another, often in the aftermath of an election in which turnout has hit a new low. It has not been the subject of sustained policy discussion and debate. A party that managed to highlight the key dimensions of the problem and its principal consequences, along with the outlines of a relevant program for change, and succeeded in generating enhanced public awareness through both conventional means and some of the Internet-based methods of political communication that savvy politicians are now adopting, might well reap significant electoral rewards. These could come from both Canadians at large, concerned about the future of our democracy, and young people in particular, made more aware of the marked estrangement of their generation from political and civic life.

Another way in which momentum could be lent to the cause would be to establish a public agency with a mandate to coordinate citizen engagement efforts across different departments and levels of government. Something of the sort has been done in recent years, as governments in Canada, both federal and provincial, have created offices of democratic reform and appointed cabinet ministers to oversee their operation.[3] The problem is that such agencies have typically been given the joint mandate of initiating and managing processes of institutional reform *and* devising methods of promoting citizen involvement in politics. The first of these has tended to take centre stage, while the latter has been something of an afterthought, either taken to be the natural consequence of updating and improving democratic institutions or limited to the enhancements that can be achieved through changes to electoral administration. But as we have seen, there are other factors that must be addressed in order to encourage citizen engagement, and more particularly the cultivation of engagement among the young, factors that are both relatively profound and diffuse. Institutionally, what is required is separation of the two objectives in recognition of the fact that reform of democratic institutions and citizen engagement are not simply opposite faces of the same coin. At the federal level, a newly minted Citizen Engagement Office should be charged with spearheading research and policy initiatives aimed at achieving robust, broad-based democratic engagement across different sections of Canadian society. This would serve to coordinate and focus efforts across different agencies with a role to play, including Elections Canada, Canadian Heritage, Human Resources and Skills Development, and Statistics Canada, as well as relevant provincial government departments (most notably education) and various partner groups in the voluntary, and possibly private, sectors.

The work to be done is thus challenging but necessary. Ensuring that today's Canadians and those to follow are committed to our democracy and engaged in its deliberations is an indispensable goal, for this is the foundation that underwrites so much of what we have done and might yet achieve together.

Appendix A
Survey Design and Methodology, Canadian Citizen Engagement Survey 2007-08

The Canadian Citizen Engagement Survey was a national telephone survey of Canadians carried out between 11 December 2007 and 8 April 2008. The survey contained a wide range of questions relating to political participation, political knowledge, news media use, and other topics as described in the text. The average length of the interviews was twenty-two minutes.

The questionnaire was written by the principal investigator, Paul Howe. The fieldwork was carried out by the Quebec polling firm Jolicoeur et associés. Translation of the questionnaire into French was undertaken by a second polling firm, Opinion Search Inc., with subsequent verification by Jolicoeur.

A total of 1,925 interviews was conducted in all provinces and territories of Canada, 1,407 in English and 518 in French. Up to twenty call-backs were made, along with refusal conversion attempts, in order to maximize response rate. The final response rate, based on the AIRMS method of calculation, was 38 percent.

Sampling and Weighting
The sample was compiled by the firm ASDE Survey Sampler. The sample was a disproportionate stratified sample. Respondents from smaller provinces (the Atlantic provinces) were oversampled by a factor of approximately 2.0, while Ontario was undersampled by a factor of 0.8. Sampling proportions for the other provinces were in the 0.9 to 1.1 range. In all calculations reported in the text, weights have been applied to correct for this disproportionate provincial sampling.

Given concerns about the under-representation of young adults in most telephone surveys conducted nowadays, efforts were made to increase the number of adults under age thirty in the sample. Oversampling was therefore undertaken of geographic areas (census dissemination areas) known to contain a higher-than-average proportion of young adults (by a factor of 1.25) and under-sampling of areas with a lower-than-average proportion (by

Provincial/territorial distribution of interviews

Province/territory	Completed questionnaires	Response rate (%)
Newfoundland	64	38
Prince Edward Island	18	42
Nova Scotia	104	34
New Brunswick	98	41
Quebec	491	44
Ontario	601	36
Manitoba	69	34
Saskatchewan	58	34
Alberta	192	38
British Columbia	223	34
Yukon	2	50
Northwest Territories	3	43
Nunavut	2	62
Total	1,925	38

a factor of 0.87). Again, in all calculations reported in the text, weights have been applied to correct for this disproportionate sampling.

Respondent Selection within Households

As a further measure to increase the representation of the under-thirty population, the standard procedure of selecting respondents within households – random selection of the adult eighteen or over with the most recent birthday – was altered. The individual answering the phone was first asked how many adults eighteen or over lived in the household. Where there was more than one, they were asked how many adults aged eighteen to twenty-nine lived in the household. On a random basis (50 percent of the time for the first 1,200 interviews; 75 percent of the time for subsequent interviewing), the household member selected for the interview was the adult aged eighteen to twenty-nine, or in cases where there was more than one adult in this age group, the adult aged eighteen to twenty-nine with the most recent birthday. In all other cases, the household member selected was the adult of any age with the most recent birthday.

This procedure could potentially raise concerns about sample bias. The concerns do not relate to the eighteen to twenty-nine age group, as the selection process for these respondents fully respected random selection procedures (random selection of telephone numbers, followed in some cases by random selection of a household member, and in other cases, randomly determined, by random selection of a household member eighteen to twenty-nine). The concern would lie with adults in other age groups residing in households with people in the eighteen to twenty-nine age group. These potential respondents would have a reduced probability of selection compared to people residing in households without anyone in the eighteen to twenty-nine age group.

More specifically, two demographic groups are apt to be under-represented by the use of this procedure: older adults with adult children still living at home; and people residing with either a spouse, partner, or housemates under the age of thirty (many of whom would probably be in their early thirties). Cognizant of this potential problem, analysis was undertaken, both in advance and after the fact, to see if such groups were in fact under-represented in the sample and whether these groups are distinctive with respect to key variables used in the study (if not, then their under-representation would have no bearing on the overall results). Some of this analysis was based on the CCES survey itself, some was based on Statistics Canada's General Social Survey (GSS 17).

With respect to older adults with adult children still living at home, there was under-representation in the CCES sample. Among those aged fifty-five to sixty-nine, 13 percent reported having children still living at home, whereas the GSS 17 data, based on a nationally representative sample, yield an estimate of 21 percent. However, there are but slight differences (on both the CCES and GSS 17) on basic measures of political engagement such as voting and following politics between those with adult children living at home and those without (controlling for respondents' age), rendering this under-representation immaterial to the overall results.

With respect to those in their thirties living with people in their twenties (apt to be in their early thirties), there does not appear to be any significant under-representation in the CCES sample. For example, of those in their thirties in the sample, 7.7 percent are thirty to thirty-four and 9.2 percent are thirty-five to thirty-nine – a relatively small discrepancy. Furthermore, 71 percent of those in the thirty to thirty-four group report living with a spouse or partner, compared to 70 percent of those thirty-five to thirty-nine, suggesting that the sampling procedure did not result in any significant oversampling of single people within the thirty to thirty-four age group as might have been anticipated.

Because there was no evidence of any significant bias resulting from selection procedure within households, weights were not applied to compensate for this.

The overall effect of the various measures designed to increase the representation of young adults (eighteen to twenty-nine) was just to bring their representation in the survey sample (18.9 percent) in line with their representation in the Canadian population (19.8 percent), underscoring the current challenges involved in securing adequate survey response rates among young adults.

Appendix B
Question Wording and Coding

Political Knowledge Questions (Table 3.2)

For data sources see Table 3.2 in text. Where question exclusions are specifically noted, the incidence of correct answers was either above 90 percent or below 10 percent. Other knowledge questions on these studies, not explicitly noted, were excluded for the same reason or because they captured different types of political knowledge (typically civics or historical knowledge).

Britain

1960a, 7 potential items: names of up to 3 Conservative party leaders; names of up to 3 Labour party leaders; name of one Liberal party leader.

1969, 3 items: Gallup polls 972d and 973a combined. Respondents asked to identify "who these people are." 972d: Jack Dash (dockers' leader). 973a: George Woodcock (trade union leader), L.K. O'Brien (head of Bank of England).

1979, 19 items: name and party of twelve politicians presented in photographs (24 potential items, 5 items excluded).

1994a, 4 items: names of president of European Commission, European Commissioner of own country, national finance minister, national foreign minister.

2001, 3 items: 3 true-false items (it is Conservative Party policy that Britain should never join the single European currency; Liberal Democrats favour proportional representation; unemployment has fallen since Labour was elected in 1997).

2005, 4 items: 4 true-false items (Liberal Democrats favour proportional representation; Chancellor of the Exchequer responsible for setting interest rates in UK; Labour wants university students to pay fees up to £3,000 each year; Conservative party favours strict limits on number of asylum-seekers).

Canada

1956: CIPO 250 and 252 combined. CIPO 250, 16 items: country and job
of 8 international figures (Krushchev, Nehru, Dulles, Bulganin, Pearson,
Ben-Gurion, Nasser, Eden; St. Laurent and Eisenhower excluded). CIPO
252, 9 items: identification of province for 9 provincial premiers (names
provided; Maurice Duplessis excluded).

1984, 9 items: names of premiers of 9 provinces (PEI excluded).

1993, 7 items: 6 party position questions (support GST; oppose GST; do away
with NAFTA; eliminate deficit in 3 years; eliminate deficit in 5 years;
increase spending on public works), Kim Campbell's cabinet job before
becoming prime minister.

1997, 6 items: 3 party position questions (lower personal income taxes by
10 percent; cut unemployment in half by 2001; against recognizing
Quebec as distinct society), name of federal finance minister, name of
premier of own province, name of US president.

2000, 10 items: 4 party position questions (single tax rate; national prescription drug plan; law to fight criminal biker gangs; law to pay back debt
in 25 years), name of premier of own province, names of 4 party leaders
(Liberals, Conservatives, Canadian Alliance, NDP), name of federal finance minister.

2004, 11 items: 5 party position questions (get rid of gun registry; increase
military spending by $2 billion each year; spend $250 million for fight-
ing AIDS in poor countries; spend $4 billion to reduce waiting times for
surgeries; inheritance tax on estates over $1 million), name of premier
of own province, names of three party leaders (Liberals, Conservatives,
NDP), name of British prime minister, name of female cabinet minister
who ran against Paul Martin for leadership of Liberal Party.

2006, 8 items: party promising to cut GST from 7 to 5 percent, name of
premier of own province, names of 3 party leaders (Liberals, Conservatives, NDP), name of British prime minister, name of a female cabinet
minister in federal government, name of judge heading inquiry into
sponsorship scandal.

United States

1960a, 6 potential items: names of up to 3 Republican Party leaders; names
of up to 3 Democratic Party leaders.

1960b, 5 items: part of country Nixon comes from, part of country Kennedy
comes from, Nixon's religion, which party had more members in Congress before election, which party had more members in Congress after
election.

1964, 7 items: part of country Goldwater comes from, Goldwater's religion,
is government of China/Cuba democratic, communist, or something
else (two items), is communist China member of UN, which party had

more members in Congress before election, which party had more members in Congress after election.

1968, 4 items: is government of China democratic, communist, or something else, is communist China member of UN, which party had more members in Congress before election, which party had more members in Congress after election.

1984, 4 items: which party had more members in House of Representatives/Senate before election, which party will now have more members in House of Representatives/Senate.

1988, 8 items: job or political office held by Ted Kennedy, George Schultz, Mikhail Gorbachev, Margaret Thatcher, Yasser Arafat, Jim Wright; which party had more members in House of Representatives/Senate before election.

1992, 5 items: job or political office held by Dan Quayle, Boris Yeltsin, Tom Foley, which party had more members in House of Representatives/Senate before election.

1996, 6 items: job or political office held by Al Gore, William Rehnquist, Boris Yeltsin, Newt Gingrich; which party had more members in House of Representatives/Senate before election.

2000, 11 items: job or political office held by William Rehnquist, Tony Blair, Janet Reno; US state Bush lives in, US state Gore is from originally, Gore's religion, US state Cheney lives in, US state Lieberman lives in, Lieberman's religion, which party had more members in House of Representatives/Senate before election.

2004, 6 items: job or political office held by Dennis Hastert, Dick Cheney, Tony Blair, William Rehnquist; which party had more members in House of Representatives/Senate before election.

Netherlands

1971, 22 potential items: names of ministers in present government (up to 14 mentions), names of members of parliament (up to 8 mentions).

1977, 30 items: name, party, and position of 11 politicians presented in photographs (33 potential items, 3 items excluded).

1981, 22 items: name, party, and position of 10 politicians presented in photographs (30 potential items, 8 items excluded).

1986, 12 items: name, party, and position of 4 politicians presented in photographs.

1989, 12 items: name, party, and position of 4 politicians presented in photographs.

1994a, 4 items: names of president of European Commission, European Commissioner of own country, national finance minister, national foreign minister.

1994b, 12 items: name, party, and position of 4 politicians presented in photographs.

1998, 17 items: name, party, and position of 4 politicians presented in photographs (12 items), which of 2 parties has more seats in parliament (4 items), parties that are members of current coalition (single item).

Norway

1965, 14 items: name and party of 7 party leaders presented in photographs.

1969, 14 items: name and party of 7 party leaders presented in photographs.

1973, 19 items: name and party of 8 party leaders presented in photographs; knowledge of 3 new EEC countries.

1997, 3 items: name of party leader of KRF, name of minister of local government and labour; party of the president of the Storting during last 4 years.

2001, 5 items: which parties formed government from 1997 to 2000 (3 items); name of minister for local government and regional development; president of the Storting for last 4 years.

Sweden

1956, 10 items: 4 party position questions (military cooperation between Sweden and NATO state; obligatory supplementary pensions; referendum on pensions issue; reducing subsidies to security installations of Swedish Rail), names of 5 party leaders from photographs, parties represented in current government (single item).

1960, 12 items: 5 party position questions (voted for introduction of general sales tax; repeal general pension system; eliminate allowance for first child; sell shares in state-owned companies to private persons; greater increase in national old-age pension), names of 5 party leaders from photographs, type of election this year (parliamentary or communal), parties represented in current government (single item).

1964, 7 items: 3 party position questions (reduction of general pension funds, maintaining connection between communal and Riksdag elections, preventing migration from rural areas), names of 3 party leaders from photographs, parties represented in current government (single item).

1985, 7 items: parties of 4 politicians (names provided); 3 true-false items (current rate of unemployment is less than 5 percent, budget deficit has increased in last year, rate of inflation in 1985 is over 9 percent).

1988, 8 items: parties of 5 politicians (names provided), 3 true-false items (current rate of unemployment is less than 5 percent, rate of inflation in 1988 is over 9 percent, parliament has decided to store most toxic radioactive waste abroad).

1991, 9 items: parties of 6 politicians (names provided), 3 true-false items (current rate of unemployment is less than 5 percent, parliament has decided to store most toxic radioactive waste abroad, Sweden accepted more than 50,000 refugees last year).

1994, 9 items: parties of 7 politicians (names provided), 2 true-false items (about 10 percent of all who live in Sweden are born abroad, parliament has decided to store highly radioactive waste abroad).

1998, 10 items: parties of 7 politicians (names provided), 3 true-false items (current rate of unemployment is less than 5 percent, about 10 percent of all who live in Sweden are born abroad, parliament has decided to store highly radioactive waste abroad).

2002, 11 items: parties of 8 politicians (names provided), 3 true-false items (current rate of unemployment is less than 5 percent, one Euro at the moment is worth more than ten Swedish kronor, last year just over 20,000 people applied for asylum in Sweden).

Political Interest Question Wording and Coding (Table 3.3)
Numbers in parentheses indicate values assigned to response categories for the purpose of calculating means.

Britain
1974: General interest in politics: a great deal (100), some (67), not much (33), none at all (0)?

1979: How much interest would you say you take in politics – a great deal (100), some (67), not much (33), or none at all (0)?

1983, 1988a, 1989, 1990, 1994a (Eurobarometer polls): To what extent would you say you are interested in politics? A great deal (100), to some extent (67), not much (33), not at all (0).

1997, 2001, 2005: How much interest do you generally have in what is going on in politics? A great deal (100), quite a lot (67), some (67), not very much (33), none at all (0).

Canada
1949, 1957: Are you interested in the coming election? [If no, coded as 0.] If yes: About how much are you interested in it, would you say very interested (100), moderately interested (50), or only interested a little (0)?

1965: How much interest do you generally have in what is going on in politics – a good deal (100), some (50), or not much (0)?

1968: Some people don't pay much attention to elections. How about you – would you that that you were very much interested (100), somewhat interested (50), or not much interested (0) in last June's election?

1974, 1979: We would also like to know whether you pay attention to politics generally. I mean from day to day, when there isn't a big election campaign going on. Would you say you follow politics very closely (100), fairly closely (50), or not much at all (0)?

1984: Do you pay much attention to politics generally – that is, from day to day, when there isn't a big election campaign going on? Would you say that you follow politics very closely (100), fairly closely (50), or not much at all (0)?

1988: We would like to know whether you pay much attention to politics generally, whether there is an election going on or not. Would you say that you follow politics very closely (100), fairly closely (50), not very closely (0), or not at all (0)?

1993: Would you say that you are very interested (100), fairly interested (50), not very interested (0), or not at all interested (0) in the campaign?

1997, 2000, 2004, 2006: And your interest in politics generally [on a 0 to 10 scale]? 8-10 (100), 5-7 (50), 0-4 (0).

United States

All years except 1964: Some people seem to follow what's going on in government and public affairs most of the time, whether there's an election going on or not. Others aren't that interested. Would you say you follow what's going on in government and public affairs most of the time (100), some of the time (67), only now and then (33), or hardly at all (0)?

1964: "never" is an additional response category (coded as 0).

Netherlands

All years: Are you very interested in political subjects (100), fairly interested (50), or not interested (0)?

Norway

Full question text not available for all years. However, response categories are available for all. Question texts below are from the 1965 and 2001 surveys.

1965, 1969, 1973, 1977, 1981: In general, would you say that you are very interested in politics (100), fairly interested (50), or not very interested at all (0)?

1985, 1989, 1993, 1997, 2001: Would you say that you in general are very interested in politics (100), fairly interested (50), not very interested (0), not interested at all (0)?

Sweden

All years: In general, how interested in politics are you? Are you very interested (100), fairly interested (67), not very interested (33), or not at all interested (0) in politics? [Earlier studies provide different English translations of response categories, but it appears that original Swedish categories were identical.]

Election Debate Wording and Coding (Tables 3.7 and 3.10)

Note: For all countries, in instances where respondents were asked how much of the debate they watched, anyone who saw at least some of the debate was coded as a viewer. In cases where there were multiple debates, those who watched at least one were coded as viewers.

Canada

1968: Did you watch the TV debate among the leaders before the election?

1979: Did you see the debates between the party leaders on television on Sunday, May 13? [debate in English only]

1984: Did you see the general debate in English on Wednesday, July 25? Did you see the general debate in French on Tuesday, July 24? [A question asking about a third debate on women's issues was not included.]

1988: Did you see the TV debate among the party leaders?

1993: Did you see the French TV debate among the party leaders? Did you see the English French TV debate among the party leaders?

1997: Did you see the English TV debate among the party leaders? Did you see the first French TV debate (which took place on May 13)? [A third question asking about a second French debate on 19 May was not included.]

2000, 2004 and 2006: Did you see the English TV debate among the party leaders? Did you see the French TV debate? [Note that in 2006, respondents asked these questions after the second English and French debates had taken place could have answered yes if they had seen any of four debates rather than the normal two.]

From 1988 to 2006, the Canadian election studies asked about debate viewing in both campaign-period and post-election surveys. Both surveys are used for these years to measure debate viewing.

United States

1960: Did you watch any of the TV debates where Kennedy and Nixon appeared on the same show together?

1976: Did you watch any of the televised debates between the presidential or vice-presidential candidates?

1980: Did you watch the televised debate between Carter and Reagan?

1984: Did you watch the first televised presidential debate held on October 7 between Ronald Reagan and Walter Mondale? Did you watch the second televised presidential debate held on October 21 between Ronald Reagan and Walter Mondale?

1996: Did you watch the first televised presidential debate held on October 6, 1996, between Bill Clinton and Bob Dole? Did you watch the second televised presidential debate held on October 16, 1996, between Bill Clinton and Bob Dole?

2000: Did you watch a televised presidential debate between Al Gore and George W. Bush?

Netherlands

1986: During the evening before the election a televised debate was held in which the leaders of the three largest political parties participated. Did you watch this debate between Den Uyl, Lubbers, and Nijpels?

1989: During the evening before the election a televised debate was held in which the leaders of the three largest political parties participated. Did you watch this debate, or parts of it?

1998: Did you watch the debate of the party leaders on the eve of the election, entirely or for the greater part?

Norway

1965: Did you follow the concluding debate between the party leaders on Friday, September 10th, on radio or on TV? [Those who followed no election programs on radio or TV were coded as not watching.]

1969: Did you follow the closing debate of the party leaders which was a combined broadcast by radio and TV, a few days before the election? [Those who followed no election programs on radio or TV were coded as not watching.]

1977: Did you follow the conclusive party leaders' debate?

2001: As always, the election campaign ended with the party-leaders' debate on NRK the Friday before the election. Did you watch the entire debate, more than half of the debate, less than half of the debate or nothing of the debate?

Sweden

1960: Radio and TV had a number of programs before this year's election. Did you listen to: the debate between the party leaders on TV and radio?

1964: Did you listen to this program? "To the polls," the concluding debate between the party leaders?

1979: Did you see the final debate among the party leaders on the Friday before the election on September 15?

After 1979, question text remains the same through to 2002.

TV News Viewing Wording and Coding (Tables 3.8, 3.10, and 3.11)
Response coded as daily/regular viewing indicated in italics.

Britain, Netherlands, and Norway (Eurobarometer polls)
All years: About how often do you watch the news on television? *Every day,*
  several times a week, once or twice a week, less often, never.

Sweden
Those who watch one specific news program 6 to 7 days a week *or* who watch
more than one program at least 3 to 5 days per week were coded as regular
viewers.

Canada
1962: Watches CBC news: *regularly*, occasionally, hardly ever.
1977: Watch news on TV: *every day*, several times a week, once a week, less
  often, no TV.
2002: How often do you do the following things, *every day*, a couple of times
  a week, a couple of times a month or less than that? Watch the news
  on television.

United States
1980: How often do you watch the national network news on early evening
  TV – *every evening*, 3 or 4 times/week, once or twice a week, or less often?
1984: How often do you watch the national network news on TV – *every
  day*, 3 or 4 times a week, once or twice a week, or less often that that?
1988, 1992: How many days in the past week did you watch the news on
  TV? *7*
1996: How many days in the past week did you watch the national news on
  TV? *7*
2000: How many days in the past week did you watch the national network
  news on TV? *7*
2004: How many days in the past week did you watch the national network
  news on TV? *7* [The 2004 study also replicated the 1988/1992
  question.]

Note: The appropriate coding of those who reported 5 or 6 days per week in
the years 1988 through 2004 is clearly debatable and would depend on where
such viewers would have placed themselves in the response categories offered in 1980 and 1984. Fourteen percent of respondents responded 5 or 6
days on the 2004 study.

Notes

Introduction

1 Relevant academic papers include: Blais et al. 2002, Rubenson et al. 2004, Howe 2006, Tossuti 2007, Anderson and Goodyear-Grant 2008, and Raney and Berdahl 2009. Relevant studies published by research institutes and government agencies include: Centre for Research and Information on Canada 2001; O'Neill 2001, 2003, 2007; Pammett and Leduc 2003a, 2003b; Gidengil et al. 2003, 2005; Howe 2003a, 2003b, 2007a, and 2007b; Milan 2005; Milner 2005 and 2007; Stolle and Cruz 2005; Turcotte 2005 and 2007; Canadian Policy Research Networks 2007; MacKinnon et al. 2007; and Bristow 2008.

2 The survey was conducted by telephone in late 2007 and early 2008, with a response rate of 37.5 percent and a final sample size of 1,925. The response rate was lower than hoped for, but this is partly a reflection of a sampling design aimed at oversampling younger respondents. Technical details of the survey are provided in Appendix A.

Chapter 1: Democratic Participation in Canada

1 Elections Alberta 2008.

2 These are unweighted figures, based on the author's calculations using Elections Canada 2002 Survey of Voters and Non-Voters. With a weight applied to correct for disproportionate regional distribution, the respective figures are 79.9 percent and 51.0 percent.

3 This figure was later updated to 64.1 percent by Elections Canada after removal of duplicate names from the voters list (though 61.2 percent remains the official turnout figure).

4 The precise numbers should be treated with some caution, as there are margins of error for all the turnout estimates in the table, generally in the range of plus or minus 3 to 6 percentage points (due to the method used to sample voters list records).

5 The survey asks about birth year rather than age. This calculation assumes that half of those born in 1974 would have been 29 at the time of being interviewed in May and June of 2004.

6 In light of the current challenges in securing the cooperation of participants for telephone surveys, some researchers are now turning to the Internet. At this stage, however, web-based surveys (in Canada at least) suffer from two key problems: Internet access remains less than universal and respondents normally volunteer themselves rather than being randomly selected for participation. With these filtering mechanisms in place, the prospects for compiling a survey sample that faithfully reflects both the politically engaged and disengaged sections of the population are slim. And for web-based surveys, there is the further complication that people must be sufficiently literate – not computer literate, just plain literate – in order to complete a written questionnaire on their computer screens, a barrier to participation for an unfortunately large number of adult Canadians (which does not arise in orally administered telephone interviews). All of this threatens to compromise our ability to tap the pool of disengaged citizens in the Canadian population in order to determine their true numbers and the reasons for their disengagement.

7 This simple distinction is surprisingly underutilized in the electoral participation literature. Examples of its application can be found in Sigelman et al. 1985, Green and Shachar 2000, Kaplan 2004, Prairie Research Associates 2004, and Howe 2007a.

8 Asking about participation in elections from several years previous has its drawbacks, as people may not accurately recall whether they voted or not. However, there is no real reason to think this inaccuracy would vary dramatically for different age groups, so this should not bias comparison of their voting habits.

9 The statistical quirk lies in the fact that there is actually one person 25 to 29 who reported voting in none of the elections. However, the weight for this case is only .125, producing a rounded weighted N of 0.

10 Calculations based on the binomial theorem.

11 This reasoning helps explain the findings of a study, based on Canadian election study data from 1979 to 1988, which concludes that statistical models are generally not very successful in predicting voter turnout because "whether or not a person votes is to a large degree random" (Matsusaka and Palda 1999, 431). This conclusion, the current analysis would suggest, is probably true of voters of the past (and older voters of today), but does not apply as readily to today's younger cohorts.

12 These results are consistent with Pammett and LeDuc's finding (2003a, 9-10) that reasons for not voting form two distinct clusters: a "lack of interest factor" and a "personal/administrative factor."

13 The relevant distinction drawn by the International Institute for Democracy and Electoral Assistance with respect to different methods of encouraging participation is between facilitating and motivating voting (1999, 44).

14 To reduce perceived pressure to give the socially acceptable response, the first voting question was prefaced with the statement "Lots of people find it difficult to get out and vote."

15 These figures are based on the percentage of immigrants remaining in each age group once recent immigrants are excluded – 10 percent among those aged 25-29 and about 24 percent among those in the three oldest age categories – and estimated naturalization rates of 85 percent and 90 percent, respectively (the latter based on data presented in Tran et al. 2005).

16 Precise Canada-wide figures for municipal turnout do not exist, but one study based on 1994 data estimated turnout rates of 37.0 percent, 43.6 percent, and 54.0 percent for small, mid-size, and large municipalities respectively (Kushner et al. 1997), while a more recent study reports an average turnout rate in the 1990s for seven of Canada's larger cities of 43.2 percent (Gidengil et al. 2004, 124).

17 The 76.1 percent figure is based on respondents 20 and older, virtually all of whom would have been eligible to vote in 2000. The 64.1 percent figure is the adjusted turnout reported by Elections Canada after corrections to the voters list.

18 The 2000 Canadian election study produces an 81 percent estimate of voter turnout among university graduates under age 30. By contrast, the Statistics Canada dataset yields a turnout estimate of 68 percent for university graduates aged 20-29 in 2003. A few in this age range would have been ineligible to vote in 2000 (precise exclusion of ineligible voters is not possible because the public dataset contains only age categories, not specific ages of respondents). However, the turnout figure for university graduates aged 25-29 is still just 72 percent.

19 The estimate of voter turnout among high school dropouts under age 30 on the 2000 Canadian election study is based on only 52 cases, whereas the sample size for the equivalent group on the 2003 Statistics Canada survey is 295.

20 Statistics Canada figures for 2001 indicate that 60.5 percent of those in the 25-34 age group had postsecondary education of some kind. See: http://www12.statcan.ca/english/census01/products/analytic/companion/educ/tables/canada/newedatt.cfm.

21 Household rather than personal income is used to allow for situations where a young adult in comfortable or affluent circumstances has little or no personal income (e.g., students).

22 Relevant Canadian research includes Barnard et al. 2003, MacKinnon et al. 2007, Turcotte 2007, O'Neill 2007, Cross and Young 2008. Outside Canada, similar arguments have been made by Norris 2003, Stolle and Hooghe 2005, Stolle et al. 2005, Henn et al. 2007, and Dalton 2008.

23 Those who said they had volunteered in the past year but for less than one hour per month are treated as non-volunteers (the same coding is used in Chapter 5, where this variable appears in further analysis).

Chapter 2: The Wellsprings of Disengagement

1 As in all voting calculations based on this study, those under 25 who might have been ineligible for some elections are omitted, along with recent immigrants.

2 One recent study, for example, cautions: "We have to be careful not to blame young people for their own marginalization from politics" (MacKinnon et al. 2007, foreword, i).

3 Relevant Canadian studies include: O'Neill 2001; Blais et al. 2002, 52-4; Howe 2006, 2007b; and Milner 2005, 2007. Studies from elsewhere include: Times Mirror Center 1990; Bennett 1998; and Wattenberg 2002, 2008.

Chapter 3: The Evolution of Political Attentiveness

1 The ESS question asked: "How interested would you say you are in politics? Very interested, quite interested, hardly interested or not at all interested?" The CCES question asked: "To what extent would you say you are interested in politics? A great deal, to some extent, not much or not at all?"

2 This is a slight reformulation. Norris speaks more broadly of the mutually reinforcing linkages between civic engagement and attention to news media, but two of her principal measures of civic engagement are political interest and political knowledge.

3 Although data for the 2002 Dutch election study were available at the time of carrying out the analysis for this chapter, it was decided not to use this study in light of certain anomalies in the sample (probably reflective of acute response rate challenges in that country). The percentage of respondents under age 30 in 2002 was 10.6 percent, only half what it had been in 1998 (20.9 percent). Meanwhile, reported voter turnout in the 2002 study was 96.9 percent, whereas actual turnout in the election was 79.1 percent, a more profound discrepancy than in years past. The latter would suggest that over-representation of politically engaged citizens was especially marked in the 2002 study, the former that the young adult sample in particular may be less representative than in previous years.

4 Items answered correctly by nearly everyone (90 percent or more correct) or no one (10 percent or less) are excluded from the analysis, as such questions generally do a poor job of distinguishing more and less knowledgeable respondents. In addition, one common question type not used involves the identification of local candidates, as the relevance of such knowledge would vary considerably from one national context to another. In places where politics has a strong local (and perhaps parochial) flavour, knowledge of local candidates would not necessarily reflect broader attentiveness to national public debates.

5 Respondents under age 21 are excluded for all time points, as there were no such respondents on the earlier surveys from the 1950s and 1960s. Their inclusion on the later surveys could serve to artificially distort the gap between young and old if those aged 18-20 differ markedly from those slightly older.

6 This calculation involves not just determining the median knowledge category for the younger age group but also the proportion of cases within that category necessary to arrive at precisely the 50th percentile, and then applying that same proportion to the relevant knowledge category for the older age group. For Canada, we use 2004 data instead of 2006 because about half the respondents on the latter study were part of a 2004-06 panel, not a new cross-sectional sample.

7 The 2000 US election study had a larger number of surveillance knowledge items (11) than the 2004 study (6), allowing for a more accurate assessment. For 2000, the median respondent in the younger age group lies at the 26th percentile of the knowledge distribution for the older age category.

8 That there is a positive impact of civic education on knowledge was questioned in the past but has been bolstered by Niemi and Junn (1998) and in subsequent studies.

9 The statement is deliberately phrased somewhat cautiously, as relevant works tracing the extent of civics teaching in different countries over time are not easily located. Certainly there is scattered evidence in various case studies and comparative databases to suggest

there has been no widespread reduction in civics instruction over the past several decades. For example, a case study of civics education in the Netherlands notes that courses aimed at "social and political education," scheduled for one hour per week in the final two years of general secondary education, were introduced in 1968 (Dekker 1999, 444). Summary information provided in the International IDEA Civic Education Research Database indicates that there remains a similar compulsory civics course at the secondary level today (http://www.civiced.idea.int). In the case of Sweden, an overview of civic education practices prepared in the early 1970s noted that "considerable instructional time is devoted to Civic Education at all age levels" (Torney et al. 1975, 41). The IDEA database confirms that there continues to be civics instruction of one to two hours per week at the primary, intermediate, and secondary levels of schooling in that country. The same source also indicates that currently in Norway there is considerable emphasis given to civics – two to three hours per week at all three levels of schooling – which is consistent with a historical overview noting the longstanding emphasis on "social studies" in the Norwegian school system (Rust 1989, 115). In Britain, a formal civics curriculum was introduced for the first time in 2002. Prior to that, there was a long tradition of offering civics instruction under the broader rubric of British history. In Canada, recent critiques point out that the formal commitment to achieving certain citizenship outcomes in most provinces is not backed up with the resources and dedicated instruction needed to produce effective results (Hughes and Sears 2008). However, an in-depth study of civics education practices from four decades ago was equally critical of the antiquated and inadequate efforts at that time, noting as well that similar concerns had been voiced for at least the past thirty years (Hodgetts 1968, 115). The US is the only case of the six where there is more clear-cut evidence of a decline in civics teaching starting in the 1960s, as measured by the proportion of secondary students who had taken a class in American government. Yet there is also evidence of a substantial increase in exposure to such classes starting in the 1980s and continuing into the 1990s (Niemi and Smith 2001).

   In brief, while there is certainly variation across countries in the time and effort devoted to civics education, there is no compelling evidence of any sharp de-emphasizing of civics education in these six countries that could explain the consistent emergence of a significant knowledge deficit among younger citizens in the past few decades.

10 Where there are three response categories, the values 0, 50, and 100 are assigned to low, intermediate, and high interest categories, respectively; where there are four, the values 0, 33, 67, and 100 are used; and so on in accordance with the number of response categories. For Canada, the same method is used, except that responses from the varying questions are first grouped into three categories with roughly equal proportions of respondents in each before assigning the values 0, 50, and 100 (all details of question wording and recoding are provided in Appendix B).

11 For further details, see http://www.timeuse.org.

12 There are some inconsistencies that should be noted. The 1965 American study was not a fully representative national sample (for details, see Putnam 2000, 424). For the UK studies, the time intervals for activity reporting have decreased considerably, from 30 minutes in 1975 to 15 minutes from 1983 to 1995, and then to 10 minutes in 2000. For Norway, there was a similar switch from 15 minutes to 10 minutes in 2000. The effect of these changes would be to pick up more short intervals of newspaper reading, which would favour younger respondents (see note 15) and therefore lead to higher estimates of reading among the young, i.e., a conservative bias.

13 Author's calculations based on Statistics Canada, GSS 19: Time Use.

14 This is despite the fact that the instructions to respondents are to not report activities of less than five minutes duration.

15 The Canadian evidence of shorter reading times for young people comes from the CCES and is detailed in the next chapter. The evidence for Europe can be found in questions on the European Social Survey, which ask respondents how long they read the paper on an average weekday. Younger respondents across all countries are much more likely to indicate the shortest time category, less than half an hour (author's calculation based on ESS 2002-03).

The latter result suggests an important problem with Wattenberg's comparative analysis of changes in regular newspaper reading among young people (2008, 21-22). His earlier data for various European countries (1981-83) are based on a question that asks whether respondents read a paper regularly (at least four out of every six issues), while his later data (2002-03) are based on the European Social Survey question asking how long respondents read the paper on an average weekday, with only those reading *for 30 minutes or more* counted as readers. Setting the bar this high in the latter instance has the effect of placing many young newspaper readers in the category of non-readers. While it is not unreasonable to take duration of reading time into account in assessing newspaper reading habits, when this is done only for the later measurement point it has the effect of significantly exaggerating the decline in readership among younger groups. So whereas Wattenberg's analysis points to dramatic changes in newspaper reading among young people between the early 1980s and early 2000s, the results presented here, based on a more consistent measurement strategy, suggest a more gradual decline.

16 Moreover, this share is somewhat greater for younger respondents, suggesting that the use of this combined measure likely inflates estimates of newspaper reading more for young respondents than older ones – and therefore represents a conservative approach to assessing the gap between young and old.

17 Age is transformed so that age 21 takes a value of 0 and 65 takes a value of 1. In other words, the regression coefficient for age indicates the estimated change in reading minutes per day between age 21 and 65.

18 In some cases, question wording was such that someone who listened to a debate on the radio instead of watching on TV would also have answered in the affirmative.

19 Also for Sweden and Norway, but figures for these countries are not used as they have only been included in a limited number of more recent Eurobarometer surveys.

20 Norris, for example, states that the audience for TV news rose substantially in five EU countries from 1970 to 1999 (2000, 84), implying that this was due to an increased penchant for news consumption. However, household penetration of TV in those five countries was well below 100 percent in 1970. Using the same method and data sources as in Table 3.4, 1970 TV penetration estimates for the five countries Norris considers are: 63 percent in Belgium, 67 percent in France, 60 percent in Italy, 74 percent in West Germany, 81 percent in the Netherlands. The fact that 49 percent of survey respondents in the five countries reported watching the news every day in 1970 becomes rather more impressive when measured against this more limited pool of potential viewers.

21 In 1988, the American National Election Study switched from asking respondents how often they watched "the national network news on early evening television" to asking them how often they watched "the news on TV," thereby bringing viewers of local news, cable news networks, and news briefs into the mix and producing a sharp spike in news viewing. In 1996, the question was switched again to "national TV news" and in 2000 and 2004 to "national network news," leading to a predictable drop in the percentage of regular news viewers.

22 In the 1977 survey, the response category following "every day" (coded as regular viewers) was "several times a week," whereas in 2002 it was "a couple of times a week." This change would presumably lead more people who watched the news about four or five times a week to place themselves in the "every day" category, thus helping to account for the apparent jump from 1977 to 2002.

23 These data, archived in two locations in Toronto and Montreal, suffer from some gaps and omissions, as noted in the text.

24 Data from 1986 to 1995 are from annual reports by Statistics Canada entitled *Culture Statistics: Television Viewing in Canada*. Data from 1998 on are from tables available at the website of Statistics Canada.

25 Since Figure 3.2 is based on average figures, it is possible that some people might have significantly increased the percentage of time spent viewing news and current affairs (due to increased news options in the cable era) while others might have significantly decreased their time, the changes cancelling one another out and leading to a roughly consistent average over time (the argument of Markus Prior [2007, 49, 113-16]). Ideally, we would

prefer to know the proportion who reported spending a given percentage of time watching news and current affairs (e.g., 10 percent) and whether this has increased or decreased over time, but such information cannot be culled from the Statistics Canada reports.

26 It should be noted that prior to the introduction of cable in 1982, some could pick up Swedish channels from across the border, but this viewing option does not account for the patterns in Table 3.9. In 1975, for example, only 25 percent of those surveyed said they could receive Swedish channels and a mere 7 percent reported watching any Swedish TV on the day they were surveyed (versus 73 percent who watched Norwegian television), with both figures consistent across age groups. Moreover, there was no difference in the incidence of watching Norwegian news between those who could access Swedish TV and those who could not.

27 The interpretation favoured by Norris (2000, 114).

28 While data for American debate viewing cover a long stretch of time, the key stumbling block is that the number of presidential debates has varied from one election to the next, and along with this the relevant question(s) asked in the American national election studies, sometimes asking about each debate, sometimes whether respondents saw any of the debates (which in one year specifically included vice-presidential debates). In Canada and Sweden, on the other hand, the number of debates has been more consistent (one on the eve of the election in Sweden, one English and one French debate part way through the campaign in Canada), as have the survey questions, which ask about each specific debate. The one exception is Canada in 2006, when there were two debates in each language and two general questions asking whether respondents had seen the English TV debate and the French TV debate.

Chapter 4: Political Attentiveness in Canada

1 A handful of "correct" responses to the second question (2.3 percent) are people who had selected the US for the first question and subsequently gave the more correct response (Canada) to the second question.

2 A handful of close responses, less than 0.5 percent, are people who spontaneously mentioned that the WTO protests revolved around globalization or anti-globalization.

3 Cronbach's alpha for the combined knowledge index is 0.85.

4 Those who reported that they did not have Internet access are included in these calculations. This represents 56 percent of those 70 and over, 25 percent of those 55-69, 11 percent of those 45-54, 6 percent of those 35-44, and 5 percent among those under 35. Obviously, if these respondents were excluded, the age trend for Internet news use would become flatter.

5 The assumed values for categories of duration of use are 45 minutes (more than half an hour), 22.5 minutes (15 to 30 minutes), and 10 minutes (15 minutes or less). For frequency of use, the assumed values are: 7 days (every day), 4.5 days (several times a week), 1.5 days (once or twice per week), 0.5 days (less often), 0 days (never). These estimates are probably truncated for high-end users (assuming there are some news buffs who spend significantly longer than 45 minutes per day using particular news media).

6 The Pew Research Center for People and the Press also includes questions about duration of use in its surveys of American news consumption habits. The most recent study produces very similar estimates to those reported here of total news consumption for different age groups: 5.4 hours per week (46 minutes per day) for those 18-29 and 8.6 hours per week (74 minutes per day) for those 50-64 (2008, 9).

7 Relevant prior studies include Newton 1999, Holtz-Bacha and Norris 2001, and Milner 2002.

8 With demographic variables removed, a necessary adjustment to gain a truer sense of the impact of media variables alone, this R^2 value remains 0.41.

9 My view is that the knowledge items from that study – asking whether crime has increased or decreased, whether pollution has become worse or better, whether the gap between rich and poor has increased or decreased, and whether Aborginal peoples are better or worse off than other Canadians – are overly broad and, therefore, less than ideal measures of political

knowledge. This point is further developed in Chapter 5, where the question concerning the well-being of Aboriginal peoples is examined more closely.

10 In the CCES data, the R^2 value for a knowledge model containing these two media variables only is 0.12.

11 Though this conclusion is subject to the same caveat invoked in the analysis of voting in Chapter 1: cohort-level stability in news media consumption does not necessarily translate into individual-level stability.

12 Where individual-level data on the media environment are gathered, the more typical practice is to inquire about aspects of people's current rather than past personal media environment (see for example Prior's comprehensive study [2007]).

Chapter 5: Political Knowledge and Canadian Democracy

1 These comparisons are generally based on voting in the most recent election for which election study data are available (in two cases, two election studies are combined to create more adequate sample sizes). For Canada, the 2004 election study is used because in 2006 about half of the respondents were part of a 2004-06 panel. For the Netherlands, the 1998 election study is used rather than 2002 because of concerns about response rate, exceptional inflation of reported turnout (96.9 percent), and a dearth of young respondents in the latter study. To ensure consistency across countries, only surveillance knowledge questions are used, as in Chapter 3.

2 Others have suggested that weaker turnout effects (for variables such as knowledge) may just reflect high overall turnout in certain countries: in such cases, it is mathematically impossible for turnout to be much below the norm in low turnout groups (Fisher et al. 2008, 94). I am not entirely persuaded by this reasoning, which can make it sound as if overall turnout is somehow driving turnout in subgroups of the electorate, rather than turnout in subgroups driving overall turnout – the puzzle remains, why do low knowledge groups vote at much lower rates in some countries than others? In any event, the relationship captured in Figure 5.2 still stands when alternative statistical methods are used. Fisher et al., rather than looking at differences in the proportion voting in low and high knowledge groups, instead examine differences in the corresponding log odds ratios (i.e., the dependent variable underlying logistic regression), a more stringent and unimpeachable test of differential knowledge effects in low and high turnout countries. Their focus is on the impact of electoral systems, so they examine the vote-knowledge relationship in various countries participating in the Comparative Study of Electoral Systems, contrasting those that use single-member plurality systems (SMP) (Canada, the UK, the US, and the Philippines, though the latter ends up being identified as an anomaly) and a larger number that use different variants of proportional representation (PR) (including all three Northern European countries in Figure 5.2). The result is consistent with that reported here, a stronger effect of knowledge on voter participation in the SMP, which is to say the three Anglo-American countries.

3 The questions on the Canadian and European surveys asked: "About how often do you [watch the news on television/read the news in the daily newspapers]? Would it be every day, several times a week, once or twice a week, less often, or never?" The questions on the American survey asked: "How many days in the past week did you [read a daily newspaper/ watch the news on TV]?"

4 The Fisher et al. study (2008), on the other hand, attempts but fails to identify any variables associated with different electoral systems that help account for the heightened impact of knowledge on voting in the SMP countries, presenting this as a puzzle still to be solved. One resolution of the puzzle is that the electoral system is not really relevant to the vote-knowledge relationship: instead, media attentiveness variables are what matter. Another, proposed by Henry Milner (2002), is that electoral systems are among the structural variables that influence the political knowledge and attentiveness of citizens, PR helping to create more knowledgeable citizens by providing them (through the party system) with a more stable and comprehensible political roadmap.

5 Question wording was randomly assigned to respondents.

6 Too often in this body of literature, higher education levels and the expansion of information sources are taken as the principal indicators of heightened political "sophistication" among citizens, with no corroborating evidence relating to actual knowledge of politics. See, for example, Dalton 2006.

7 Admittedly, specific reform proposals are typically accompanied by an explicit "no opinion" option, as it is anticipated that many respondents will not be familiar with the issue, whereas more general queries about politics and democracy are not. To verify that the latter really do elicit opinions more readily from all respondents, it would be useful if they were sometimes posed with an explicit "no opinion" option.

8 The specific questions are from the mail-back survey component of the 2000 study: questions a4, a11, a14, b1, c6, c11, e3.

Chapter 6: Community Attachments

1 For a similar argument with respect to the US, see Kersh 2007.

2 The specific groups are: school group/neighbourhood associations, service club/fraternal organizations, religious-affiliated groups, cultural/educational/hobby organizations, sports/recreation organizations, and other groups.

3 Those who say they have volunteered in the past year but volunteer less than one hour per month are treated as non-volunteers, since their reported attitudes and behaviour seem more in line with non-volunteers than with more active volunteers.

4 These are the "standard" trust question ("Generally speaking, would you say that most people can be trusted or that you cannot be too careful in dealing with people?") and another asking respondents to use a five-point scale to indicate their level of trust in strangers (where 1 means strangers "cannot be trusted at all" and 5 means they "can be trusted a lot"). Respondents saying most people can be trusted and giving a rating of at least 3 to the trustworthiness of strangers are coded as high in trust.

5 The reader may notice an inconsistency here with the earlier analysis in Chapter 2. There (Figure 2.9), community attachments were treated as an independent variable influencing involvement in groups and volunteering. Now, community attachments are treated as the dependent variable potentially influenced by these same civic activities that are reflective of social connectedness. The fact is that causation could run either or both ways, from social connectedness to community sentiment and/or from community sentiment to social connectedness (just as others have investigated whether causation runs from social connectedness to trust, or vice versa – see Brehm and Rahn 1997). Subsequent analysis in this chapter suggests, however, that the first is a more plausible interpretation for the two variables that show the strongest relationship to social connectedness – trust and local community attachments – while the second is a more plausible interpretation of the two that show the weaker connection – national and provincial attachments. This is because the former variables exhibit significant change over the life cycle in lockstep with the changes in social connectedness associated with aging processes, whereas the latter sentiments appear to be more invariant over the adult years, i.e., unaffected by changes in social connectedness. This, of course, only strengthens the conclusion that social connectedness has relatively little bearing on large-scale attachments to nation and province.

6 Trust is defined in the same manner as in Figure 6.1 (see note 4 for details).

7 The inclusion of the youngest age categories in the graph for lower education levels might be questioned, as these groups include virtually all respondents, some of whom will go on to higher levels of educational attainment, whereas the older age groups include only the subset of respondents who did not (and most of whom will not) pursue any further education. The key issue is whether or not it is educational experiences per se that foster higher levels of social trust, or whether the pursuit of higher education simply serves as a proxy for other background variables – such as social class and parental influence – that would already differentiate individuals within the youngest age categories, serving to make some more trusting and others less so. If the latter is the case, then higher trust levels within the "less-educated" youngest cohorts (relative to those in their twenties) might simply reflect the fact that virtually everyone is included – both less trusting individuals who are less likely to continue their education and more trusting individuals likely to stay in school longer.

One way to probe this potential problem is to assess whether there are, in fact, significant variations in levels of trust within the youngest age categories across socioeconomic categories associated with the pursuit of higher education. The simplest relevant measure, available in the GSS data, is parental educational attainment. Creating four categories for parental education (using both father's and mother's education), the analysis reveals only slight differences in trust levels between fifteen- to nineteen-year-olds with the least educated parents (25.1 percent are highly trusting; $N = 255$) and those with the most educated parents (28.3 percent; $N = 460$). This difference pales next to the trust gap associated with respondents' own level of education (for all respondents combined, 20.9 percent are highly trusting in the lowest of four education categories compared to 50.6 percent in the highest education category; $N = 5,083$, $N = 4,914$, respectively). It would seem, in other words, that differences in social trust are rather minimal among adolescents of different social backgrounds and only grow larger as some move on to pursue higher education and others do not – in other words, that education itself does make a genuine contribution to social trust. This being the case, the approach adopted in Figure 6.3 – comparing adolescents as a whole, who have not yet had the opportunity to pursue higher education, to less-educated older respondents – seems reasonable.

8   While there was a panel component to this study, for present purposes only the cross-sectional samples for particular years are used.

9   There is some inconsistency in the documentation for the Social Change in Canada study: sometimes the question wording is "problem," sometimes it appears as "problems." It would appear however, that the 1981 version was "problems." The singular was used on the CCES question, but this slight difference in wording is unlikely to explain the sharp increase in involvement levels over time. Other question wordings were identical.

10 Analysis of a further question appearing on both the CCES and the Social Change in Canada studies revealed that the mean number of years respondents had been living in their current neighbourhood was significantly higher on the CCES than on the earlier survey (likely a reflection of a lower response rate on the CCES and attendant oversampling of residentially stable respondents). To compensate for this important difference, the CCES data were weighted to reflect the pattern of residential longevity in the earlier data set. This has the effect of reducing levels of social connectedness in the CCES data.

11 In this case, details of question wording and other questions included on the surveys are not available.

12 It is the personal autonomy reflected in the choice of which city or town to live in that underlies Richard Florida's analysis of the different character and development prospects of various urban centres across North America (2008).

13 Fukuyama is sensitive to the liabilities of living at the "end of history" and indeed outlines a more ominous possibility in his book-length treatment of the theme: "Experience suggests that if men cannot struggle on behalf of a just cause because that just cause was victorious in an earlier generation, then they will struggle *against* the just cause ... [against] peace and prosperity, and against democracy" (1992, 330).

14 On the GSS, the tau-b value for strength of provincial and national attachments is 0.43.

15 Again based on 2003 GSS data, for Quebec respondents only, tau-b = 0.28.

Chapter 7: Ascendant Individualism

1   The specific phrase appears in the title of an earlier paper (Putnam 1995), but the same stylization runs through *Bowling Alone* (2000), especially section III on the causes of declining social capital.

2   In fairness, individualism is invoked explicitly in a couple of chapters: "From Generation to Generation" and "The Dark Side of Social Capital." In the first of these, attention is given to the changing values of younger generations – individualism, heightened materialism – which in turn are linked to the absence of social solidarity in their formative years (in contrast to older generations who came of age during times of hardship and crisis such as the Second World War), as well as the pernicious effects of television.

3   The distinction is, however, occasionally rendered explicit. See, for example, Rokeach's classic study of human values (1973, 3-25).

4   Since levels of agreement with statements are high in many cases, we concentrate on levels of total agreement, which are more revealing of age-related variation.

5   The general depth of scepticism towards the views of the average citizen is itself a striking result and a stark contrast to the relatively high levels of confidence respondents express in their own opinions. As Figure 7.2 indicates, whereas more than 50 percent totally agree that "I am generally confident in my own opinions and ideas," a mere 5 percent totally agree that the "average citizen's opinions on issues are sound and carefully considered" (the gap for those agreeing either "totally" or "somewhat" is equally striking: 95 percent versus 31 percent). Clearly, most who believe in the soundness of their own opinions do not extend this confidence to the views held by others. This disjuncture, not closely considered in political science research invoking the concept of cognitive mobilization, merits closer attention. The consequences of the discrepancy are potentially quite negative: a society of self-confident citizens deeply sceptical of one another's views is likely to hinder rather than facilitate democratic deliberation and debate.

6   I would acknowledge a discrepancy between these results and those obtaining for a more commonly used survey item designed to measure the cognate quality of "internal efficacy": "Sometimes politics seems so complicated that a person like me can't really understand what's going on." For the latter measure, posed on various Canadian election studies, those with higher education levels are more apt to express disagreement, i.e., express greater self-confidence. This result may be attributable to the more explicitly political focus of the item. Importantly, however, there is again no evidence of greater internal efficacy among the young, as younger respondents are neither more nor less likely to disagree with the statement (results are based on the 2004 Canadian election study).

7   In 1996, the question asked how important it was to "to earn more money than most people."

8   The measurement of openness to experience by psychologists is based on more extensive probing with shorter and longer questionnaires deployed in different contexts. Costa and McCrae (1992) provide details of specific items. Some examples of cognate items used to measure openness to experience are as follows. Emotions: "Without strong emotions, life would be uninteresting to me"; "I experience a wide range of emotions or feelings." New opportunities: "I'm pretty set in my ways" (reverse-coded); "I think it's interesting to learn and develop new hobbies." Personality exploration: numerous items gauging receptiveness to aesthetics (music, dance, art) and ideas (puzzles, abstract ideas, philosophical arguments).

Chapter 8: Social Integration and Political Engagement

1   For both Figures 8.3 and 8.5, it could reasonably be asked whether the differential effects across age groups might represent a life-cycle rather than cohort pattern – that is to say, a greater impact of interest and knowledge (on following the news and voting) among younger adults that diminishes steadily as they grow older. In the case of Figure 8.5, I have elsewhere analyzed the knowledge-vote relationship across age groups at different points in time (1956, 1984, 1990, 1993, 1997, and 2000) and found that the knowledge-vote relationship was consistent across age groups at the earliest point and has since grown more pronounced among rising cohorts (Howe 2003a, 2003b). In other words, the longitudinal evidence supports a cohort, not life-cycle, interpretation. In the case of Figure 8.3, I am not aware of earlier datasets containing sufficiently similar questions that might be used to look at the relevant relationships over an extended period.

2   Figure 8.5 reiterates an earlier finding from Chapter 5, which examined the effects of knowledge on voting by age group across different countries, using election study data. There, it was reported that in Canada the effect of knowledge on young people's participation is elevated compared to certain Northern European countries. This result was explained by the fact that political attentiveness levels are relatively low in Canada and the effects of knowledge on voting are greatest at the low end of the knowledge scale. Here, emphasis is placed on the fact that knowledge effects on voting are greater among those with a weak sense of civic duty (Figure 8.6). Thus, the overall argument about the impact of knowledge on voting is effectively twofold: the effects are greater where attentiveness levels are gener-

ally low (Canada) *and* among groups with a weak sense of civic duty (younger generations). This twofold account is developed further in Howe 2006.

3 The analysis is limited to those between the ages of 25 and 69 who are not recent immigrants to Canada (1995 or later). The lower ages boundary is necessary to include only those old enough to have been eligible to vote in all three elections. The upper boundary reflects the fact that the percentage living alone starts to increase considerably around age 70 due to spousal death, leading to significant collinearity of age and living alone. Respective sample sizes for those living with and without other adults in the household are 12,590 and 2,874.

4 The survey had a sample size of 812 split equally between voters and non-voters.

5 Investigation of factors relating to partisan persuasion (people coaxing others to vote for their preferred party) stands as the principal exception.

6 As in the previous chapter, respondents whose pattern of response suggests acquiescence bias – those agreeing with twelve or more agree-disagree statements out of thirteen – are eliminated from the calculations for the background dimensions of individualism.

7 Other investigations of the effects of declining social connectedness on US voter turnout have yielded mixed results. Miller and Shanks (1996, 100-6) reach the conclusion that this is not a significant reason for turnout decline, while Teixera accords it greater significance (1992, 36-39 and 47).

Chapter 9: Political Culture in the Age of Adolescence

1 This has the additional benefit of breaking down the perfect collinearity of age and birth year in pure cross-sectional data.

2 Birth year can be included because the surveys with the political discussion question span a thirty-year period, making it feasible to separate out life cycle and cohort effects with some measure of confidence. For political interest, the shorter time span of the surveys (twelve years) produces high levels of collinearity when age and birth year are both included, and associated problems of inflated standard errors. Thus, the political discussion results represent a purer reflection of the life cycle pattern alone, whereas the political interest results may conflate life cycle and cohort patterns. To reiterate, however, when focusing on a narrow age span over which there is great variation, cohort effects are unlikely to be a principal source of the observed differences.

3 To be more specific, the characteristics of the average 30-year-old are: living in France (the country closest to the EU average on these measures) in the year 1988 and born in 1958.

4 More technically, education is an intervening variable between age and political attentiveness, which therefore, in keeping with the reasoning of King et al. (1994, 173-74), should not be included in seeking to estimate the effects of age.

5 Evidence that this pattern is not unique to the period or countries considered can be found in Hyman's classic work on political socialization, which references two studies from the early 1950s, one American, the other German. Both reveal sharp increases in political interest and attentiveness from adolescence through early adulthood (1959, 41-42).

6 It should be noted that the IEA Civic Education Study (see http://www.wam.umd. edu/~jtpurta) has examined and compared younger and older adolescents on a variety of civic engagement measures and found some evidence of significant change occurring through adolescence. One concern with these surveys, however, is the bias introduced by those who drop out of high school: samples of younger students are more complete in their coverage of the population than samples of older students. The Eurobarometer polls do not have this problem as they survey the general population, not just students.

7 An interesting cross-sectional study (Hart et al. 2004) providing evidence consistent with these assertions looks at the effect of "youth bulges" in communities and countries on young people's level of political knowledge. The study reasons that "an adolescent living in a community in which a large fraction of the population is composed of children and adolescents ... will interact more often with peers, and consequently will be more influenced by them, than will an adolescent in a community with relatively few children and many adults" (591). Since youth typically have less civic knowledge than adults, the hypothesis is that young people in more "youthful" communities will be less knowledgeable than

those in more adult-dominated places (592). This expectation is borne out in the empirical analysis, which looks at variations in civic knowledge with the prevalence of youth in local communities within the US (using data from the National Household Educational Survey) as well as variations in knowledge with the prevalence of youth in countries as a whole (using IEA Civic Education data).

8   All that has been done here is to re-jig the age categories used in Figure 7.7 to reveal the sharp distinctiveness of adolescent respondents.

9   The argument of Nie et al. (1996), on the other hand, draws on the distinction between absolute and relative levels of education. In brief, they suggest absolute levels of education influence support for democratic principles, principally tolerance, whereas relative levels of education influence engagement and participation. Since absolute levels of education have increased over time, but relative levels have not, this explains why tolerance and engagement have followed different trajectories.

Chapter 10: Engendering Engagement among Young Canadians

1   The teacher's testimonial is available at: http://www.sacsc.ca/upload/pdf/The percent20ABCs percent20of percent20Canada-Social percent20Studies percent2016.1.pdf.

2   Information on these programs can be found in the programs section of http://www. katimavik.org.

3   Two provincial governments that have established such offices are Ontario and Quebec.

Works Cited

Adams, M. 1998. *Sex in the snow: Canadian social values at the end of the millennium.* Toronto: Penguin Canada.
–. 2003. *Fire and ice: The United States, Canada and the myth of converging values.* Toronto: Penguin Canada.
Adelson, J., and R.P. O'Neil. 1966. Growth of political ideas in adolescence. *Journal of Personality and Social Psychology* 4(3): 295-306.
Althaus, S.L. 2003. *Collective preferences in democratic politics: Opinion surveys and the will of the people.* Cambridge: Cambridge University Press.
Anderson, B. 1991. *Imagined communities: Reflections on the origin and spread of nationalism,* revised edition. London: Verso.
Anderson, C., and E. Goodyear-Grant. 2008. Youth turnout: Adolescents' attitudes in Ontario. *Canadian Journal of Political Science* 41(3): 697-718.
Andersson, B.E. 1979. Developmental trends in reaction to social pressure from adults versus peers. *International Journal of Behavioural Development* 2(3): 269-86.
Archer, K. 2003. Increasing youth voter registration: Best practices in targeting young electors. *Electoral Insight* 5(2): 26-30.
–. 2008. *The voter identification card: Advantages and disadvantages.* ACE Electoral Knowledge Network. http://aceproject.org/ace-en/topics/vr/vra/vra08/vra08a.
Arneil, B. 2006. *Diverse communities: The problem with social capital.* Cambridge: Cambridge University Press.
Arnett, J. 2004. *Emerging adulthood: The winding road from the late teens through the twenties.* New York: Oxford University Press.
–. 2005. *Emerging adults in America: Coming of age in the 21st century.* Washington, DC: American Psychological Association.
Avineri, S., and A. de-Shalit, ed. 1992. *Communitarianism and individualism.* Oxford: Oxford University Press.
Balthazar, L. 1993. The faces of Québec nationalism. In *Quebec: State and society,* 2nd edition, ed. A. Gagnon, 2-17. Toronto: Nelson Canada.
Barber, B.R. 1992. *An aristocracy of everyone.* New York: Ballantine.
–. 2003. *Strong democracy: Participatory politics for a new age.* Berkeley: University of California Press.
Barnard, R., D.A. Campbell, and S. Smith with D. Embuldeniya. 2003. *Citizen regeneration: Understanding active citizen engagement among Canada's information age generations.* Toronto: D-Code.
Baum, M.A., and S. Kernell. 1999. Has cable ended the golden age of presidential television? *American Political Science Review* 93(1): 99-114.
Baxter, Steven. 2003. Don't let school get in the way of your education. *Verge* (summer). http://www.vergemagazine.ca/.

Beck, P.A., R. Dalton, S. Greene, and R. Huckfeldt. 2002. The social calculus of voting: Interpersonal, media, and organizational influences on presidential choices. *American Political Science Review* 96(1): 57-73.

Bellah, R.N., R. Madsen, W.M. Sullivan, A. Swidler, and S.M. Tipton. 1996. *Habits of the heart: Individualism and commitment in American life*, updated edition. Berkeley: University of California Press.

Bennett, S.E. 1988. "Know-nothings" revisited: The meaning of political ignorance today. *Social Science Quarterly* 69(2): 476-90.

–. 1998. Young Americans' indifference to media coverage of public affairs. *PS: Political Science and Politics* 31(3): 535-41.

Bennett, S.E., R.S. Flickinger, and S.L. Rhine. 2000. Political talk over here, over there, over time. *British Journal of Political Science* 30: 99-119.

Billig, M. 1995. *Banal nationalism*. London: Sage.

Bissoondath, N. 2002. *Selling illusions: The cult of multiculturalism in Canada*. Toronto: Penguin.

Black, J. 2005. From enumeration to the national register of electors. In *Strengthening Canadian democracy*, ed. P. Howe, R. Johnston, and A. Blais, 161-219. Montreal: Institute for Research on Public Policy.

Blais, A., A. Dobrzynska, and P. Loewen. 2007. *Potential impacts of extended advance voting on voter turnout*. Elections Canada, Working Paper Series.

Blais, A., E. Gidengil, R. Nadeau, and N. Nevitte. 2002. *Anatomy of a Liberal victory: Making sense of the vote in the 2000 Canadian election*. Peterborough, ON: Broadview Press.

Blais, A., E. Gidengil, N. Nevitte, and R. Nadeau. 2004. Where does turnout decline come from? *European Journal of Political Research* 43(2): 221-36.

Bliss, M. 2003. The multicultural North American hotel. *National Post*, 15 January.

Bourdeau, A., S. Tremblay, and J. Valois. 2004. La tournée des mousquetaires. http://www.politiquebec.com/forum.

Boyte, H.C., and J. Farr. 1997. The work of citizenship and the problem of service-learning. In *Experiencing citizenship*, ed. R. Battistoni and W. Hudson, 35-48. Washington, DC: American Association of Higher Education.

Brehm, J., and W. Rahn. 1997. Individual-level evidence for the causes and consequences of social capital. *American Journal of Political Science* 41(3): 999-1023.

Bristow, J. 2008. *The next west generation: Young adults, identity and democracy*. Canada West Foundation, 11 March. http://www.cwf.ca (Publications).

British Columbia Ministry of Education. 2005. *Civic studies 11 (Final draft: April 2005): Integrated resource package 2005*. Victoria: Ministry of Education, Province of British Columbia.

Brown, S.D., A. Meinhard, K. Ellis-Hale, A. Henderson, and M. Foster 2007a. *Community service and service learning in Canada: A profile of programming*. Draft Research Report to the Knowledge Development Centre Imagine Canada. http://www.wlu.ca/lispop/workingpaperseries.html.

Brown, S.D., S.M. Pancer, A. Henderson, and K. Ellis-Hale. 2007b. *The impact of high school mandatory community service programs on subsequent volunteering and civic engagement*. Draft Research Report to the Knowledge Development Centre Imagine Canada. http://www.wlu.ca/lispop/workingpaperseries.html.

Bureau of Broadcast Measurement. Various years, 1968 to 1994. *Television network program reports*.

Byers, M. 2007. *Intent for a nation: A relentlessly optimistic manifesto for Canada's role in the world*. Toronto: Douglas and McIntyre.

CBC/Radio Canada. 2007. *What's next? How we're meeting the changing needs of Canadians*. http://www.cbc.radio-canada.ca/submissions/plan/2007/pdf/plan2007-e.pdf.

Campbell, D. 2006. *Why we vote: How schools and communities shape our civic life*. Princeton, NJ: Princeton University Press.

Canadian Policy Research Networks. 2007. *Charting the course for youth civic and political participation: CPRN youth workshop summary report*. http://www.cprn.org/documents/48533_EN.pdf

Cassel, C., and D. Hill. 1981. Explanations of turnout decline. *American Politics Quarterly* 9(2): 181-95.

Centre for Research and Information on Canada. 2001. *Voter participation in Canada: Is Canadian democracy in crisis?* Montreal: Centre for Research and Information on Canada.

Chaffee, S.H., and J. Schleuder. 1986. Measurement and effects of attention to media news. *Human Communication Research* 13(1): 76-107.

Clarke, H.D., D. Sanders, M.C. Stewart, and P.F. Whiteley. 2003. Britain (not) at the polls, 2001. *PS: Political Science and Politics* 36(1): 59-64.

Cohen, A. 2003. *While Canada slept: How we lost our place in the world.* Toronto: McClelland and Stewart.

Coleman, J.S. 1961. *The adolescent society: The social life of the teenager and its impact on education.* New York: Free Press.

Costa, P.T., and R.R. McCrae. 1992. *Revised NEO personality inventory (NEO PI-R) and NEO five-factor inventory (NEO-FFI) professional manual.* Odessa, FL: Psychological Assessment Resources.

Côté, J.E., and A.L. Allahar. 2007. *Ivory tower blues: A university system in crisis.* Toronto: University of Toronto Press.

Cross, W., and L. Young. 2004. The contours of political party membership in Canada. *Party Politics* 10(4): 427-44.

–. 2008. Factors influencing the young politically engaged to join a political party: An investigation of the Canadian case. *Party Politics* 14(3): 345-69.

Culture Statistics: Television viewing in Canada. Various years, 1986 to 1995. Ottawa: Statistics Canada, Education, Culture and Tourism Division.

Cutler, F., and P. Fournier. 2007. Why Ontarians said no to MMP. *Globe and Mail,* 25 October, A21.

Dalton, R. 2004. *Democratic challenges, democratic choices: The erosion of political support in advanced industrial democracies.* Oxford: Oxford University Press.

–. 2006. *Citizen politics: Public opinion and political parties in the advanced industrial democracies,* 4th edition. Washington, DC: CQ Press.

–. 2008. *The good citizen: How a younger generation is reshaping American politics.* Washington, DC: CQ Press.

Dalton R.J., and M.P. Wattenberg. 2000. *Parties without partisans: Political change in advanced industrial democracies.* Oxford: Oxford University Press.

Dekker, H. 1999. Citizenship conceptions and competencies in the subject matter "society" in the Dutch schools. In *Civic education across countries: Twenty-four national case studies from the IEA Civic Education Project,* ed. J. Torney-Purta, J. Schwille, and J. Amadeo, 437-62. Amsterdam: International Association for the Evaluation of Educational Achievement.

Delli Carpini, M. 2000. Gen.com: Youth, civic engagement and the new information environment. *Political Communication* 17(4): 341-49.

Delli Carpini, M., and S. Keeter. 1991. Stability and change in the US public's knowledge of politics. *Public Opinion Quarterly* 55(4): 583-612.

–. 1996. *What Americans know about politics and why it matters.* New Haven, CT: Yale University Press.

De Tocqueville, A. 1969. *Democracy in America,* ed. J.P. Mayer. Garden City, NY: Anchor.

Deutsch, K. 1969. *Nationalism and social communication,* 2nd edition. Cambridge, MA: MIT Press.

Deutsch, K., L.J. Edinger, R.C. Macridis, and R.L. Merritt. 1967. *France, Germany and the western alliance.* New York: Scribner's.

De Vreese, C.H., and H. Boomgaarden. 2006. News, political knowledge and participation: The differential effects of news media exposure on political knowledge and participation. *Acta Politica* 41(4): 317-41.

Dey, E.L. 1997. Undergraduate political attitudes: Peer influence in changing social contexts. *Journal of Higher Education* 68(4): 398-413.

Dionne, E.J. Jr., K.M. Drogosz, and R.E. Litan, eds. 2003. *United we serve: National service and the future of citizenship.* Washington, DC: Brookings Institution Press.

Directeur Général des Élections du Québec. 2008. *Elections générales au Québec, 1867-2008.* http://www.electionsquebec.qc.ca (Chercheur; Statistique Sur Les Résultats Électoraux).

Dworkin, R. 1985. *A matter of principle.* Cambridge, MA: Harvard University Press.

Eisner, J. 2003. First vote. In *United we serve: National service and the future of citizenship,* ed. E.J. Dionne Jr., K. Meltzer Drogosz, and R.E. Litan, 169-74. Washington, DC: Brookings Institution Press.

Ekos Research Associates. 2008. *Canadian views on volunteer service and a national youth service policy: Draft report.* http://www.katimavik.org (Facts).

Elections Alberta. 2008. *2008 General report.* http://www.elections.ab.ca (Reports; General Elections).

Elections BC. 2001. *Report of the chief electoral officer: 37th provincial general election, May 16, 2001.* http://www.elections.bc.ca (Resource Centre; Reports).

–. 2005. *Report of the chief electoral officer: 38th provincial general election, 2005 Referendum on Electoral Reform, May 17, 2005.* http://www.elections.bc.ca (Resource Centre; Reports).

Elections Canada. 2005. *Estimation of voter turnout by age group at the 38th federal general election (June 28, 2004).* http://www.elections.ca (Electoral Law, Policy and Research; Research Documents).

–. 2008. *Estimation of voter turnout by age group at the 39th federal general election, January 23, 2006.* http://www.elections.ca (Electoral Law, Policy and Research; Research Documents).

–. 2009. *Voter turnout at federal elections and referendums, 1867-2008.* http://www.elections. ca (Past Elections).

–. 2010. *Estimation of voter turnout by age group at the 2008 federal general election.* http:// www.elections.ca (Electoral Law, Policy and Research; Research Documents).

Elections Nova Scotia. 2009. *Comparative statistics – Nova Scotia provincial general elections – 1960-2009.* http://www.electionsnovascotia.ns.ca (Results and Stats; Election Statistics; Comparative Statistics).

Elections Ontario. 2007. *2007 General election statistical summary.* http://www.elections. on.ca (Past Election Results; 2007 General Election).

Elkind, D. 1998. Egocentrism in adolescence. In *Adolescent behaviour and society: A book of readings,* 5th edition, ed. Rolf E. Muuss and Harriet D. Porton, 91-97. New York: McGraw-Hill.

Elkins, D.J., and R. Simeon. 1979. A cause in search of its effect, or what does political culture explain? *Comparative Politics* 11(2): 127-45.

Environics. 2003. *Preliminary qualitative exploration of the values and priorities of the next generation of community leaders, qualitative research, a summary report.* Ottawa: Centre for Research and Information on Canada.

Epstein, R. 2007. *The case against adolescence: Rediscovering the adult in every teen.* Fresno, CA: Quill Driver Books.

Erikson, E. 1968. *Identity, youth, and crisis.* New York: Norton.

Eveland, W.P. Jr., A.F. Hayes, D.V. Shah, and N. Kwak. 2005. Understanding the relationship between communication and political knowledge: A model comparison using panel data. *Political Communication* 22(4): 423-46.

Fasick, F.A. 1994. On the "invention" of adolescence. *Journal of Early Adolescence* 14(1): 6-23.

Fendrich, J.M., and K.L. Lovoy. 1988. Back to the future: Adult political behaviour of former student activists. *American Sociological Review* 53(5): 780-84.

Fisher, S.D., L. Lessard-Phillips, S.B. Hobolt, and J. Curtice. 2008. Disengaging voters: Do plurality systems discourage the less knowledgeable from voting? *Electoral Studies* 27(1): 89-104

Florida, R. 2008. *Who's your city?* New York: Basic Books.

Franklin, M. 2004. *Voter turnout and the dynamics of electoral competition in established democracies since 1945.* Cambridge: Cambridge University Press.

Fukuyama, F. 1989. The end of history? *National Interest* 16: 3-18.

–. 1992. *The end of history and the last man.* New York: Free Press.

Galston, W.A. 2001. Political knowledge, political engagement, and civic education. *Annual Review of Political Science* 4(1): 217-34.

–. 2007. Civic knowledge, civic education, and civic engagement: A summary of recent research. *International Journal of Public Administration* 30(6-7): 623-42.

Geddes, J. 2006. Pride in the country has dropped significantly. *Maclean's*, 23 January, 22.

Gerber, A.S., D.P. Green, and C.W. Larimer. 2008. Social pressure and voter turnout: Evidence from a large-scale field experiment. *American Political Science Review* 102(1): 33-48.

Gidengil, E., A. Blais, J. Everitt, P. Fournier, and N. Nevitte. 2005. Missing the message: Young adults and the election issues. *Electoral Insight* 7(1): 6-11.

Gidengil, E., A. Blais, N. Nevitte, and R. Nadeau. 2003. Turned off or tuned out? Youth participation in politics. *Electoral Insight* 5(2): 9-14.

–. 2004. *Citizens*. Vancouver: University of British Columbia Press.

Gray, M. 2003. *In the midst of fellows: The social context of the American turnout decision.* PhD dissertation, University of California, Irvine.

Green, D.P., and A.S. Gerber. 2004. *Get out the vote! How to increase voter turnout.* Washington, DC: Brookings Institution Press.

Green, D.P., and R. Shachar. 2000. Habit formation and political behaviour: Evidence of consuetude in voter turnout. *British Journal of Political Science* 30(4): 561-73.

Greenstein, F.I. 1969. *Children and politics*. New Haven, CT: Yale University Press.

Griffiths, Rudyard. 2009. *Who we are: A citizen's manifesto*. Vancouver: Douglas and McIntyre.

Hamilton, R., and M. Pinard. 1976. The bases of Parti Québécois support in recent Quebec elections. *Canadian Journal of Political Science* 9(1): 3-26.

Hart, D., R. Atkins, P. Markey, and J. Youniss. 2004. Youth bulges in communities: The effects of age structure on adolescent civic knowledge and civic participation. *Psychological Science* 15(9): 591-97.

Henn, M., M. Weinstein, and S. Hodgkinson. 2007. Social capital and political participation: Understanding the dynamics of young people's political disengagement in contemporary Britain. *Social Policy and Society* 6(4): 467-79.

Hess, R.D., and J.V. Torney. 1968. *The development of political attitudes in children*. New York: Anchor Books.

Highton, B. 2000. Residential mobility, community mobility, and electoral participation. *Political Behavior* 22(2): 109-20.

Highton, B., and R.E. Wolfinger. 2001. The first seven years of the political life cycle. *American Journal of Political Science* 45(1): 202-9.

Hillygus, D.S. 2005. Campaign effects and the dynamics of turnout intention in election 2000. *Journal of Politics* 67(1): 50-68.

Hobsbawm, E. 1990. *Nations and nationalism since 1780: Programme, myth and reality*. Cambridge: Cambridge University Press.

Hodgetts, A.B. 1968. *What culture? What heritage? A study of civic education in Canada*. Toronto: Ontario Institute for Studies in Education.

Hollander, B. 1997. Television news exposure and foreign affairs knowledge. *Gazette: International Journal for Communication* 59(2): 151-62.

Holtz-Bacha, C., and P. Norris. 2001. To entertain, inform and educate: Still the role of public television. *Political Communication* 18(2): 123-40.

Honoré, C. 2008. *Under pressure: Rescuing childhood from the culture of hyper-parenting*. Toronto: Knopf Canada.

Hooghe, M. 2004. Political socialization and the future of politics. *Acta Politica* 39(4): 331-41.

Howe, P. 1998. *National identity and political behaviour in Quebec, Scotland and Brittany*. PhD dissertation, University of British Columbia.

–. 2001. The sources of campaign intemperance. *Policy Options* 22(1-2): 21-24.

–. 2003a. Where have all the voters gone? *Inroads: The Canadian Journal of Opinion* 12: 74-83.

–. 2003b. Electoral participation and the knowledge deficit. *Electoral Insight* 5(2): 20-25.

–. 2005. Nationalist idealisation and the state. *National Identities* 7(1): 79-102.

–. 2006. Political knowledge and electoral participation in the Netherlands: Comparisons with the Canadian case. *International Political Science Review* 27(2): 137-66.

–. 2007a. *The electoral participation of young Canadians.* Elections Canada: Working Paper Series on Electoral Participation and Outreach Practices. http://www.elections.ca (Electoral Law, Policy and Research; Research Documents).

–. 2007b. Voter participation in New Brunswick and the political disengagement of the young. In *Democratic reform in New Brunswick,* ed. W. Cross, 240-72. Toronto: Canadian Scholars' Press.

Howe P., and J. Fletcher. 2002. The evolution of Charter values. In *Canadian political culture(s) in transition,* ed. H. Telford, and H. Lazar, 265-91. Montreal and Kingston: McGill-Queen's University Press.

Howe, P., R. Johnston, and A. Blais, ed. 2005. *Strengthening Canadian democracy.* Montreal: Institute for Research on Public Policy.

Hughes, A.S., and A. Sears. 2008. The struggle for citizenship education in Canada: The centre cannot hold. In *SAGE handbook of education for citizenship and democracy,* ed. J. Arthur, I. Davies, and C. Hahn, 124-38. London: Sage.

Hyman, H. 1959. *Political socialization: A study in the psychology of political behaviour.* New York: Free Press.

Hyman, H., and P. Sheatsley. 1947. Some reasons why information campaigns fail. *Public Opinion Quarterly* 11(3): 412-23.

Inglehart, R. 1990. *Culture shift in advanced industrial society.* Princeton, NJ: Princeton University Press.

–. 1997. *Modernization and postmodernization: Cultural, economic, and political change in 43 societies.* Princeton, NJ: Princeton University Press.

International Institute for Democracy and Electoral Assistance. 1999. *Youth voter participation: Involving today's young in tomorrow's democracy.* Stockholm: International IDEA.

Ipsos-Reid/Dominion Institute. 2007. National citizenship exam, 10 year benchmark study. 29 June. http://www.dominion.ca (Polling).

Jennings, M.K. 1996. Political knowledge over time and across generations. *Public Opinion Quarterly* 60(2): 228-52.

Jennings, M.K., and R.G. Niemi. 1974. *The political character of adolescence: The influence of families and schools.* Princeton, NJ: Princeton University Press.

Johnson, C., and B. Marshall. 2004. *Political engagement among young people: An update. Research paper prepared by the Electoral Commission.* London: Electoral Commission.

Johnston, R.J., and J.S. Matthews. 2004. Social capital, age, and participation. Paper presented at Youth Participation Workshop at annual meeting of Canadian Political Science Association. Winnipeg, 3 June.

Jowell, R., and A. Park. 1998. *Young people, politics and citizenship.* Centre for Research into Elections and Social Trends, Working Paper 67. London: Citizenship Foundation.

Kahne, J., B. Chi, and E. Middaugh. 2006. Building social capital for civic and political engagement: The potential of high school government courses. *Canadian Journal of Education* 29(2): 387-409.

Kahne, J., and S. Sporte. 2007. Developing citizens: A longitudinal study of school, family, and community influences on students' commitments to civic participation. Paper delivered at 2007 Annual Meeting of the American Political Science Association, 30 August–2 September.

Kam, C. 2005. Who toes the party line? Cues, values, and individual differences. *Political Behavior* 27(2): 163-82.

Kanji, M. 2002. Political discontent, human capital, and representative governance in Canada. In *Value Change and Governance in Canada,* ed. N. Nevitte, 71-106. Toronto: University of Toronto Press.

Kaplan, N. 2004. *Episodic voting: The logic of electoral participation in the context of multiple elections.* PhD dissertation, Columbia University.

Kersh, R. 2007. Civic engagement and national belonging. *International Journal of Public Administration* 30(6-7): 595-613.

Kimberlee, R.H. 2002. Why don't British young people vote at general elections? *Journal of Youth Studies* 5(1): 85-98.

King, G., R.O. Keohane, and S. Verba. 1994. *Designing social inquiry: Scientific inference in qualitative research*. Princeton NJ: Princeton University Press.

Klofstad, C. 2005. *The art of associating: The central role of peers in civic life*. PhD dissertation, Harvard University.

Kroger, J. 2007. *Identity development: Adolescence through adulthood*, 2nd edition. Thousand Oaks, CA: Sage.

Kunkel, J., C. Johnson, H. Bakke, and J. Miller. 2001. Public achievement: Collaboration, action and civic education. National Council for the Social Studies, Bulletin 98: 95-105.

Kushner, J., D. Siegel, and H. Stanwick. 1997. Ontario municipal elections: Voting trends and determinants of electoral success in a Canadian province. *Canadian Journal of Political Science* 30(3): 539-59.

Kusiek, J. 2007. *Addressing youth (dis)engagement through age-integrated activity*. Major research project submitted to Faculty of Arts, University of New Brunswick, 20 August.

Kymlicka, W. 1989. *Liberalism, community and culture*. Oxford: Clarendon Press.

Laselva, S. 1996. *Moral foundations of Canadian federalism: Paradoxes, tragedies and achievements of nationhood*. Montreal and Kingston: McGill-Queen's University Press.

Lauf, E. 2001. Research note: The vanishing young reader. *European Journal of Communication* 16(2): 233-43.

Lazarsfeld, P.F., B. Berelson, and H. Gaudet. 1968. *The people's choice: How the voter makes up his mind in a presidential campaign*, 3rd edition. New York: Columbia University Press.

Leger Marketing. 2008. *Elections Alberta, survey of voters and non-voters, research report*. http://www.elections.ab.ca (Reports; Research).

Lijphart, A. 1997. Unequal participation: Democracy's unresolved dilemma. *American Political Science Review* 91(1): 1-14.

Lynd, R.S., and H.M. Lynd. 1929. *Middletown: A study in American culture*. New York: Harcourt Brace.

MacKinnon, M.P., S. Pitre, and J. Watling. 2007. *Lost in translation: (Mis)understanding youth engagement. Synthesis report*. Ottawa: Canadian Policy Research Networks. http://www.cprn.org/documents/48800_FR.pdf.

Macedo, S., Y. Alex-Assensoh, J.M. Berry, M. Brintnall, D.E. Campbell, L. Ricardo Fraga, A. Fung, W.A. Galston, C.F. Karpowitz, M. Levi, M. Levinson, K. Lipsitz, R.G. Niemi, R.D. Putnam, W.M. Rahn, R. Reich, R.R. Rodgers, T. Swanstrom, and K. Cramer Walsh. 2005. *Democracy at risk: How political choices undermine citizen participation, and what we can do about it*. Washington, DC: Brookings Institution Press.

Marcus, G.E., J.L. Sullivan, E. Theiss-Morse, and S.L. Wood. 1995. *With malice toward some: How people make civil liberties judgments*. Cambridge: Cambridge University Press.

Marwell, G., M.T. Aiken, and N.J. Demerath. 1987. The persistence of political attitudes among 1960s civil rights activists. *Public Opinion Quarterly* 51(3): 359-75.

Matsusaka, J.G., and F. Palda. 1999. Voter turnout: How much can we explain? *Public Choice* 98: 431-46.

McAdam, D. 1988. *Freedom summer*. New York: Oxford University Press.

McAllister, I. 1998. Civic education and political knowledge in Australia. *Australian Journal of Political Science* 33(1): 7-24.

McCrae, R.R. 1996. Social consequences of experiential openness. *Psychological Bulletin* 120(3): 323-37.

McCrae, R.R., P.T. Costa, Jr., M.P. de Lima, A. Simões, F. Ostendorf, A. Angleitner, I. Marusić, D. Bratko, G.V. Caprara, C. Barbaranelli, J.-H Chae, and R.L. Piedmont. 1999. Age differences in personality across the adult life span: Parallels in five cultures. *Developmental Psychology* 35(2): 466-77.

McFayden, S., C. Hoskins, and D. Gillen. 1980. *Canadian broadcasting: Market structure and economic performance*. Montreal: Institute for Research on Public Policy.

McKenna, P. 2006. Opting out of electoral reform: Why PEI chose the status quo. *Policy Options* 27(5): 58-61.

McLean, S. 2006. Patriotism, generational change, and the politics of sacrifice. In *Social capital: Critical perspectives on community and "Bowling Alone,"* ed. S.L. McLean, D.A. Schultz, and M.B. Steger, 147-66. New York and London: New York University Press.

Mettler, S. 2007. Bringing government back into civic engagement: Considering the role of public policy. *International Journal of Public Administration* 30(6-7): 643-50.

Mick, H. 2007. He ain't heavy, he's my buddy. *Globe and Mail*, 2 October, L1-L3.

Milan, A. 2005. Willing to participate: Political engagement of young adults. Statistics Canada: *Canadian Social Trends* 79.

Miller, D. 1995. *On nationality*. Oxford: Oxford University Press.

Miller, W.E., and J.M. Shanks. 1996. *The new American voter*. Cambridge, MA: Harvard University Press.

Milner, H. 2001. Civic literacy in comparative context: Why Canadians should be concerned. *IRPP Policy Matters* 2(2): 3-40.

–. 2002. *Civic literacy: How informed citizens make democracy work*. Hanover, NH: University Press of New England.

–. 2005. Are young Canadians becoming political dropouts? A comparative perspective. *IRPP Choices* 11(3): 1-26.

–. 2007. Political knowledge and participation among young Canadians and Americans. *IRPP Working Paper Series* 2007-01.

Mindich, D.T.Z. 2005. *Tuned out: Why Americans under 40 don't follow the news*. New York: Oxford University Press.

Mutz, D.C. 2006. *Hearing the other side: Deliberative versus participatory democracy*. Cambridge: Cambridge University Press.

Nadeau, R., and T. Giasson. 2005. Canada's democratic malaise: Are the media to blame? In *Strengthening Canadian democracy*, ed. P. Howe, R. Johnston, and A. Blais, 229-67. Montreal: Institute for Research on Public Policy.

Nevitte, N. 1996. *The decline of deference*. Peterborough, ON: Broadview Press.

Newton, K. 1999. Mass media effects: Mobilization or media malaise? *British Journal of Political Science* 29(4): 577-99.

Nickerson D.W. 2008. Is voting contagious? Evidence from two field experiments. *American Political Science Review* 102(1): 49-57.

Nie, N.H., J. Junn, and K. Stehlik-Barry. 1996. *Education and democratic citizenship in America*. Chicago: University of Chicago Press.

Niemi, R.G. 1999. Editor's introduction. *Political Psychology* 20(3): 471-76.

Niemi, R.G., and M.A. Hepburn. 1995. The rebirth of political socialization. *Perspectives on Political Science* 24(1): 7-16.

Niemi, R.G., M.A. Hepburn, and Chris Chapman. 2000. Community service by high school students: A cure for civic ills? *Political Behavior* 22(1): 45-69.

Niemi, R.G., and J. Junn. 1998. *Civic education: What makes students learn*. New Haven and London: Yale University Press.

Niemi, R.G., and J. Smith. 2001. Enrollments in high school government classes: Are we short-changing both citizenship and political science training? *PS: Political Science and Politics* 34(2): 281-87.

Niven, D. 2001. The limits of mobilization: Turnout evidence from state house primaries. *Political Behavior* 23(4): 335-50.

–. 2002. The mobilization calendar: The time-dependent effects of personal contact on turnout. *American Politics Research* 30(3): 307-22.

–. 2004. The mobilization solution? Face-to-face contact and voter turnout in a municipal election. *Journal of Politics* 66(3): 868-84.

Norris, P., ed. 1999. *Critical citizens: Global support for democratic governance*. Oxford: Oxford University Press.

–. 2000. *A virtuous circle: Political communications in postindustrial societies*. Cambridge: Cambridge University Press.

–. 2003. Young people and political activism: From the politics of loyalties to the politics of choice. Paper presented to the Council of Europe Symposium, Young People and Democratic Institutions: From Disillusionment to Participation, Strasbourg, 27-28 November.

O'Neill, B. 2001. Generational patterns in the political opinions and behaviour of Canadians: Separating the wheat from the chaff. *Policy Matters* 2(5): 1-48. http://www.irpp.org (Publications).

–. 2003. Examining declining electoral turnout among Canada's youth. *Electoral Insight* 5(2): 15-19.

–. 2007. Indifferent or just different? The political and civic engagement of young people in Canada. Ottawa: Canadian Policy Research Networks, June. http://www.cprn.org/documents/48504_EN.pdf

O'Toole, T., M. Lister, D. Marsh, S. Jones, and A. McDonagh. 2003a. Tuning out or left out? Participation and non-participation among young people. *Contemporary Politics* 9(1): 45-61.

O'Toole, T., D. Marsh, and S. Jones. 2003b. Political literacy cuts both ways: The politics of non-participation among young people. *Political Quarterly* 74(3): 349-60.

Page, B.I., and R.Y. Shapiro. 1992. *The rational public: Fifty years of trends in Americans' policy preferences*. Chicago: University of Chicago Press.

Pammett, J.H., and L. Leduc. 2003a. *Explaining the turnout decline in Canadian federal elections: A new survey of non-voters*. Ottawa: Elections Canada.

–. 2003b. Confronting the problem of declining voter turnout among youth. *Electoral Insight* 5(2): 3-8.

Park. A. 2005. Has modern politics disenchanted the young? In *British social attitudes, the 21st century report: Continuity and change over two decades*, ed. K. Thomson, 23-48. London: Sage.

Peiser, W. 2000. Cohort replacement and the downward trend in newspaper readership. *Newspaper Research Journal* 21(2): 11-22.

Pew Research Center for People and the Press. 2004. *Cable and Internet loom large in fragmented political news universe*. Washington, DC: Pew Research Center for People and the Press.

–. 2007. *What Americans know: 1989-2007. Public knowledge of current affairs little changed by news and information revolutions*. Washington, DC: Pew Research Center for People and the Press.

–. 2008. *2008 Pew Research Center for People and the Press news consumption and believability study*. Washington, DC: Pew Research Center for People and the Press.

Plutzer, E. 2002. Becoming a habitual voter: Inertia, resources, and growth in young adulthood. *American Political Science Review* 96(1): 41-56.

PMRS Response Rate Committee. 2003. Telephone refusal rates still rising: Results of the 2002 response rate survey. http://www.mria-arim.ca (Committees; Response Rate Committee; Published Articles).

Policy Research Initative. 2005. *Social capital as a public policy tool: Project report*. Ottawa: Policy Research Initiative.

Popkin, S.L., and M. Dimock. 1999. Political knowledge and citizen competence. In *Citizen competence and democratic institutions*, ed. S.L. Elkin and K.E. Soltan, 117-46. University Park, PA: Pennsylvania State University Press.

Prairie Research Associates. 2004. *Low voter turnout: A survey of voters and non voters*. Report prepared for Elections Manitoba, 10 March. http://www.electionsmanitoba.ca (Publications; Other Publications).

Price, V., and J. Zaller. 1993. Who gets the news: Measuring individual differences in likelihood of news reception. *Public Opinion Quarterly* 57(2): 133-64.

Print, M., L. Saha, and K. Edwards. 2004. *Youth electoral study report 1: Enrolment and voting*. http://www.aec.gov.au (About Us; AEC Research; Youth Electoral Study).

Prior, M. 2007. *Post-broadcast democracy: How media choice increases inequality in political involvement and polarizes elections*. New York: Cambridge University Press.

Pryor, J.H., S. Hurtado, V.B. Saenz, J.S. Korn, J.L. Santos, and W.S. Korn. 2006. *The American freshman national norms for fall 2006*. Prepared for Higher Education Institute, Graduate School of Education and Information Studies, University of California, Los Angeles. http://www.gseis.ucla.edu/heri/index.php (Publications; Publications Archive).

Putnam, R.D. 1995. Tuning in, tuning out: The strange disappearance of social capital in America. *PS: Political Science and Politics* 28(4): 664-83.

–. 2000. *Bowling alone: The collapse and revival of American community*. New York: Simon and Schuster.

–. 2002. Bowling together: The United State of America. *American Prospect* 13(3): 20-22.

–. 2008. The rebirth of American civic life. *Boston Globe*, 2 March.

Raeymaeckers, K. 2002. Research note: Young people and patterns of time consumption in relation to print media. *European Journal of Communication* 17(3): 369-83.

Rahn, W.M., and J.E. Transue. 1998. Social trust and value change: The decline of social capital in American youth, 1976-1995. *Political Psychology* 19(3): 545-65.

Raney, T., and L. Berdahl. 2009. Birds of a feather? Citizenship norms, group identity, and political participation in western Canada. *Canadian Journal of Political Science* 42(1): 187-209.

Rawls, J. 1999. *A theory of justice*, revised edition. Cambridge, MA: Belknap Press.

Renan, E. 1996. What is a nation? In *Becoming national: A reader*, ed. G. Eley and R. Suny, 42-56. New York: Oxford University Press.

Richie, R. 2007. Leave no voter behind: Seeking 100 percent voter registration and effective civic education. *National Civic Review* 96(3): 39-45.

Riedel, E. 2002. The impact of high school community service programs on students' feelings of civic obligation. *American Politics Research* 35(5): 499-527.

Robinson, J.P. 1980. The changing reading habits of the American public. *Journal of Communication* 30(1): 141-52.

Robinson, M.J. 1976. Public affairs television and the growth of political malaise: The case of "the selling of the Pentagon." *American Political Science Review* 70(2): 409-32.

Rokeach, M. 1973. *The nature of human values*. New York: Free Press.

RoperASW (2002). *National Geographic – Roper 2002 global geographic literacy survey*. Report prepared for National Geographic Education Foundation. http://www.nationalgeographic. com (Search).

Rosenstone, S.J., and J.M. Hansen. 2003. *Mobilization, participation and democracy in America*. New York: Longman.

Rubenson, D., A. Blais, P. Fournier, E. Gidengil, and N. Nevitte. 2004. Accounting for the age gap in turnout. *Acta Politica* 39(4): 407-21.

Rust, V.D. 1989. *The democratic tradition and the evolution of schooling in Norway*. Westport, CT: Greenwood Press.

Saul, J.R. 1998. *Reflections of a Siamese twin: Canada at the end of the twentieth century*. Toronto: Penguin.

Schudson, M. 1998. *The good citizen: A history of American civic life*. Cambridge, MA: Harvard University Press.

Sciadis, G. 2002. *Unveiling the digital divide*. Catalogue No. 56F0004MIE, no.7. Ottawa: Statistics Canada.

Seidle, F.L. 2005. Lessons from PEI's plebiscite on electoral reform. *Opinion Canada* 7(40).

Shea, D.M., and R. Harris. 2006. Why bother? Because peer-to-peer programs can mobilize young voters. *Political Science and Politics* 39(2): 341-45.

Sigelman, L., P.W. Roeder, M.E. Jewell, and M.A. Baer. 1985. Voting and nonvoting: A multi-election perspective. *American Journal of Political Science* 29(4): 749-65.

Skocpol, T. 2002. Will 9/11 and the war on terror revitalize civic democracy? *PS: Political Science and Politics* 35(3): 537-40.

Statistical Abstract of the United States. 1999. Chief of the Bureau of Statistics, Treasury Department. Washington, DC: Government Printing Office.

Stock, S, C. Miranda, S. Evans, S. Plessis, J. Ridley, S. Yeh, and J. Chanoine. 2007. Healthy buddies: A novel, peer-led health promotion program for the prevention of obesity and eating disorders in children in elementary school. *Pediatrics* 120(4): e1058-e1068.

Stolle, D., and C. Cruz. 2005. Youth civic engagement in Canada: Implications for public policy. In *Social capital in action: Thematic policy studies*, 82-114. Ottawa: Policy Research Initative.

Stolle, D., and M. Hooghe. 2004. The roots of social capital: Attitudinal and network mechanisms in the relation between youth and adult indicators of social capital. *Acta Politica* 39(4): 422-41.

–. 2005. Review article: Inaccurate, exceptional, one sided or irrelevant? The debate about the alleged decline of social capital and civic engagement in western societies. *British Journal of Political Science* 35(1): 149-67.

Stolle D., M. Hooghe, and M. Micheletti. 2005. Politics in the supermarket: Political consumerism as a form of political participation. *International Political Science Review* 26(3): 245-69.

Strate, J.M., C.J. Parrish, C.D. Elder, and C. Ford. 1989. Life span civic development and voting participation. *American Political Science Review* 83(2): 443-64.

Strategic Counsel. 2008. A report to the *Globe and Mail* and CTV. 2008 federal election: pre-election national poll, 12 October. http://www.thestrategiccounsel.com (Our News; Globe and Mail/CTV polls).

Sullivan, J.L., G.E. Marcus, S. Feldman, and J.E. Piereson. 1981. The sources of political tolerance: A multivariate analysis. *American Political Science Review* 75(1): 92-106.

Taras, D. 2001. *Power and betrayal in the Canadian media*, updated edition. Peterborough, ON: Broadview Press.

Taylor, C. 1991. *The malaise of modernity*. Toronto: House of Anansi Press.

–. 1992. *Multiculturalism and "the politics of recognition,"* ed. Amy Gutmann. Princeton, NJ: Princeton University Press.

Teixeira, R.A. 1992. *The disappearing American voter*. Washington, DC: Brookings Institution Press.

Times Mirror Center. 1990. *The age of indifference: A study of young Americans and how they view the news*. Washington, DC: Times Mirror Center for the People and the Press.

Torney, J.V., A.N. Oppenheim, and R.F. Farnen. 1975. *Civic education in ten countries: An empirical study*. Stockholm: Almqvist and Wiksell International.

Tossuti, L.S. 2007. Voluntary associations and the political engagement of young Canadians. *Journal of Canadian Studies* 41(1): 100-27.

Tran, K., S. Kustec, and T. Chui. 2005. Becoming Canadian: Intent, process and outcome. *Canadian Social Trends* 76: 8-13.

Turcotte, A. 2005. Different strokes: Why young Canadians don't vote. *Electoral Insight* 7(1): 12-16.

–. 2007. *"What do you mean I can't have a say?" Young Canadians and their government*. Ottawa: Canadian Policy Research Networks. http://www.cprn.org/documents/48799_EN.pdf

Twenge, J. 2006. *Generation me: Why today's young Americans are more confident, assertive, entitled – and more miserable than ever before*. New York: Free Press.

Twenge, J., and K. Campbell. 2009. *The narcissism epidemic: Living in the age of entitlement*. New York: Free Press.

Van den Broek, A. 1994. Political involvement in the Netherlands. *Acta Politica* 29(2): 173-97.

Van Deth, J. 2000. Political interest and apathy: The decline of a gender gap? *Acta Politica* 35(3): 247-74.

Verba, S., K.L. Schlozman, and H.E. Brady. 1995. *Voice and equality: Civic voluntarism in American politics*. Cambridge, MA: Harvard University Press.

Verba, S., K.L. Schlozman, and N. Burns. 2005. Family ties: Understanding the intergenerational transmission of political participation. In *The social logic of politics*, ed. A. Zuckerman, 95-114. Philadelphia: Temple University Press.

Von Drehle, D. 2008. It's their turn now. *Time* 171(6): 34-48.

Von Hahn, K. 2007. I like to hang out with my teenager. What's wrong with that? *Globe and Mail*, 1 September, L3.

UNESCO statistical yearbook. Various years. Paris: United Nations Educational, Scientific and Cultural Organization.

United Nations demographic yearbook. Various years. New York: Statistical Office of the United Nations.

Walker, T. 2000. The service/politics split: Rethinking service to teach political engagement. *PS: Political Science and Politics* 33(3): 647-49.

Watson, W. 1998. *Globalization and the meaning of Canadian life*. Toronto: University of Toronto Press.

Wattenberg, M.P. 2002. *Where have all the voters gone?* Cambridge, MA: Harvard University Press.

–. 2003. Electoral turnout: The new generation gap. *British Elections and Parties Review* 13: 159-173.

–. 2008. *Is voting for young people?* New York: Pearson.

Waterman, A. 1984. *The psychology of individualism.* New York: Praeger.

Watts, M.W. 1999. Are there typical age curves in political behavior? The "age invariance" hypothesis and political socialization. *Political Psychology* 20(3): 477-99.

Weber, E. 1976. *Peasants into Frenchmen: The modernization of rural France, 1870-1914.* Stanford, CA: Stanford University Press.

Weinrib, L. 2001. The activist constitution. In *Judicial power and Canadian democracy,* ed. P. Howe and P. Russell, 80-86. Montreal and Kingston: McGill-Queen's University Press.

Welsh, J. 2004. *At home in the world: Canada's global vision for the 21st century.* Toronto: HarperCollins.

White, C., S. Bruce, and J. Ritchie. 2000. *Young people's politics. Political interest and engagement amongst 14-24 year olds.* York: Joseph Rowntree Foundation.

Whiteley, P. 2007. Are groups replacing parties? A multi-level analysis of party and group membership in the European democracies. Paper presented at the conference On Britain after Blair, sponsored by the British Politics Group of the American Political Science Association, University of Chicago, 29 August.

Wolfe, A. 1998. *One nation, after all.* New York: Penguin Putnam.

Young, L., and W. Cross. 2007. *A group apart: Young party members in Canada.* Ottawa: Canadian Policy Research Networks. http://www.cprn.org/documents/48499_EN.pdf.

Zaller, J. 2002. The statistical power of election studies to detect media exposure effects in election campaigns. *Electoral Studies* 21(2): 297-329.

Zuckerman, A.S., ed. 2005. *The social logic of politics.* Philadelphia: Temple University Press.

Zuckerman, A.S., and L.A. Kotler-Berkowitz. 1998. Politics and society: Political diversity and uniformity in households as a theoretical puzzle. *Comparative Political Studies* 31(4): 464-97.

Zukin, C., S. Keeter, M. Andolina, K. Jenkins, and M.X. Delli Carpini. 2006. *A new engagement? Political participation, life and the changing American citizen.* New York: Oxford University Press.

Zussman, D. 1997. Do citizens trust their government? *Canadian Public Administration* 40(2): 234-54.

Data References

In light of the large number of survey datasets used in the book, abbreviated references are provided with essential information about each: the title of the survey, the principal investigator(s), the distributing agency or website, and the study number (where applicable). Further documentation is available from the distributing agencies. The standard disclaimer applies across the board, that none of the original investigators or distributors bears any responsibility for the data analysis or interpretations contained herein.

Election Studies

Britain
(All but 2001 and 2005 distributed by the Inter-university Consortium for Political and Social Research)
British Election Study: October 1974 Cross-Section. I.M. Crewe, B. Sarlvik, and J. Alt. SN7870.
British Election Study: May 1979 Cross-Section. I.M. Crewe, B. Sarlvik, and D.R. Robertson. SN8196.
British Election Study: June 1983. A.F. Heath, R.M. Jowell, J.K. Curtice, and E.J. Field. SN8409.
British Election Study: Cross-Section 1987. A.F. Heath, R.M. Jowell, and J.K. Curtice. SN6452.
British General Election Cross-Section Survey, 1992. A.F. Heath, R.M. Jowell, J.K. Curtice, J.A. Brand, and J.C. Mitchell. SN6453.
British General Election Cross-Section Survey, 1997. A.F. Heath, R.M. Jowell, J.K. Curtice, and P. Norris. SN2615.
British Election Study 2001. H. Clarke, M. Stewart, D. Sanders, and P. Whiteley. British Election Study website: http://www.essex.ac.uk/bes/Default.htm.
British Election Study 2005: Face-to-Face Survey. H. Clarke, M. Stewart, D. Sanders, and P. Whiteley. British Election Study website: http://www.essex.ac.uk/bes/Default.htm

Canada
(All but 2004 and 2006 distributed by the Inter-university Consortium for Political and Social Research)
Canadian Federal Election Study 1968. John Meisel. SN7009.
Canadian National Election Study 1974. H. Clarke, J. Jenson, L. Leduc, and J. Pammett. SN7379.
Canadian National Elections and Quebec Referendum Panel Study, 1974-1979-1980. H. Clarke, J. Jenson, L. Leduc, and J. Pammett. SN8079.
Canadian National Election Study 1984. R.D. Lambert, S.D. Brown, J.E. Curtis, B.J. Kay, and J.M. Wilson. SN8544.
Canadian National Election Study 1988. R. Johnston, A. Blais, H. E. Brady, and J. Crête. SN9386.
Canadian Election Study 1993: Incorporating the 1992 Referendum Survey on the Charlottetown Accord. R. Johnston, A. Blais, H. Brady, E. Gidengil, and N. Nevitte. SN6573.

Canadian Election Study 1997. A. Blais, E. Gidengil, R. Nadeau, and N. Nevitte. SN2593.
Canadian Election Study 2000. A. Blais, E. Gidengil, R. Nadeau, and N. Nevitte. SN3969.
Canadian Election Study 2004. A. Blais, E. Gidengil, N. Nevitte, P. Fournier, and J. Everitt.
    Canadian Election Study website: http://ces-eec.mcgill.ca/ces.html.
Canadian Election Study 2006. A. Blais, E. Gidengil, N. Nevitte, P. Fournier, and J. Everitt.
    Canadian Election Study website: http://ces-eec.mcgill.ca/ces.html.

Netherlands
(All but 1977 distributed by the Inter-university Consortium for Political and Social
Research)
Dutch Parliamentary Election Study, 1971. R. J. Mokken and F. M. Roschar. SN7311.
Dutch Parliamentary Election Study, 1977. G.A. Irwin, J. Verhoef, and C.J. Wiebrens. Steinmetz
    Archive. PO354.
Dutch Parliamentary Election Study, 1981. C. van der Eijk, B. Niemoller, and A. Th. J. Eggen.
    SN7912.
Dutch Parliamentary Election Study, 1986. C. van der Eijk, G.A. Irwin, and B. Niemoller.
    SN8876.
Dutch Parliamentary Election Study, 1989. H. Anker and E.V. Oppenhuis. SN9950.
Dutch Parliamentary Election Study, 1994. H. Anker and E.V. Oppenhuis. SN6740.
Dutch Parliamentary Election Study, 1998. K. Aarts, H. van der Kolk, and M. Kamp. SN2836.

Norway
(All but 1965 distributed by Norwegian Social Science Data Services)
1965 Norwegian Election Study. H. Valen. ICPSR. SN7256.
1969 Norwegian National Election Study. H. Valen.
1972-73 Norwegian National Election Study. H. Valen and W. Martinussen.
1977 Norwegian National Election Study. H. Valen.
1981 Norwegian National Election Study. H. Valen and B. Aardal.
1985 Norwegian National Election Study. H. Valen and B. Aardal.
1989 Norwegian National Election Study. H. Valen and B. Aardal.
1993 Norwegian National Election Study. H. Valen and B. Aardal.
1997 Norwegian National Election Study. H. Valen and B. Aardal.
2001 Norwegian National Election Study. H. Valen and B. Aardal.

Sweden
(All distributed by the Swedish National Data Service)
Swedish Election Study 1956. B. Sarlvik and J. Westerstahl. SND 0020.
Swedish Election Study 1960. B. Sarlvik. SND 0001.
Swedish Election Study 1964. B. Sarlvik. SND 0007.
Swedish Election Study 1968. B. Sarlvik. SND 0039.
Swedish Election Study 1970. B. Sarlvik. SND 0047.
Swedish Election Study 1973. B. Sarlvik and O. Petersson. SND 0040.
Swedish Election Study 1976. O. Petersson. SND 0008.
Swedish Election Study 1979. S. Holmberg. SND 0089.
Swedish Election Study 1982. S. Holmberg. SND 0157.
Swedish Election Study 1985. S. Holmberg and M. Gilljam. SND 0217.
Swedish Election Study 1988. S. Holmberg and M. Gilljam. SND 0227.
Swedish Election Study 1991. S. Holmberg and M. Gilljam. SND 0391.
Swedish Election Study 1994. S. Holmberg and M. Gilljam. SND 0570.
Swedish Election Study 1998. S. Holmberg. SND 0750.
Swedish Election Study 2002. S. Holmberg. SND 0812.

United States
(All distributed by the Inter-university Consortium for Political and Social Research)
American National Election Study, 1956. A. Campbell and P. Converse. SN7214.
American National Election Study, 1960. A. Campbell and P. Converse. SN7216.

American National Election Study, 1964. University of Michigan, Survey Research Center. SN7235.
American National Election Study, 1968. University of Michigan, Survey Research Center. SN7281.
American National Election Study, 1972. A. Miller and W. Miller. SN7010.
American National Election Study, 1976. A. Miller and W. Miller. SN7381.
American National Election Study, 1980. W. Miller. SN7763.
American National Election Study, 1984. W. Miller. SN8298.
American National Election Study, 1988. W. Miller. SN9196.
American National Election Study, 1992. W. Miller, D.R. Kinder, and S. J. Rosenstone. SN9549.
American National Election Study, 1996. W. Miller, D.R. Kinder, and S. J. Rosenstone. SN6869.
American National Election Study, 2000. N. Burns, D.R. Kinder, S.J. Rosenstone, and V. Sapiro. SN3131.
American National Election Study, 2004. University of Michigan, Center for Political Studies. SN4245.

Other Studies

Britain
Gallup Poll 972d. March 1969. UK Data Archive.
Gallup Poll 973a. April 1969. UK Data Archive.

Canada
CIPO [Canadian Institute of Public Opinion] Poll 186. May 1949. Carleton University Library Data Centre.
CIPO Poll 189. May 1949. Carleton University Library Data Centre.
CIPO Poll 250. July 1956. Carleton University Library Data Centre.
CIPO Poll 252. October 1956. Carleton University Library Data Centre.
CIPO Poll 257. May 1957. Carleton University Library Data Centre.
CIPO Poll 258. May 1957. Carleton University Library Data Centre.
CIPO Poll 299. November 1962. Carleton University Library Data Centre.
CROP Socio-Cultural Surveys, 1989-96. Canadian Opinion Research Archive, Queen's University.
Elections Canada 2002 Study of Voters and Non-Voters. J. Pammett and L. Leduc. Elections Canada website (http://www.elections.ca), Electoral Law, Policy and Research section.
General Social Survey, Cycle 17: Social Engagement. 2003. Statistics Canada. University of New Brunswick, Data Services.
General Social Survey, Cycle 19: Time Use. 2005. Statistics Canada. University of New Brunswick, Data Services.
Quality of Canadian Life: Social Change in Canada, 1977. T. Atkinson, B. Blishen, M. Ornstein, and H.M. Stevenson. Institute for Social Research, York University.
Social Change in Canada, Phase 3, 1981. T. Atkinson, B. Blishen, M. Ornstein, and H.M. Stevenson. Institute for Social Research, York University.

Norway
Norwegian National Broadcasting System, viewer surveys (*Radio og fjernsynsundersøkelse*), 1975 and 1983. Norwegian Social Science Data Services.

Multi-country
Civic Culture Study, 1959-1960. G. Almond and S. Verba. ICPSR. SN7201.
European and World Values Survey Four Wave-Integrated Data File, 1981-2004, v. 20060423. European Values Study Group and World Values Survey Association. World Values Survey website: http://www.worldvaluessurvey.org.
European Communities Study 1970. R. Inglehart and J-R. Rabier. ICPSR. SN 7260.
European Election Study 1994. H. Schmitt, C. van der Eijk, E. Scholz, and M. Klein. ICPSR. SN3014.

European Social Survey Round 1, 2002/2003. R. Jowell, and the Central Co-ordinating Team. European Social Survey website: http://www.europeansocialsurvey.org.

European Social Survey Round 2, 2004/2005. R. Jowell and the Central Co-ordinating Team. European Social Survey website: http://www.europeansocialsurvey.org.

European Social Survey Round 3, 2006/2007. R. Jowell and the Central Co-ordinating Team. European Social Survey website: http://www.europeansocialsurvey.org.

Eurobarometer 65.2: The European Constitution, Social and Economic Quality of Life, Avian Influenza and Energy Issues, March-May 2006. A. Papacostas. ICPSR. SN20322.

Mannheim Eurobarometer Trend File, 1970-2002. H. Schmitt and E. Scholz. ICPSR. SN4357.

Multinational Time Use Study, Version 5.5.2. J. Gershuny, K. Fisher and A. H. Gauthier, with A. Borkosky, A. Bortnik, D. Dosman, C. Fedick, T. Frederick, S. Jones, T. Lu, F. Lui, L. MacRae, B. Monna, M. Pauls, C. Pawlak, N. Torres, and C. Victorino. Centre for Time Use Research website: http://www.timeuse.org.

Index